Free Will, Agency, and Selfhood in Indian Philosophy

Free Will, Agency, and Selfhood in Indian Philosophy

Edited by
MATTHEW R. DASTI
and
EDWIN F. BRYANT

OXFORD
UNIVERSITY PRESS

OXFORD
UNIVERSITY PRESS

Oxford University Press is a department of the University of Oxford.
It furthers the University's objective of excellence in research, scholarship,
and education by publishing worldwide.

Oxford New York
Auckland Cape Town Dar es Salaam Hong Kong Karachi
Kuala Lumpur Madrid Melbourne Mexico City Nairobi
New Delhi Shanghai Taipei Toronto

With offices in
Argentina Austria Brazil Chile Czech Republic France Greece
Guatemala Hungary Italy Japan Poland Portugal Singapore
South Korea Switzerland Thailand Turkey Ukraine Vietnam

Published in the United States of America by
Oxford University Press
198 Madison Avenue, New York, NY 10016

Library of Congress Cataloging-in-Publication Data
Free will, agency, and selfhood in Indian philosophy / edited by Matthew R. Dasti and Edwin F. Bryant.
pages cm
Includes index.
ISBN 978–0–19–992275–8 (pbk. : alk. paper) — ISBN 978–0–19–992273–4 (hardcover : alk. paper) — ISBN 978–0–19–992274–1 (ebook) 1. Philosophy, Indic. 2. Self (Philosophy)—India. 3. Free will and determinism—Religious aspects. I. Dasti, Matthew R., editor of compilation. II. Bryant, Edwin F. (Edwin Francis), 1957– editor of compilation.
B131.F76 2014
126.0954—dc23
2013017925

9 8 7 6 5 4 3 2 1
Printed in the United States of America
on acid-free paper

Dedicated to Anasuya,
Leela, and Mohini

Contents

Acknowledgments

THIS VOLUME AROSE from a long-standing friendship between the editors, often centered on shared appreciation and dedication to the interconnected universe of the premodern Indic intellectual traditions. In many conversations probing various aspects of Hindu philosophy, we often puzzled over the nature of free will and personal agency as construed in the various schools. We found ourselves grappling again and again with the philosophical resources available to the Indian thinkers on this issue given the parameters of their metaphysical commitments and presuppositions. From these conversations, this volume was born.

That the exercise of personal agency depends on a variety of factors and conditions beyond the individual agent is brought home in a most personal way as we reflect on the people whose sacrifices and generosity have put us in a position to develop this volume. Matthew Dasti would like to thank his family, especially his wife, Nandanie, for her constant support and love, and his mother, Lynn, for a lifetime of care. He has also benefitted from a number of remarkable teachers, and would like to express a particular debt of gratitude to Matt K. Matsuda, Edwin Bryant, Paul Woodruff, Rob Koons, David Sosa, and Stephen H. Phillips. He would finally like to thank his colleagues in the Philosophy Department of Bridgewater State University, for creating and sustaining an atmosphere of profound collegiality and friendship. Edwin Bryant, too, would like to thank all of his mentors and teachers, whose guidance, examples, and encouragement over the years have afforded him the luxury of pursuing his life's interest. He would also like to express his gratitude to Rutgers University for its generous sabbatical program, which allowed this volume to reach its finalized form. The editors would both like to thank David Buchta for his Sanskrit editing of the volume. Finally, many thanks to Cynthia Read of OUP, for her willingness to take on this project.

Contributors

Edwin F. Bryant received his Ph.D. in Indic languages and cultures from Columbia University. He has taught Hinduism at Harvard University and is presently a professor of Hindu Religion and Philosophy at Rutgers University. His areas of specialization are Indian proto-history, the Krishna Tradition and Indian Philosophy, especially Sāṃkhya/Yoga. He is the author of *The Quest for the Origins of Vedic Culture* (2001); translated the *Srīmad Bhāgavata Purāṇa Book X* (2003); translated and wrote an extensive commentary on the *Yoga Sūtras* of Patañjali (2009); and has published three edited volumes on Indian religion and history. He is presently translating further selections from the *Bhāgavata Purāṇa*.

David Buchta is Lecturer in Sanskrit in the Department of Classics at Brown University and is currently a doctoral candidate in the Department of South Asia Studies at The University of Pennsylvania. His research focuses on Vaiṣṇava Vedānta traditions, particularly examining where theology and Vedānta exegesis intersect with poetry, literary theory, and the concept of *rasa* (aesthetic delight). His research, especially on the 18th-century Vedāntin, Baladeva Vidyābhūṣaṇa, has been published in the *Journal of Hindu Studies* and the *Journal of Vaiṣṇava Studies*, and he has contributed to the *Brill Encyclopedia of Hinduism*.

George Cardona is Emeritus Professor of Linguistics at The University of Pennsylvania. He received his doctorate in linguistics, with a specialization in Indo-European, from Yale University in 1960. He also studied Sanskrit grammar (*vyākaraṇa*) and allied areas, principally *nyāya* and *mīmāṃsā*, in India with traditional scholars, receiving various honors and titles from institutions of Sanskritic learning. His works include *Pāṇini: His Work and its Traditions (Volume 1)*, *Pāṇini: A Survey of Research*, and *Recent Research in Pāṇinian Studies*. He has also published dozens of essays on Pāṇinian grammar and historical Indo-Aryan linguistics in leading scholarly journals and collections.

Christopher Key Chapple is Doshi Professor of Indic and Comparative Theology at Loyola Marymount University in Los Angeles. He has published more than fifteen books, including *Karma and Creativity* (1986), *Nonviolence to Animals, Earth, and Self in Asian Traditions* (1993), *Jainism and Ecology* (2002), *Reconciling Yogas* (2003), *Yoga and the Luminous* (2008), and *In Praise of Mother Earth* (2012).

Satyanarayana Dasa holds a Ph.D. in Sanskrit from Agra University. His scholarly training is Indian philosophy, and his specialty is the theology and philosophy of Gauḍīya Vaiṣṇavism. He has been a visiting professor at Rutgers University and Mississippi State University and is founder and director of the JIVA Institute in Vrindavan, India. He has authored and translated several books on Gauḍīya Vaiṣṇava philosophy, including the *Śrī Tattva Sandarbha* (1995), the *Bhakti Sandarbha* (2005–2006) and the *Bhagavat Sandarbha* (forthcoming). He is currently engaged in the project of translating the rest of Jīva Gosvāmin's *Six Treatises* into English.

Matthew R. Dasti is Assistant Professor of Philosophy at Bridgewater State University. He received his doctorate from the University of Texas, Austin, in 2010. His research to date has focused on classical Indian philosophy, and especially the Nyāya tradition. He has published in various journals and collections including *Philosophy East and West, Asian Philosophy, History of Philosophy Quarterly*, and *The Routledge Companion to Theism.*

Jonathan Edelmann is Assistant Professor of Religion at Mississippi State University in the Department of Philosophy and Religion. Edelmann was a 2009–2011 Luce Summer Fellow with the American Academy of Religion and a winner of the John Templeton Prize for Theological Promise. He is the author of *Hindu Theology and Biology: The Bhāgavata Purāṇa and Contemporary Theory* (2012).

Elisa Freschi received her Ph.D. from Rome, "La Sapienza," and holds degrees in both Sanskrit and Western Philosophy. She focuses on issues of epistemology, deontics and hermeneutics (see her *Duty, language and exegesis in Prābhākara Mīmāṃsā*, 2012). Her historical approach also engages with the topic of intertextuality and of the re-usage of texts in Indian philosophical literature (about which she is currently editing a volume). She is the head of a project on Veṅkaṭanātha between Mīmāṃsā and Viśiṣṭādvaita Vedānta at the Austrian Academy of Sciences (IKGA, Vienna).

Martin Ganeri is Lecturer in Theology and Director of the Centre for Christianity and Interreligious Dialogue at Heythrop College, University of London. He research has focused on the theology of Rāmānuja and Thomas Aquinas. His recent publications include, "Two Pedagogies for Happiness: Healing Goals and Healing Methods in the *Summa Theologiae* of Thomas Aquinas and the *Śrī Bhāṣya* of Rāmānuja" in *Philosophy as Therapeia* (2010), "Theology and Non-Western Philosophy" in *Religion and the University: Theology, Philosophy and the Disciplines*, Vol. 1 (2012) and "Tradition with a New Identity: Thomist Engagement with Non-Christian Thought as a Model for the New Comparative Theology in Europe," in *Religions* 3, no. 4 (2012). He is currently working on a monograph, *Indian Philosophy and Western Theism: Rāmānuja and Aquinas.*

Jay Garfield is Doris Silbert Professor in the Humanities, Professor of Philosophy, and Director of the Logic Program and of the Five College Tibetan Studies in India Program at Smith College; Professor in the Graduate Faculty of Philosophy at the University of Massachusetts; Professor of Philosophy at Melbourne University; and Adjunct Professor of Philosophy at the Central Institute of Higher Tibetan Studies. He teaches and pursues research in the philosophy of mind, foundations of cognitive science, logic, philosophy of language, Buddhist philosophy, cross-cultural hermeneutics, theoretical and applied ethics and epistemology. Garfield's most recent books are his translation, with the Ven. Prof. Geshe Ngawang Samten, of the 14th–15th-century Tibetan philosopher Tsong Khapa's commentary on Nāgārjuna's *Mūlamadhyamakakārikā (Ocean of Reasoning)* and *Empty Words: Buddhist Philosophy and Cross-Cultural Interpretation* (2002 and 2006, respectively). Garfield is also working on projects on the development of the theory of mind in children with particular attention to the role of pretence in that process; the acquisition of evidentials and its relation to the development of theory of mind (with Jill deVilliers, Thomas Roeper and Peggy Speas), the history of 20th-century Indian philosophy (with Nalini Bhushan), and the nature of conventional truth in Madhyamaka (with Graham Priest and Tom Tillemans). He recently co-directed, with Peter Gregory, a year-long research institute, *Trans-Buddhism: Transmission, Translation and Transformation* investigating the interaction of Buddhist societies with the West. Other books in progress include the *Oxford Handbook of World Philosophy* (editor), *Readings in Buddhist Philosophy* (co-editor with William Edelglass), *Trans-Buddhism: Transmission, Translation and Transformation* (co-editor with Nalini Bhushan and Abraham Zablocki), and *Sweet*

Reason: A Field Guide to Modern Logic (co-authored with Jim Henle and the late Thomas Tymoczko).

David Peter Lawrence received his Ph.D. from the University of Chicago, and has taught at universities in Hong Kong, Canada, and the United States. Presently, he is Associate Professor in the Department of Philosophy and Religion at the University of North Dakota. He specializes in nondual Kashmiri Śaivism and related areas of Hindu and Buddhist philosophy and religion, and is more broadly concerned with the use of philosophy as a mode of cross-cultural dialogue. His publications include *Rediscovering God with Transcendental Argument: A Contemporary Interpretation of Monistic Kashmiri Śaiva Philosophy* (1999); and *The Teachings of the Odd-Eyed One: A Study and Translation of the Virūpākṣapañcāśikā with the Commentary of Vidyācakravartin* (2008). During academic year 2011–2012, Dr. Lawrence was recipient of a Fulbright-Nehru Senior Research Fellowship for work in India toward completion of a new annotated translation of Abhinavagupta's *Īśvarapratyabhijñāvimarśinī*.

Karin Meyers received her Ph.D. from the University of Chicago in 2010 for her dissertation *Freedom and Self-Control: Free Will in South Asian Buddhism*. She is a Lecturer at Kathmandu University Centre for Buddhist Studies at Rangjung Yeshe Institute. Her current research focuses on the relationship between theory and meditative practice in the Abhidharma.

Sthaneshwar Timalsina completed his Masters degree at Sampurnananda Sanskrit University, Benares, and received his Ph.D. from Martin Luther University, Halle, Germany. He is currently teaching Indian religions and philosophies as Associate Professor at San Diego State University. His books, *Seeing and Appearance* (2006) and *Consciousness in Indian Philosophy* (2009), excavate classical Sanskrit texts to examine different modalities of consciousness within the Advaita school. His publications include multiple essays and book chapters in the areas of Indian philosophy, Tantric studies, yoga, and ritual studies. He is currently working on memory, imagination, and other related aspects of the Indian philosophy of mind.

Free Will, Agency, and Selfhood in Indian Philosophy

Introduction

Matthew R. Dasti

IF ONE WERE to make a list of the leading topics of debate in classical Indian philosophy, contenders might include the existence and nature of the self; the fundamental sources of knowledge; the nature of the engagement between consciousness and reality; the existence and nature of God/Brahman; the proper account of causation; the relationship between language and the world; the practices that best ensure future happiness; the most expedient method for any soteriological attainment (or not); or the fundamental constituents of reality. We might also include the various debates engendered by the skeptical challenges to philosophy itself. But, as typically formulated, the problem of free will would not make the cut. As a number of our contributors note, classical Indian philosophy simply does not have an overarching debate about free will that neatly corresponds to that within the Western tradition, where it is a prominent, enduring feature of the philosophical landscape. While there are various debates over the existence and proper construal of agency and individual freedom, the "free will debate" does not have this central position.

What then is the motive behind a book centered on the themes of agency and free will in classical Indian philosophy? As illustrated in the following chapters, the lack of a dialectical isomorphism does not entail a lack of shared concerns. In lieu of a clear, genre-defining debate over free will in classical Indian philosophy, discussion of related issues is scattered throughout various topics and ramifies in a number of peculiarly Indian contexts. Commonly, they flow from concerns with agency: what

---

An earlier draft of this introduction was composed during a writing retreat sponsored by the Bridgewater State University Office of Teaching and Learning, for which I would like to express my gratitude. While conceptualizing this introduction, I have benefitted from discussion with and/or comments by various participants in the writing retreat, as well as David Palmer, Edwin Bryant, Matthew O'Brien, Ed James, and Jim Crowley.

it is and whether we truly have it. The purpose of this volume is to highlight these discussions and bring them into focus. Taken as a whole, this volume illustrates that concerns surrounding the intersection of free will, agency, and selfhood are not unimportant in, or negligible to, the leading schools of Indian philosophy. It also reveals the way in which the concepts of agency and free will provide a helpful context to explore issues within Indian philosophical thought.

For our purposes, "classical Indian philosophy" refers to the philosophical developments in and around India from roughly 100 to 1800 CE. This period is bracketed on one side by the earlier proto-philosophical period centered on the late Vedic culture and its discontents (in the form of the Buddhist and Jaina revolts and the other *śramaṇa* movements of first millennium BCE), and on the other side, the modern period, characterized by a self-conscious attempt to reconsider and rearticulate Indian tradition in response to Western culture and science, and the problems of modernity more generally. Features that distinguish classical Indian philosophy include the common use of Sanskrit as the philosophical lingua franca; the consolidation of various schools of systematic thought (typically called *darśanas*, "viewpoints") with burgeoning commentarial traditions upon the ur-texts of each school; and a concern with the rational justification of one's beliefs or the holdings of one's school, which in turn hinges on examinations of legitimate sources of knowledge (*pramāṇas*).

In the classical period, we find that individual schools try to marshal their philosophical resources to reflect upon and defend the goals of life that they take on from traditional cultural and religious authorities. These various schools were in constant dialogue. Philosophical development often involves inter-school debate, with mutually inspired refinement throughout the generations of commentators and respondents. An individual *darśana's* arguments and positions cannot, in fact, be fully understood without determining who its disputants are, whether or not such interlocutors (*pūrvapakṣins*) are stated explicitly or left unmentioned. This fact has guided our approach in this book. Each chapter centers on a specific tradition of thought, but we have encouraged authors to consider points of intersection and to refer to other chapters when relevant. Our hope is that the various chapters reveal a greater perspective not only on specific *darśanas*, but also on the range of responses and debates on core issues which transcend individual schools.

Free Will, Agency, and Selfhood

Free will, agency, and *selfhood* are terms with rich histories. They have been defined, refined, and debated for centuries. To ground the ensuing discussions, we would like to provide fairly general treatments of each; different chapters will employ them with varied shades of nuance and meaning. **Will** is a capacity to choose certain courses of action. Having **free will** is often understood in terms of one's being able to choose otherwise or in terms of a person being the proper source of her choice. The Sanskrit term that perhaps best approximates "free will" is *svātantrya,* "independence," which suggests the capacity for self-determined action. From a psychological perspective, *cikīrṣā,* "desire to act" is analogous to "will" in that it refers to the component of one's inner life through which one initiates and directs intentional actions.

One key reason that philosophers have typically been interested in free will is that it is often considered a necessary condition for moral responsibility: only those beings that exercise free will can be morally responsible for their actions. Such interest also flows from reflection on human goals and achievement. Do we truly have the ability to freely direct ourselves toward those objectives we deem desirable? Or are we rather powerless, merely driven by the causal currents that envelop us?

An **agent** is someone or something that performs actions. And thus, **agency** is the capacity to perform actions. A stone may roll down a hill and land in a stream. In doing so, it enters into various causal relations and produces various effects, including, for example, splashing water in the air as it falls into the stream. But these are not actions proper, in the sense of being manifestations of agency. Compare this to my jumping into a stream to cool down on a hot summer day. This is an action, which has me, the agent, as its source. The term "agency" is well captured by the Sanskrit term *kartṛtva.*

Whether or not agency requires a robust capacity for reflection and choice, the kind typically associated with human beings, is debated. Some philosophers have argued that the possession of agency ranges beyond human beings—that spiders, for example, perform actions despite their lacking the rational powers we associate with human agency.[1] Others

1. See Frankfurt 1978. Further, a tradition that may be traced to Aristotle and Aquinas contends that agency is merely the expression of a thing's nature, which is oriented toward some *telos.* From this perspective, agency may even be possessed by insentient things. Thanks to Matthew O'Brien for calling my attention to this.

have argued that "full-blooded agency" requires rationality and the capacity for reflection and choice.[2] We (the editors) are not interested in settling this issue here. Nor are we interested in arguing for a specific account of the relationship between agency and free will. We are, however, most interested in the way that agency is manifested by rational agents, and this specific manifestation of agency will be the dominant construal of the notion in the following chapters. Human beings have the ability to intentionally produce certain outcomes that we select as worthy in accordance with our values and desires. And thus, our agency not only allows for ownership of our actions, but a distinctive responsibility for our choices and behaviors. Problems or concerns about agency motivate a host of philosophical questions that naturally intersect with questions about free will.

As a first approximation, we may consider **selfhood** to be the condition of being a locus of various psychological states, that is, being the kind of thing which possesses and synthesizes such states such that they are co-located. This notion of the self is defended by Hindu schools like Mīmāṃsā and Nyāya, which develop metaphysics grounded in common experience.[3] Beyond this, however, a number of influential Indian traditions contend that this conception of selfhood is superficial or even false. We have our roots in a deeper self, which transcends the empirical ego and is our truest essence. The famous meditative quest of the Upaniṣadic and yogic traditions is to unearth and fully invest in the deep self. Classical Buddhists, in contrast, while engaged in a similar search, report that there is ultimately no self to be found; there are merely bundles of properties or states beneath which we tend to project the fiction of an enduring self. Debates between Hindus and Buddhists over the existence of the self, and between various schools of the Hindu fold over the nature of the self, are some of the richest veins of philosophical development within the Indian tradition. As is well known, *ātman* is the Sanskrit term which corresponds to "self," and is invested with a similarly wide range of meanings.

2. See Velleman 1992.

3. "Hindu" is of course, a problematic term for various reasons, including the fact that it refers to hundreds of philosophical and religious movements under a single heading. For our purposes, it refers to persons and traditions that accept the authority of the Vedas and Upaniṣads—if only nominally—along with allied texts, cultural norms, and practices.

The Indian Context

A number of intellectual currents inform the classical Indian treatments of free will, agency, and selfhood and provide a distinctive problem space within which the Indian thinkers operate. Our philosophers inherit questions and a wide range of precursor views from the proto-philosophical period about the efficacy of human action in the grand scheme of things. Amid the *śramaṇa* revolts of pre-classical India, the Ājīvika ascetic Makkhali Gosāla famously argued that human effort is useless; fate rules the lives of all, and our lot is to accept what we are destined to suffer and enjoy until we have exhausted our personal allotment. The Buddha and Mahāvīra, the Jaina luminary, both his contemporaries, vigorously condemned Gosāla and extolled personal effort in the pursuit of the supreme good. In a related development, the Upaniṣadic sages developed the doctrine of karma to account for the way in which small decisions collectively form one's character and future self.[4] Despite their other differences, Buddhism, Jainism, and the Upaniṣadic tradition agree that one's decisions and actions create a sort of momentum that continues after death and into one's next lifetime, and have consequences that unfold over the course of multiple embodiments. Classical philosophers largely accepted that a person's karmic inheritance determines the range of options she has in her current life, and they seek to articulate the role of human effort in light of both the causal weight of the past and the complicated set of current relationships that impinge upon individual agency. The Mīmāṃsā ("Exegesis") school is, of all classical traditions, most devoted to the preservation of ancient Vedic ritual culture, and its concern with agency stems from concerns with ritual obligations and consequences. Mīmāṃsakas appeal to both common experience and the nature of obligation itself to articulate the notion that individuals are indeed agents and possess the freedom necessary for agency. Nyāya philosophers agree that the enduring individual self must be the locus of agency and moral responsibility, and correspondingly attack Buddhist no-self theories. They argue that rejection of an enduring self makes it impossible to explain moral responsibility over time: if there is no enduring self, I am not the same individual that I was last week, or, for that matter, in my previous birth. This disassociation, Nyāya argues, would make me free of moral responsibility for what

4. See Ganeri 2007: 223–228 for a concise discussion of the philosophical origins of the karma doctrine.

"he" did back then as much as I am currently not responsible for what my neighbor does right now. Madhyamaka Buddhists conversely argue that moral responsibility is not to be found in an enduring self, but in the network of relationships, states, and interconnections that constitute our rich identities. Only by navigating these connections will we understand the fact that human agency and the responsibilities that go along with it are multivalent and narrative-dependent aspects of conventional reality.

Traditions of contemplative practice are inherited and developed by a number of classical schools including Sāṃkhya, Yoga, Buddhism, Vedānta, and Kashmiri Śaivism. These schools' analyses of free will and agency are profoundly influenced by such practice, which is taken to reveal a more accurate picture of selfhood and its capacities than ordinary experience. By appeal to both meditational experience and philosophical analysis, these schools deconstruct the empirical ego into various components and tie such components to more fundamental metaphysical realities and causal processes. Given such a deconstruction, where, if anywhere, are agency and responsibility to be located? Where is the seat of human willing and the origin of human action? Abhidharma Buddhists argue personal agency and free will make sense from the conventional perspective but not according to the fundamental reality of momentary *dharmas*. Part of their challenge is to navigate between both registers to make sense of our felt sense of agency and its importance in the pursuit of enlightenment. Sāṃkhya and Advaita Vedānta conclude that the will is ultimately extrinsic to selfhood, part of a psychological apparatus covering the *ātman* with which we identify in our unenlightened way of thinking. These schools typically say that mistakes about agency are a fundamental part of spiritual ignorance. The notion that we are in control, that we are beings who act, is somehow a crucial aspect of the cognitive and affective disorders collectively called *avidyā*, existential ignorance. Though it too is a monistic school, Kashmiri Śaivism radically differs from Advaita Vedānta over the issue of individual freedom. For the Advaitins, Brahman, the ultimate reality, does not act, as action implies change and Brahman does not undergo modification of any kind. Therefore, since we are identical to that fundamental reality, the notion of ourselves as volitional beings that can generate change is an illusion. For the Śaivas, however, our individual freedom is an expression of the creative spontaneity of the single reality of Śiva. The error that belies our unenlightenment is not our sense of volitional freedom, but rather our failing to see the identity of our freedom with God's own power. Somewhat akin to the Śaivas, a number of theistic Vedāntins argue that our problem is not that we think we are agents, but rather that we ignore the fact that our agency is derivative of, and in constant negotiation with, the agency of God, who is the supreme Self. They further reflect on individual freedom in relation to a God who creates, sustains, and oversees the universe, yet responds to the loving entreaties of his devotees.

A further concern carried over from traditional authorities in the proto-philosophical period is the possibility of liberation or enlightenment. Though the details are developed in very different ways, typically liberation is thought of as the ultimate and final goal of life, an achievement that brings freedom from the cycle of rebirth and, at minimum, freedom from the pain of ordinary embodied existence. Though concern with liberation is not at the forefront of every school, classical *darśanas* tend to constrain their metaphysical analyses to allow for its possibility. Any account of agency or individual effort must therefore cohere with this possibility. This is perhaps most starkly seen in the Sāṃkhya school's rejection of agency as a property of the self, arguing that such would entail that the self undergoes change and therefore be impermanent. It could not, therefore, be the subject of liberation, understood of as a kind of eternal, unchanging self-awareness.

A final significant influence to mention is that of the Grammarian tradition (*vyākaraṇa*) on Indian philosophical analysis generally and questions of agency in particular. It would be difficult to overstate this influence. Led by Pāṇini's epochal work in linguistics, the Grammarian school seeks to excavate the structure of the Sanskrit language. Commonly, Grammarian accounts are cited and modified by other thinkers as they perform conceptual analysis. Most relevantly, the Grammarians introduce the system of *kārakas*, the individual components of an action as expressed by a sentence (e.g., the agent of the act, the object of the act, the location of the act). This system provides a vocabulary that facilitates the analysis of agency in relation to the other components of an action.

The Western Context

This book is not formally a work of comparative philosophy. Our authors are fundamentally concerned with exploring the richness of the Indian schools on their own terms and according to their own distinct set of concerns. This should be underscored. And yet, as will be evident, our authors are sensitive to the ways in which conceptions of agency and free will have been informed by the sensibility of what we may loosely call the Western philosophical tradition. Some cite specific analyses from Western thinkers for the sake of explanation or comparison. Others make distinctions in order to recognize that the Indian thinkers should not be forced into Western categories or concerns that are an imprecise fit. Still others use the Indian discussions to motivate an important meta-philosophical critique of Western approaches to free will: what appears to be an obvious and natural philosophical problem may, when seen in the light of a separate tradition of thought, be found to rely on contingent presuppositions or concerns that are provincial to a particular historical context. Given this kind of engagement, it may help us to take note of some of the key figures, options, and motivations in the Western tradition. To that end, let us very briefly, and without trying to get at all of the nuances or competing interpretations, mention some of these key figures and options. The idea, to repeat, is to provide us with some footholds that may be helpful in situating the issues that will be discussed throughout the book. (We would direct readers interested in a more focused investigation of the genesis of the free will debate to the initial sections of Garfield's chapter.)

In the ancients, we find a concern to identify the factors that contribute to autonomy and robust agency that is motivated by both ethical inquiry and investigations into the metaphysics of personhood. Plato repeatedly argues that the best kind of life is governed by a reflective knowledge of what is good. He famously—and perhaps shockingly—contends that the most politically powerful individuals of his time were in a deeper sense powerless; slaves to their passions and ignorant of what is truly good, they were incapable of achieving what they actually wanted, happiness. True autonomy—genuine agency—requires an understanding of the good, with a corresponding rational control over one's desires and actions, aligning them with it. In this light, the Socratic *elenchus* may be seen as a method of integration, of helping an individual gain reflective, critical awareness of his formerly unacknowledged attitudes and beliefs. Plato's concern about autonomy, knowledge, and self-possession iterates in various forms but continues in contemporary action theory insofar as it seeks to understand the way in which actions are motivated by and explicable according to the cognitive and affective states of an individual. Following Plato, Aristotle focuses his characteristically keen eye on the question of human autonomy, identifying conditions that impair or undermine it. In such situations, the origin of action is external to the individual: in cases of deception, for example, one unwittingly acts for something one would avoid if fully knowledgeable. In simple compulsion, the individual is turned into a mere instrument of some external agent. Aristotle calls attention to a range of important cases of self-caused lack of autonomy. A man whose character strongly inclines him to vice is not necessarily free from blame: his character may be the product of his decisions over the years. Likewise, a drunk person may be culpable for his drunken behavior despite his lack of self-possession; after all, it is he who chose to drink.

For the medieval thinkers, concerns relating to free will and human agency are typically generated by theological reflection. Augustine's response to the problem of free will is grounded in the attempt to assign responsibility to human beings for the Fall, despite God's omnipotence. So long as Adam and Eve truly had free will, even as a gift of God, Augustine contends that they may be properly responsible for their choice. God is off the hook, so to speak. The theological problem of free will is further compounded by God's omniscience: if God already knows the future, how is it possible that my current choices actually make a difference in what happens? Boethius (and following him, Aquinas) solves the problem of God's foreknowledge by situating God outside of time. Our free choices take place within time, and as God is outside of time, it makes little sense to say that "Today, God knows what I will do tomorrow." God's existence cannot be confined to today or tomorrow, and his knowledge is not foreknowledge, but a simultaneous and atemporal immediate awareness of the entirety of reality. Medieval philosophers also continue the tradition of philosophical analysis of human psychology initiated by Plato and Aristotle. Aquinas thus famously develops the notion of the will as rational appetite, a motivation for goal-directed action that is informed by intellectual cognition.

In the early modern period, discussion of free will and human agency starts to transition from a theological to a naturalistic context. Modern thinkers often consider human agency and responsibility as being embedded within a causally determined natural world and provide a corresponding formulation of the problem of free will. Every event in the natural world is causally determined by some prior event(s). We may trace out the ancestry of an event or thing, finding the causal antecedents that collectively necessitate its occurrence. But human animals are part of the natural world, beings whose biological and physiological functioning is subject to strict causal law. How then could we be autonomous agents, possessors of free will? Though the source of external or prior necessity has shifted from God to nature, the problem remains functionally similar. A number of thinkers respond by embracing determinism while criticizing the very notion of "free will." Hobbes influentially argues that the term "freedom" simply means a lack of physical impediments to movement, and as such, may only be applied to physical bodies. Therefore, people, as physical things, may or not be free to pursue specific courses of action, but it is incoherent to speak of a will as free or bound. Spinoza argues that while free will as commonly conceived is an illusion, a kind of freedom is possible in the very act of accepting our complete embeddedness within the network of relationships that comprise this deterministic universe. Kant's famous distinction between the phenomenal and noumenal realms allows him to concede the world of experience to scientific determinism while allowing the possibility of free will from a noumenal perspective.

The history of philosophical engagement, informed by recent scientific discovery, has led to a fairly clear array of contemporary responses to the problem of free will. In short: determinists accept that human behavior is necessitated by prior causes. Some of them, compatibilists, contend that despite determinism, there are ways in which we may speak of ourselves as possessing free will that are important and valuable for human life. Others argue that free will is incompatible with causal determinism. The only non-compatibilist option for such defenders of free will is to deny causal determinism and take up what is typically called the libertarian position on free will. Thus, three primary options remain: rejection of free will, compatibilism, or libertarian free will.

The Papers

Bryant explores the axiom central to Sāṃkhya, perhaps the oldest speculative tradition to emerge in ancient India: if something is eternal, that thing cannot change. Accepting the eternality of the *ātman* that had long been established in the Upaniṣadic tradition, Sāṃkhya's inflexible position on changelessness causes it to develop an uncompromising dualism: the self is little more than a quantum of consciousness, and all fluctuating features of personhood, such as agency, desire, and propositionally structured cognition, are relegated to the subtle but inert material (*prakṛtic*) coverings enveloping the *ātman*. Thus, the deep self is entirely devoid of agency and will. The chapter engages Nyāya's much more substantive notion of selfhood as its primary *pūrvapakṣa* and explores the tension inherited by the exegetes of the *Bhagavad Gītā* in their attempt to reconcile the seemingly conflicting views of agency in the Vedānta and Sāṃkhya traditions.

As with other contributions, Meyers's chapter strives to locate cross-cultural correspondences to frame her discussion of Abhidharma Buddhism. This is complicated by the Buddhist traditions' absence of any semantic correspondence to Western notions of free will and any enduring entity that might be considered an agent who could be considered free or not. Meyers reconstructs a compatibilist stance consistent with the axioms of the tradition and grounded in the notion of the "two truths": on the one hand, the individual as construed conventionally who is exhorted to endeavor to pursue the Eightfold Path, and the other, the ultimate reality of the individual as a psychophysical vortex in the flow of interdependent momentariness. She considers the tensions to be faced as Buddhist thinkers must negotiate between these two accounts in order to make sense of not only ordinary experience, but also the Buddhist pursuit of enlightenment.

The Jaina tradition places great emphasis on prescribed voluntarist action, albeit directed at a very different goal than the ritually centered directives of the Mīmāṃsā school we will encounter in Freschi's chapter. While emphatically a soteriological tradition, the Jaina notion of liberation entails removing karmic coverings from the soul, but a karma much more physically construed than the contemporary Hindu or Buddhist soteriological traditions. These karmic coverings are to be extirpated through assiduous adherence to very strict ethical rules; indeed, the commitment to nonviolent regulatory action defines Jainism. The Jaina precepts covered in Chapple's chapter, culled from the primary early and medieval sources, exhaustively outline the types of behaviors required to purge this karma, all predicated on the correct utilization of the individual's will.

Cardona analyzes the Grammarian conception of agency, centered on Pāṇini's discussion of the application of *kāraka* category names. *Kārakas* are the direct participants in the accomplishment of an action, and their category names are assigned according to the kind of role they play. The relevant *sūtra* in this regard (*Aṣṭādhyāyī* 1.4.54) simply notes that the *kāraka* that is independent (*svatantra*) has the category name "agent" (*kartṛ*). In the act of cooking rice, for example, various participants contribute to its accomplishment, including the fire, wood, pot, grains of rice, et cetera. But the cook is the agent proper, the "independent" participant who manages the other factors, setting them in motion and causing them to cease functioning when the act is accomplished. Much of Cardona's chapter is devoted to unpacking this notion of agential independence in the work of leading Grammarians, culminating in Bhartṛhari's explicit criteria for agency. Since a paradigmatic agent would seem to be a person, as in the example of cooking rice, Grammarians further consider the best analysis of well-attested statements like "the river flows" that seem to allow nonsentient entities to play role of agent. Cardona explores these and highlights the centrality that Grammarians place on common linguistic usage to guide conceptual analysis. Grammarians thus affirm that things that lack volition, cognition, and effort may be spoken of as agents in a straightforward, non-metaphorical manner and thus oppose Nyāya's contention that agency belongs only to sentient beings.

Dasti explores Nyāya's conception of the self as a substance that bears psychological properties like cognition, desire, and volition as well as characteristics such as agency. He focuses on Nyāya's view that that these properties, along with others like karmic merit and moral responsibility, function interdependently and therefore require a self to serve as their shared location. Dasti's chapter provides a further example of the engaged *pūrvapakṣa* characteristic fundamental to the development of the Indian intellectual traditions, focusing on Nyāya's refutations of Sāṃkhya's "frictionless self," which never truly participates in the world or bears world-engaging properties like volition or intention. Dasti also explores Nyāya's contention that as knowing is itself an expression of cognitive agency, Sāṃkhya's dualism of knowing and acting is ultimately unsustainable.

Freschi investigates the intersection of subjectivity, agency, and freedom in the Mīmāṃsā school. Mīmāṃsā takes a common-sense approach to volition, considering felt experience as sufficient to assign agency to the subject. It also implicitly rejects the Sāṃkhya axiom examined by Bryant. Even if the subject truly undergoes change and engages directly with the world, it may still maintain a dynamic identity. This position is due to the Mīmāṃsā emphasis on the moral and epistemological aspect of the subject over the ontological permanence of the *ātman*. Freschi further explores Mīmāṃsā accounts of motivation, focusing on the complex interplay of the Veda as ultimate moral authority, individual desire, the varieties of ritualistic injunctions, and the adjudication of possible conflicts between sources of moral motivation, including apparent conflicts between Vedic injunctions themselves.

Garfield's chapter is both an examination of Madhyamaka Buddhist accounts of free will and a critique of the very problem of free will as developed in Western philosophy. Beginning with a genealogy of the free will problem in the West, Garfield argues that it is not in fact an inescapable outcome of reflection on common beliefs. Rather, it is dependent on a handful of contingent historical factors that are, as seen by comparison with classical Buddhist thought, far from being mere givens. Garfield reflects on how the free will problem dissolves under scrutiny informed by the Madhyamaka notion of dependent origination and concludes by discussing how Madhyamaka thought can account for responsibility and agency within its own framework.

Timalsina's chapter reminds us that like the Mādhyamikas, Śaṅkara (ca. 710 CE), the great Advaita Vedāntin, argued from two perspectives, the conventional and the absolute. While willing to countenance the categories of agent and agency from a conventional view, Śaṅkara follows Gauḍapāda by arguing that from the absolute perspective, agency and free will are nonexistent. They require the possibility of causation, which itself is absent in the ultimate reality. Given that the possibility of genuine causal interaction is central to this issue, Timalsina explores Śaṅkara's arguments against the possibility of causation from the absolute perspective. He further explores Sureśvara's arguments that liberation cannot depend on any kind of action, even meditative practice. Finally, he provides a consideration of alternate models of causation developed by Advaitins that may provide context for our felt sense of agency from a phenomenal level.

While Śaṅkara's nondualism has no scope for agents or agency, Lawrence examines the way in which Kashmiri Śaivas, particularly the Pratyabhijñā philosophers Utpaladeva (ca. 900–950 CE) and Abhinavagupta (ca. 950–1000 CE) wed nondualism with an affirmation of agency. Nondual Śaiva traditions identify Śakti, the Goddess, as the integral creative power and consort of God, Śiva. Lawrence calls attention to the way in which Pratyabhijñā thinkers identify Śakti with "Supreme Speech," which allows them to understand the creation as linguistic in nature and to adopt categories created by the Grammarian school to develop their robust metaphysics. Given this context, the Pratyabhijñā thinkers deploy the *kāraka* analysis to conceive of all of reality as an action directed by the ultimate agent, God, reducing all causality to the syntax of agency. Lawrence calls special attention to the fact that this ultimate affirmation of agency is in stark contrast to a general Indian tendency to denigrate the role of agents in causal processes. Finally, he elaborates the way in which Kashmiri Śaiva cosmology may be understood to be a spectrum of degrees of agency. As beings' awareness of their identity with God is obscured, their dualistic vision of the world is wed to an imperfect and limited agency.

Ganeri examines the conception of agency in the work of Rāmānuja (11th century CE), arguably the most influential philosopher amongst the theistic Vedāntins. Ganeri begins with a discussion of Rāmānuja's metaphysics of selfhood—both individual selfhood and the selfhood of God—that allows for a much more robust notion of self-world interaction than Sāṃkhya or Advaita Vedānta. God is, in Rāmānuja's schema, the self of the world insofar as he sustains it, directs it, and is its purpose-giving end. And his agency serves to sustain and delimit all other expressions of personal freedom. Against this background, Rāmānuja takes pains to stress that the agency of individual selves is indeed real, though it is clearly dependent upon and mediated by a host of factors which are external to the individual—chiefly, of course, God's own power. Rāmānuja accordingly must chart the delicate relationship between the individuals' agency and the sovereign power of God. Ganeri focuses on Rāmānuja's notion of God's agency in the form of oversight and sanction of an individual's acts. He concludes by considering both the apparent renunciation of agency advocated by Rāmānuja in the discipline of *karma-yoga* and the complete unfolding of individual agency in the state of liberation.

The last of the three great traditions of Vedānta was founded by Madhva (1238–1317), who is the subject of Buchta's chapter. Buchta illustrates that in many ways—including his approach to agency—Madhva is an exception to major trends in Indian thought. Against the traditional definition of an agent as a causal participant who is independent, Madhva defines individual beings as "dependent agents." Given the all-encompassing independence of God, nothing else is independent. Further, Madhva holds that different individuals possess different innate natures, eternally established and inexorable, which necessitate their moral decisions and ultimate destination, whether Viṣṇu's heaven, eternal sojourning within *saṃsāra*, or eternal hellish damnation. Buchta provides close analyses of key passages in Madhva's work to illustrate the development of his views. He further considers, somewhat skeptically, whether Madhva possesses the resources for a successful theodicy, as claimed by contemporary Madhva apologists and scholars. Finally, Buchta reflects on later developments in Indian philosophy that adopt or borrow from Madhva.

Our final chapter takes us the closest to the rise of modernity that marks the close of our volume chronologically. Dasa and Edelmann focus on the 16th-century *bhakti* school of Gauḍīya Vaiṣṇavism as expressed by its principal exponent, Jīva Gosvāmin. Prioritizing the testimony of the Bhāgavata Purāṇa as its highest epistemological authority, this school accepts features of Sāṃkhya that countenance an individual enduring self, upon which it grafts aspects of Nyāya, arguing that it must be this very self that possesses latent powers of agency, and knowledge, et cetera. Given that certain verses in the *Bhāgavata* and *Bhagavad Gītā* appear to deny agency in the self, in harmony with the Advaita Vedānta perspective, the chapter engages Advaita Vedānta as Jīva's primary *pūrvapakṣa*. Jīva proceeds further than Nyāya, however, by arguing that these latent capacities must have access to a real body in order to find expression not only in the state of *saṃsāra*, but, as with other Vaiṣṇava schools, in the liberated state as well. Here we encounter the notion of transcendent embodiment through a personalized *siddharūpa*, or *brahman* body, that reflects one's personal devotional relationship with God in a dynamic and eternal spiritual realm.

References

Frankfurt, Harry G. 1978. "The Problem of Action." *American Philosophical Quarterly* 15 (2): 157–162.

Ganeri, Jonardon. 2007. *The Concealed Art of the Soul*. New York: Oxford University Press.

Velleman, J. David. 1992. "What Happens When Someone Acts?" *Mind* 101 (403): 461–481.

I

Agency in Sāṃkhya and Yoga

THE UNCHANGEABILITY OF THE ETERNAL

Edwin F. Bryant

nāsato vidyate bhāvo
nābhavo vidyate sataḥ
—BHAGAVAD GĪTĀ II.16

WE BEGIN THE volume with Sāṃkhya since it is likely the oldest speculative philosophical tradition in ancient India, with clear roots in the Upaniṣads (e.g. *Śvetāśvatara Upaniṣad* VI.13). While, in places, the Upaniṣads exhort their audience to seek the transcendent *ātman* (e.g., *Bṛhadāraṇyaka* II.4.5) and extricate it from its embeddedness in the temporal, only the roots of proto-speculations concerning the metaphysical composition of physical reality within which the *ātman* is embedded are to be found there, and only a couple of brief skeletal passages to a practical method of extrication called Yoga (e.g., *Kaṭha* VI.11–18; *Śvetāśvatara* II.8–15). Sāṃkhya seems to have been the first systematic philosophical tradition to have emerged from that matrix to fill this metaphysical lacuna. Indeed, it has permeated the dominant subsequent Hindu traditions such as Vedānta, Purāṇa, Vaiṣṇava, Śaiva, Tantra and even the medicinal traditions such as *āyurveda*. Larson goes so far as to say: "Buddhist philosophy and terminology, Yoga philosophy, early Vedānta speculation, and the great regional theologies of Śaivism and Vaiṣṇavism are all, in an important sense, footnotes

My thanks to Matthew Dasti and Satyanarayana Dasa for their valuable comments on earlier drafts of this paper.

Some preliminary thoughts on this issue were expressed by the author in Bryant, 2009, 462–466.

and/or reactions to a living 'tradition text' of Sāṃkhya" (1999: 732). One could, indeed, profitably explore the extent to which some of the other subsequent systematized philosophical traditions were in some ways responses to the perceived shortcomings of Sāṃkhya's position on a variety of philosophical issues.

One such issue is that of agency and its location. In Sāṃkhya, there are two discrete and ultimately irreducible ontological entities underpinning all reality: the conscious, eternal, and changeless *ātman* (also known as the *puruṣa*) and *prakṛti*, the unconscious matter underpinning the physical world of change. We will briefly note here that, unlike the Platonic and Abrahamic notions of soul, there are no psychic functions inherent in the *ātman* in Sāṃkhya. As will be discussed further below, the *ātman* is covered by *buddhi*, intelligence; *ahaṃkāra*, ego; and *manas*, mind; but these are distinct, separable, and inanimate coverings of subtle *prakṛti* (and to be ultimately and ideally uncoupled from *ātman*, for the latter's liberation from *saṃsāra*, the cycle of birth and death, to take place). When extricated from its coverings, the liberated *ātman/puruṣa* itself, in its pure autonomous state, has no intentionality (or, more precisely, is devoid of any object of consciousness external to itself, indeed, devoid of any instrument or faculty of cognition). Who (or what), then, in this type of dualistic metaphysics foundational to Sāṃkhya and Yoga, is the agent of action?

Sources

Although Sāṃkhya and Yoga eventually emerged as two of the six schools of Indian philosophy, they were not considered as distinct in the earlier period.[1] The earliest doxographies do not identify Yoga as a separate school (Nicholson 2011: 144); in fact, the first reference to Yoga itself as a distinct school seems to be the writings of Śaṅkara in the 9th century CE (Bronkhorst 1981).[2] We thus utilize as source material for the first section

1. In the *Mahābhārata* epic, for example, none of the 1100-odd total combined references to the two approaches indicate any other difference between them than one of method in attaining the same goal: Yoga seeks the vision of *ātman* through practice and mental concentration, and Sāṃkhya through knowledge and the inferential reasoning power of the intellect (Edgerton 1924).

2. In fact, Yoga is much less a philosophical school than a meditative technique adopted as a sort of generic meditative blueprint for all soteriological schools. Thus Nyāya has no problem deferring to Yoga when it comes to praxis (*Nyāya Sūtras* IV.2.42) and directs its philosophical rebuttals against Sāṃkhya, which it considers its metaphysical opponent, *pūrvapakṣa*, from amongst the Vaidika ("orthodox") traditions (see Dasti in this volume).

of this chapter the primary extant sources for (what came in later times to be known as) the Sāṃkhya and Yoga traditions: the *Yoga Sūtras* (ca. 2nd–3rd century CE) with some of its principle commentaries (Vyāsa 4–5th century; Vācaspati Miśra, 9–10th century; Vijñānabhikṣu, 16th century); the *Sāṃkhya Kārikās* (4–5th century) and three of its commentaries (Gauḍapāda, 6–7th century; Vācaspati Miśra; and a text called the *Yuktidīpikā* 7–8th century); and the *Sāṃkhya Sūtras* (15–16th century) and two of its commentaries (Aniruddha, 15–16th century and Vijñānabhikṣu).[3] For convenience, and following the canonical *Yoga Sūtras* commentator Vyāsa,[4] we will label all these traditions "Sāṃkhya."

For our specific purpose and delimited focus here, we do not require any chronological nuancing in presenting these sources, since there is very little development in the later texts or commentaries to the essential Sāṃkhya notion of free will and agency, later sources simply providing metaphors or elaborations on a long-established Sāṃkhya position. We must note that the *Sāṃkhya Kārikās* (henceforth, *Kārikās*) becomes the "primary" text of the Sāṃkhya tradition in the *darśana* period by default: we have no extant copies of earlier or other primary works, although we know there were numerous early schools of Sāṃkhya, some with significant differences.[5]

The chapter also briefly considers the Sāṃkhya sections of the *Bhagavad Gītā*, which, though a text that becomes incorporated into the *prasthāna trayī*, "three sources of scriptural authority," for the Vedānta school, might just as well be considered a Sāṃkhya text (as it more or less declares itself to be). Our task, here, is not to poach on the Vedānta sections of this volume, but to briefly foreground the tensions that might be inherited for the thinkers represented in those sections, who, given the differences between Sāṃkhya and Vedānta on agency, are obliged to come up with ways to reconcile the *Bhagavad Gītā's* prima facie Sāṃkhya view

---

3. All dates from Larson and Bhattacharya (1987 & 2008).

4. Vyāsa, whose commentary is historically an indispensible canonical extension of Patañjali, explicitly concludes the chapters of his commentary with the colophon *pātañjala-sāṃkhya-pravacana-yoga-śāstra*, "Patañjali's Yoga treatise, an exposition on Sāṃkhya."

5. As with the cluster of Yoga traditions, there were numerous variants of Sāṃkhya, amply attested in the 12th book of the *Mahābhārata* epic. The Chinese Buddhist pilgrim Hsöen Tsang's disciple in the 7th century CE reports 18 schools, and the *Bhāgavata Purāṇa* refers to a plethora of competing taxonomies [XI.22.2]. Only fragments quoted by other authors have survived from the works of the original teachers of the system.

with that of the Vedānta Sūtras, which is explicitly opposed to it. The two Sanskrit terms primarily engaged in this chapter are *kartṛ*, the agent, and *kartṛtva*, agency.

The Problem: The Axiom of Changelessness in Sāṃkhya Metaphysics

As with any human intellectual endeavor dedicated to probing the truths of manifest reality by means of philosophy, religion, or science, one of the main challenges confronting ancient Indian thinkers was how to infer causal explanations to adequately account for the manifest ever-changing world as perceivable effect. For our purposes here, a well-known axiom central to much Indian philosophizing becomes pivotal in this regard:

If something is eternal, then that thing cannot change.

And by the principle of *anvaya-vyatireka*, the contrapositive holds true: if something undergoes change, it cannot be eternal. This, then, for Sāṃkhya, requires that if an *ātman* be deemed an entity that is eternal, as it is construed in the Upaniṣads and subsequently derived Hindu *mokṣa* (soteriological) traditions, its essence or nature must also be eternal; they can never change or "move": "because of the unchanging-ness of that which is the very nature of a thing" (*Sāṃkhya Sūtras* I.8).[6]

The Location of Agency in Sāṃkhya Sources

With these axiomatic presuppositions in place, then, free will and agent-hood, in their basic sense as cause of action and thus, by definition, changeable catalyst triggering temporal action, could only belong to *prakṛti's* sphere of reality for Sāṃkhya. It could not belong to the eternal, changeless *puruṣa*, the synonym for *ātman* preferred by the Sāṃkhya school (the terms will be used here interchangeably).

In the *Sāṃkhya Kārikās* (XIX), Iśvara Kṛṣṇa, the author, lists the five attributes of the *puruṣa*: *sākṣitva*, witness; *kaivalya*, autonomous; *mādhyasthya*, indifferent; *draṣṭṛtva*, seer; and *akartṛbhāva*, non-agent. To

6. *Svabhāvasya-anapāyitvāt*. All translations my own. Because of limitations of space, only Sanskrit for select translations provided.

be an agent, of course, can only transpire in a context of changeability and responsiveness: agency presupposes the potential to make choices (and change one's choice if one so determines), some form of investment in choice, and determinative or discriminative faculties with which to adequately select the desirable choices between options. And all such potential change, as Vācaspati reminds us in his commentary to LVI, "cannot be brought about by *brahman*, because of the unchangability of *citiśakti* (pure consciousness)."[7] Consequently, in the phraseology of the *Sāṃkhya Sūtras*, "action is not a property of the *puruṣa*....which cannot move" [I.48–52].[8]

In the *Yuktidīpikā* commentary to XIX a number of conceptualizations of agency are rejected as applicable to the *puruṣa*;[9] the common concern of all these inapplicable forms of agency is outlined in a further passage in this section:

> The nature of not being an agent (*akartṛ*) is non-production.[10] The nature of production is change and movement. He is not an agent because he is devoid of action; he is not an agent because he is not productive...And also, [*puruṣa* is not an agent] because he has the nature of being unmixed.

To be an agent means to be able to "produce" an action, and this either entails the agentive entity undergoing some internal change or its "mixing" with some other external entity and thereby also undergoing change. If production is due to the entity's latent inherent dynamic, its eternal nature is compromised, as it will undergo change from a non-actualized pre-productive state to an actualized productive (or post-productive) state—worse, in fact, as, if production were its inherent nature, it would as a consequence

---

7. *Citiśakter apariṇāmāt.*

8. *Niṣkriyasya tad-[gati-]asambhavāt....na karmaṇāpy ataddharmatvāt.*

9. "It does not directly ascertain objects it contacts through the external and internal sense organs; it does not become a subordinate constituent of the *guṇas* (the three 'strands' or qualities that compose *prakṛti*); it does not sustain the object produced by others (the *guṇas*) as a nurse does with a child; it does not engage others to activity, while situated in connection, like one who sets the chariot, car or machine in motion [and then sits inactively as a passenger]; it does not create something from itself like a lump of clay, since unconscious things cannot be produced from conscious things [due to dissimilarity between cause and effect]; it does not do something with something else like a potter does; it does not do something through its command, like a magician does; nor does it actively work jointly [with the *guṇas*] like a father and mother together."

10. *Aprasava-dharmī.*

always be producing, and thus always undergoing change. If that entity has to come in some sort of contact with an external entity or force to produce, thereby becoming "mixed," its unchanging nature is again compromised (i.e., milk with a souring agent and with motion, which causes its production of, but also transformation into, yogurt). By such reasonings, which will be further extended in Sāṃkhya's rebuttal to Nyāya, action can only occur in the world of mixture and change, not in any changeless entity like *puruṣa*, which, having no internal parts and nothing mixed in with it, and producing nothing from itself, can never change.

This raises the obvious question, which Gauḍapāda echoes from the *Vedānta Sutras* (II.3.34–40): "if *puruṣa* is not an agent, then how does it determine that 'I will perform *dharma* and not engage in *adharma*?' "(Gauḍapāda to *Sāṃkhya Kārikā* XIX). For some of the reasons noted above, agency, in the Sāṃkhya perspective, has to be consigned to an entity other than *puruṣa*, which must be "unmixed" with such changeable qualities as agency, and Sāṃkhya assigns this function either to *buddhi*, its covering of discrimination, or to the second evolute emanating from *prakṛti*, *ahaṃkāra*, ego (literally: "I maker"), defined as the function of conceit or ego (*abhimāna*, *Kārikā* XXIV).[11] As noted, *buddhi*, *ahaṃkāra*, and *manas* cover the *puruṣa* like a multilayered lampshade covers a bulb:

"The ego is the agent, not the *puruṣa*." (*Sāṃkhya Sūtras* VI.54).

Aniruddha: Since there is the immediate cognition that 'I do,' the doubt arises whether *ahaṃkāra* (ego) is the agent, or whether, by the word *ahaṃkāra*, the self be denoted and it be the agent. In regard to this the author says [the former]: "Because *puruṣa* is not liable to transformation."

Vijñānabhikṣu: The internal organ possessing the mental state of *abhimāna* (conceit) is *ahaṃkāra*. It is that which possesses activity, as exertion is generally seen to follow immediately after *abhimāna*; it is not *puruṣa* since he is not constituted for change.

---

11. The ego is the faculty of *abhimāna*, "false conceit" or "conception" (in this case an erroneous one regarding one's self). In this regard, the *Yoga Sūtra* (II.6) defines its very close synonym, *asmitā*, as the confusing of the instruments and powers of sight with the seer, that is, of one's *ātman* self as pure consciousness with the body/mind instrumentation through which consciousness cognizes and becomes aware of external objects (subtle or gross). The "conceit" points to the illusion of thinking that it is one's self (*ātman*) that is acting, when, in fact, all action is performed by *prakṛti* (as the *Gītā* will assert in verses quoted in the second section).

The Nyāya view that consciousness and cognition must be co-locational, hinted at by Aniruddha here, will be discussed below, but for Sāṃkhya, in conjunction with the ego noted in the verse above, it is *buddhi* (the first evolute of *prakṛti* enveloping the *ātman*) that cognizes. *Buddhi* provides the faculty of determination or discrimination that governs choices (*adhyavasāya*, its primary characteristic), and some Sāṃkhya sources prefer to associate *buddhi* with agency:

> "*Buddhi* is determination [quoting *Kārikā* XXIII]"; this means that there is no difference between the action [of determining] and the active agent [that which determines]. It is known in the world that anyone who is an agent of action, reflects, thinks, decides "I am qualified in this matter," determines that "this will be done by me," and then does it. Now "determination" consists in the decision that "this should be done," and it belongs to, and forms the characteristic function of, *buddhi*, which obtains consciousness from its proximity[12] to consciousness. (Vācaspati Miśra on *Sāṃkhya Kārikā* XXIII)

Buddhi is also the locus of knowledge, *jñāna*, and other behavior regulating functions, called *bhāvas*, with which to enact choice and free will (XXIII).[13] But the point is that anything other than the function of inactive awareness is *prakṛti-kṛta* (LVI), an activity of *prakṛti* (whether in its manifestation of *ahaṃkāra* or of *buddhi*) undertaken for the sake of *puruṣa*. Since to be an agent is to effect activity, and thus undergo change, the *puruṣa/ātman*, if it is to be unchanging, can do nothing other than be aware ("see"). As Gauḍapāda puts it: "just like a *saṃnyāsin* is indifferent toward the villagers engaged in tilling, so the *puruṣa* remains indifferent" (commentary on *Sāṃkhya Kārikā* XIX). It cannot be overstressed that *puruṣa* is *anupakārin*, "plays no part" (LX), other than being proximate to the source of action.

---

12. We will return to Vācaspati's comment about "proximity" shortly.

13. *Buddhi* is the receptacle for three additional *bhāvas* "states," in addition to *jñāna*, knowledge, as well as their opposites, totaling eight possible states. These are the behavior-governing functions of: *dharma*, virtue; *virāga*, non-attachment; and *aiśvarya*, possession of power (XXIII). Manifesting its higher potential (*sattva*), leads to higher embodied forms and, ultimately, through to the highest expression of *jñāna*, enlightenment. The opposites of these (non-virtue, etc.) are *buddhi's* lower potential, which leads to lower forms of embodiment (*tamas*).

Sāṃkhya Objections to a Nyāya Pūrvapakṣa

While Sāṃkhya's position on agency is taken to task by Vedānta and other systems due to the moral implications it raises, it is Nyāya that primarily engages and challenges the metaphysical axioms that seem to mandate the intractability of the Sāṃkhya position (Vedānta, after all, shares Sāṃkhya's *satkāryavāda* presuppositions[14]). Nyāya seeks to ascribe agency (and other psychological qualities) to the *ātman*, while simultaneously preserving its changelessness, by separating the categories of substance and qualities. We will consider some responses from the later Sāṃkhya tradition to such proposals (since Indian philosophy rarely proceeds without a rebuttal to the *pūrvapakṣa*).

We begin with the realist Nyāya argument (outlined in Dasti, and inherited by Mīmāṃsā, as mentioned by Freschi in this volume), sandwiched in the quotation below, that consciousness and cognition must be co-located in the same substratum, simply because common-sense experience makes this appear to be true, and common sense should be upheld in the absence of compelling contrary evidence. Vācaspati articulates the Nyāya view: "But from experience, after determining what is to be done, we think: 'I am conscious, and, desiring something, I will act.' In this way, it is established that the experience of consciousness and activity occurs in the same locus.... The seed of this error is the union (*saṃyoga*)" (commentary to *Kārikā* XIX–XX; we will take up the important notion of "union" later). The *Yuktidīpikā* also takes up this theme in its comments to the same verse:

> [**Sāṃkhya view**] Because there is the absence of [the qualities of] happiness and unhappiness in the *puruṣa*, therefore it is the witness of their activities.... It has the nature of being a seer, because it is devoid of qualities.
>
> [**Nyāya *Pūrvapakṣa***]... This is incorrect, because if this were so then there would be a difference of location in a unitary sentence involving the "I-maker (*ahaṃkāra*)." But it is seen that it is the "I" that is happy and the "I" that is unhappy....

---

14. *Satkāryavāda* is the view that all effects in visible reality are present in one cause. Nyāya is *asatkāryavāda*: effects are new entities not present in their causes; reality is to be understood as the product of seven distinct causes.

> [**Sāṃkhya response**]. This is not conclusive. There is the difference of location involving the qualities of body and soul in single sentences involving the use of "I," such as in the case of the sentence: "I am white" and "I am black." Likewise would be the case with pleasure, pain, etc.; those, too, would not be the qualities of the same self. (XIX)

Nyāya (contra, e.g., the materialist Cārvāka), does not accept "I-am" bodily qualities (e.g., whiteness or blackness) as being co-located in the *ātman*, but as objects external to its awareness, so, by the same logic, for Sāṃkhya, I-am qualities of agency and feelings, too, are similarly objects of consciousness. Nyāya, at this point, would likely protest that it is only apperceptive states of I-am-ness that pertain to the *ātman*—the internal states of agency, happiness, and distress, et cetera—not external perceptive states such as the bodily color of whiteness or blackness. Vācaspati probes the fault-lines with this position:

> There is a *puruṣa* because of the existence of experience. By "the existence of experience" is intended the objects of experience, happiness and distress. The objects of experience, happiness and distress, which are felt by everyone, are experienced as agreeable and disagreeable. But there must be someone other than the feelings themselves, for whom the feelings can be agreeable or disagreeable or otherwise. They cannot be agreeable and disagreeable to *buddhi* etc. [i.e., ego, mind], as *buddhi* etc. are themselves composed of pleasure and pain, and so [positing this] would violate the principle of things acting on themselves. (Vācaspati to *Kārikā* XVII)

Vācaspati is here invoking the "anti-reflexivity" principle (*svātmani vṛtti-virodhāt*), which is widely accepted in Indian philosophy, namely, that a thing cannot act on itself—cutting cannot cut itself or, in this case, there cannot be a feeling of pleasure and pain by pleasure and pain, that is, the *ātman* cannot feel itself. Feelings are as much objects of experience as bodily states and also require a distinct subject, or "experiencer."

The most common objection to the Nyāya view, predictably, is that assigning changeable qualities to the *ātman* compromises its eternality:

> It is not possible to say that the desire, et cetera, of the *puruṣa* should be eternal, because they are found by perception to be producible;

> and if you admit a producible attribute in the case of *puruṣa*, it would entail his liability to transformation. (Vijñānabhikṣu to *Sāṃkhya Sūtras* I.145)

As we know, the only qualities of the *ātman* that Sāṃkhya will entertain are the eternal (i.e., not "producible") ones of being-ness and consciousness (*sat* and *cit*); producible ones, that is, qualities that are everywhere perceived as coming and going temporally, such as agential choice and desire, cannot belong to an eternal entity. Apart from anything else, soteriological problems present themselves, from a Sāṃkhya perspective, if qualities are to be entertained as belonging to the *ātman*. In what may be an ironic response to the charge directed against them (outlined in Dasti's chapter) that liberation would be impossible in their changeless-*puruṣa* ontology, Sāṃkhya retorts that this very corollary is endemic to the Nyāya position, not theirs:

> [if the qualities of agency and happiness and distress were in the soul] there would arise the undesirable consequence that the *puruṣa* would not attain *mokṣa*. Because a quality can never be separated from its substance, if happiness and distress were the qualities of the *ātman*, there would be the undesirable consequence that the *ātman* could never attain liberation from them. Therefore their being qualities of the soul is not correct... Therefore it is impossible that the *ātman* has the qualities of desire, aversion, endeavor, *dharma*, knowledge, *saṃskāra*, which are of varied nature and mutually contradictory. (*Yuktidīpikā* XIX)

Qualities such as agency and desire, then, must belong to a substratum such as that proposed by Sāṃkhya: an inanimate and changeable *buddhi*, which can never attain liberation as it can never be free from its inherent qualities, and so is distinct from (but animated by) the changeless *ātman*, which can free itself from that which is not inherent to it:

> Liberation can never belong to *buddhi*, et cetera, ... since happiness and suffering constitutes its nature, so how could it ever be separated from its inherent nature (*svabhāva*)? It is only when something is distinct from *buddhi* and does not have such a nature, that liberation is possible.... Therefore, for there to be liberation, the *ātman* must be something other than *buddhi*. (Vācaspati to *Kārikā* XVII)

And again:

> The knowledge of the self propounded by [those who ascribe agency to the self] is misleading argumentation. The knowledge of the self propounded by them is not reasonable, because of its contradictoriness to the *śruti*, because the self does not possess agency of itself, and because (on the basis of this theory) non-release would be entailed, since there is the saying:
>
> > If the *ātman* had the form of the agent, et cetera.
> > Then do not desire its liberation
> > For the inherent essence of entities cannot be separated from them
> > Like heat from the sun.
> > (Aniruddha to *Sāṃkhya Sūtra* VI.34, verse untraced)

One is tempted to wonder whether the format of Aniruddha's quotation here is provocatively (mischievously?) turning on its head the following verse, composed by the Naiyāyika Udayana, situating agency in *ātman*:

> An agent's own merit fixes his place
> Cognition is his alone
> Else liberation would be a fancy
> Or seeds of bondage never sown.
> (Udayana, quoted in Dasti, in this volume)

Thus, where Nyāya sees the Sāṃkhya view as incompatible with liberation, Sāṃkhya deems that it is Nyāya's view that is soteriologically incoherent: it is precisely because the *ātman* is in reality "unmixed" by such qualities, as in a Sāṃkhya metaphyics, that it can be extracted from them and attain liberation.

As touched on in Aniruddha's quotation, above, the same soteriological impasse of the Nyāya position is pursued by Sāṃkhya on the basis of other epistemological means:

> Moreover, with those logicians who desire the agency of the Self, there can be no proof or possibility of release, since it is this modification of *buddhi* (the covering of intelligence), namely, "I am the agent" that has been declared in the *Gītā* [III.27] as being the cause of the production of *adṛṣṭa*, or merit and demerit [i.e., *karma* and bondage in *saṃsāra*]. Again, as in their opinion, this particular

> modification of *buddhi* or idea does not constitute the nature of false knowledge, it is not possible that it should be removed by knowledge of Truth. Hence, seeing as how the release taught in the Veda is not possible on any other theory, it is desired by us that the self is not an agent. And from its not being the agent follows the non-existence of pleasure, etc.,.... [in the *ātman*]. And thereafter *manas* (mind) having to be conceived as the cause of deeds to be done, etc.... It follows, therefore, that the self is devoid of attributes (Vijñānabhikṣu I.145, Sinha translation).

This argument resorts to an appeal to scriptural authority (*āgama/śabda/śruti*); while this is not a reason-based (inferential) form of epistemology, it was standard for the "orthodox" (Vedic) schools, which included Nyāya, to accept the epistemological validity of the sacred texts (even if only nominally). Vijñānabhikṣu's point is that the *Bhagavad Gītā* (III.27) explicitly states that considering agency to be in the *ātman* occurs in one who is deluded by ego. Since a Nyāya ontology explicitly postulates such agency in *ātman*, it opposes scripture and thus cannot be rectified by knowledge of Truth in the form of the teachings of the *Bhagavad Gītā* (which will be examined in some detail below).

Objections (Pūrvapakṣa) *to the Sāṃkhya Position*

If *puruṣa*'s eternality exempts it from any form of action, Sāṃkhya is now left with the problem of accounting for how an unconscious entity, *prakṛti*, acting purely mechanistically, can be an agent. In his preamble to the *Kārikā*'s response to this, Gauḍapāda lays out part of the problem: "how can *prakṛti*, which is non-conscious, act like the conscious *puruṣa* and say: 'I must provide the *puruṣa* with the objects of the senses in the three worlds like sound, et cetera, and at the end liberation?' " Sāṃkhya offers in response a metaphor: "just as the non-conscious milk functions for the nourishment of the calf, so does *prakṛti* function for the sake of *puruṣa*." In other words, *prakṛti* just acts spontaneously due, as will be discussed further below, to the proximity of the *puruṣa* (*Kārikā* LVII).

This radical changeless non-involvement of *puruṣa*, then, leads Sāṃkhya inexorably to the famous climax of the *Kārikās*: "no one, therefore, is bound, no one liberated: only *prakṛti* in her various evolutes (*āśraya*) transmigrates, is bound, and is released" (LXII). Gauḍapāda spells this out: "it is the practice in this world to say the *puruṣa* is bound or liberated, but it is neither.... It is always liberated and all-pervading. It is only *prakṛti* that is bound or liberated" (commentary to LXII).

Prakṛti binds herself with her own *bhāvas*[15] (LXIII), and releases herself through them (LXV). Vacaspati offers more metaphors: "this is just as victory or defeat, although actually occurring to his soldiers, are attributed to a king, so the effects of sorrow or gain occur to the king" (commentary to LXII).

Aniruddha's *vṛtti* commentarial preamble to *Sāṃkhya Sūtra* I.105 considers a further concomitant problem: "if *pradhāna* [*prakṛti*] is the *kartṛ*, and *puruṣa* the *bhoktṛ*, then one entity would be experiencing the karmic consequences of acts performed by someone else." The text and its commentaries do not engage the moral or judicial problem implicit in such a state of affairs, but concern themselves with establishing its possibility by analogy:

> "A non-agent (*a-kartṛ*) can be the experiencer of results; just as is the case with food et cetera."
>
> **Aniruddha**: Just as in the case where the nature of being an agent in the cooking of food, et cetera [i.e., the cook], is not the [same as the] agent in the form of the master who enjoys it, so is the case here [with *puruṣa* and *prakṛti*]. (*Sāṃkhya Sūtras* I.105)
>
> Additionally, to account for this, the notion that the results belong to the agent is because of a lack of discrimination"
>
> **Aniruddha**: The *puruṣa* is neither the agent nor the *bhoktṛ* (experiencer), but because of having the material nature [*prakṛti*] reflected in it, it has the notion of being the agent. It is because of not attaining the discrimination of the difference between *prakṛti* and *puruṣa* that the notion that it is the agent of the fruit of action comes about. (*Sāṃkhya Sūtras* I.106)
>
> So when the Truth of reality is explained, there is neither [the agent nor experiencer] (*Sāṃkhya Sūtras* I.107)

The common Sāṃkhya and Vedānta trope of "reflection" is invoked here in Aniruddha's commentary to I.106. To accommodate the notion of *puruṣa's* changelessness and total unconnectedness with the world of change, *buddhi* is typically analogized with a mirror. As the changes (such

15. See footnote 12.

as warps) occurring in a mirror do not occur "in" the person gazing at his reflection in the mirror, yet the person is nonetheless aware of his distorted image, so *buddhi* "reflects" the world of change back to *puruṣa*, who is aware of yet aloof from it. Thus, commenting on *Sāṃkhya Sūtra* III.56, which refers to the *ātman* as "the knower of everything and the agent of everything," Aniruddha states: "such conceit (*abhimāna*), of all-knowingness and doing-ness arises through its being reflected in *prakṛti*."

This notion of reflection is then coupled with that of conjunction and proximity:

> "Superintendence belongs to the *antaḥ-karaṇa*, which is illuminated by *puruṣa* like an iron." (*Sāṃkhya Sūtras* I.99)
>
> **Vijñānabhikṣu**: The illumination of the *antaḥ-karaṇa*, psychic body,[16] consists merely of a particular conjunction with consciousness, which is eternally shining, that is, is nothing but the reflection of consciousness produced through a particular conjunction.

Sāṃkhya runs into various problems with this analogy: how can consciousness, which is one kind of an entity, be "reflected" in a completely different metaphysical entity with which it has no causal connection; *puruṣa* and *prakṛti* are ontologically completely distinct sorts of things with diametrically opposed natures?[17] Conceptualizing how consciousness can impact matter (and, in this case, be reflected back to its source), in other words accounting for ignorance of the real nature of the self, *avidyā*, is a famously recondite area of Indian philosophy (and philosophy in general, although Indic dualism has arguably an advantage over Cartesian dualism here[18]), so one cannot single out Sāṃkhya on this score. But this does lead to an exegetical scramble to construe "single reflection" theories (Vācaspati) that are later countered by "double reflection" theories (Vijñānabhikṣu) in Yoga exegesis.[19] Yoga's response to this metaphysical

16. The *antaḥ-karaṇa* consists of the *buddhi, ahaṃkāra, manas,* and other subtle cognitive elements.

17. The *Sāṃkhya Kārikā* describes the various qualities of *prakṛti*, and then simply states that the *puruṣa's* nature is the opposite of them all (XI).

18. The mind, in Sāṃkhya, is simply a subtler form of matter than the body and sense objects, and hence can effect them, being constituted of essentially the same stuff. Consciousness, in this model, does not effect anything; it simply pervades the mind with its consciousness, thus animating it. See Larson (1983) for brief discussion, here.

19. See, for discussion, Rukmani (1988).

dilemma is that *buddhi* is made of the finest potential of *prakṛti*, *sattva*, which can attain a translucence equal (*sāmya*) to that of consciousness (*Yoga Sūtra* III.55). Leaving aside the philosophical vagueness of a qualifier such as "equal to," the fact is, even the highest state of *sattva* (i.e., *sattva* as free from the influence of *rajas* and *tamas* as possible), is, nonetheless, unconscious matter, and the problem invites criticism from rival schools.

Also tricky, from a philosophical point of view, is using the language of conjunction or proximity (*sannidhi*/*saṃyoga*), to account for the spontaneity of *prakṛti's* agentive evolutionary fecundity and *puruṣa's* lack thereof. The notion is hinted at in the *Kārikās*,[20] where it is stated that because of their proximity, the unconscious one (*prakṛti*) appears conscious,[21] because of the agency of the *guṇas*, while the neutral one (*puruṣa*) appears as if it were the agent (XX). The *Sāṃkhya Sūtras* expands on this: "[Apparent] agency in *puruṣa* is from the influence [of *prakṛti*] through proximity to consciousness, through proximity to consciousness (*sic*, I.164)." On the other side of the metaphysical divide, *buddhi* likewise appears as if conscious due to the same proximity. As always, analogies are offered:

> "Because of the conjunction (*samyogāt*) between them, the unconscious one appears as if (*iva*) characterized by consciousness, and the indifferent one (*puruṣa*) appears as if the agent, when it is the *guṇas* that have agency." (*Kārikā* XX)
>
> **Gauḍapāda**: Just as in the world a jar becomes cold when it comes in contact with coolness, and becomes hot when it comes in contact with heat, so the... *mahat* et cetera [synonym of *buddhi*], by coming in contact with *puruṣa*, becomes as if intelligent... And [from its side], though activity resides in the *guṇas* [constituents of *prakṛti*] yet the indifferent *puruṣa* becomes as if an agent, although it is not an actual agent. There is an illustration of this: as a person who is not a thief, when arrested along with thieves, becomes a thief. So the [real] agent is the *guṇas*, but the *puruṣa*, although indifferent,

---

20. In the famous analogy of the blind man (*prakṛti*) and the lame man (*puruṣa*), *Kārikā* XXI uses the term *saṃyoga*, proximity, to account for how creation (*sargaḥ*) takes place from the association of these two. The concept takes up several aphorisms in the *Yoga Sūtras* (e.g., II.23).

21. *Tasmāt tat-saṃyogād acetanaṃ cetanāvad iva... karteva bhavati udāsīnaḥ.*

> becomes active by coming in contact with them, by coming in contact with the [actual] agent (on XX).

Ātman is potentially omnipresent and infinite (see, e.g., *Yoga Sūtra* I.45; IV.23), and it has no spatial geography: how then, are notions such as "nearness" or "conjunction" to be understood for something that potentially at least has the ability to pervade everything? Vācaspati Miśra, in his commentary to *Yoga Sūtra* I.4, states: "the nearness of the *puruṣa* is not in space, nor yet in time, on account of the absence of juxtaposition. It is defined by suitability (*yogyatā*): the *puruṣa* possesses the potential (*śakti*) of enjoying as subject, while the mind possesses the potential of being enjoyed." In using nebulous categories such as *yogyatā*, Vācaspati is implicitly acknowledging the limits of philosophical thought in conceptualizing the perennially problematic relationship between consciousness and matter (more famously expressed in terms such as *anirvacanīya*, beyond the ability of words to convey [Śaṅkara], and *acintya*, inconceivable [the Gauḍīya school], both represented later in this volume).

If we read "nearness" neither spatially nor temporally but as a metaphoric indicator of consciousness "pervading" *prakṛti*, other questions are raised. How can this pervasion or "nearness" between *puruṣa* and *prakṛti* ever be terminated in the liberated state as Sāṃkhya and Yoga requires it to be (*Kārikās* LIX & LXI; *Yoga Sūtras* II.22)? How can one all-pervading consciousness, once regained, be autonomous and exclusively immune from *prakṛti* (*Yoga Sūtras* I.4, II.25, III.50, IV.34) if the latter is also all-pervasive (*Kārikā* X)? Although both entities are two radically distinct kinds of things, they are both "reals," eternal and omnipresent, so how can *puruṣa*, which is inherently conscious, not be conscious of that with which it is eternally and infinitely co-terminus and co-extensive, so to speak?! Thus, as an aside, when we are informed by the *Yoga Sūtras* that *prakṛti* is "destroyed" for one who has "seen" the truth (II.22), the metaphysical gap between Sāṃkhya and Advaita Vedānta, which resolves this dilemma by simply accepting the reality of *puruṣa* and dispensing with *prakṛti* altogether, seems not so vast, even as Vedānta takes Sāṃkhya to task more than any other school[22] (Burley 2004).

---

22. Section IV of chapter I and section I of chapter II. Sāṃkhya heads the list of inadequate *pūrvapakṣas*, significant in itself in Sanskrit hermeneutics by dint of beginning the list, and takes up more aphorisms than any other school.

Yet another obstacle to the Sāṃkhya view is represented in Aniruddha's commentary to *Sāṃkhya Sūtra* I.164, this time hermeneutical rather than philosophical:

> But some may say: "we hear of the agency of the Self from the scripture: how is this?" To this the author replies: "Agency" is the fancy or assumption of agency from the influence of *prakṛti* by means of her proximity to consciousness.

Aniruddha here is referring to the *Vedānta Sūtras* (II.3.33–39) as the scripture in question (discussed in the Vedānta contributions to this volume). This leads to a different sort of problem for the Vaidika exegetes of the *Kārikās* and *Sāṃkhya Sūtras*, who must not only accept the epistemological authority of the *Upaniṣads/Vedānta* texts,[23] but, who, in several instances, wrote commentaries on, them.[24] How to reconcile the clear statement in the *Vedānta Sūtras* that *ātman* must be an agent (II.3.33), with the equally clear statements of the *Kārikās* and *Sāṃkhya Sūtras* that it can certainly not be so? Aniruddha here is reworking *Kārikā* XX quoted above ("the neutral one appears as if it were the agent," because of proximity) into a response to the Vedānta position in an attempt at an exegetical resolution: the agency indicated in the Vedānta is not factual, but fanciful.

In this regard, Vijñānabhikṣu, noteworthy in his attempt to reconcile the various *darśana* philosophical traditions (Nicholson 2011), offers the following comments in his commentary to *Sāmkhya Sūtras* II.29:

> *Puruṣa,* although itself immutable, through the instruments of eye, et cetera, becomes the seer, the speaker, the thinker, et cetera, in as much as he incites them to action simply by his mere proximity to them, which is called *saṃyoga,* as is the case with the magnet, which moves iron by itself by mere proximity to it, without actively exerting any force. And here agency (*kartṛtva*) consists in that which sets in motion the wheel (*kāraka-cakra*) of all that helps toward the accomplishment of action.

---

23. The *śruti,* "that which is heard," consists of the four strata of the old Vedic corpus: the four Vedas, Brāhmaṇas, Āraṇyakas, and Upaniṣads. These are highest epistemological source for Vaidikas (those who accept the authority of these texts).

24. From the scholastics quoted here who wrote commentaries on Sāṃkhya, Gauḍapāda, Vācaspati, and Vijñānabhikṣu also wrote on Vedānta texts.

The magnet metaphor works less problematically than the "cow spontaneously producing milk" metaphor of *Kārikā* LVII noted above—the *Vedānta Sūtra* II.2.3 and its commentaries point out that, in the cow example, it is the sentient principle in the cow that causes the milk to flow, not inanimate matter, hence this analogy for a spontaneously productive but insentient *prakṛti* is defective. Introducing an inanimate magnet as an example of something that can cause action in another entity without being a conscious agent sidesteps this particular objection. Thus, a reconciliatory form of passive agency is allotted to *puruṣa* without requiring it to be an agent in any sort of manner that is active (with its concomitant and undesirable corollary, change). Vijñānabhikṣu thus at least offers a coherent harmonization of the Vedāntic and Sāṃkhya viewpoints.

Agency in the Sāmkhya of the Bhagavad Gītā*: Hermeneutical Dilemmas*

This problematic of reconciling these Sāṃkhya and Vedānta statements on agency becomes even more conspicuous in what we might term a Vedānto-Sāṃkhyan text, the *Bhagavad Gītā*. While the *Gītā* is construed as part of the *prasthāna trayī* of the Vedānta tradition,[25] one might just as well consider it a Sāṃkhya text expressing the theism of the older Sāṃkhya traditions[26] as well Vedānta. Two and a half of the *Gītā's* 18 chapters are dedicated to (and are one of the best sources for) the expressions of the three *guṇas* of Sāṃkhya (XIV, XVII, and much of XVIII), another chapter to the Sāṃkhya binaries of *puruṣa* and *prakṛti*[27] (chapter XIII), and the text is pervaded with Sāṃkhya language and taxonomy. Indeed, the text not only explicitly accepts Sāṃkhya (V.4–5; XIII.24), but specifically claims to be transmitting (II.39; XVIII.13), and indeed, of Kṛṣṇa originally teaching Sāṃkhya himself (III.3). The text, in fact, is consciously appropriating and subsuming the dominant intellectual currents of its time under a higher principle of *bhakti* to Kṛṣṇa as the Supreme Being, but, for our purposes here, we feel justified in claiming it to be as much of a Sāṃkhya as a Vedānta text.

---

25. The three sources are: the Upaniṣads themselves, the *Vedānta Sūtras*, and the *Gītā*.

26. It is erroneous to generically label Sāṃkhya non-theistic, as many, in fact most, strains of Sāṃkhya were theistic, as evident in the *Mahābhārata* epic and entire Purāṇic genre (for the theism of Sāṃkhya, see Bronkhorst 1981).

27. The synonyms of *kṣetra* and *kṣetra-jña*, the field and the knower of the field, are used for *prakṛti* and *puruṣa* in chapter XIII.

The *Bhagavad Gītā* appears to unequivocally adhere to the Sāṃkhya position: "In all instances, action is performed by the qualities of *prakṛti*; one who is deluded by ego thinks 'I am the agent'" (III.27); "One who sees that all actions are performed by *prakṛti* only, and that the *ātman* is a non-agent, that person sees" (XIII.29); "The Lord does not create either the agency or the deeds of people, nor the connection with the resulting fruits of work. It is spontaneous *prakṛti* that produces this" (V.14).

Elsewhere, Kṛṣṇa teaches the five Sāṃkhya causes of action, one of which is the agent, along with the body as seat, instruments, efforts, and the presiding deities (of the senses). All action, he states, stems from these five (XVIII.13–15). Indeed, "one who sees the *ātman* as the sole agent, has imperfect intelligence; such a person is a fool and does not see" (XVIII.16). Rather, "He whose state of mind is that 'I am not the agent,' his intelligence is not tainted..." (XVIII.17). The text then proceeds to discuss the agent, action, and the instruments of knowledge according to the three *guṇas* (XVIII.20-36), with the agent, in all instances, construed as a product of *prakṛti*.[28]

While *puruṣa* is not here rendered an agentive cause in any sort of an active way, it is a cause in so far as *puruṣa's* presence is causal in the phenomenology of "being the experiencer," (*bhoktṛtve*): "*prakṛti* is said to be the cause in the matter of agency (*kartṛtve*), the act to be done, and the instrument of action; *puruṣa* is said to be the cause in the experiencing of happiness and distress" (XIII.20). Experience requires consciousness, and this, of course, *puruṣa* provides (in fact it is all it can provide, constitutionally, for Sāṃkhya). But this is a very passive type of causality and is not assigned the term *kartṛ*, agent, which implies the performer of an action. The section concludes that: "the one who truly sees, is the one who sees that all actions are being done by *prakṛti* and that the *puruṣa* is not the agent" (*akartāram*, XIII.29); "*puruṣa* does not act" (*na karoti*, XIII.31).

Again, we do not wish to trespass on the Vedānta contributions to this volume, but we must note that all the Vedānta schools accommodate some variant of the Sāṃkhya schema into their metaphysics, in addition to appropriating the *Bhagavad Gītā* into their primary canon. We will thus simply state here that, at least in their commentaries on these *Gītā* verses,

---

28. After listing the threefold impulses to action (knowledge, object of knowledge, and the knower, XVIII.18), Kṛṣṇa lists the three constituents of action: the agent, action, and the instruments of action (XVIII.19). Merging these latter two lists, he selects knowledge, action, and the agent for analysis according to the three *guṇas* (XVIII.19–26). The *kartṛ* influenced by *sattva* has such qualities as detachment from the fruits; the one by *rajas*, qualities such as attachment to the fruit; and the one by *tamas*, such qualities as disregard for other, etc.

some commentators follow the Sāṃkhya position on agency-in-*prakṛti* (e.g., Śaṅkara, Jñāneśvara, Śrīdhara, Viśvanātha Cakravartī), and some the Vedānta position of agency-in-*puruṣa* (e.g. Rāmānuja, Madhva, Baladeva), with a clear but not quite exact divide between the *advaita* exegetes and the Vaiṣṇava ones[29] (but note the differences here between Baladeva and Viśvanātha, who share the same Gauḍīya Vedānta lineage). To illustrate this exegetical dilemma, we will content ourselves with one example (but see Dasa and Edelmann in this volume) the later 18th-century Gauḍīya commentator Baladeva Vidyābhūṣaṇa, who is well aware of some of the sources we have quoted.

While, in places, Baladeva seems to follow the Sāṃkhya view explicit in the *Gītā*,[30] elsewhere, he assigns a more robust sense of agency to *puruṣa*, most notably in XIII.22:

> The followers of Sāṃkhya, taking isolated meanings from such statements [viz., some of the various *Gītā* verses noted above], state that *prakṛti* alone is the agent. That is an over-hasty claim, because it is not possible for *prakṛti*, which is unconscious, to be an agent, just as it is not possible for metal or wood. Agency means having direct perception of the means [to accomplish an act], the desire to act, and volition, and this occurs only in a conscious entity. Therefore the sacred texts state.... "the *puruṣa* is the seer, toucher, hearer, taster, smeller, thinker, knower, and agent" [*Praśna Upaniṣad* IV.9].... Some [Sāṃkhya followers] say that *prakṛti* has this nature [of agency] because of the nearness of *puruṣa*, and because of the

29. While this is problematic, we use this term for succinctness of phraseology only. It is difficult to succinctly categorize the Vedānta commentators in a non-cumbersome manner for reasons that would take us too far afield to consider here in depth (but, e,g, rubrics of "non-dualists" vs. "dualists" would be contested by most opponents of nondualism, all of who other than Madhva promote some expression of nondualism; and rubrics of "nondualists" vs. "Vaiṣṇavas" that we have adopted here are unsatisfactory for different reasons: most nondualist commentators of the text including Śaṅkara were, conventionally at least, Vaiṣṇavas).

30. "The *jīva* does not become an agent.... Then who or what acts or makes others act? *Svabhāva* (nature). This word indicates the impressions of matter that function without beginning. The *jīva* possessing a material body becomes the doer and the cause of others acting. The *jīva* as isolated entity is not the doer. Even when it is pure, there is some degree of agency in the *jīva*, since it was previously stated [V.13] that he is an agent in the state of happiness. However, this agency should be understood like the agency in light and the like, for being the primary element in an action, which is the meaning of a verbal root, is called being an agent" [commentary to V.14].

> superimposition of consciousness [upon it]. This is not the case. For it is well said that the agency that [ostensibly] belongs to that [*prakṛti*] because of the consciousness imposed on it from nearby, really belongs only to that nearby entity—it is seen that the ability of hot iron to burn is not due to iron, but to fire... [Therefore] agency belongs to the *jīva*. When it is said "agency belongs to *prakṛti*," this is because of the abundance of her transformations. This is just like when a person carries something in his hand: it is said in common parlance that "the hand is carrying"; similarly, when a *puruṣa* acts through *prakṛti*, [it can be said that] "*prakṛti* acts." Thus some say that he [the *jīva*] should be [understood as the agent].

Thus, following Rāmānuja,[31] Baladeva here assigns to the *ātman* not only agency, but what can be argued to be its indispensable corollary, desire. Later, in XVIII.13–14 (the five Sāṃkhya causes of action cited previously), Baladeva accommodates the two scriptural traditions by suggesting that "here, Sāṃkhya means the Vedānta." He then glosses "agent" with *jīva* (quoting the aforementioned statements from both the *Vedānta Sūtras* and the *Praśna Upaniṣad* as justification) and concludes that "the *jīva* rules over his mind and body by his desires alone, for accomplishing his actions."

There are, in fact, grounds to suppose certain Upaniṣadic thinkers did assign agency and desire to the *ātman*—we can add, here, to the *Praśna Upaniṣad* verse Baladeva quotes, a further example of *Chāndogya* (VII.7.1): "the self has real desires and real intentions."[32] But again, as with Rāmānuja, in Baladeva's commentary to these sections of the *Bhagavad Gītā*, at least, there seems to be more concern with honoring the Vedānta/Upaniṣadic position on agency than with addressing the underlying concern of Sāṃkhya pertaining to eternality and change. Additionally (and curiously), there is no attempt to reconcile this assignment of desire by these commentators to the *ātman* with the *Gītā's* location of desire and all its synonyms to the prākṛtic mind and senses (III.34–40; XIII.6), nor a nod of possible acknowledgment to Nyāya in this move, even as some of Nyāya's *ātman*-related qualities seem to have been adopted.[33]

---

31. See Rāmānuja's commentary to, e.g., *Gītā* XVIII.15.

32. *satya-kāmaḥ satya-saṃkalpaḥ*.

33. For example, see Rāmānuja's assignment of *prayatna* (volition, will, effort) to the *ātman* in XIII.20, one of the primary qualities of the *ātman* in Nyāya.

We leave a fuller discussion of these Vedāntins for the later chapters, our task here being to set the stage for this tension, but we can again draw attention to the difference in the construal of agency, *kartṛtva*, at least in their *Bhagavad Gītā* commentaries, between the *advaita* (nondualist) commentators of the text and those defending some ultimate reality to the individuality of the *ātman* and of eternal devotion to Viṣṇu/Kṛṣṇa in the liberated state (in addition to the fact that these later Vaiṣṇava Vedāntins opted to assign primary agency to Īśvara). Whereas for the advaitins, when liberated, the *ātman* experiences an eternal but completely passive state of *sat-cit-ānanda*, for the Vaiṣṇava traditions, the highest state is an eternal but active state of blissful service to Īśvara. While there are a number of different types of liberated states in Vaiṣṇavism,[34] they mostly involve the *ātman* attaining a *brahman* pyscho-physical, body mind mechanism, the form with which the *ātman* engages in devotion to Viṣṇu/Kṛṣṇa in the divine realms of Vaikuṇṭha/Goloka. Thus, these more robust notions of *ātman* noticed in the Vaiṣṇava commentaries seem to be precursory to the far more active notions of liberation posited by these traditions. Indeed, Baladeva, in XVIII.14, raises the *pūrvapakṣa*: "but then at least the liberated soul should not be the agent because he no longer has a body, senses, and life airs." He responds: "No, that is not so, because the liberated souls have spiritual senses and body, which are established according to their desires." While he is in line here with the Vaiṣṇava reading of the *Vedānta Sūtra's* IV.4th *pāda*, clearly, we have come a very long way from the content-less awareness in the liberated state of Sāṃkhya.

Conclusion

In conclusion, then, Sāṃkhya's non-negotiable commitment to an axiom of unchangeability in the form of an eternal, and therefore, *ex hypothesi*, unchanging *ātman* leaves it with various corollaries, which expose it to criticism from the rival schools. We might add as an aside, here, that the school has no problem accepting *prakṛti* herself as eternal (*Kārikā* I.3; *Yoga Sūtras* II.22), yet nonetheless capable of, and indeed, inherently bound to,

34. The *Bhāgavata Purāṇa*, for example, speaks of five types of liberation (overlapping with options expressed in the 4th *pāda* of the *Vedānta Sūtras*): living in the same realm as Viṣṇu (*sālokya*); having equal powers as Viṣṇu (*sārṣṭi*); staying close to Viṣṇu (*sāmīpya*); having a similar form to Viṣṇu (*sārūpya*); and becoming one with Viṣṇu (*ekatva*) (III.29.13).

constant change, so the presupposition of the eternal equals non-changing equation does not seem to apply to *prakṛti*.[35] Sāṃkhya's insistence is on the unchanging *ātman*. But this leaves it with the corollary of an *ātman* that is not responsible for the specifics of its material embeddedness, for it possesses no agency or means to effect it: all decisions are made by the prākṛtic covering of mind. While the problem may be waved away by stating that *puruṣa* has always been free and never bound, *puruṣa* is nonetheless "the spectator," and its awareness is absorbed in the "performance" put on by *prakṛti* (*Kārikā* LIXLXI) rather than absorbed in its own nature (*Yoga Sūtras* I.3–4). Why one *ātman* is, if not bound, then surely associated with a mind that opts to pursue worldly experiences, while another with a mind that pursues the path to liberation, is not due to any merits or choices ensuing from either *ātman*: it is the prākṛtic mind that makes these choices: yet the *ātman* is, in some very real sense at least, bound by the choices made by a completely distinct metaphysical entity.

Why one mind makes a particular set of choices is, according to Sāṃkhya, due to the memory imprints (*saṃskāras/vāsanās*[36]) dominant in the mind, which in turn are the product of previous *sāṃskāras*, and so on, in a never ending vicious concatenation of *sāṃskāra*-influenced decisions that, in turn, flavor, and to a great extent determine, subsequent decisions (with no initial causality, as all Indic traditions construe saṃsāric existence as *an-ādi*, "beginningless"). While one must always keep in mind the fact that much earlier Sāṃkhya material is lost, it is nonetheless curious to find very little discussion, if any at all, with any moral or justice-related questions that could be raised here pertaining to why one *ātman* is bound by (associated with?) one *citta*, and thus by the consequences of that *citta's* choices, rather than by another more enlightened *citta* (other than by stating that it is not really bound at all). In short, there are no grounds inherent in the *ātman* as to why one *ātman* is liberated and not another.

Thus, to a great extent, the unwelcome corollaries of Sāṃkhya's hard-line position on such issues act as a trigger for much subsequent development in Indian philosophy. Unhappy with the Sāṃkhya position, Nyāya seeks to couple an eternal unchanging *ātman* as substance with

35. The *guṇas* are the very form of *prakṛti*, not its qualities in a Nyāya sense (*Sāṃkhya Sūtras* VI.39).

36. All sensual and mental activity, in Sāṃkhya, leaves a memory imprint embedded on the mind. These are transferred from life to life, and thus formative of personality, disposition, etc.

separable changing qualities such as agency; Buddhism to jettison notions of any eternal entities in the first place, and Advaita Vedānta of non-eternal ones; and the theists to conclude that unresolvable philosophical problems of this sort mandate the existence of an Īśvara who is beyond comprehension. All run into philosophical difficulties of their own.[37] We are thus left with the choice of, on the one hand, an ongoing chronological history of philosophical debate between the various schools that seek to improve on the weaknesses perceived by them in other schools—but always at the cost of creating further corollary philosophical problems from the perspective of how *laghutva* (Occam's razor) gets applied by their opponents—or, on the other hand, of accepting the will of an inconceivable Īśvara beyond the boundaries of philosophical resolution. Sāṃkhya, as the earliest expression of systematic philosophy evidenced in Sanskrit texts, has, in many ways, set the stage for both options.

References

PRIMARY SOURCES

Āraṇya, Swāmi Hariharānanda. 1963. *Yoga Philosophy of Patañjali.* Calcutta: Calcutta University (reprint, New York: SUNY, 1977).

———. 1984. *Yoga Philosophy of Patañjali [with the Commentary of Vyāsa].* Albany: State University of New York Press.

Ballantyne, James Robert. 1852. *The Aphorisms of the Yoga Philosophy of Patañjali with Illustrative Extracts from the Commentary by Bhoja Rājā.* Allahabad: Presbyterian Mission Press.

Jha, Gangantha. 1934. *The Tattva Kaumudī.* Poona: Oriental Book Agency.

Kumar, Shiv & Bhargava, D. N. 1980. *Yuktidīpikā.* Delhi: Eastern Book Linkers.

Manikar, T. G. 1972. *Sāṃkhya Kārikā of Īśvarakṛṣṇa with Gauḍabhāṣya* Poona: Oriental Book Agency.

Pandeya, Ram Chandra. 1967 *Yuktidīpikā.* Delhi: Motilal Banarsidass.

37. Thus, for example, from a theological point of view, Kṛṣṇa may very well say that he is not responsible for anyone's pious or impious behavior, since living entities are enveloped in ignorance (V.15). But given that this very ignorance is his own power (VII.14), and that the intelligence, ego, mind, and senses with which to formulate and enact choices are his own *prakṛti* (VII.4) and given all the verses from the text on *prakṛti* being the agent and not the *ātman*, quoted above, it is not so easy to respond to the old *nir-īśvara-vādin* (non-theistic) charge that any postulated supreme being is cruel and partial, other than by resorting to a position of God's inconceivability (a position with extensive precedents in the Upaniṣads; see Dasa in this volume for later expressions of this).

Rukmani, T. S. 1981. *Yogavārttika of Vijñānabhikṣu*. 4 vols. Delhi: Munshiram Manoharlal.

Sharma, Har Dutt. 1933. *The Sāṃkhya Kārikā [with the Commentary of Gauḍapāda]*. Poona: Oriental Book Agency.

Woods, James Haughton. 1912. *The Yoga System of Patañjali* [*with the Commentary of Vācaspati*]. Delhi: Motilal Banarsidass (reprint, 1998).

SECONDARY SOURCES

Bronkhorst, Johannes. 1981. "Yoga and Seśvara Sāṃkhya." *Journal of Indian Philosophy* 9: 309–320.

———. "God in Sāṃkhya." 1983. *Archiv Für Indische Philosophie* 27: 149–164.

Bryant, Edwin. 2009. *The Yoga Sūtras of Patañjali*. New York: North Point Press.

Burley, Mikel. 2004. " 'Aloneness' and the Problem of Realism in Classical Sāṃkhya and Yoga." *Asian Philosophy* 14.3: 223–238.

Edgerton, Franklin. 1924. "The Meaning of Sāṃkhya and Yoga." *American Journal of Philology* 45.1: 1–46.

Hopkins, E. W. 1901. "Yoga Technique in the Great Epic." *Journal of the American Oriental Society* 22: 333–379.

King, Richard. 1995. *Early Advaita Vedānta and Buddhism*. Albany, New York: State University of New York Press.

Larson, Gerald James. 1979. *Classical Sāṃkhya*. Delhi: Motilal Banarsidass.

——— 1983. "An Eccentric Ghost in the Machine: Formal and Quantitative Aspects of the Sāṁkhya-Yoga Dualism." *Philosophy East and West* 33.3: 219–33.

——— & Bhattacharya, Ram Shankar, eds. 1987. *Sāṃkhya. Encyclopedia of Indian Philosophies*, vol. 4. Delhi: Motilal Banarsidass.

——— & Bhattacharya, Ram Shankar, eds. 2008. *India's Philosophy of Meditation. Encyclopedia of Indian Philosophies*, vol. 12. Delhi: Motilal Banarsidass.

Nelson, Lance. 2007. "Krishna in Advaita Vedanta: the Supreme Brahman in Human Form." In *Krishna: A Sourcebook*. New York: Oxford University Press.

Nicholson, Andrew J. 2011. *Unifying Hinduism*. Ranikhet: Permanent Black.

Rukmani, T. S. 1988. "Vijñānabhikṣu's Double Reflection Theory of Knowledge in the Yoga Sūtras." *Journal of Indian Philosophy* 16: 367–375.

Schreiner, Peter. 1999. "What Comes First (in the Mahābhārata): Sāṃkhya or Yoga?" *Asiatische Studien Études Asiatiques* 52.3: 755–777.

2

Free Persons, Empty Selves

FREEDOM AND AGENCY IN LIGHT OF THE TWO TRUTHS

Karin Meyers

Something peculiar happens when we view action from an objective or external standpoint. Some of its most important features seem to vanish under the objective gaze. Actions seem no longer assignable to individual agents as sources, but become instead components of the flux of events in the world of which the agent is a part. The easiest way to produce this effect is to think of the possibility that all actions are causally determined, but it is not the only way. The essential source of the problem is a view of persons and their actions as part of the order of nature, causally determined or not. That conception, if pressed, leads to the feeling that we are not agents at all, that we are helpless and not responsible for what we do. Against this judgment the inner view of the agent rebels. The question is whether it can stand up to the debilitating effects of a naturalistic view.

—NAGEL 1989: 110

This article represents a summary and further development of the argument presented in Meyers 2010. The interested reader may refer there for a more comprehensive review of the secondary literature and a more technical discussion of Buddhist accounts of karma and causation in light of the problem of free will.

Note: The first number in references to Pāli *suttas* are to the *sūtra* numbers so that non-specialists may consult translations in the print editions by the Pāli Text Society, Buddhist Publication Society, or the online resource, Access to Insight (http://www.access-toinsight.org). The translations, however, are mine, so with the second number I have included the volume and page number for the original-language Pāli Text Society editions.

THE IDEA THAT we have the capacity to choose or control our actions, that our actions are, in some important sense, *up to us*, is deeply intuitive, part of our common-sense view of the world and perhaps even essential to human rationality. Despite this, doubt as to the nature and extent of this freedom has made the problem of free will an abiding topic in Western philosophy. The problem typically arises when our capacity to choose or control our actions is thought to be threatened by some variety of determinism, such that God knows what we will do before we act or that our actions are the inevitable result of causes beyond our control.[1] But the basic existential anxiety that fuels doubt about these capacities is not contingent upon any particular metaphysical thesis concerning the faculty of the will, agency, God, or causation. All that is required is some reason to doubt that our actions are truly up to us coupled with notion that things would be better if they were.

If this is right, then there is no prima facie reason to suppose that Buddhists shouldn't find some version of the free will problem worth thinking about—despite the fact that there is no Buddhist term or concept equivalent to "free will." One might object that given the doctrine of non-self (*anātman*), which explicitly denies that actions originate from an agent (*kartṛ*), Buddhists ought not be bothered by the doubt that our actions may not be up to us. But this oversimplifies the matter. Much of Buddhist discourse endorses the view that things are better, indeed *much better*, when our actions are up to us and so provides practical instruction as to how to cultivate a certain kind of agency, that is, how to achieve consummate control over our bodily, vocal, and mental actions. While this suggests that some version of the free will problem may be relevant to the Buddhist project, there is no evidence that premodern Buddhists were concerned about the problem as typically defined in the West, that is, in terms of the debate over whether the relevant sense of agency, control, or choice required for moral responsibility is compatible with causal determinism. The central concern in Buddhism is not moral or metaphysical, but soteriological: how to attain a specific kind of freedom, namely, liberation from suffering. That said, the fact that our actions are—in some significant sense—*up to us*, that we have some capacity to choose or control

1. Some philosophers distinguish between "free will" and "free action," using the latter to indicate cases in which physical action is compelled or constrained in such a way that it cannot be considered free even when the will to act is not constrained. In this chapter, I use the term "free will" for the general capacity to engage in "free action."

what we do and can even achieve an optimal level of self-control, that is, control over our own mental states, is sine qua non for the realization of this soteriological goal as it is conceived in classical Buddhist sources. In other words, Buddhist liberation requires *some variety* of free will.

But, as hinted at above, there seems to be a problem here. There appears to be a contradiction between the notion that we enjoy free will, that we have some degree of choice or control over our actions, and the doctrine of non-self, which denies that actions are caused by agents. In the context of early Buddhism and the Abhidharma, this amounts to an apparent contradiction between the two truths: between the conventional truth (*saṃvṛti-satya*) reflected in discourse about persons, and the ultimate truth (*paramārtha-satya*) reflected in discourse about *dharmas*, the impersonal, ephemeral mental and physical events that constitute the basic elements of existence or experience.[2] According to the former, persons are the agents or causes of their actions; according to the latter, there are no agents, and actions issue from a combination of *dharmas*.[3] I submit that the tension between these two perspectives (rather than any presumed contradiction between agent causation or moral responsibility, on the one hand, and causal determinism or indeterminism, on the other) is the proper frame for thinking about the problem of free will in the Buddhist context. Operating within this frame helps us avoid imposing Western metaphysical or theological concerns onto Buddhist discourse, while still allowing us to formulate a Buddhist response to the doubt about our capacity to choose or control our actions prompted by reflection on the concept of non-self.

In what follows, I argue that while it does not make sense to say that *dharmas* enjoy free will or that *dharmas* make choices or control action, one can, and Buddhists often do, explain the freedoms conventionally attributed to persons in terms of the particular *dharmas* operative in the

---

2. According to both the Sarvāstivāda and Theravāda Abhidharma traditions, a *dharma* is something that bears its own nature (*svabhāva*). While the mature Sarvāstivāda Abhidharma tends to conceive of *dharmas* in ontological terms, as the final real things or ultimate building blocks of existence, the Theravāda Abhidhamma tends to conceive of them in more phenomenological terms, as the basic elements of (meditative) experience. For more on the term *dharma* in Abhidharma thought, see Cox 2004, Gethin 2004, and Ronkin 2005.

3. Indian Buddhist schools differ as to how they frame the two truths. In the Madhyamaka school, for example, *dharmas* are merely conventional, and the ultimate truth is the fact or reality that all things, including *dharmas*, are empty of any intrinsic nature (*svabhāva*). This necessitates a different response to the problem of free will.

sequence of events (specifically, the mental states, *citta*) issuing in an action. On this view, persons enjoy the freedom to choose or control action, not *despite* the fact that their actions issue from *dharmas*, but *when* their actions issue from certain kinds of *dharmas*.[4] This version of a Buddhist "compatibilist" solution to the problem of free will is neutral with respect to the truth of causal determinism[5] and consistent with the basic concerns and categories internal to Buddhist discourse, but it is important to note that this solution is not described in any classical source. Rather, it is a solution a Buddhist could offer in light of what these sources say about persons and *dharmas*. Before presenting this solution ("Freedoms Enjoyed by Ordinary Persons and Noble Beings"), I address some common misconceptions about the relationship between Buddhist conceptions of karma, free will, and moral responsibility and explain how the freedoms Buddhists understand persons to enjoy relate to the conceptions of free will at work in the contemporary free will debate ("Karma, Free Will, and Moral Responsibility"). I conclude ("The Two Truths: About Persons and *Dharmas*") with a brief sketch of how this solution relates to Buddhist practice: how dharmic analysis works in conjunction with a personal view of action to promote optimal self-control while simultaneously eroding the self-grasping[6] Buddhists regard as the source of suffering.

In this chapter, I focus on basic Buddhist doctrines as presented in the Pāli *suttas* and the *dharma* theory elaborated in the subsequent traditions of Buddhist scholasticism known as the "Abhidharma" (literally, "higher *dharma*"), the traditions in which the basic terms of Buddhist doctrine were first systematized.[7] When I refer to "Buddhists" I am referring to the authors of these classical texts and theories, but much of what I say applies to Buddhist traditions more broadly. Except for where I directly

---

4. I take this to be the key difference between my account of Buddhist compatibilism and Mark Siderits's Buddhist "paleo-compatibilism." See Siderits 1987, 2005, 2008.

5. It is compatible with both a causal determinism in which there is exactly one metaphysically possible future and an indeterminism in which there is more than one metaphysically possible future, but a sufficient degree of regularity to ensure that our actions are not the outcome of mere chance but issue from our reasons, desires, etc.

6. By "self-grasping" I mean the range of cognitive and affective attitudes related to the innate view of self, an implicit belief in a discrete, unchanging, and enduring personal identity.

7. Here I draw on the Abhidharma theories of the Theravāda, Sarvāstivāda, and Sautrāntika. These traditions disagree on many points, but I will note only those disagreements that are directly relevant to the problem of free will.

quote or paraphrase a Pāli source, I provide the Sanskrit spellings of Buddhist terms.[8]

Karma, Free Will, and Moral Responsibility

In the West, the problem of free will is typically defined as the problem of accounting for the freedoms a person must enjoy in order to be considered a morally responsible agent, that is, as an apt target for praise or blame. While philosophers disagree as to the meaning and metaphysics of free will, most agree that it is this connection to moral responsibility (and related interpersonal attitudes) that makes the problem of free will worth thinking about. The search for an analogue in Buddhist thought has lead some scholars to infer that free will is implied in the Buddha's statement that karma (i.e., action) is *cetanā*.[9] Although they debate over the details, Buddhists generally agree that *cetanā*, which is variously translated as "volition," "intention," "will," or "an intending," is itself a form of karma, namely, mental action, and also what distinguishes bodily and vocal action from mere movement. Insofar as it is the essential, defining feature of karma, what distinguishes it as an action as opposed to a mere accident or happening, *cetanā* serves as a necessary and often sufficient condition for karmic fruition. Drawing an analogy between karmic fruition and moral responsibility or deserts, some interpreters take this to imply that *cetanā* is equivalent to a faculty of free will or that its presence entails that an action is freely willed. The problem is that in classical Buddhist sources, facts about moral responsibility do not always map directly onto facts about karma: a person is not necessarily morally responsible for his karma or morally deserving of its results. In contexts where something like moral responsibility is a central concern, as in the case of transgression of a monastic rule, culpability requires the presence of other mental

8. I make an exception for "karma" which I treat as an English loan-word. I do not italicize it or use its Pāli equivalent, *kamma*, even when referring directly to theories found in Pāli sources. It should also be noted that while in popular English usage, the word "karma" has come to refer almost exclusively to the results of action, the primary meaning in classical Buddhist discourse is "action." In this chapter I will use the term "karma" in this primary sense.

9. AN 6.63 (A iii.415): *Cetanāhaṃ, bhikkhave, kammaṃ vadāmi; cetayitvā kammaṃ karoti kāyena vācāya manasā.* "I say, oh monks, karma is an intending (*cetanā*). Intending, one acts with the body, speech, or mind."

factors[10] in addition to *cetanā*, such as (non-confused) mindfulness (*sati*) and clear awareness (*sampajāna*).[11] Moreover, *cetanā* does not entail free will under any of the common descriptions of free will. In its most basic sense, *cetanā* is simply the movement of a mind (*citta*) toward an object or goal.[12] It also connotes appetitive or conative exertion and has a cognitive dimension, such that it is often amenable to verbal expression in the form of such statements as, "I will do X," but as a factor present in every instance of mind (*citta*), including deep sleep, *cetanā* is not always conscious, deliberate, voluntary, or subject to choice—some combination of which is typically regarded as essential for free will. In sum, because it is the distinguishing feature of action, we can say that *cetanā* is a necessary condition for moral responsibility, but it is not sufficient; it does not, in itself, make a person an apt target of praise or blame and it is not, in itself, equivalent to free will.

Another problem that arises when we attempt to assimilate Buddhist concerns about karma to Western concerns about moral responsibility is that this tends to obscure the aspects of Buddhist doctrine that make free will a potential problem and, I might add, *one worth thinking about* from a Buddhist perspective. While there are contexts in which Buddhists worry about moral responsibility, the fundamental concern with respect to karma is soteriological. Insofar as it is conditioned by self-grasping, karma and specifically *cetanā* perpetuate suffering. It is this self-grasping that impels a mind toward a particular object or goal, such that when self-grasping ceases, *cetanā* ceases as well.[13] This does not entail that persons do not

---

10. Mental factors (*caitta* or *cetasika*) are the cognitive and affective elements (*dharmas*) that define the qualities of a particular mental state (*citta*). Abhidharma schools disagree on some of the details, but generally agree that there are certain factors present in every mental state (e.g., *cetanā*) as well as those peculiar to wholesome or unwholesome mental states, such as faith and anger, respectively.

11. The Vinaya attests to cases in which *cetanā* is present, but a person is not held culpable. For example, a monk who has a wet dream does not commit an offense, owing to forgetting or, literally, "confused mindfulness" (*muṭṭhassati*) and lack of awareness (*asampajāna*), despite there being an intending (*cetanā*). See Harvey 1999: 6.

12. *Cetanā* is a highly polyvalent term. For more on *cetanā*, see Heim 2003, Devdas 2008, and Meyers 2010.

13. This does not necessarily mean that liberated beings do not engage in any volitional activity. In fact, classical Buddhist thought admits a wide range of views on the degree to which a liberated mind is analogous to an ordinary mind in this and other respects, but because the term *cetanā* implies self-grasping and effort, there is a general reluctance to label the volitional activity of liberated beings as *cetanā*.

enjoy some variety of free will, only that they cannot be considered free in the ultimate sense valued by Buddhists so long as their actions are informed by the desire and delusion associated with an implicit identification with a substantial or autonomous self. All of this suggests that if we want to decide what a Buddhist should say about the problem of free will and, specifically, about the doubt that our actions are truly up to us, (1) we might do better to begin our inquiry by examining what Buddhists say about the freedoms a person requires in order to become liberated rather than those he requires in order to be held morally responsible, and (2) we ought to examine how free will might look in light of the tension between the self-grasping or delusion of autonomy implied in goal-oriented action, including the practice of the path, and the self-less point of view cultivated through this practice.

Freedoms Enjoyed by Ordinary Persons and Noble Beings

Whatever their metaphysical views, few philosophers would dispute the empirical fact that much of human endeavor involves choosing one course of action over another, that when these choices lie behind us, it often appears that we could have done otherwise, and that when they lie ahead of us, it appears that there is more than one possible future or course of action open to us. Similarly, few would deny the empirical fact that we enjoy some degree of control over our actions. While we sometimes feel that we are "out of control"—when we act against our better judgment or get the sense that no one has been "behind the wheel" after engaging in some mindless activity—such instances stick out as problems or as just plain odd because of the conviction that we can and regularly do control our actions. That we enjoy these freedoms to choose and control our actions—however imperfectly we wield them—is integral to our interpersonal relationships as well as our sense of ourselves and of our life's endeavors.

Although "free will" originated as a term for a discrete faculty or power, contemporary philosophers typically define it in terms of these capacities to choose or control our actions. However, they disagree as to what precisely it means to say that we "choose" or "control" our actions, over the metaphysics that make the relevant senses of choice or control possible, and as to whether these capacities are real or merely illusory. As indicated above, the debate typically revolves around whether the sort of choice or control needed to make sense of moral responsibility is compatible with causal determinism. I have already suggested that it is a mistake to overemphasize concerns about moral responsibility when interpreting Buddhist accounts of karma. Below I will suggest that it is also a mistake to read concerns about causal determinism into Buddhist accounts of dependent origination and that the thesis of causal determinism is not directly relevant to the problem of free will in the Buddhist context. Nevertheless, insofar as this solution depends on the coherence of compatibilism over and against common libertarian objections, it will be helpful to outline some of the basic contours of the contemporary debate over free will.

Causal determinism can be defined as the view that there is *exactly one metaphysically*[14] *possible future* as determined by prior events or states of affairs according to causal laws. This poses an immediate intuitive threat to the notion that we are free to choose between alternative possibilities or that, in any particular situation, we "could have done otherwise" than what we actually did. Because it entails that our actions are the consequences of events in the remote past, events over which we had no control, causal determinism also appears to threaten the notion that we are in control of our actions (Ginet 1966; Van Inwagen 1983). Broadly speaking, so-called "incompatibilists" either take this to mean that free will exists and causal determinism is false, in which case they are called "libertarians," or that causal determinism is true and free will does not exist, in which case they are called "hard determinists." While hard determinists are willing to abandon the notion of moral responsibility, libertarians typically argue that because we cannot be held responsible for actions that we do not choose or control, at least some of our actions must originate with us or in us[15] in such a way that they are not determined by previous causes.

14. I use "metaphysically possible" as a substitute for the more common "physically possible." The latter reveals the physicalist bias that permeates the modern free will debate, namely, the view that causal law or determinism is tantamount to physical law or determinism. There is no reason, however, that causal determinism could not include mental as well as physical events. Because Buddhists take mental events to be real and causally efficacious, the Buddhist determinist would have to be committed to this more inclusive variety of causal determinism. In either case, the qualification ("metaphysically" or "physically") helps distinguish the notion that there is only one possible future *as determined by prior events* from the notion that there is only one *epistemically* possible future (that we can only know or imagine one future) or only one *logically* possible future. As we will see, it is important to the compatibilist that the former does not entail the latter two.

15. "Agent-causal" libertarians hold that the agent must be the cause of free action, while "event-causal" libertarians hold that the cause must be some non-deterministic process

Although causal determinism poses an intuitive threat to free will, many philosophers hold that the relevant senses of control and choice are compatible with or even *require* causal determinism.[16] So-called "compatibilists" argue that while actions compelled by external causes cannot be considered subject to a person's control, those that proceed from internal causes in accordance with a person's own reasons, volitions, or desires can.[17] Some further argue that control is impossible unless action is determined by these causes, otherwise action would be subject to mere chance. Because there are also internal causes, such as overwhelming desire, that compel action in such a way that we would not consider it free, compatibilists typically distinguish between internal causes that undermine control and those that are conducive to it by placing various sorts of rational constraints on the latter. Naturally, much of the debate between compatibilists (and also event-causal libertarians) concerns the proper delineation of these causes.

While some compatibilists doubt that the freedom to choose between alternative possibilities is required for moral responsibility (Frankfurt 1969; Fischer and Ravizza 2000), many take seriously the intuition that such freedom is essential to our conception of free will and so attempt to explain how this freedom is consistent with causal determinism. Daniel Dennett, for example, argues that the relevant sense of the notion that one "could have done otherwise" does not lie in the *metaphysical fact* of there being more than one physically possible future, but in the *epistemic fact* that one is able to imagine more than one possible future (Dennett 1984, 2004; cf. Parfit 2011: 11.38). This is a *subjectively* open as opposed to an objectively open future. Metaphysically speaking, all that free will requires, according to this view, is that this epistemic freedom plays a role in determining one's action, and that had the situation been slightly

within the agent. They will not concern us here, but it ought to be mentioned that there are also non-causal libertarian theories. For an overview of the various kinds of libertarianism and an assessment of their conceptual adequacy, see Clarke 2003.

16. It should be noted that while many compatibilists are committed to the truth of causal determinism and believe free will is only possible if causal determinism is true, others are agnostic with respect to the truth of causal determinism or do not think free will requires its truth. There are also a few so-called "compatibilists" who merely aim to provide an account of free will and/or moral responsibility that is independent from and thus not falsified by the truth of determinism (Strawson 1960).

17. In classical compatibilism, the agent was considered the cause of action, but in contemporary or "neo-compatibilism," events within the agent are considered the cause of action. In this chapter, I am concerned with the latter variety of compatibilism.

different; if slightly different reasons or circumstances had been obtained, one could have done otherwise. The reasoning is that because we never find ourselves in precisely the same situation twice, this epistemic freedom suffices to explain our intuition of an open future and to support the interpersonal practices grounded in this intuition.

As noted above, Buddhists do not have a term equivalent to "free will" or any concept of a discrete faculty of the will, but they clearly recognize the empirical freedoms persons enjoy in choosing and controlling their actions as well as the essential roles these freedoms play in the project of liberation from suffering. Indeed, the Buddha's message is predicated on the fact that human beings can choose one course of action over another. We can choose to nurture wholesome (*kuśala*) qualities and abandon unwholesome ones, to take up the path, or to go forth into the life of a renunciant. In so doing, we can change our personalities, achieve greater well-being, and even eliminate suffering altogether. Moreover, according to Buddhist cosmology, the human realm is a particularly good environment for this endeavor. Because we do not experience the consistently painful or pleasant sensations that attend rebirth in the lower or heavenly realms and, unlike animals, have an ability to use language, we are able to understand the Buddha's teachings, reason, and reflect upon our actions without being completely overwhelmed by attraction, aversion, or delusion. Encoded in this cosmological framework is the optimistic anthropology Buddhist soteriology demands: although our actions are conditioned by self-grasping, we have the freedom to reflect on this situation and extricate ourselves from it. This why the Buddha gives advice such as to pause to consider whether an action might be harmful to oneself or others prior to acting (Majjhima Nikāya, English [MN] 61, Pāli [M] i.415) or to reflect upon how one becomes fettered (*saṃyutta*) by desirous rumination (Aṅguttara Nikāya, English [AN] 3.109–110, Pāli [A] i.263–264). The implication is that this moment of reflection enables one to choose a better course.

While the Buddhist path is premised on the empirical fact that persons enjoy the freedom to choose one course of action over another, control seems to be the preferred idiom for describing the freedom cultivated through the practice of the path. In the Pāli *suttas*, we find expressions such as "a monk controls his mind, and is not controlled by his mind" (MN 32, M i.214). A person who has undertaken the training is described as "one who goes against the stream" (*paṭisotagāmin*) as opposed to "one who follows the stream" (*anusotagāmin*), and a person who has "perfected the training" (*paripuṇṇasekha*) as "having mastery over his mind" (*cetovasippatta*) (AN 4.5, A ii.4). Removing unwholesome thoughts is described as "restraining, crushing, and scorching the (unwholesome) mind with the (wholesome) mind" in the same way a strong man overpowers a weaker man, and the monk who has thoroughly trained his mind in this way is described as being able to think whatever thought he wishes to think and not any thought he does not wish to think (MN 20, M i.120–121). Finally, it is significant that the qualities cultivated through the path, namely, faith (*śraddhā*), energy (*vīrya*), mindfulness (*smṛti*), concentration (*samādhi*), and discernment (*prajñā*), are referred to as ruling or controlling faculties (*indriya*) and powers (*bala*).

Owing to their commitment to the doctrines of dependent origination and non-self, Buddhists cannot regard the freedoms enjoyed by ordinary or noble persons (*ārya*)[18] as contra-causal powers or attribute them to an autonomous or substantially existent agent, but, as seen above, they clearly accept that ordinary beings enjoy some degree of choice or control over their actions and understand the path to result in a particular sort of agency, a consummate kind of self-control. Cultivating this self-control involves both critical reflection and conscious choice of the sort described above, and a training of habit, affection, and moral sentiment, such that the supremely self-controlled individual is no longer capable of engaging in unwholesome action (Saṃyutta Nikāya, English [SN] 25.7, S iii.227; Pāli [AN] 4.37, A ii.39). This control is enhanced and ultimately perfected through knowledge and meditative insight into how *cetanā* and the other mental factors or *dharmas* that contribute to action are conditioned by self-grasping. The idea is that by seeing how action arises from these conditions and perpetuates suffering, the practitioner is able to dis-identify from this process, gain greater control over it, and eventually let go of it altogether. In other words, the logic of liberation not only presumes the empirical freedoms of choice and control recognized by libertarians and compatibilists alike, but involves the cultivation of *greater* freedom and self-control through the recognition of non-self.

This brings us to the theoretical-metaphysical problem outlined in the introduction: how can Buddhists explain the choice and control enjoyed by ordinary or noble persons when they deny that actions are caused by agents? There is also a related practical-existential problem: what prevents the concept of non-self from undermining the sense of agency or autonomy critical to the personal initiative and effort needed to extricate oneself

---

18. A person who has already or will shortly attain one of the four stages of awakening.

from self-grasping and also essential to the morally reactive attitudes that are supposed to support this endeavor, such as shame (*hrī*) and apprehension (*apatrāpya*)?[19] Most interpreters who take up the problem of free will in the Buddhist context assume that the critical issue with respect to either of these problems is whether or not the Buddhist theory of causation is deterministic. They assume that if karma or *cetanā* is not causally determined, a person can be said to enjoy free will, but the problem—if there is one—is deeper than this. It is the problem to which Thomas Nagel refers in the passage from *The View From Nowhere* quoted at the beginning of this essay. Nagel explains that the essential source of the problem of free will is not causal determinism per se, but "a view of persons and their actions as part of the order of nature," and the resultant "feeling that we are not agents at all, that we are helpless and not responsible for what we do" (Nagel 1989: 110). Whereas Nagel characterizes this impersonal, external, or objective view of action as disturbing and even "debilitating" insofar as it threatens our sense of autonomy and responsibility, Buddhists understand an impersonal analysis of action to be therapeutic and to even enhance our ability to control our actions, namely, to increase our autonomy with respect to the influence of unwholesome tendencies. In order to understand how this works in practice, it is necessary to first examine the solution to the theoretical problem, for the solution to both problems hinges upon the Buddhist notion of the two truths.

The Two Truths: About Persons and Dharmas

In the early discourses, the Buddha speaks in two semantic registers, one that countenances persons (and the freedoms they enjoy) and another in which persons, their experiences, and their actions are analyzed in terms of individual, ephemeral mental and physical elements (*dharmas*) or aggregates (*skandhas*) of these elements.[20] A single discourse or passage typically shifts back and forth between these two registers. In the *Anupada sutta*, for example, Sāriputta is praised (personal register) for having discerned the arising and passing away of the mental *dharmas* (impersonal register) that constitute his own meditative states (personal and impersonal registers)

19. These attitudes are regarded as essential to the cultivation of virtue, which serves as the foundation of the path.

20. Namely, physical form (*rūpa*), feeling (*vedanā*), cognition (*saṃjñā*), conditioning forces (*saṃskāra*), and consciousness (*vijñāna*).

and for recognizing the possibility of his (personal register) escape therein (MN 111, M iii.25).[21] These two registers work in concert to illustrate the means by which the practitioner may learn to dis-identify with or "lay down the burden" of the aggregates (SN 22.22, S iii.25). Concerns about the potential contradiction between these two registers eventually led to a codification of their respective scopes and values in the doctrine of the "two truths."[22] Here truth (*satya*) refers to the veracity of statements as well as the reality of the referents of these statements,[23] such that there can be true statements about persons or *dharmas* and both persons and *dharmas* can be said to exist. Thus, while persons disappear and there is no entity to which we might ascribe agency, choice or control from the perspective of *dharma* analysis or ultimate truth (*paramārtha-satya*), this does not entail that persons do not exist or that they do not enjoy these freedoms from the perspective of conventional truth (*saṃvṛti-satya*).[24] In the wake of this hermeneutic innovation, the challenge for the Buddhist exegete is to sort out precisely how these two perspectives are supposed to relate to each other (and much of the history of Buddhist philosophy can be understood as attending to this task in one way or another).

---

21. Here "escape" (*nissaraṇa*) does not refer directly to liberation, but rather a meditative state that is more refined than the current (or recent) one. In the *sutta*, Sāriputta progresses through the four principle absorptions (*jhāna*) and then through the immaterial states (*āruppa-āyatana*) discerning the mental factors associated with these states and becoming ever less attached to the world.

22. Some of the earliest references to "two truths" are Nāgārjuna's *Mūlamadhyamakakārikā* XXIV.8 (c. 150–250 CE) and the commentary on the Kathāvatthu (*Kathāvatthuppakaraṇaṭṭh akathā*). While the latter was redacted in the fifth century, the Sinhalese commentaries on which it was based are considerably older. The two truths are also discussed in the great Sarvāstivāda Abhidharma compendium, the *Mahāvibhāṣā* (c. 150 CE).

23. For a good summary of the hermeneutic origins of the doctrine, see Cowherds 2010: 5–11.

24. Here it should be noted that while the Pāli term for conventional truth, *sammuti* (derived from the verbal root √*man*), means something like "think together" or "consensus" and does not connote falsehood, the Sanskrit term, *saṃvṛti*, comes to be understood as derived from the verbal root √*vṛ* ("to cover over"). While the primary meaning in the AKBh (AKBh vi.4 & vii.2) and many Yogācāra works is "conventional," the sense of "concealing" is emphasized in many Madhyamaka works. This affects the conception of the relationship between the two truths and the status of the conventional truth. Thus, while the Mādhyamika could not easily endorse the view that the free will conventionally attributed to persons is consistent with the ultimate truth (regardless of whether the latter be understood in terms of *dharmas* or emptiness), the Theravādin would be less inclined to speak of delusion with respect to the conventional attribution of agency to persons, regarding this as a manner of speaking that is consistent with the ultimate truth and the Buddha's message.

While it is debatable whether the personal and impersonal registers represent an explicitly ontological doctrine in the context of the early discourses (Thanissaro 2012), they take on a distinctively ontological character as the Abhidharma schools elaborate and systematize the terms of the ultimate truth (Cox 2004). According to this ontological project, facts about persons, their experiences, or their actions ultimately reduce to facts about *dharmas*. Thus, in response to the grammatically informed objection that action (*karman*) requires an agent (*kartṛ*), Vasubandhu explains:

> That which is the primary cause of action is called an "agent." The self is not seen to have any causal efficacy. Therefore it is also inappropriate to regard it as an agent. From memory arises desire; from desire thought; from thought there is effort; from effort there is a wind; and from that there is [bodily] action. What is there for a self to do here (Abhidharmakośabhāṣya [AKBh] ix, Pradhan 1975: 476–477)?

This kind of reductionism entails that if the empirical freedoms enjoyed by persons are not merely illusory, they must be *explained* in terms of facts about *dharmas*, but this does not mean that facts about persons and facts about *dharmas* are the *same* facts. There are certain facts about persons that only make sense from the perspective of conventional truth, the shared reality of interpersonal experience.[25] Because they *require* persons they cannot be ascribed to *dharmas*. While we might isolate certain aspects of a personality and view them from an objective, impersonal perspective, observing, for example, whether a feeling (*vedanā*) is pleasant or painful, or the aim and intensity of desire (*chanda*) quite apart from the person who feels or desires, attributes like moral responsibility and freedom require persons, that is, *complex entities that endure over time*. Although it does not make sense to say that *dharmas* enjoy free will or that *dharmas* make choices, control action, or are morally responsible for the actions they cause, these person-properties can be explained, in theory, in terms of facts about the *dharmas* operative in the sequence of mental states (*citta*) issuing in an action. Before presenting an outline of this Buddhist

25. Collins 1997 explains that this is not merely because the discourse of ultimate truth fails to be an expedient means to achieve certain ends, but because certain features of conventional truth, such as those displayed in narrative and monastic jurisprudence, require persons (479).

"compatibilist" account of free will, however, it will be instructive to examine some of the ways in which traditional libertarian assumptions about freedom and agency have led interpreters to misconstrue the relationship between *dharmas* and persons and to reexamine the significance of determinism with respect to free will in the Buddhist context.

Because the libertarian understanding that we enjoy a freedom to choose between more than one metaphysically possible future is more intuitive than the compatibilist view that this sort of freedom is illusory and/or unnecessary, most interpreters who have addressed the problem of free will in Buddhism have simply assumed that libertarian choice is definitional of free will and so have sought some analogy (or disanalogy) in Buddhist thought. Noting the connection between *cetanā* and karma mentioned above, some have attempted to locate free will in the indeterminism of *cetanā* and/or related psychological factors (e.g., Aung 1910: 43; Jayatilleke 1972: 6–8; Nanayakkara 1979: 280; Walshe 1987: 34; Harvey 2007: 68). On some versions of this theory (e.g., Jayatilleke, Nanayakkara, Walshe), *cetanā* is simply treated as the choice or power of choice exercised by persons, but as indicated above, *cetanā* is not necessarily conscious, deliberate, or voluntary, and so even if it were appropriate to conceive of it as a kind of "choice" this would not be sufficient to account for some of the empirical freedoms Buddhists attribute to persons. A more serious problem with this approach is that in treating *cetanā* as something persons do or a power they wield, it does not resolve the apparent contradiction between the personal and impersonal levels of discourse with regard to action. Rather than explaining the freedom attributed to persons *in terms of dharmas*, it simply inserts persons into the dharmic level of explanation or ignores the tension between the two discourses altogether.

Out of respect for the reductive imperative of *dharma* theory, other interpreters have suggested that *cetanā* itself is responsible for choice, that is, for deciding between two courses of action or between the influence of wholesome and unwholesome motives (Aung 1910: 43–44; Payutto 1993: 7). The problem with this approach is that if *cetanā* exercised the freedom and agency we generally suppose ourselves to enjoy, this would seriously undermine rather than explain our freedom. On this view, *cetanā* becomes a kind of homuncular agent capable of acting autonomously.[26]

---

26. A view that is perhaps encouraged by the *Atthasālinī* (and *Visuddhimagga*) analogy between *cetanā* and a landowner who directs and works alongside his laborers (the other mental factors constituting a mental state) toward a particular end. Whereas this analogy

Even if it were correct to understand the process by which *cetanā* comes to be directed toward a particular end as indeterministic, having a little man inside of us making our decisions for us would be just as deleterious to our freedom as having our actions be the outcome of chance. In both scenarios there would be an insufficient connection between our reasons or desires and actions.

The problem with these theories is not their commitment to indeterminism per se, but their failure to jettison the agent-causal paradigm implicit in traditional versions of libertarianism. Whether they posit *cetanā* as a power or faculty belonging to the person as agent or as itself a kind of agent or prime mover (or uncaused cause), these theories do not explain free will in terms of the impersonal perspective, but merely confuse or postpone sorting out the relationship between the personal and impersonal perspectives. Moreover, it should be noted that whereas focus on a single *dharma* as the explicans for libertarian choice reveals an unconscious allegiance to an agent-causal paradigm, *dharma* theory holds that action is the result of a complex of *dharmas* produced in a longitudinal causal process comprised of the synchronic and diachronic conditioning relations of dependent origination. Any Buddhist theory of free will must take account of these conditioning relations and, as we will see below, doing so makes it easier to account for the freedoms enjoyed by ordinary persons and noble beings.

Although most interpreters assume that the Buddhist theories of causation, action, or soteriology entail a commitment to indeterminism, a few have supposed that the respect for the principle of universal causation, the principle that everything has a cause, at work in the theory of dependent origination implies a commitment to determinism (Siderits 1987, 2008; Goodman 2002). Regardless of where they fall on the issue, however, most interpreters believe that a commitment one way or another is significant with respect to the problem of free will in Buddhism. One problem with this approach is simply exegetical: while early Buddhist sources demonstrate a persistent concern with the various sorts of fatalism, they do not address the problem of determinism. Whereas determinism is the view that there is only one metaphysically possible future, fatalism is the

---

conveys the influence of *cetanā* on the other mental factors, it does not imply that *cetanā* "freely chooses" an object or end in the to the way we suppose persons choose their ends.

further view that our efforts make no difference to this future.[27] Because the former does not entail the latter, the Buddha's arguments against theories that propose that the future is decided by something other than our own efforts do not tell us anything about a commitment to causal determinism except that he would reject any determinism in which our efforts had no causal efficacy. Moreover, when Abhidharma schools elaborate upon the causal theories at work in dependent origination, they also do not speak directly to the thesis of determinism.[28]

The other and more significant problem with focusing on determinism is that once Buddhists eliminate agent-causation, the critical issue is no longer how to explain free will in light of the fact or illusion of alternative metaphysical possibilities; it is identifying the kinds of *dharmas* and relationships between *dharmas* whose salience in the mental process (*citta-santāna*) issuing in action accounts for the empirical distinction between free and compelled or constrained action. In other words, persons can be said to choose or control an action when it issues from the right sort of causes in the right sort of mental state (*citta*) with the right sort of causal history, regardless of the truth of causal determinism. In an indeterministic world with a sufficient degree of regularity, this explanation will account for how one metaphysically possible future is decided over another, and in a deterministic world, for how the one metaphysically possible future is decided. As in the case of contemporary compatibilist (and event-causal libertarian) theories, the challenge is deciding precisely what kinds of causes and causal histories are required for free will.

Before providing a sketch of how the Buddhist might approach this challenge, I think it is important to pause to note that while the free will solution I propose is neutral with respect to the truth of causal determinism, and classical Buddhist sources do directly address the issue of determinism, there is, in fact, good reason to doubt whether the epistemic freedom proposed by Dennett is consistent with the notion of alternative possibilities assumed in Buddhist soteriology. Even if epistemic freedom is conceptually adequate to explain the kind of alternative possibility

27. See Dennett 1984 and 2004 for a particularly clear explanation of the distinction between determinism and fatalism.

28. The combination of efficient and final causation or diachronic and synchronic conditioning involved in the Theravāda theory of conditioning relations makes a commitment to determinism unlikely. There is perhaps more scope to see determinism in the AKBh (where Vasubandhu rejects synchronic causation), but I think a commitment to determinism is also unlikely there for, among other things, the reasons described below.

required for liberation (and I tend to think it is), the view that there is only one metaphysically possible future is so counterintuitive to the project of liberation that if it were ever widely held among premodern Buddhists, one would expect to see a rigorous explanation and defense of it (just as we see for the counterintuitive view of non-self), lest this Buddhist determinism be misinterpreted as fatalistic. Such a defense may exist, but I have not seen it. Again, I do not mean to suggest that Buddhists must be committed to indeterminism in order to offer a philosophically coherent account of the empirical freedoms they attribute to persons, merely that it is difficult to imagine, on exegetical and psychological grounds, that they would have understood dependent origination as a form of causal determinism. Putting the issue of determinism aside, let us now turn to the solution to the Buddhist problem of free will, the apparent contradiction between the two truths.

There is not space here for an extensive account of the kinds of *dharmas* and conditioning relationships that might underlie the empirical distinction between free and compelled or constrained action, but a few general remarks are in order. Because it is the defining feature of action, *cetanā* must be present in order for there to be action, but since *cetanā* is present in every mental state (*citta*), additional conditions must obtain in the case of free action. In order to decide what these conditions are, we might start by examining those Buddhists cite to explain the difference between action and accident. The primary concern for Buddhists is typically the conditions that must be in place for karmic fruition (or the "accumulation of karma"), but this generally has to do with whether an action is voluntary.[29] In the case of verbal or bodily action, for example, Vasubandhu explains that there must be an appropriate relationship between *cetanā* and verbal utterance or bodily movement, such that the latter (or what is to be accomplished by the latter) is the object or aim of *cetanā* (AKBh iv.120, 271–272). Other conditions that must obtain in the grave action of murder, for example, are an absence of cognitive error or doubt about the identity of the victim (AKBh iv.73ab, 243–244). Elsewhere, Vasubandhu also explains that an action is distinguished from autonomic processes (Tib. *so so pa'i nus pa*), such as the movement of an eye, in virtue of the fact that it is endowed with exertion (Tib. *rtsol ba, *vyāyāma*) (Karmasiddhiprakaraṇa

29. According to my reading of Vasubandhu, there are, in fact, karmic repercussions for what we would consider involuntary actions, but only when they correspond to enduring personality traits, not if they are "out of character."

[KSP] 145a). There are cases in which voluntary action might still be compelled in ways we would not consider free,[30] but these conditions provide a foundation from which one might build an account of the freedoms of choice or control analogous to those offered by contemporary compatibilists (or event-causal libertarians).

To account for the critical distinction between internal conditions that limit and those that conduce to freedom, we would likely want to add to this account factors like clear awareness and mindfulness, which we saw figure into Buddhist accounts of moral culpability. Elsewhere, Buddhists present madness and severe pain as factors that mitigate culpability, so we might also include the absence of these as among the critical conditions for free will.[31] There are, in fact, a variety of mental factors that pick out the sort of cognitive, affective, and conative conditions that might figure into the distinction between free and compelled or constrained action, such as attention (*manaskāra*), approbation (*adhimokṣa*), desire for action (*chanda*), discernment (*mati*), reflection (*vitarka*), examination (*vicāra*), doubt (*vicikitsā*), delusion (*moha*), and anger (*krodha*).

In sum, given the richness of Buddhist psychological vocabulary, Buddhists ought to be able to account for the sorts of affective and rational processes featured in contemporary compatibilist accounts of free will, such as Dennett's epistemic freedom, Harry Frankfurt's second order desires (Frankfurt 1969), or John Fischer and Mark Ravizza's reasons-responsiveness (Fischer and Ravizza 2000).[32] In addition to examining the ways in which actions relate to immediate reasons, intentions, or desires, these theories take into consideration the historical dimension of action, how these immediate internal causes relate to past decisions or long-standing habits and beliefs. Without this historical information, it can be difficult to decide whether an action might be internally or externally compelled or constrained in ways we would not consider free. If these compatibilisms are coherent, then there is no reason to suppose that

30. See Garfield on defenestration in this volume.

31. For example, the Theravāda Vinaya explains that a monk who is mad (*ummattaka*), temporally unhinged (*khitta-citta*), or severely afflicted by pain (*vedanaṭṭa*) is not necessarily culpable for his actions (Harvey 1999: 2–3).

32. For a recent analysis of the Buddhist theory of non-self in light of Frankfurt's theory, see Adam 2011. For a positive assessment of free will in Theravāda Buddhism in light of Dennett's compatibilism, which is somewhat different from my own, see Federman 2010. For an overview of the secondary literature on Buddhist compatibilism, see Repetti 2010.

we couldn't propose a version consistent with Buddhist *dharma* theory.[33] But, as we have seen, Buddhists are less interested in the minimal freedom required for moral responsibility than in the enhanced freedom or self-control cultivated through the path. While *dharma* theory might be utilized to explain the former, it was designed to illustrate and *facilitate* the latter.

Whereas most compatibilists would not consider persons incapable of reasoning, such as the insane or developmentally immature, to act with sufficient freedom to be held morally responsible for their actions, from the Buddhist perspective, all ordinary persons are children (*bāla*) and functionally insane insofar as our actions are compelled by the greed, hatred, and delusion associated with self-grasping. We might act voluntarily insofar as we endorse our actions or have coherent reasons for what we do. We might also deliberate and make judgments about the best course of action for accomplishing a desired end, but so long as we are afflicted by self-grasping, and thus continue to perpetuate our own suffering, our actions will appear less than fully rational or self-controlled to one who has overcome these afflictions.

It is natural to suppose that escaping the bondage of *saṃsāra* requires alternative possibilities, and that reversing the process of habituation governed by self-grasping, turning around to swim "against the stream," requires a moment in which the future is undecided, a moment in which there is an equal opportunity for things to go one way or another. But this need not be the case. All that liberation requires is for our efforts to make a difference to our future and for the causal processes with which we identify to be sensitive and responsive to influence of wholesome mental factors or, put another way, for these factors to play a role in the mental series (*citta-santāna*) issuing action. A series conditioned by self-grasping and other unwholesome factors can also be sensitive and responsive to wholesome factors like faith (*śraddhā*), shame (*hrī*), tranquility (*praśrabdhi*), or wisdom (*prajñā*), resulting in action conducive to greater well-being and a weakening of self-grasping. Moreover, dependent origination ensures that the wholesome influence that sets this reversal in motion need not come, in the first instance, from within the series. All that is needed is

33. In fact, our Ābhidharmika will have one distinct advantage over contemporary compatibilists (and event-causal libertarians), most of whom are committed to physicalism. Because consciousness or the intentional quality of the mental factors is part of his basic metaphysic, he is not immediately confronted with the problem of explaining the relationship of mind to physical brain processes.

a mind that is able to attend to the Buddha, his teaching, or his representatives with some degree of understanding or affection. And this can happen even if the mental series is under the sway of unwholesome motivations (namely, greed, hatred, or delusion) or other unwholesome mental factors. In his *Mahāyānasaṃgraha*, for example, Asaṅga explains that the supramundane mind, which marks entry into the path of seeing and the first bodhisattva ground, is the result of the impression left by hearing (*śruta-vāsanā*) the Buddha's teaching, such that the wisdom born of hearing gradually develops by way of reflection and meditation (Mahāyānasaṃgraha [MSg] i.45–49).[34] The enhanced self-control that results from this development is not a freedom to do whatever one desires or wills, but a freedom from the unwholesome mental factors that result in manifestly painful experience and from the self-grasping that causes subtle forms of suffering even in highly refined and wholesome states of consciousness. This does not require something outside of the causal nexus, but merely causal processes that are intelligent, that is, responsive to information. It might, however, require a *distortion* in this information processing, namely, a delusion of autonomy.

Conclusion: Free Persons, Empty Selves

The kind of goal-oriented action, effort, and initiative involved in taking up and practicing the path seems to require, psychologically speaking, a certain kind self-grasping, specifically, the kind of self-grasping in which one regards oneself as an autonomous agent. From an impersonal perspective, we might say that this is just a glitch in the information-processing mechanism such that there is a mismatch between how things really are (*yathābhūtam*) and how the mechanism responds. But it also seems to be the case that this process cannot be corrected or reversed without the energy (*vīrya*) produced by this delusion of autonomy. In personal terms, this is the energy or empowerment we feel when we take responsibility for our situation and commit to doing something about it. Nagel is not wrong to suggest that an impersonal view of action can undermine this.

---

34. In both the Mahāyāna and non-Mahāyāna shools, the path of seeing (*darśana-mārga*) is the point at which a practitioner is transformed from an ordinary to noble being (*ārya*) on account of direct meditative insight into the ultimate nature of things. There are technical reasons internal to Yogācāra theory as to why Asaṅga has to introduce this explanation in the way he does, but it is consistent with general Buddhist views regarding the transformative power of the Buddha and his teaching.

Dennett also recognizes this problem and so cautions against dwelling upon things from an impersonal perspective:

> Since there will always be strong temptations to make yourself really small, to externalize the causes of your actions and deny responsibility, the way to counteract these is to make people an offer they can't refuse: If you want to be free, you must *take* responsibility. (Dennett 2004: 292)

I suggest that the Buddha and our Ābhidharmikas would agree with this, *up to a point*. The Buddhist canon is full of exhortations to take responsibility for one's own liberation, and this is clearly the impulse behind the Buddha's consistent message regarding the indispensability of effort.

While the Buddha was not explicitly concerned about causal determinism (the view that there is only one metaphysically possible future), he was deeply concerned about the enervating effects of fatalism (the view that one's efforts make no difference to the future) and so reserved his deepest censure for the views of the Ājīvika, Makkhali Gosāla, who held the view that purification and defilement were without cause, that nothing is done by oneself (*attakāra*), another (*parakāra*), or man (*purisakāra*); that living beings are without power (*bala* and *vasa*), energy (*viriya*), steadfastness (*thāma*), or exertion (*parakkama*) and experience pleasure and pain as the result of fate (*niyati*) (Dīgha Nikāya, English [DN] 2, Pāli [D] i.53).[35] Elsewhere, the Buddha says that among the many (erroneous) views of the ascetics and *brāhmaṇas*, Makkhali's view is the (most) vile (*paṭikiṭṭha*), that while all the Buddhas and *arahants* teach the reality of karma, the efficacy of action (*kiriya*) and energy (*viriya*), Makkhali teaches the opposite. He continues,

> Just as one might set a trap at the mouth of a river for the harm, suffering, distress, and loss of many fish, so I believe, Makkhali is a useless man (*moghapurisa*), who has arisen in the world in the manner of a mantrap (*manussakhippa*) for the harm, suffering, distress, and loss of many beings. (AN 3.135, A i 286–287)

35. In addition to fate (*niyati*), the *sutta* lists *saṅgati* (sometimes translated as "serendipity" or "chance") and *bhāva* ("nature") as determining experience. There is some debate about the precise meaning of these two other terms, but they also seem to imply some kind of fatalism. See Kalupahana 1975: 32–43 for a discussion of these terms.

Makkhali's view is singled out as particularly pernicious because he directly attacks the notion that individual effort and endeavor make a difference not only to one's experience of pleasure and pain, but to one's liberation.[36] Alongside this emphasis on the importance of effort, the Buddha endorses personal initiative and ridicules those who think that his teaching entails a person can't do anything. When a Brahmin approaches the Buddha and claims that nothing is done by oneself (*attakāra*) or others (*parakāra*), the Buddha asks how one who has himself stepped forward can say this, for isn't there an element (*dhātu*) of initiative (*ārabbha*), exertion (*nikkama*), striving (*parakkama*), resistance (*thāma*), stability (*ṭhiti*), and undertaking (*upakkama*), when one steps forward or retreats (AN 6.38, A iii.337–338)?[37] While this does not imply libertarian choice, as some have supposed, it does suggest the psychological importance of maintaining a view of oneself as an autonomous agent (and hints at a dharmic explanation of this agency).

While effort and initiative speak to the importance of the idea of personal autonomy, the morally reactive attitudes of shame (*hrī*) and apprehension (*apatrāpya*) concern the interpersonal and moral sphere. Whereas Buddhist texts condemn unwholesome morally reactive attitudes like anger (*krodha*) and hatred (*dveṣa*), shame and apprehension—that is, respect for oneself and the personal consequences of one's actions—are regarded as the basis for virtue, and thus the foundation of the path to liberation.[38] From the perspective of ultimate truth, these are impersonal mental factors, but like *cetanā*, they are self-referencing: they presuppose the notion of oneself as a morally responsible agent. Despite their entanglement with the delusion of self, great emphasis is placed on their cultivation owing to their power to attract the kinds of wholesome qualities that will eventually destroy this delusion. Specifically, in helping perfect discipline (*śīla*), they help create the calm mind needed to cultivate the

36. Makkhali is said to hold the view of "purification through wandering on" (*saṃsāra-suddhi*), the view that the wise and foolish alike come to an end of suffering without any cause, just like a ball of string comes to an end by unwinding (DN 2, D i.53–54).

37. The Pāli terms, *nikkama*, etc., carry both the figurative meanings I have given above, as well as literal meanings having to do with bodily movement, but these double entendres are clearly intended to convey the idea that individuals perform these movements by way of their own exertions.

38. Visuddhimagga, 464–465; AKBh ii.25–26cd, ii.32ab, iv.9c. For an excellent analysis of shame and apprehension in Pāli sources, see Heim 2008. For more on morally reactive attitudes in relation to the problem of free will, see Goodman 2002, Siderits 2005, Harvey 2007, and Meyers 2010.

concentration (*samādhi*) necessary for the discernment (*prajñā*) of reality. In other words, the idea that *we* choose or control our actions, rather than that the choice and control we enjoy are the result of impersonal dharmic processes, is a useful delusion, *up to a point*.

This delusion can only take us so far. In order to gain the kind of consummate control over our body, speech, and mind enjoyed by noble beings, we must also learn to let go, to dis-identify with the process and stop trying to control it, for there is a subtle sort of self-grasping in trying or making an effort. This dis-identification, which is facilitated by the impersonal view of action, erodes habitual self-grasping and helps loosen the grip of unwholesome motivations and factors. It won't do, however, to simply let go from the outset and to wholeheartedly embrace the impersonal view of action and abdicate responsibility.[39] The impersonal flow of psycho-physical elements must be set on the right course, and this requires, at first, alternation between personal and impersonal perspectives, lest the view of non-self have the kind of stultifying effect Nagel and Dennett fear, or worse, cause harm to oneself or others. Thus, at first, the ultimate perspective must be confined to rarefied moments of deep reflection, meditation, and the period just after meditation. Meanwhile, the practitioner cultivates her freedom by, as Dennett puts it, "taking responsibility" for her actions. Gradually, however, as wholesome habits take hold and self-grasping loosens, there is no need for self-conscious effort. Just as the music plays itself when a master musician is at her instrument, the psycho-physical process flows expertly and effortlessly for the well-trained individual. Should the musician or *ārya* pause to reflect, it will seem exactly as if the action is not her own, as if it were spontaneous. For the Buddhist, of course, this is not "debilitating"; it is liberating.

Does this mean that free will is an illusion? I do not see any reason to conclude this. From the ultimate perspective, there is no free will because there are no persons to enjoy it; there is merely the flow of *dharmas*. From the conventional perspective there is most decidedly free will, of exactly the sort the Buddhist will find "worth wanting" to borrow Dennett's phrase. There is the freedom persons enjoy to choose the path over continued bondage to suffering and the freedom to cultivate a supreme degree of control over body, speech, and mind. These personal freedoms are not at

39. That some might arrive at this conclusion is a recurrent Buddhist concern as is evidenced in Buddhist reactions to annihilationism and the perennial debate between gradual and sudden conceptions of the path.

odds with the fact that when we look for the self, we come up empty, but are grounded in the reality of the dharmic processes we find instead.

References

Adam, Martin T. 2011. "No Free Will, No Problem: Implications of the *Anattalakkhaṇa Sutta* for a Perennial Philosophical Issue." *Journal of the International Association of Buddhist Studies* 33: 239–265.

Aung, Shwe Zan, trans. and Caroline Augusta Foley Rhys Davids, ed. 1910. *Compendium of Philosophy: Being a Translation Now Made for the First Time from the Original Pali of the Abhidhammattha-sangaha.* London: Pali Text Society (reprint, 1979).

Clarke, Randolph. 2003. *Libertarian Accounts of Free Will.* New York: Oxford University Press.

Collins, Steven. 1997. "A Buddhist Debate About Self; and Remarks on Buddhism in the Work of Derek Parfit and Galen Strawson." *Journal of Indian Philosophy* 25/5: 467–493.

Cox, Collett. 2004. "From Category to Ontology: The Changing Role of Dharma in Sarvāstivāda Abhidharma." *Journal of Indian Philosophy* 32: 543–597.

Cowherds. 2010. *Moonshadows: Conventional Truth in Buddhist Philosophy.* New York: Oxford University Press.

Davids, T.W. Rhys and J. Estlin Carpenter, eds. 1966. *The Dīgha Nikāya.* 3 vols. London: Pali Text Society.

Dennett, Daniel C. 1984. *Elbow Room: The Varieties of Free Will Worth Wanting.* Cambridge, MA: MIT Press.

———. 2004. *Freedom Evolves.* London: Penguin Books.

Devdas, Nalini. 2008. *Cetanā and the Dynamics of Volition in Theravāda Buddhism.* Delhi: Motilal Barnarsidass.

Federman, Asaf. 2010. "What Kind of Free Will did the Buddha Teach?" *Philosophy East and West* 60/1: 1–19.

Feer, M. Leon, ed. 1973–1980. *The Saṃyutta Nikāya of the Sutta-piṭaka.* 6 vols. London: Pali Text Society.

Fischer, John and Mark Ravizza. 2000. *Responsibility and Control: A Theory of Moral Responsibility.* Cambridge: Cambridge University Press.

Frankfurt, Harry. 1969. "Alternate Possibilities and Moral Responsibility." *Journal of Philosophy* 66: 829–839.

Gethin, Rupert. 2004. "He Who Sees Dhamma Sees Dhammas: Dhamma in Early Buddhism." *Journal of Indian Philosophy* 32: 513–542.

Ginet, Carl. 1966. "Might We Have No Choice?" In *Freedom and Determinism*, edited by Keith Lehrer, 87–104. New York: Random House.

Goodman, Charles. 2002. "Resentment and Reality: Buddhism on Moral Responsibility." *American Philosophical Quarterly* 39/4: 359–372.

Harvey, Peter. 1999. "Vinaya Principles for Assigning Degrees of Culpability," *Journal of Buddhist Ethics* 6: 271–291.

Harvey, Peter. 2007. "Free Will in Light of Theravāda Buddhism." *Journal of Buddhist Ethics* 14: 34–98.

Heim, Maria. 2003. "Aesthetics of Excess," *Journal of the American Academy of Religion* 71/3: 531–554.

———. 2008. "Shame and Apprehension: Notes on the Moral Value of *Hiri* and *Ottappa*." In *Embedded Religions: Essays in Honor of W. S. Karunatillake*, edited by Carol Anderson, Susanne Mrozik, and R. M. W. Rajapakse. Colombo, Sri Lanka: S. Godage and Brothers: 237–260.

Jayatilleke, K. N. 1972. "Ethics in Buddhist Perspective." *The Wheel* 175/6. Kandy: Buddhist Publication Society.

Kalupahana, David. 1975. *Causality: The Central Philosophy of Buddhism*. Honolulu: University Press of Hawaii.

Kane, Robert. 1998. *The Significance of Free Will*. New York: Oxford University Press.

La Vallée Poussin, Louis de. 2001. *La Morale Bouddhique*. Saint Michel en l'Herm: Editions Dharma (reprint of 1927 Paris edition).

Meyers, Karin. 2010. "Freedom and Self-Control: Free Will in South Asian Buddhism." PhD dissertation, University of Chicago.

Morris, Richard and Edmund Hardy, eds. 1961–1981. *The Aṅguttara-Nikāya*. 5 vols. London: Pali Text Society.

Nagel, Thomas. 1989. *The View From Nowhere*. New York: Oxford University Press.

Nanayakkara, S. K. 1979. "Free Will." In *Encyclopaedia of Buddhism*, edited by G. P. Malalasekera, vol. 5: 277–280. Colombo: Dept. of Government Printing.

Parfit, Derek. 2011. *On What Matters*. Vol. 2. New York: Oxford University Press.

Payutto, Venerable P. A. 1993. *Good, Evil and Beyond: Kamma in the Buddha's Teachings*. Bangkok: Buddhadhamma Foundation. Page reference is to the freely distributed English translation by Bruce Evans (no publication date), available online: http://www.buddhanet.net/pdf_file/good_evil_beyond.pdf.

Pradhan, P., ed. 1975. *Abhidharmakośabhāṣyam of Vasubandhu*. 2nd ed. Tibetan Sanskrit Works Series Vol. 8. Patna: K.P. Jayaswal Research Institute.

Repetti, Riccardo. 2010. "Earlier Buddhist Theories of Free Will." *Journal of Buddhist Ethics* 17: 279–310.

Ronkin, Noa. 2005. *Early Buddhist Metaphysics: The Making of Philosophical Tradition*. New York: RoutledgeCurzon.

Rhys Davids, C. A. F., ed. 1975. *The Visuddhi-magga of Buddhaghosa*. London: Pali Text Society, 1975.

Siderits, Mark. 1987. "Beyond Compatibilism: A Buddhist Approach to Freedom and Determinism." *American Philosophical Quarterly* 24: 149–159.

———. 2005. "Freedom, Caring and Buddhist Philosophy." *Contemporary Buddhism* 6: 87–116.

———. 2008. "Paleo-Compatibilism and Buddhist Reductionism." *Sophia* 47: 29–42.

Strawson, P. F. 1960. "Freedom and Resentment." In *Freedom and Resentment and Other Essays*. New York: Routledge (reprint, 2008).

Thanissaro, Bhikkhu. 2012. "The Not-Self Strategy." *Access to Insight*, 12 February 2012, http://www.accesstoinsight.org/lib/authors/thanissaro/notself.html. Retrieved on April 3, 2012.

Trackner, V., ed. 1991–1994. *The Majjhima Nikāya*. 4 vols. London: Pali Text Society.

Van Inwagen, Peter. 1983. *An Essay on Free Will*. New York: Clarendon Press.

Vasubandhu. 1986. *Las grub pa'i rab tu byed pa (Karmasiddhiprakaraṇa)*. sDe dge bsTan 'gyur series. Delhi: Karmapae Choedhey, Gyalwae Sungrab Nyamso Publishing House.

Walshe, Maurice, trans. 1987. *The Long Discourses of the Buddha*. Boston: Wisdom Publications (reprint, 1995).

3

Free Will and Voluntarism in Jainism

Christopher Key Chapple

THIS CHAPTER WILL explore notions of will and voluntarism in the Jaina tradition by examining passages from early and medieval literature. The earliest extant text of the Jaina tradition, the *Ācārāṅga Sūtra*, espouses adherence to vows as the primary way of achieving its intended spiritual goals. This text, dating from 300 BCE, is accepted by the adherents to the Śvetāmbara or White-clad group of Jainas but rejected by the other main group of Jainas, the Digambara or Sky-clad. Both agree on the authority of a later text, the *Tattvārtha Sūtra* of Umāsvāti, thought to have been composed in the fifth century of the common era. This text expounds on the foundational principles of Jaina belief, particularly its description of the soul (*jīva*), how it becomes sullied through self-effort with karma, and how it can be purified and set free from karmic bondage. In addition to these sources, literature from each tradition will be considered on the topic of will, including the *Yogadṛṣṭisamuccaya* of Haribhadra Yākinī-putra (ca. 8th century Śvetāmbara) and the *Pravacanasāra* and *Samayasāra* of Kundakunda (ca. 5th century Digambara).

Jainism, like Buddhism and the Yoga tradition, emphasizes karmic causality in its philosophy. It does not posit a creator deity such as Brahmā or Prajāpati, nor does it advance the notion of an originating matrix such as *prakṛti*, the source of all manifestation in Sāṃkhya philosophy. The Jaina worldview asserts the existence of innumerable souls or *jīvas* that become obscured by cloakings of karma. These karmas, like the *jīvas* themselves, are particular and individual, and the path of Jaina purification requires that they be expelled or extirpated through assiduously adhering to strict ethical rules. By sloughing off these karmas, one attains increasingly rarefied spiritual states. Ultimately, this process culminates in liberation and the ascent of the undying, conscious soul to a beatific state. According to this system, will reigns supreme in both the accumulating and shedding of karma. Through acts of will vitiated by violent intent, karmas adhere to the soul. Through acts of will inspired by a desire to do no harm, karmas fly away, leaving the soul lighter and less burdened and ultimately free to soar into endless energy, consciousness, and bliss.

The Ācārāṅga Sūtra

Jainism traces its origins back to the teacher Pārśvanātha, who lived approximately 850 BCE in northeast India. Three to four hundred years later, Mahāvīra codified the teachings of Pārśvanātha. These two religious leaders are considered within the Jaina tradition to be the 23rd and 24th of a long line of liberated guides known as Tīrthaṅkaras, which means "one who has forded the stream." This epithet indicates that these Jinas, or "great victors," have conquered the stream of karma and reached the banks of the other shore. From their place of splendid luminosity, they dwell in perpetual consciousness, energy, and bliss, perched atop their own mountain, endlessly surveying the play of karma below. To emphasize the singular, heroic nature of this achievement, the Sanskrit term for this ascent, *kevala*, means "simple, pure, uncompounded, unmingled, entire, whole, all."[1]

From the onset, the *Ācārāṅga Sūtra* sets forth a voluntarist view. It begins with an exhortation to know one's orientation within the four directions and to accept the premise that the "soul is born again and again." The opening passage goes on to state that a Jaina "believes in the soul, believes in the world, believes in reward, believes in action (acknowledged to be our own doing in judgments such as these: 'I did it;' 'I shall cause another to do it;' 'I shall allow another to do it'). In the world, these are all the causes of sin which must be comprehended and renounced."[2] The translator adeptly points out that the belief in a soul sets Jainism apart from the materialist Cārvākas, that the reference to the reality of the world distinguished the Jainas from the Vedāntins, and that the cause of all suffering lies in action (*kiriyā/kriyā*). Similarly, the ideas of Jainism also contrast with the emphasis on ritual activity found in the Mīmāṃsakas. By purification of action, the soul purifies itself.

---

1. Monier Monier-Williams, *A Sanskrit-English Dictionary* (Oxford: Clarendon Press, 1899), s.v. *kevala*.

2. Jacobi 1968: 2. Hereafter abbreviated as *AS*.

The commitment to nonviolent action defines Jainism. Acts of nonviolence are willfully undertaken. The *Ācārāṅga Sūtra* states: "a wise person should not commit violence nor order others to commit violence, nor consent to the violence done by somebody else" (*AS* 1:2,3). The text repeatedly extols "penance, self-restraint, and control" as the means of purification. It also lauds the Jaina practitioner as a hero:

> The hero should conquer wrath and pride.. .
> the hero, knowing bondage, knowing sorrow,
> should exercise self-restraint.
> Having risen to human birth,
> the hero should not take the life of living beings. (*AS* 1:3,3)

The use of the term "conquer" plays a preeminent role in the text, with regard to conquering negative actions or karmas such as "wrath, pride, deceit, and greed" (*AS* 1:4.1).

It is important to note that this effort is not exerted to create or engage in worldly activities, but to purge oneself of karmas that bind one to the cycle of birth, life, death, and rebirth. The goal is to follow assiduously Jaina precepts protecting all forms of life, not necessarily for the sake of those life forms themselves, but to purify oneself of karmic accretions. The meticulous articulation of the places that contain life requires utmost attentiveness. The *Ācārāṅga Sūtra* begins with a thorough analysis of the elemental presences of life before turning to the more obvious presence of life in vegetation, in bacteria, and in animals. Hence, the Jaina monk is advised to be vigilant not to commit harm to earth bodies, water bodies, as well as to the forms of life in fire and air. The following passage conveys a sense of the care to be observed:

> There are beings living in the earth, living on grass, living on leaves, living in wood, living in cowdung, living in dust heaps, and jumping beings which coming near fire fall into it. Some certainly, touched by fire, shrivel up [and] die there.... a wise person should not act sinfully towards fire, nor cause others to do so, nor allow others to do so. The one who knows the causes of sin relating to fire is called a reward-knowing sage. (*AS* 1:1.4.6–7)

The text goes on to itemize the eight ways in which life takes form, including from eggs, fetuses, fetuses with amniotic sacs, fluid (worms), sweat (lice), coagulation (locusts, ants), sprouts (butterflies), and by regeneration (animals, humans, gods, hell-beings; *AS* 1:1.6.1).

Punishments due to past action can be severe. The *Ācārāṅga Sūtra* attributes such problems as "boils and leprosy, consumption, falling sickness, blindness and stiffness, lameness and humpbackedness, dropsy and dumbness, epilepsy, eye disease, trembling and crippledness, elephantiasis, and diabetes" to "the fruits of their own acts" (1:6.2). In order to rid oneself of the afflictions that cause such unpleasant experiences, Mahāvīra urges taking up the monastic life. Practicing austerities, the monk or nun "neither injuring nor injured, becomes a shelter for all sorts of afflicted creatures, even as an island, which is never covered with water, is so" (1:6.5.4). Detailed rules are given governing the life of the monks and nuns, specifying that one may own at most only three robes and one begging bowl and perhaps a broom. The ideal observance of Digambara male monasticism includes the option of total nudity and renunciation of even the begging bowl (I:7.7). Enduring great hardship and discomfort, including reviling blows from non-believers, the monk or nun bears "the pains caused by cold, heat, flies, gnats, and . . . miserable beds and miserable seats" as did Mahāvīra (1:8.3.2).

The second book of the *Ācārāṅga Sūtra* expands the list of ways in which the Jaina monk or nun must exert his or her will in order to best adhere to the precepts of the faith, including how and where and when to beg for food, the requirement that one avoid various specific forms of entertainment or festivals that might stir the passions, and that one should not point accusingly at anyone. Detailed lists are provided regarding unacceptable food, including "bulbous roots . . . ginger . . . raw mango . . . unripe wild rice, honey, liquor, ghee" and many others (2:1.8.3–4). Places to avoid lodging include those "used by the householder, in which there are women, children, cattle, food, and drink. This is the reason: A mendicant living together with a householder's family may have an attack of gout, dysentery, or vomiting; or some other pain, illness, or disease may befall him" (2:2.1.8). Other reasons to avoid living with householders, for monks, include becoming sexually aroused by "the householder's wives, daughters, daughters-in-law, nurses, slave-girls or servant girls" (2:2.1.12). Monks and nuns are restricted from traveling in the rainy season due to potential harm caused to living beings. They must take care to avoid thieves, guard their speech, and avoid acquiring anything beyond essential clothing.

The text concludes with a summary account of the life of Mahāvīra, the exemplar for adherents to the faith.

In reading the *Ācārāṅga Sūtra*, one finds not only a philosophy and way of life based on voluntary action, but also exhaustive and somewhat exhausting detail in regard to behaviors to be avoided and allowed behaviors to be cultivated.

The Tattvārtha Sūtra

Whereas earlier Prakrit texts such as the *Ācārāṅga Sūtra* and the *Kalpa Sūtra* provide narrative accounts of how best to practice the Jaina faith, the fifth-century *Tattvārtha Sūtra* falls within the genre of Sanskrit philosophical texts that set forth premises and assertions, exposing the reader to a comprehensive worldview that encourages religious practice culminating in freedom. Thus, reflection upon cosmology leads to insight; insight leads to religious commitment; religious commitment delivers one into a life of purified action and ultimately freedom. Authored by the scholar Umāsvāti, this text has earned acceptance from both Śvetāmbaras and Digambaras, who have disagreed on many other issues since their separation, most likely due to famine, 2300 years ago. They disagree on the details of Mahāvīra's biography and on the potential spiritual status of women. Śvetāmbaras proclaim that women can attain release; Digambaras say they need to reincarnate as a man to do so. Both groups agree on the principles set forth by Umāsvāti: karma causes rebirth; vows cleanse one of karma; through diligent adherence to Jaina vows, one can purge karma and gain release.

Umāsvāti composed ten chapters that describe the progression from cosmology to karma to ethics to liberation. The first chapter includes a summary view of Jainism that reveals the fundamental commitment to a philosophy of free will. It works with an ascending hierarchy of three binaries leading to liberation, contrasting soul with matter, and contrasting the inflow and binding of karma with the stoppage and expulsion of karma. This ascension results in "liberation from worldly (karmic) bondage."[3] Each soul authors its own future existence, inviting karma to stick to and occlude its true nature or actively expelling karma through the performance of purifying vows.

3. Tatia 1994: 6. Hereafter abbreviated as *TS*.

According to Umāsvāti, souls and matter have existed since time without beginning. Individuals determine their present state, generally sullied with the presence of karmic matter. Karmas flow onto the soul, sticking to it and shrouding the soul with tendencies and predispositions. Through taking up the religious life, one is able to first stop the influx of more karma, and then gradually slough off the karmas that have accrued over time. Though the stories of great heroic spiritual teachers such as Mahāvīra may inspire an individual to be steady in his or her religious practice, each soul creates and follows a solitary destiny. Vows must be observed and performed from within; no human being and no god or demon can effect either adherence to or straying from the commitment to expel all the fettering karmas.

In the second chapter of the *Tattvārtha Sūtra*, Umāsvāti describes the eight forms of karma that shape reality: (1) knowledge-covering; (2) intuition-covering; (3) sensation-covering; (4) deluding; (5) lifespan-determining; (6) body-making; (7) status-determining; (8) obstructive (Tatia 1994: 33). Details follow that describe all the various forms of life, divided into mobile and non-mobile forms, that fall sway to the influences of these karmas. Unlike Aristotle, who defined life in terms of respiration and growth, Umāsvāti, following the ideas of earlier Jaina teachers such as Mahāvīra in the *Ācārāṅga Sūtra*, sees life in particles of earth, drops of water, flickering flames, and gusts of wind. To each life form is attributed at least one sense. Souls trapped by karma in the form of earth or plants possess the consciousness of touch. Worms and leeches add taste, bugs add smell, flying insects add sight, and larger beings including fish, mammals, humans, and gods add hearing and mind.

The text delineates three domains: the infernal region, the middle realm of earth, and the heavenly region. The liberated soul can only attain release from containment in these zones into a place of liberation known as the Siddha Loka by attaining human birth and then entering and completing the Jaina path of purification. Chapter three describes the lower and middle region, comprising a remarkable geography interwoven with moral implications. If one performs evil actions, one descends into the various hells. On earth, known as Jambūdvīpa, elements, plants, as well as non-human animals are given the opportunity to cultivate virtue.

The heavenly realm, described in chapter four, includes many varieties of gods and goddesses. In the lower realms of heaven, they enjoy sexual activity (Tatia 1994: 100), while in the higher realms they find sexual pleasure through sight, sound, and thought. Ten "mansion gods" are listed as follows: "fiendish youths, serpentine youths, lightning youths, vulturine youths, fiery youths, stormy youths, thundering youths, oceanic youths, island youths, and youths who rule the cardinal points" (TS 4.11). Other types of gods include forest gods and luminous gods, located in more than two dozen heavens. These heavenly domains are not destinations but way stations; in order to advance toward freedom, each soul must eventually re-inhabit human form through the accumulation of merit and virtue, regardless of its abode.

The fifth chapter describes substances, considering the soul and karma alike to be substantial. It additionally names categories that are non-sentient: matter, motion, rest, and space. Soul has consciousness; matter, motion, rest, and space have no consciousness. Within this amalgam of ingredients, reality takes form as individual consciousnesses interact with the material environment. According to the commentaries, vibrations (*spanda*) of the soul attract particular forms of karma, clustering into body-making karma, mind-covering karma, and the rest. The sixth chapter specifies: "Good actions cause the inflow of beneficial karma. Evil actions cause the inflow of harmful karma" (*TS* 6:3–4). The commentary gives details on the various "doors" of karma, such as the five senses, the four passions (anger, pride, deceit, greed); the five indulgences (causing harm, lying, stealing, licentiousness, possessiveness); and the 25 urges, from seeking the enlightened view to harboring passions and possessiveness. These 25 urges provide a roadmap to understanding human will. The assessment of the innate human condition is actually quite grim. Only the first urge leads to the enlightened worldview. The other 24 urges cause delusion; various forms of evil; malicious, torturous, and murderous activities; disrespect for scriptural teachings; and more (Tatia 1994: 153).

The *Tattvārtha Sūtra* specifies the causes that inhibit consciousness:

> Slander, concealment, envy, obstructiveness, and disregard or condemnation of the scripture, its keepers and instruments, cause the inflow of knowledge-covering and intuition-covering karma. (*TS* 6.11)
>
> Causing pain, grief, agony, crying, injury or lamenting in oneself or others or both, attracts pain karma. (*TS* 6.12)
>
> The inflow of view-deluding karma is caused by maligning the Jinas, their scripture, religious order and doctrine, and the gods and goddesses. (TS 6.14)

> The inflow of conduct-deluding karma is caused by the highly-strung state of the soul due to the rise of the passions. (*TS* 6.15)

In addition to the four passions listed above, the commentaries list nine "quasi-passions: laughter, relish, ennui, grief, fear, abhorrence, feminine sexuality, masculine sexuality, hermaphroditic [*sic*] sexuality" (Tatia 1994: 158).

The text then specifies that varying degrees of these karmas lead to infernal, animal, and human births:

> Virulent aggression and extreme possessiveness lead to birth in the infernal realm. Deceitfulness leads to birth in animal realms. Attenuated aggression, attenuated possessiveness, and a soft-hearted and straightforward nature, lead to birth in the human realm. (*TS* 6.16–18)

The text also states that self-restraint and purging of karma "lead to birth in the realm of the gods" (*TS* 6.20), though this is not the same as the ultimate goal of freedom from all karma. The qualities required for this freedom are sixteen-fold, including purity; humility; virtue; knowledge; dread of repeated rebirth; charity; austerity; harmony; service; devotion to the Jina, the living teacher, fellow monks, and scripture; performance of vowed duties; promotion of the spiritual path; and "adoration of the learned ascetics in the scripture" (*TS* 6.23). Each of these qualities, whether of the negative type listed above or those that lead to the realm of the gods or to freedom, affirm the philosophy of voluntarism and free will that characterizes Jainism.

The seventh chapter of the *Tattvārtha Sūtra* explains the five major vows, the seven supplementary observances, and the ultimate act of Jaina will: the fast unto death. Just as willful karma delivers individual souls into repeated births in the infernal, elemental, microbial, plant, animal, human, and heavenly realms, the practice of vows reverses this process. The five major vows are "abstinence from violence, falsehood, stealing, carnality and possessiveness" and the seven supplementary vows to be followed by lay persons are "refraining from movement beyond a limited area; restricting movement...even more...; refraining from wanton destruction of the environment by thought, word, or deed; keeping aloof from sinful conduct for a set period of time; fasting on sacred days.... ; limiting the use of goods; and offering alms to wandering ascetics" (*TS* 7.1,

16). Specific details are given for monastics and laypersons for the practice of these vows, including dietary and hygiene requirements.

The commentary on the eighth chapter states that there are 180 forms of activity that cause bondage and the adherence of karmic particles that obscure the purity of the soul. Due to one's actions, one obtains status within the realms of hell beings, subhumans, humans, and gods. The text states that good karmas result in "pleasure, auspicious lifespan, auspicious body, and auspicious status" (*TS* 8.25). The ninth chapter advocates moral behavior as the key to spiritual advancement along the fourteen stages that lead to freedom.[4] The text defines morality as "perfect forgiveness, humility, straightforwardness, purity, truthfulness, self-restraint, austerity, renunciation, detachment and continence" (*TS* 9.6). Additionally, karma can be sloughed off by enduring 22 hardships such as "hunger, thirst, cold, heat, and insect bites." (*TS* 9.9).

The text also specifies six external austerities, six internal austerities, and nine types of penance. Two types of meditation are prescribed for liberation, "analytic and white" (*TS* 9.3), which are said to arise among those who have perfected self-restraint and have eliminated passions. Will is required to adhere to the vows and to overcome the influence of past karmas. One is then able to enact the four varieties of white meditation: "multiple contemplation, unitary contemplation, subtle infallible physical activity, and irreversible stillness" (Tatia 1994: 241).[5] All of this effort finds its crescendo when "there is no fresh bondage because the causes of bondage have been eliminated and all destructive karmas have worn off" (*TS* 10.2). With this moment of freedom, the efforts of all spiritual exertion have borne fruit, delivering the soul forever more from the cycle of rebirth.

The *Tattvārtha Sūtra*, in a philosophy, style, and genre similar to that found in the *Yoga Sūtra*, the *Sāṃkhya Kārikā*, and the *Visuddhi Magga*, asserts that human action determines the nature of how one feels about the world one occupies. Karma theory in all these texts allows no space for external agency. No creation narrative is offered. Although great figures such as Mahāvīra, or the unnamed Īśvara, or Buddha may serve as exemplars and provide inspiration, they cannot intervene to create or alter

4. See Chapple 2003, chapter two.

5. Greater study is needed of these states of Jaina meditation. They perhaps may correspond to *savitarka, nirvitarka* and *savicāra, nirvicāra* as described in Patañjali's *Yoga Sūtra*. See Chapple 2003, chapter two, "Haribhadra and Patañjali" and especially the chart on p. 38.

karmas. Responsibility for one's karma lies solely within the creative powers of each individual.

The Yogadṛṣṭisamuccaya

Haribhadra Yākinī-putra (ca. 700–770 CE) composed a text on comparative approaches to spiritual discipline called the *Yogadṛṣṭisamuccaya.* In this work he provides a critique of various non-Jaina schools, including Tantra, Advaita Vedānta, and Buddhism, along with a criticism of unclear, muddled thinking. He gently asserts that steady practice in accord with scripture is required for spiritual advancement. Following the tradition of Mahāvīra and Umāsvāti summarized above, Haribhadra proclaims the reality of the soul, the reality of karma, and the centrality of action both in terms of worldly creation and freedom.

Haribhadra criticizes aspects of Tantra. Referring to the rituals that require forbidden behavior as part of a purification process, he states that "stepping into licentiousness is not stepping toward the highest goal. Indeed, the only step to be taken by Yogis is toward sanctioned behavior" (*YDS* 72).[6] With great emotion, he writes, "Like baited meat on a fishhook, they are addicted to vanity, decadent pleasures, and cruel behavior. Cruel and lethargic, they renounce the true object of desire. What a pity!" (*YDS* 84).

In regard to unclear thinking, Haribhadra makes the following observation:

> Fallacious argument produces in the mind
> sickness of intellect, destruction of equanimity,
> disturbance of faith and cultivation of pride.
> In many ways, it is the enemy of existence. (*YDS* 87)
> The proponents of liberation
> are not tied to the pursuit of these fallacious arguments.
> Instead, the great-souled ones are joined
> to scripture, good action, and *samādhi.* (*YDS* 88)

In opposition to the teachings of Buddhism that deny abiding self-nature (*sva-bhatu*), Haribhadra claims that Buddhist doctrines comprise an

6. Translation by Chapple and Casey in Chapple 2003. Hereafter abbreviated as *YDS*.

incipient form of illusionism. For Jainas, the reality of soul and matter cannot be denied. Haribhadra states that "something that is always being destroyed cannot be posited" (*YDS* 195). He holds a similar critique for the monism espoused in Advaita Vedānta: "If any singular essence is proclaimed, then there could never be the two states of life" (*YDS* 198), implying that without the reality of happiness and misery there would be no incentive to take up spiritual purifications. He writes:

> If an ailment is an illusion (as per the Vedāntins), or is always changing into something else (as the Buddhists claim),.... then a liberated one is not liberated! (*YDS* 204–205)

According to Jainism, both Vedānta and Buddhism fall short of the mark because of their reluctance to take the pains of the world sufficiently seriously.

Haribhadra asserts the efficacy of human action in the world:

> Effort Yoga is known as the highest Yoga.
> It arises from an abundance of power
> stemming from the steadfast observance of the precepts.
> It is the dwelling place of the accomplished ones. (*YDS* 5)

Spiritual practice, generally referred to by the term Yoga, requires dropping away all attachments to karma, a process known as disjunction or *ayoga* or *nirjarā*. This can only take place through assiduous adherence to the purifying vows. Haribhadra writes, "The Yoga of total freedom (*ayoga*) is declared the highest of Yogas. Characterized by the renunciation of all things, it is truly the path of liberation" (*YDS* 11).

The religious life is summarized as a process of willful activity in the following verse:

> Bringing about positive (*sat*) activity
> by battling negative (*asat*) activity
> is considered an awakened view.
> From this, one is joined to true faith. (*YDS* 17)

Several activities are prescribed to cultivate these positive behaviors, including the advice that "through books, worship, giving, listening, and speaking, one is uplifted, as well as through teaching study, reflection, and meditation" (*YDS* 28). Using the metaphor of eight different forms of fire, Haribhadra sets forth eight different pathways that lead one toward freedom from all karma.[7] Through these Yogas, one achieves "freedom from all adversity":

> With the various species of karma purified,
> the soul becomes established in a cool, moonlike radiance.
> In respect to the world, ordinary consciousness
> is like a cloud concealing the moonlight.
> It is said that at the time when the clouds of destructive karma
> are destroyed by the winds of Yoga, that is the escape.
> Then the glory of singular knowledge is born. (*YDS* 183–184)

For Haribhadra, Yoga entails human spiritual effort. By engaging the ascetic practices of Jaina Yoga, one is able to dispel the clouds of karma and rise up into a space of total freedom.

Divine Will? Human Will!

The question of divine will does not arise in the Jaina tradition. In his introduction to the *Paramātmaprakāśa* of Yogīndu, A. N. Upadhye states:

> neither Arhat nor Siddha has on him the responsibility of creating, supporting, and destroying the world. The aspirant receives no boons, no favours, and no curses from him by way of gifts from the divinity. The aspiring souls pray to him, worship him and meditate on him as an example, as a model, as an ideal that they too might reach the same condition.[8]

Those souls who have achieved liberation dwell in the highest state possible. However, they hold no power over those who remain mired in the cycle of life and death and rebirth. Their example may inspire others to

7. The eight include Friendliness, Protection, Power, Shining, Firmness, Pleasing, Radiance, and Highest Yoga. These correspond to Patañjali's eight limbs of Abstinence, Observance, Postures, Breath Control, Inwardness, Concentration, Meditation, and *Samādhi*. Haribhadra takes the further step of using the names of goddesses to describe these stages: Mitrā, Tārā, Balā, Diprā, Sthirā, Kāntā, Prabhā, Parā.

8. As quoted in Sogani 2001: 199.

hasten in their process on the path to release. As noted by Kamal Chand Sogani:

> The ultimate responsibility of emancipating oneself from the turmoils of the world falls upon one's own undivided efforts, upon the integral consecration of energies to the attainment of divine life. Thus every soul has the right to become Paramātman, who has been conceived to be the consummate realization of the divine potentialities. (Sogani 2001: 200)

The only god to be worshipped is an indwelling god. By purifying and releasing all karmic obstructions, human beings have the potential to connect with that point of consciousness. Though few have done so,[9] the liberated souls remain inspiring for those that follow them.

Soul Without Attachment According to Kundakunda

Kundakunda, an important early Digambara writer, most likely lived no earlier than the third century of the common era and no later than the fifth century. His two primary texts, the *Pravacanasāra* and the *Samayasāra*, attribute qualities to the soul that underscore its independent and self-determining nature. He also clearly articulates themes well known in other traditions of India: the undying nature of the soul and the existence of two realms of existence: the provisional and transient (*vyavahāra*), in contrast with the undying consciousness, bliss, and energy (*caitanya, sukha, vīrya*) of the liberated soul (*niścaya*).

The *Pravacanasāra* asserts that impure actions result from one's own efforts. W. J. Johnson notes that "bondage—life in *saṃsāra*—is the direct result of particular states of consciousness which are self-generated" (Johnson 1995: 120).[10] Human beings make decisions that lead to impure actions (*aśubha-karma*). In order to reverse this process, purification (*śuddha*) through adherence to vows is needed. Negative undertakings cause molecules or atoms (*skandha*) to adhere to the soul, which itself is without form or materiality. In other words, acts of will cause the soul

9. According to Jaina tradition, the last human to achieve total liberation was the monk Jambū, who died in 463 BCE, 64 years after the death of Mahāvīra. See Jaini 1991: 98.

10. Johnson 1995: 120. Subsequent references to the two texts, the *Pravacanasāra* (*PS*) and the *Samayasāra* (*SS*), are drawn from Johnson's translations.

to partake in *saṃsāra* and perpetuate its own difficulties. Acts of will are needed to reverse course and move toward freedom.

As found in other systems of Indian thought, attraction (*rāga*), repulsion (*dveṣa*), and delusion (*moha*) are at the heart of all fettering karmas according to Kundakunda. This brew of karmas results in the emergence of a fixed sense of ego. Johnson translates verse 2:91 of the *Pravacanasāra*:

> Who does not know thus the *paramātman*, encountered in their own natures, conceives through delusion the idea "I am (this), this is mine."

In other words, the presence of *rāga*, *dveṣa*, and *moha* results in attachment to a fixed identity which covers over the true or highest self.

As with the Sāṃkhya system and the descriptions of freedom in Pāli Buddhist literature, Kundakunda sees the abandonment of ego as the key to freedom:

> He who does not abandon the idea of "mine" with regard to body and possessions—[thinking] "I am [this], this is mine"—gives up the state of being a *śramaṇa* and becomes one who has resorted to the wrong road. He who meditates in concentration, thinking "I am not others and they are not mine; I am one [with] knowledge," comes to be a meditator on the [pure] self. (*PS* 2.98–99)

Internal purity (*śuddhopayoga*), enacted through adherence to nonviolence, brings the aspirant away from karmic bondage. Eventually, meditation itself becomes the vehicle for release.

Kundakunda emphasizes equanimity (*sāmāyika*) as the path that leads to realization of the highest self. He indicates that even being self-pleased with one's virtuous behavior must be abandoned:

> Free from inauspicious manifestation of consciousness, not joined to auspicious (manifestation of consciousness)...let me be indifferent (i.e. neutral); I meditate on the self whose self is knowledge.
>
> I am neither body, nor mind, nor speech, nor the cause of these, neither the agent, nor the instigator, nor the approver of doers/actors. (*PS* 2.67–68)

In the final analysis, the last verse of the *Pravacanasāra* proclaims that inner purity, which is also reflected in one's activities in the external world, results in faith, knowledge, and freedom:

> He, who is pure, is said to be a *śramaṇa*; to the pure one belong faith and
> knowledge; the pure one attains liberation; he alone is a siddha: my salutation to him. (*PS* 3.74)

Right knowledge and right action purify the soul. Kundakunda's *Samayasāra* elaborates on the theme of overcoming attachment within the realm of conventional reality or *saṃsāra*. The three core practices of right view, right thought, and right action must be practiced, though; from an ultimate point of view, attachment to their "rightness" must also be renounced:

> Right belief, knowledge, and conduct should always be practiced by a *sādhu* [from the *vyavahāra*, conventional, point of view]; but know that these three are in reality the [pathway to] self. (*SS* 16)[11]

In the *Pravacanasāra*, Kundakunda explains attachment in terms of the adherence (*upayoga*) of karmas. In the *Samayasāra* the term *bhāva* indicates emplacement and attachment within the morass of karmas. As Johnson points out, "the liberated self is... *bhāva*-less" (Johnson 1995: 267). The text states:

> When the *jīva* has this true knowledge, then the self, which is pure consciousness, produces no *bhāvas* whatsoever. (*SS* 183)

Kundakunda states that the liberated one's *bhāva* consists of knowledge, much as stated in verse 63 of the *Sāṃkhya Kārikā*:

> The *bhāva* of an ignorant person consists of ignorance; through that he produces karmas. But the knower's *bhāva* consists of knowledge and therefore he does not produce karmas. (*SS* 127)

---

11. The Jainas use the term *niścaya* for what the Buddhist refer to as *pāramārthika*.

Returning to the earlier theme of freedom from possession and ego, Kundakunda poses the following question:

> What wise man, indeed, knowing all *bhāvas* to have arisen from non-self (*para*), and knowing that the self is pure, would utter the words, "This is mine"? (*SS* 300)

By abandoning all claims to the self bound by hatred (*dveṣa*), greed (*rāga*), and delusion (*moha*), one moves toward purity and freedom.

Kundakunda's assessment of will, while acknowledging its power in the creation and manipulation of the realm of phenomena (*vyavahāra*), states that even will or intention to follow the rules must eventually be discarded. The practices must become automatic. The vows play an important role in the process of purification, but Kundakunda implies that while from all outward appearances a *sādhu* will continue to live according to the vows, all pride and attachment to their perfection must disappear:

> Bondage is brought about by what is resolved (*adhyavasāna*) whether one kills beings or not... Similarly, the resolution to lie, to take what is not given, to be unchaste, and to acquire property leads to the bondage of bad (*pāpa*) karma, whereas the resolution to be truthful, to take only what is given, to be chaste, and not to acquire possessions leads to the bondage of good (*puṇya*) karma. For *jīvas*, resolution occurs with reference to an object, but bondage is not caused by that object; bondage is caused by resolution [i.e., by the attitude toward the object]. (*SS* 262–265)

The power of will entangles one in *saṃsāra*; enactment of will through the performance of action in accord with the five great vows helps release one from *saṃsāra*. Kundakunda states that the true nature of the soul is that of the knower, and that "in reality it cannot and can never have been associated with the impure knowledge-restricting not-self" realm of karma (Johnson 1995: 282). Through action, one becomes trapped in karma; through action one can start to regain a sense of one's true identity as not having any claim on anything, including the notion of self. Meditation, an act of will to undo the will, provides the path to that realization.

Conclusion

The earliest literature of the Jaina faith asserts the efficacy of a vowed life for the purpose of overcoming karmic fetters. Accrued over several lifetimes, these impediments to highest human potential require asceticism to effect their extirpation. Although acknowledging the helpfulness of developing a religious attitude and feeling of reverence for the great teachers of Jainism, both living and dead, Jaina philosophy espouses a thorough voluntarist outlook. Human action attracts negative karmas; human action and commitment to a life regulated by the vows of nonviolence, truthfulness, not stealing, sexual propriety, and non-possession set the contours not only for a life well lived, but also for a life oriented toward eventual total freedom. In contrast to more grace-oriented philosophies, Jainism stands starkly at the existential edge, proclaiming that each individual carries ultimate control over his or her own life. Karma determines all things, and each soul faces, moment to moment, the decision to continue in patterns of behavior that densify karma and hence obscure the soul or to take up the steady path to purification.

References

Chapple, Christopher Key. 2003. *Reconciling Yogas: Haribhadra's Collection of Views on Yoga with a New Translation of Haribhadra's Yogadṛṣṭisamuccaya by Christopher Key Chapple and John Thomas Casey.* Albany: State University of New York Press.

Jacobi, Hermann, trans. 1968. *Jaina Sutras Translated from the Prakrit in Two Parts: Part I: The Ākārāṅga Sūtra, the Kalpa Sūtra.* New York: Dover; originally published in 1884 by Clarendon Press.

Jaini, Padmanabh S. 1991. *Gender and Salvation: Jaina Debates on the Spiritual Liberation of Women.* Berkeley: University of California Press.

Johnson, W. J. 1995. *Harmless Souls: Karmic Bondage and Religious Change in Early Jainism with Special Reference to Umāsvāti and Kundakunda.* New Delhi: Motilal Banarsidass.

Sogani, Kamal Chand. 2001. *Ethical Doctrines in Jainism.* Solapur: Jaina Samskriti Samrakshaka Sangha.

Tatia, Nathmal, trans. 1994. *That Which Is: Tattvārtha Sutra/Umāsvāti/Umāsvāmi with the Combined Commentaries of Umāsvāti/Umāsvāmi, Pūjyapāda and Siddhasenagaṇi.* San Francisco: HarperCollins.

4

Pāṇinian Grammarians on Agency and Independence

George Cardona

śabdapramāṇakā vayam / yac chabda āha tad asmākaṃ pramāṇam/
—MAHĀBHĀṢYA 2.1.1 (1.366.12–13)

The limits of my language are the limits of my mind. All I know is what I have words for.
—LUDWIG WITTGENSTEIN, Philosophical Investigations

Introduction

Pāṇini's rule assigning the category name *kartṛ*

In his *Aṣṭādhyāyī*, Pāṇini (**A** 1.4.54: *svatantraḥ kartā* [*kārake* 23]) provides that a direct participant in the accomplishment of an action (*kāraka*) that is independent (*svatantra*) has the category name *kartṛ* ("agent"). In his *sūtra* Pāṇini uses *svatantraḥ* but does not specify what constitutes an agent's independence. He appears to assume a commonly accepted meaning of the term *svatantra*, known to students of his grammar.

This accords with how Pāṇini proceeds in other instances, where he also takes as given accepted meanings of particular terms. Especially noteworthy among these is *adya* "today," which Pāṇini uses as part of *anadyatana* when he provides (**A** 3.2.111: *anadyatane laṅ* [*bhūte* 84]) that the *l*-affix *lAṄ* is introduced after a verbal base if the act this signifies is referred to a past (*bhūte*) time that excludes the day on which one speaks, as in *akarot* (← *kṛ-lAṄ*) "…made, did" (3sg. impfct.). The same term is used in a rule (**A** 3.3.15: *anadyatane luṭ* [*bhaviṣyati* 3]) whereby *lUṬ* is introduced if an act is referred to future (*bhaviṣyati*) time excluding the day on which one speaks, as in *kartā* (← *kṛ-lUṬ*) "…will make, do" (3sg. distant fut.). A *sūtra* that is not strictly attributable to Pāṇini, moreover, says that a statement defining particular times (*kāla*) need not be taught, since these are common knowledge.[1] The *Kāśikā* remarks that other grammarians do formulate statements concerning time. Some say that the time spoken of as *adyatanaḥ kālaḥ* "time pertaining to today" stretches from the normal time one gets up to the normal time one retires. Others say this time includes the last two and first two stretches of two-hours in the previous and following night relative to a day.[2]

Patañjali on *Aṣṭādhyāyī* 1.4.54

In the *Mahābhāṣya* on **A** 1.4.54, Patañjali also does not go into much detail concerning what is meant by *svatantra*. His brief discussion[3] begins on the assumption that *svatantra* is a *bahuvrīhi* compound referring to someone who has his own *tantra*, which tentatively allows the term to refer to a weaver (*tantuvāya*). The presumed fault is then shown not to obtain because *tantra* in this context is understood to have a particular meaning. This term can be used of a mass of threads stretched on a loom (*vitāna*), as when one says

(1) *āstīrṇaṃ tantram* "the *tantra* stretched from side to side"

or

(2) *protaṃ tantram* "the *tantra* stretched lengthwise.' "

---

1. **A** 1.2.57: *kālopasarjane ca tulyam*; see Cardona 1997: 604.

2. Kāś. 1.2.57: *ihānye vaiyākaraṇāḥ kālopasarjanayoḥ paribhāṣāṃ kurvanti | ā nyāyyād utthānād ā nyāyyāc ca saṃveśanād eṣo'dyatanaḥ kālaḥ | apare punar āhuḥ ahar ubhayatordharātram eṣo'dyatanaḥ kāla iti.*

3. Bh. I.338.17–20: *kiṃ yasya svaṃ tantraṃ sa svatantraḥ | kiṃ cātaḥ | tantuvāye prāpnoti | naiṣa doṣaḥ | ayaṃ tantraśabdo'sty eva vitāne vartate | tad yathā āstīrṇaṃ tantram protaṃ tantram | vitāna iti gamyate | asti prādhānye vartate | tad yathā svatantro'yaṃ brāhmaṇa ity ucyate | svapradhāna iti gamyate | tad yaḥ prādhānye vartate tantraśabdas tasyedaṃ grahaṇam.*

One understands a mass of threads stretched in one direction or the other on a loom. The same term is also used with respect to the property of being a principal entity (*prādhānya*), as when one says

(3) *svatantro'yaṃ brāhmaṇaḥ* "This Brāhmaṇa is *svatantra*."

Here one understands *svatantra* to mean "one who has himself as the principal person." **A** 1.4.54 comes in a section of rules headed by **A** 1.4.23: *kārake*, which establishes the domain in which subsequent name-assigning rules will apply: with respect to a *kāraka*, that is, a direct participant in bringing an action to accomplishment. In this context, one understands *svatantra* to denote a participant that is independent.

Nevertheless, Patañjali also does not tell us here just what are the semantic properties of a *kāraka* that is eligible to be given the name *kartṛ*.

Patañjali on Participants in Actions

The Roles of Direct Participants (*Kāraka*)

In the *Bhāṣya* on **A** 1.4.23, Patañjali does have more to say on this topic. The thesis is entertained that the *sūtra* assigns the class name *kāraka* to entities specified by following rules and that name is an analytic term consisting of the base *kṛ* "do, make" and the suffix *ṆvuL*, which is introduced on condition that an agent is to be signified:[4] a *kāraka* is an agent that performs the act signified by *kṛ*.[5] A participant such as the pot (*sthālī*, loc. sg. *sthālyām*) spoken of in

(4) *devadattaḥ sthālyām odanaṃ pacati* "Devadatta is cooking rice in a pot"

functions as a locus (*ādhāra*) relative to the complex of activities denoted by *pac*, so that it is assigned the category name *adhikaraṇa*.[6] On the other

4. **A** 3.1.133: *ṇvultṛcau* (*dhātoḥ* 91) introduces *ṆvuL* (→ *aka*) and *tṛC*, alternatively, after any verbal base (*dhātoḥ*). These are affixes of the *kṛt* class (**A** 3.1.93: *kṛd atiṅ*), hence introduced if an agent is to be denoted (**A** 3.4.67: *kartari kṛt*).

5. Bh. I.324.8–9: *tatra mahatyāḥ saṃjñāyāḥ karaṇa etat prayojanam anvarthaṃ yathā vijñāyeta: karotīti kārakam.*

6. **A** 1.4.45: *ādhāro'dhikaraṇam*. By **A** 2.3.36: *saptamy adhikaraṇe ca*, nominal endings of the seventh triplet (*saptamī*) of endings—*Ṅi os suP*—follow a nominal if an *adhikaraṇa* is to be signified. (4) also involves softened rice (*odana*), a participant that is given the category name

hand, with respect to each *kāraka* (*pratikārakam*), there is a distinct constituent act (*kriyābhedāt* "because of a difference in action"), so that a locus also has the status of being an agent (*kartṛbhāvaḥ*).[7] And indeed, one can also say

(5) *sthālī pacati* "The pot is cooking"
(6) *droṇaṃ pacati* "(The pot) is cooking a *droṇa* (of rice)"
(7) *āḍhakaṃ pacati* "(The pot) is cooking an *āḍhaka* (of rice)."

(4) speaks of the composite act of cooking—putting a pot on the fire, pouring water and rice grains into this, putting firewood under the pot—which is now denoted by *pac* and is cooking of the main agent (*pradhānakartuḥ pākaḥ*), Devadatta; his performing this complex act constitutes his being an agent.[8] (5), on the other hand, is used to speak of a pot as it does certain constituent acts when it cooks a *droṇa* or an *āḍhaka* of rice grains—as expressed in (6)–(7)—by holding them in and supporting them. This is the cooking of the *adhikaraṇa*, which *pac* now is used to signify, and the *adhikaraṇa's* carrying this out constitutes its being an agent.[9]

Primary Agents

Now, once an agent such as Devadatta has put a pot on the fire and performed other acts that set cooking in process, even in his absence a pot may go on cooking, as expressed in (5). Thus, Patañjali also remarks that a

---

karman ("primary goal"). According to **A** 1.4.49 (*kartur īpsitatamaṃ karma*) that participant which an agent most wishes to reach through his action is assigned to this category.

7. 1.4.23 vt. 7: *siddhaṃ tu pratikārakaṃ kriyābhedāt pacādīnāṃ karaṇādhikaraṇayoḥ kartṛbhāvaḥ.*

8. 1.4.23 vt. 8: *adhiśrayaṇodakāsecanataṇḍulāvapanaidhopakarṣaṇakriyāḥ pradhānasya kartuḥ pākaḥ.* Bh I.324.19–20: *adhiśrayaṇodakāsecanataṇḍulāvapanaidhopakarṣaṇakriyāḥ kurvanneva devadattaḥ pacatīty ucyate | tatra tadā pacir vartate | eṣa pradhānakartuḥ kartṛtvam.* Commenting on NS 2.1.42, Vātsyāyana gives a larger set of constituent acts: placing a pot on a *culli*, pouring water into the pot, putting rice grains in it, setting firewood under it, lighting a fire, stirring with a spoon, letting the scum that forms flow off, and taking down the pot: ... *nānāvidhā caikārthā kriyā pacatīti: sthālyadhiśrayaṇam udakāsecanaṃ taṇḍulāvapanam edhovasarpaṇam agnyabhijvālanaṃ darvīghaṭṭanaṃ maṇḍasrāvaṇam adhovatāraṇam iti* (NBh. 2.1.42 [83.7–10]).

9. 1.4.23 vt. 9: *droṇaṃ pacaty āḍhakaṃ pacatīti sambhavanakriyā dhāraṇakriyā cādhikaraṇasya pākaḥ.* Bh I.324.23–25: *droṇaṃ pacaty āḍhakaṃ pacatīti sambhavanakriyāṃ dhāraṇakriyāṃ ca kurvatī sthālī pacatīty ucyate | tatra tadā pacir vartate | eṣo'dhikaraṇasya pākaḥ | etad adhikaraṇasya kartṛtvam.*

pot is said to be dependent (*paratantrā*) when it accompanies the principal participant in an action, and it functions as independent participant when it is not so accompanied. A parallel is drawn with the relation that holds between a king and his ministers and other subordinates. If they are in the company of the king, the ministers and others accompanied by him have the status of being dependent on him, but when the king is not present, the same ministers and other subordinates have the status of acting independently. The principal participant is, of course, the agent of the complex act. Patañjali explains, moreover, that one knows this is the principal participant because, when all participants that serve to bring about an action are present at once, it is the agent that sets the others into play.[10]

Summary

The main points brought out in the *Bhāṣya* on **A** 1.4.23 are: there is a principal agent in a composite action such as cooking, and this action includes component acts in which other *kārakas*, such as a pot, play the role of agent; the principal agent has this status because he sets into action the other participants, which have the status of being dependent when he is present.

Bhartṛhari on the Semantic Properties of Agents

Based on what Kātyāyana and Patañjali had said, Bhartṛhari gives six properties on account of which an agent is said to have the property of being independent (*svātantryaṃ kartur ucyate*), as follows:[11]

(a) It enters into play as a *kāraka* (*śaktilābhāt* "because of gaining its capacity") before any other (*prāg anyataḥ*) *kāraka* involved in a given act. An agent takes on the status of acting as a participant in an action out of a

10. Bh. I.326.7–10: *evaṃ tarhi pradhānena samavāye sthālī paratantrā vyavāye svatantrā | tad yathā amātyādīnāṃ rājñā saha samavāye pāratantryaṃ vyavāye svātantryam | kiṃ punaḥ pradhānam | kartā | kathaṃ punar jñāyate kartā pradhānam iti | yat sarveṣu sādhaneṣu sannihiteṣu kartā pravartayitā bhavati.* I have selected parts of the arguments presented in *vārttikas* and the *Bhāṣya* on 1.4.23; full details are given in volume III.4 of my work on Pāṇini, now nearing completion.

11. VP 3.7.101–102: *prāg anyataḥ śaktilābhān nyagbhāvāpādanād api | tadadhīnapravṛttitvāt pravṛttānāṃ nivartanāt || adṛṣṭatvāt pratinidheḥ praviveke ca darśanāt | ārād apy upakāritve svātantryaṃ kartur ucyate.* The second *pāda* of verse 102 is cited with *vyatireke* instead of *praviveke* in Harivallabha's *Darpaṇa* (VBhSD 195).

desire to accomplish the result of such an act, not on account of accompanying participants such as an instrument, which he brings into play for this purpose, and he does so before the other participants take part in the act. The remaining participants, on the other hand, act as agents in their component acts only because the agent sets them into play.[12]

(b) It makes others subordinate to it (*nyagbhāvāpādanāt*). This and (c) follow from (a). Since the principal agent sets other participants into play, their acting is dependent on it, so that they acquire subordinate status. The principal agent, on the other hand, is active on his own, aiming for the result of his action.[13]

(c) Others act dependent on it (*tadadhīnapravṛttitvāt*).

(d) It causes the others to cease acting after they have played roles (*pravṛttānāṃ nivartanāt*). The principal agent, on the other hand, stops acting on his own, once he has accomplished his goal.[14]

(e) It is not seen to have a substitute (*adṛṣṭatvāt pratinidheḥ*).[15]

---

12. VPHel. 3.7.101–102 (312.9–12): *karaṇādipravṛtteḥ prāg evārthitvāder aparasmān nimittān na tu sahakāribhya eva sāmarthyam āsādayati | phalakāmo hi kartā karaṇādīny upārjayate | tathā ca pūrvam eva śaktimān svatantraḥ | karaṇādīnāṃ tu kartṛviniyogād eva svavyāpāre svātantryaṃ na tv anyataḥ.*

13. VPHel. 3.7.101–102 (312.12–13): *ata eva kartrā nyagbhāvam ātmādhīnatām āpādyante tadāyattavyāpārāś ca | kartā tu phalārtham īhamānaḥ svayaṃ vyāpāravān.*

14. VPHel. 3.7.101–102 (312.13–14): *atipravṛttāny ca karaṇādīni nivartyante kartrā | sa tu phalaprāptau svayam eva nivartate.*

15. At the beginning of his comments on this point (VPHel. 3.7.101–102 [312.14–15]: *coditāsambhave karaṇādīnāṃ pritinidhir uktaḥ | kartuḥ sa nāsti*), Helārāja remarks that in case the things in question are not available, a substitute is stated for something that is enjoined to serve as a means or such, but there is no such replacement for an agent. He thus indicates that this has to do with ritual performance, where, if a particular thing to be used is not available, it may be replaced by another. For example if a rite calls for offering a cake made with domestic rice (*vrīhi*) and this is not available, a variety of wild rice, called *nīvāra*, may be offered instead. But a master of a sacrificial rite (*svāmin*), who hires priests, is not replaceable. In his commentary on JMS 6.3.7.21, Śabara explains that a master of a rite is not replaced because he is the one directly connected with the result obtained by the performance of the rite and shows how someone else who plays this role is also a *svāmin*, so that there is no replacement for the role. A *svāmin* is the one who wishes to obtain a result and hires ritual officiants with his own money and possessions. If someone else played this role, so that he would perform all the acts required, he too would be a *svāmin*, since he would now be associated with the result, so that there would not truly be a substitution for the *svāmin*. ŚBh. 97.5.258: *tathā svāminaḥ syāt | ko'rthaḥ | na pratinidiḥ | kutaḥ | phalasamavāyāt | yo'rthī svatyāgena ṛtvijaḥ parikrīṇīte yaś ca svaṃ pradeyaṃ tyajati sa svāmī | yadi sa prati nidhīyate svāminā yat kartavyaṃ tat sarvaṃ kuryāt tat sarvaṃ kurvan svāmy eva syān na pratinidhiḥ | sa eva hi phalena sambadhyate | ya utsargaṃ karoti sa phalavān bhavati... tasmān na svāminaḥ pratinidhiḥ.* Helārāja alludes to this, remarking that if another agent carries out an act, he is not said to be a substitute, if he is one with the right to do this, desirous of gaining

(f) It may be the sole participant spoken of in an act, so that one observes it even in the absence of others (*praviveke ca darśanāt*). For example, the endings *tiP*, *te* in

(8) *asti* (9) *bhavati* (10) *vidyate* "…is"

refer to an unspecified single agent.[16]

Under the viewpoint that every participant other than the main agent of a composite action plays the role of agent with respect to a component action, the main agent acts as manager, so to speak, who sets these into play. He is thus viewed as contributing to the act from afar (*ārāt*).[17] Nevertheless, by virtue of the characteristics (a)–(f), this participant is said to have independence, so that it is classed as agent, with respect to a composite action.

Helārāja rightly notes that what Bhartṛhari says when he gives the properties that constitute an agent's independence is meant to explain Patañjali's earlier statement *yat sarveṣu sādhaneṣu sannihiteṣu kartā pravartayitā bhavati* (see note 10), on the assumption that the *Bhāṣya's* is a summary formulation that leaves unsaid what is implied.[18]

---

the result of the act, capable of doing it, and not excluded from doing so: *kartuḥ sa nāsti | kartrantaraṃ hi kriyāṃ nirvartayat pratihitaṃ nocyate tasyārthinaḥ samarthasyāparyudastasyādhikārāt* (VPHel. 3.7.102–103 [312.15–16]).

16. VPHel. 3.7.101–102 (312.16–17): *praviveke ca kārakāntarāṇām abhāve dṛśyate kartā | tadyathā asti bhavati vidyata ity ādau.* Each of the endings replaces *lAṬ*, and a feature common to all such *l*-affixes is that they are introduced on condition that an agent (*kartari*), an object (*karmaṇi*), or, in the case of objectless verbs, an action (*bhāve*), is to be signified: A 3.4.69: *laḥ karmaṇi ca bhāve cākarmakebhyaḥ* (*kartari* 67); an *l*-affix introduced under the last two conditions is replaced by an affix of the *ātmanepada* set (A 1.3.13: *bhāvakarmaṇoḥ* [*ātmanepadam* 12]); see Cardona 1997:148–150.

17. This obtains specially with respect to the participant given the category name *karaṇa* ("instrument"), which A 1.4.42 (*sādhakatamaṃ karaṇam*) assigns to the *kāraka*, which more than any other participant in a given composite act serves as that which brings it about (*sādhakatamam*). Bhartṛhari (VP 3.7.90: *kriyāyāḥ pariniṣpattir yadvyāpārād anantaram | vivakṣyate yadā yatra karaṇatvaṃ tadā smṛtam*) accordingly says: that participant whom one speaks of as being one immediately after whose activity an action comes about is then said to have the property of being a *karaṇa*.

18. VPHel. 3.7.101–102 (312.21–25): *etena cedaṃ bhāṣyaṃ vyākhyātam: yat sarveṣu sādhaneṣu sannihiteṣu kartā pravartayitā bhavatīti | etac ca bhāṣyaṃ garbhīkṛtanāntarīyakārthaṃ saṅkṣipyoktam iti garbhīkṛtārthavyaktīkāraṇenātra vyākhyātam.* Helārāja goes on to note that the other conditions noted are consequences of (c), since other participants' taking part in an act depends on a main agent. By stating (c), Bhartṛhari explicitly explains what the *Bhāṣya* said, namely that the principal agent of a composite action causes other participants

Animate and Inanimate Agents

The six properties that are associated with the independence of a *kāraka* to which the category name *kartṛ* is assigned apply for an individual such as Devadatta spoken of in (4) (§ "The Roles of Direct Participants (*Kāraka*)"). They do not hold, however, for a pot spoken of in (5). This does not pour water or rice grains into itself. Nevertheless, (5) is a perfectly acceptable Sanskrit utterance, and **A** 1.4.54 (§ 'Pāṇini's Rule Assigning the Category Name *Kartṛ*") provides for assigning the name *kartṛ* to the participant in question. Similarly, in Pāṇini's derivational system the endings *tiP* and *anti* of *dahati* "burns, is burning," *pacanti* "cook, are cooking" in

(11) *agnir dahati* "The fire is burning"
(12) *edhāḥ pacanti* "The pieces of firewood are cooking"

are replacements for *lAṬ* introduced on condition that an agent is to be signified (see note 16). The pot and firewood of (5) and (12) cannot, nevertheless, be spoken of as independent participants without simultaneously fulfilling the roles of locus (*ādhāra*) in which something being cooked is held and principal means (*sādhakatama* "most means") of burning to produce the fire for cooking.

Pāṇini's Formalism Regarding Inanimate Agents

Pāṇini reconciles the semantics of what one may say using utterances such as (5), (11), and (12) by organizing his *kāraka* classification rules in a particular order and providing both that only one of these category names may apply to a given entity at once and that, in case of conflict, that which applies by the later rule—in this instance a *kāraka* category name—takes precedence.[19] Thus, **A** 1.4.45 (note 6) assigns the *kāraka* category name *adhikaraṇa* to a direct participant in the accomplishment of an action that

---

to act; that these are made subordinate to the principal agent as well as other properties listed are inferred therefrom as consequences: *tathā hi tadadhīnapravṛttitvād ity anena sākṣāt pravartakatvam vyākhyātam | sāmarthyākṣiptaṃ ca nyagbhāvādi nirdiṣṭam* (VPHel. 3.7.101–102 [312.25–26]). It is not necessary for my presentation to give the full details of Helārāja's exposition of how this is true.

19. **A** 1.4.1–2: *ā kaḍārād ekā saṃjñā, vipratiṣedhe paraṃ kāryam*; see Cardona 1974: 231–238.

plays the role of a locus with respect to the act in question, by serving as a place where its agent or primary goal (*karman*) is located, and by **A** 1.4.54 (§ "Pāṇini's Rule Assigning the Category Name *Kartṛ*") a direct participant spoken of as independent is given the category name *kartṛ*. In case of conflict, the latter takes precedence over the former.

Semantic/Ontological and Grammatical Criteria

General Considerations

An issue nevertheless remains open. If a participant such as a pot in which one cooks is given the category name *kartṛ* by **A** 1.4.54, because it is spoken of as independent, this independence cannot be due to the six properties enumerated in VP 3.7.101–102 (note 11), unless these properties are not meant to hold for agents that act truly independently in the world as we experience it. Bhartṛhari is aware of this. For he immediately goes on to say[20] that the restriction (*niyamaḥ*) whereby the above-mentioned properties (*abhyuditair dharmaiḥ*) must apply for a participant to be understood as independent holds with respect to speech (*śabde*), but not with respect to any actual thing (*na tu vastuni*); it is from speech (*śabdāt*) that something is understood as an agent (*kartā pratīyate*), when one wishes to express for that entity an agent's properties (*kartur dharmavivakṣāyām*).

In his commentary on this *kārikā*, Helārāja emphasizes that one is to consider as agent a participant of whom the properties in question (*ete dharmāḥ*) are conveyed (*pratyāyyante*) by a speech form (*śabdena*). One should not seek the possibility (*na tu...sambhavo'nveṣaṇīyaḥ*) of these properties (*dharmāṇām eṣām*) having things as such for their domains (*vastuviṣayatayā*), that is, as necessarily pertaining to real world objects as we experience and use them. This would have as a consequence that agency would not obtain for an insentient objects (*acetanaviṣaye*) such as fire, firewood, or a pot, so that one would not appropriately consider that (5), (11), (12) as well as

(13) *kūlaṃ patati* "The river bank is falling"
(14) *nadī vahati* "A river flows"

20. VP 3.7.103: *dharmair abhyuditaiḥ śabde niyamo na tu vastuni | kartṛdharmavivakṣāyāṃ śabdāt kartā pratīyate.*

speak of agents.[21] For, he goes on to say, when one wishes to speak of these properties (*dharmā vivakṣyante*) in order to characterize a participant, by rule, as an agent (*kartṛlakṣaṇāya*), and they are conveyed in accordance with this intention (*yathāvivakṣaṃ pratyāyyante*), then an agent with a well-founded characteristic (*supratiṣṭhita-lakṣaṇaḥ kartā*) is understood from the speech form in question, so that an agent too is conveyed as one wishes to express it, just as is the case for an instrument.[22] Moreover, remarks Helārāja, by the same token, the agency attributed to insentient objects in (5), (11)–(14) is not metaphorical (*upacaritam*), since in all instances where one speaks of agents it is possible to have the usage faultlessly apply (*askhaladvṛttitvāt*) on the basis of the main meaning (*mukhyatāsambhavāt*).[23]

Finally, Helārāja makes his capital point. In the grammar with which Bhartṛhari deals—Pāṇini's system—a meaning dealt with is a meaning associated with speech units (*śabdārthaḥ*) as conventionally used, not a meaning that pertains to real things (*vastvarthaḥ*) as we see and use them.[24] Moreover, he draws a contrast between this grammar and another, in which two rules are stated assigning the category name *kartṛ* separately to sentient beings capable of conscious acts and others: a participant who has an objective to accomplish (*arthī*) is called *kartṛ*, as is also one that is associated similarly (*tathāyuktaḥ*) with an action. Helārāja remarks that what is said in VP 3.7.103 serves to reject this view as infelicitous.[25]

The same point is to be made with respect to utterances such as

(15) *kūlaṃ pipatiṣati* "The river bank is about to fall"

---

21. VPHel. 3.7.103 (313.10–13): *śabdena yasyaite dharmāḥ pratyāyyante sa kartā boddhavyaḥ | na tu vastuviṣayatayā dharmāṇām eṣāṃ sambhavo'nveṣaṇīyaḥ yenācetanaviṣaye agnir dahati edhāḥ pacanti sthālī pacatītyādau kūlaṃ patati nadī vahatītyādau ca kartṛtvaṃ na syāt.*

22. VPHel. 3.7.103 (313.13–15): *ete hi dharmā yadā kartṛlakṣaṇāya vivakṣyante śabdena ca yathāvivakṣaṃ pratyāyyante tadā śabdāt kartā supratiṣṭhitalakṣaṇaḥ pratīyata iti karaṇam iva kartāpi vaivakṣikaḥ pratipāditaḥ.*

23. VPHel. 3.7.103 (313.15–16): *evaṃ ca kṛtvācetaneṣūpacaritaṃ na bhavati kartṛtvam sarvatrāskhaladvṛttitvāt prayogasya mukhyatāsambhavāt.*

24. VPHel. 3.7.103 (313.16): *vyākaraṇe hi śabdārtho'rthaḥ na tu vastvarthaḥ.* Helārāja emphasizes this point elsewhere also, e.g., VPHel. 3.8.1 (5.6–7: *iha vyākaraṇe na vastvartho'rthaḥ api tu śabdārthaḥ*), 3.8.2 (8.1–11: *śabdaś ca svārthe yathābhidhānaṃ pramāṇam iti niścitam etat | tathā hi śabdārtho'rtho na vastvartha ity asakṛd uktam*).

25. VPHel. 3.7.103 (313.16–19): *tataś ca vyākaraṇāntare arthī kartā tathāyuktaś ceti lakṣaṇadvayaṃ cetanācetanaviṣayatayā yat praṇītaṃ tan na kauśalam ity uktaṃ bhavati.* Helārāja does not specify the other grammar in question, nor does the *Vārarucasaṅgraha* (VāS 6).

in which a form of the desiderative *pipat-iṣa* "wish to fall" is used. Pāṇini simply provides that a verbal base (*dhātoḥ*), the action signified by which is the primary object (*karmaṇaḥ*) of wishing, optionally be followed by the suffix *saN* if both the act signified by the base and the act of wishing have the same agent (*samānakartṛkāt*). In terms of his derivational system, then, (15) speaks of a river bank as an agent of wishing.[26]

Similarly,

(16) *bhikṣā vāsayanti* "Alms cause (mendicants) to stay'

(17) *kārīṣo'gnir adhyāpayati* "A cowdung fire allows (students) to study'

with forms from the causative bases *vās-i* "cause to stay, have... stay," *āp-i* with the preverb *adhi* ("cause to study, allow to study"). Such bases are derived by introducing the suffix *ṆiC* to form a base denoting an action that has a causal agent (*hetumati*).[27] The name *hetu* is assigned to a participant who causes an independent agent to carry out his act (*tatprayojaka*).[28] In his discussion of **A** 3.1.26, Kātyāyana suggests that the term *hetu* used in *hetumati* of the *sūtra* should be considered to denote merely any cause (*nimittamātra*)—so that *hetumati* would be equivalent to *nimittavati* or *kāraṇavati*—since it is observed that forms with *ṆiC* are used with respect to things such as alms for which one begs.[29] The question is posed: why does the rule not succeed in providing properly for *ṆiC* of the instances at issue if *hetu* of **A** 3.1.26 refers to a causal agent as provided for in **A** 1.4.55 (note 28)? The answer is that the reinterpretation proposed for **A** 3.1.26 presupposes that the act of causing—prompting an inferior to act (*preṣaṇam*) or respectfully asking someone to act (*adhyeṣaṇam*)—relates to a sentient being, and food given to someone is not a sentient being

26. **A** 3.1.7: *dhātoḥ karmaṇaḥ samānakartṛkād icchāyāṃ vā* (*san* 5); on this issue, see Cardona 1974: 270–273. In English too, a usage such as *This car doesn't want to start* is part of common usage, not metaphoric.

27. **A** 3.1.26: *hetumati ca* (*ṇic* 25).

28. **A** 1.4.55: *tatprayojako hetuś ca*; see Cardona 1997: 137–138.

29. 3.1.26 vt. 2: *hetunirdeśaś ca nimittamātraṃ bhikṣādiṣu darśanāt*. Bh. II.33.2–4: *hetunirdeśaś ca nimittamātraṃ draṣṭavyam | yāvad brūyān nimittaṃ kāraṇam iti | kiṃ prayojanam | bhikṣādiṣu darśanāt | bhikṣādiṣu hi ṇij dṛśyate: bhikṣā vāsayanti kārīṣo'gnir adhyāpayatīti*. As shown, Patañjali (Bh. II.33.3–4) illustrates with (16)–(17).

capable of these acts.[30] This in turn is met with the retort that there is no such fault under the interpretation that *hetu* of *hetumati* refers to a participant that causes an independent agent to act: it is not solely a person who says *uṣyatām* "stay" (3sg. pass. pres. imper.) that causes someone to stay somewhere; something that provides what is required for making another act possible, while not saying anything, also causes the act of staying to be carried out. Food given as alms, when it is plentifully available and tastily spiced, causes someone to remain. Similarly, a fire made using cowdung, when well lit in an out of the way place without any wind, allows for studying by keeping a student warm.[31]

Sentences of the Type "The Rice is Cooking"

The passive counterpart of (4) (§ "The Roles of Direct Participants (*Kāraka*)") is

(18) *devadattena sthālyām odanaḥ pacyate* "Rice is being cooked by Devadatta in a pot."

To account for such an utterance, Pāṇini lets the *l*-affix *lAṬ* follow the base *pac* on condition that a primary goal (*karman*) is to be signified; this affix is replaced by the *ātmanepada* ending *ta* (see note 16), whose *-a* is replaced by *-e*. When a verbal base is followed by an ending such as *te*—technically assigned to the class called *sārvadhātuka*—introduced under the conditions noted, the suffix *yaK* is introduced after the base.[32] There are also sentences of the type

(19) *devadattena supyate*

corresponding to

(20) *devadattaḥ svapiti* "Devadatta is sleeping"

with verb forms *supyate* and *svapiti* comparable to *pacyate* and *pacati*. The base *svap* used here, however, denotes an act without a participant classed as

---

30. Bh. II.33.4–5: *kiṃ punaḥ kāraṇaṃ pāribhāṣike hetau na sidhyati | evaṃ hi manyate: cetanāvata etad bhavati preṣaṇam adhyeṣaṇaṃ ceti bhikṣāś cācetanāḥ.*

31. Bh. II.33.5–8: *nāvaśyaṃ sa eva vāsaṃ prayojayati ya āhoṣyatām iti | tūṣṇīm apy āsīno yas tatsamarthāny ācarati so'pi vāsaṃ prayojayati | bhikṣāś cāpi pracurā vyañjanavatyo labhyamānā vāsaṃ prayojayanti | tathā kārīṣo'gnir nivāta ekānte suprajvalito'dhyayanaṃ prayojayati.*

32. A 3.1.67: *sārvadhātuke yak* (*bhāvakarmaṇoḥ* 66, *dhātoḥ* 22); see Cardona 1997: 100.

karman (see note 6), and in Pāṇini's system, to derive (19), *lAṬ* is introduced after *svap* on condition that the act in question is signified, not the primary object (*karman*) of an action. In addition, one can say

(21) *odanaḥ pacyate* "The rice is cooking"

which pairs with

(22) *odanena pacyate*

comparable to (19).

Although (21) has *pacyate*, this form is not derived in the same manner as *pacyate* in (18). For (21) concerns cooking in which the only participant is rice, which is now spoken of as an independent participant, given the class name *kartṛ* by **A** 1.4.54 (§ "Pāṇini's Rule Assigning the Category Name *Kartṛ*"). The act signified by *pac* thus has no primary object, and (22) is derived by introducing *lAṬ* on condition that the act in question is to be signified. Accordingly, Pāṇini accounts for (21) by introducing *lAṬ* to signify an agent (*kartṛ*). In addition, he provides that when there is an agent that behaves with respect to an act in the same manner (*tulyakriyaḥ*) as it did at a stage where it played the role of an object (*karmaṇā*), this is treated as though it were a *karman* (*karmavat*).[33] That is, operations that apply when a *karman* is signified apply also in this instance: *lAṬ* is replaced by an *ātmanepada* ending and *yaK* is introduced to derive (21).

Pāṇini formulates **A** 3.1.87 (note 33) because he grants that the rice spoken of in (21) plays the role of an independent participant in cooking, so that it is classed as an agent (*kartṛ*).[34]

33. **A** 3.1.87: *karmavat karmaṇā tulyakriyaḥ*; see Cardona 1974: 242.

34. Kātyāyana notes the reason why **A** 3.1.87 is formulated. A participant such as the rice of (21), which was a *karman* and is now spoken of as an agent (*karmakartari* "object agent"), has the property of being an agent (*kartṛtvam*) because one wishes to speak of its independence (*svātantryasya vivakṣitatvāt*): Bh. II.67.10: *kimarthaṃ punar idam ucyate.* 3.1.87 vt. 5: *karmakartari kartṛtvaṃ svātantryasya vivakṣitatvāt*; Bh. II.67.12–13: *karmakartari kartṛtvam asti | kutaḥ | svātantryasya vivakṣitatvāt.* Patañjali goes on to ask whether the wish to speak of independence here pertains to actual independence (*sataḥ svātantryasya vivakṣā*) or is merely a desire to speak of such independence (*vivakṣāmātram*), to which he replies that it pertains to actual independence and illustrates this with the example *bhidyate kuśūlena* "The grain holder is breaking apart." Here no other agent is seen and an action is perceived. Moreover, the possible claim that, although there is no corporeal human agent involved here, there might

Grammatically pertinent contrasts between sentient and insentient beings

It is incontrovertible that Pāṇini's grammatical system includes a category agent (*kartṛ*), that this corresponds to a participant in an action said to be independent (*svatantra*), and that an agent need not be a sentient entity capable of a conscious effort to carry out an action, so that it meets all the criteria set forth in VP 3.7.101–102 (§ "Bhartṛhari on the Semantic Properties of Agents").

There are also usages that distinguish between sentient and insentient beings. For example, forms of the derivates *trivarṣīṇa*, *trivārṣika*, and *trivarṣa* can be used interchangeably with reference to an illness (*vyādhi*) that has lasted for three years: *trivarṣīṇo vyādhiḥ*, *trivārṣiko vyādhiḥ*, *trivarṣo vyādhiḥ*. Accordingly, Pāṇini provides that a *dvigu* compound such as *trivarṣa*, with *-varṣa* "year," can take a *taddhita* suffix *īna* or *ika* or no suffix.[35] If, however, the derivate formed is to signify a sentient entity (*cittavat*), the absence of a suffix is not optional but obligatory (*nityam*);[36] for example, *dvivarṣo dārakaḥ* "a young boy, a son of two years."

Moreover, the contrast between sentient and insentient can pertain to agents. Thus, a causative derivate with the suffix *ṆiC* (see note 27) is

---

be agents such as the wind, heat of the sun, and time that break up the grain container is refuted: this could be established if there were indeed any one of these agents; but a grain container that was made recently and breaks up when there is no wind and no downpour of rain does so by itself (*svayam eva*). There is no agent here except the grain container. Bh. II.67.13–18: *kiṃ punaḥ sataḥ svātantryasya vivakṣāhosvid vivakṣāmātram | sata ity āha | kathaṃ jñāyate | iha bhidyate kuśūleneti na cānyaḥ kartā dṛśyate kriyā copalabhyate | kiṃ ca bho vigrahavataiva kriyāyāḥ kartrā bhavitavyam na punar vātātapakālā api kartāraḥ syuḥ | bhavet siddhaṃ yadi vātātapakālānām anyatamaḥ kartā syāt | yas tu khalu nivāte nirabhivarṣe'cirakālakṛtaḥ kuśūlaḥ svayam eva bhidyate tasya nānyaḥ kartā bhavaty anyad ataḥ kuśūlāt.*

35. According to **A** 5.1.88: *varṣāl luk ca* (*dvigoḥ* [86]), after a *dvigu* compound ending with *varṣa*, zero (*luk*) occurs. This is in addition (*ca* "also") to what is otherwise provided for. **A** 5.1.86: *dvigor vā* (*khaḥ* [85]) lets a *dvigu* compound optionally (*vā*) take the *taddhita* (**A** 4.1.76: *taddhitāḥ*) suffix *kha*. The heading **A** 5.1.18: *prāg vateṣ ṭhañ* provides that the suffix *ṭhaÑ* is valid in subsequent rules up to 5.1.115 (*tena tulyaṃ kriyā ced vatiḥ*), which introduces *vat*. Thus, **A** 5.1.88 allows for *kha*, *ṭhaÑ*, or a zero replacement of these. The conditions for introducing the possible *taddhita* affixes are given in **A** 5.1.80: *tam adhīṣṭo bhṛto bhūto bhāvī*. Affixes introduced by subsequent rules follow an accusative term (*tam*) to form derivates designating entities that have been requested respectfully (*adhīṣṭa*), hired for a salary (*bhṛta*), which have occurred (*bhūta*), or will occur (*bhāvin*) for a given duration. The resulting derivates are classed as nominal bases (*prātipadika*: **A** 1.2.46: *kṛttaddhitasamāsāś ca* [*prātipadikam* 45]), so that a nominal ending included therein is dropped (**A** 2.4.71: *supo dhātuprātipadikayoḥ* [*luk* 58]). Initial *kh* and *ṭh* of the suffixes introduced are cover symbols, replaced respectively by *īn* and *ik* (**A** 7.1.2: *āyaneyīnīyiyaḥ phaḍhakhachaghāṃ pratyayādīnām*, **A** 7.3.50: *ṭhasyekaḥ*). Other details concerning the derivates noted are not pertinent to my discussion.

36. **A** 5.1.89: *cittavati nityam.*

followed by affixes of the *ātmanepada* or *parasmaipada* sets, depending on whether the result of the causal act in question is or is not intended for its agent;[37] for example, the *ātmanepada* ending *te* is used with the causal base *pāc-i* in

(23) *odanaṃ pācakena pācayate* "...is having the cook cook some rice"

because the person in question has rice cooked for his consumption. If he did this to feed others, one would use *pācayati*, with the *parasmaipada* ending *ti*. Consider now

(24) a. *āste devadattaḥ* "Devadatta is sitting" b. *āsayati devadattam* "...has Devadatta sit"
(25) a. *śuṣyanti vrīhayaḥ* "The rice is drying out" b. *śoṣayate vrīhīn* "...is drying out the rice."

(24a) involves an objectless act (*akarmaka*) and is performed by a sentient being, Devadatta. The corresponding causal sentence (24b) has *āsayati*, with the causal base *ās-i* from *ās* "sit, be seated." (25a) also involves an act without an object, but this is now performed by rice (*vrīhayaḥ* [nom. pl.]), and *śoṣ-i*, the causative corresponding to the base *śuṣ*, can take *ātmanepada* affixes, as in *śoṣayate* of (25b). Accordingly, Pāṇini provides that, contrary to **A** 1.3.74 (see note 37), *parasmaipada* affixes alone follow a base in *ṆiC* if the following conditions are met: the causal suffix follows a base signifying an objectless action (*aṇāv akarmakāt*) and this act has for its agent a sentient being (*cittavatkartṛkāt*).[38]

Vivakṣā *and Conventions of a Speech Community*

In sum, for Pāṇini and Pāṇinīyas an agent (*kartṛ*) need not be an intelligent sentient being capable of conscious effort. It is a participant in an action that one wishes to speak of as acting independently in the accomplishment of an action. Note, moreover, that the notion of *vivakṣā*—the wish to speak, to express oneself in a certain manner—which Pāṇinīyas invoke is not an individual's arbitrary attitude. Patañjali distinguishes between two

37. **A** 1.3.74: *ṇicaś ca* (*kartrabhiprāye kriyāphale* 72, *ātmanepadam* 12); see note 54.

38. **A** 1.3.88: *aṇāv akarmakāt cittavatkartṛkāt* (*parasmaipadam* 78).

kinds of *vivakṣā*. There is the *vivakṣā* of an individual speaker (*prāyoktrī vivakṣā*), who may wish to speak in a particular manner, in effect, to use Prakrit forms: out of individual preference, a speaker utters soft, smooth, pleasing sounds with a soft, smooth, and pleasing tongue. On the other hand, there is the viviakṣā of the speech community (*laukikī vivakṣā*).[39] That is, one conforms to the speech conventions of a community of speakers. Sanskrit speakers conventionally use utterances like (5) and (11)–(17) without intending any metaphor.

True Agents Considered to be Sentient Intelligent Beings

Patañjali speaks of the principal agent of a composite act as one who causes other participants to act (*pravartayitṛ*; see § "Primary Agents" with note 10). He is also careful to distinguish between this agent and other participants that may be considered to act as agents in component acts that make up a major composite act, such as the pot of (5). The pot spoken of here is not said to be a *pravartayitṛ*. In effect, of the six properties Bhartṛhari mentions (§"Bhartṛhari on the Semantic Properties of Agents"), the last one best fits this participant: it is the sole participant spoken of in (5), spoken of as acting independently.[40] As noted above (§ "General Considerations"), moreover, Pāṇinīyas accept, on the basis of language usage, not only that inanimate, insentient beings may be spoken of properly as agent but also as things that cause other agents to act.

The Nyāya Position

On the other hand, some early Indian scholars maintained that a true agent is a sentient, intelligent being capable of conscious effort (*kṛti, yatna*).[41] According to one characterization of agency in harmony with this

39. Bh. II.342.26–343.3 (on **A** 5.1.16): *vivakṣā ca dvayī | asty eva prāyoktrī vivakṣāsti laukikī | prāyoktrī vivakṣā: prayoktā hi mṛdvyā snigdhayā ślakṣṇayā jihvayā mṛdūn snigdhāñ ślakṣṇāñ śabdān prayuṅkte | laukikī vivakṣā yatra prāyasya sampratyayaḥ | prāya iti loko vyapadiśyate.* Patañjali here remarks that the community (*lokaḥ*) of speakers is referred to by saying *prāyaḥ* "generally."

40. Later Pāṇinīyas accordingly maintain that an agent is the locus of an activity denoted by a verbal base. Thus, for example, ŚK 1.4.54 (p. 139): *kriyāyāṃ svātantryeṇa vivakṣito'rthaḥ kartā syāt | dhātūpāttavyāpārāśrayatvaṃ svātantryam.*

41. This is the view of Naiyāyikas, who argue on the basis of paraphrasing that a verb ending signifies such effort. See Cardona 1975.

position, that *kāraka* is an agent (*kartṛkārakam*) that causes other participants to take part in an action (*itarakārakaprayoktṛ*) while not so caused by any other (*aparāprayojyam*). Uddyotakara articulates this formulation more than once.[42] One passage concerns Vātsyāyana's use, in his introduction to NS 1.1.1 of *pramātṛ* ("one who experiences correct cognition") in relation to *pramāṇa* ("means of gaining correct knowledge") and *prameya* ("object of cognition").[43] Uddyotakara here remarks that a *pramātṛ* is an independent participant in the act of cognizing, then goes on to note different characterizations of independence. One of these is: an independent agent sets into activity a series of participants, known to be capable of serving to bring an action to its accomplishment, while he himself is not caused to act by them.[44]

In another passage, concerning a single entity's being either a *pramāṇa* or a *prameya*, Vātsyāyana not only explains the example of a scale, given in NS 2.1.16 (*prameyā ca tulā prāmāṇyavat*), but also adds an example from mundane usage. In this realm, *kāraka* words apply equally to a single object, depending on circumstances, and one can properly say

(26) *vṛkṣas tiṣṭhati* "The tree is standing"
(27) *vṛkṣaṃ paśyati* "... is looking at the tree"
(28) *vṛkṣeṇa candramasaṃ jñāpayati* "...points out the moon by means of a tree"
(29) *vṛkṣāyodakam ā siñcati* "...is pouring water intended for the tree"
(30) *vṛkṣāt parṇaṃ patati* "A leaf is falling from the tree"
(31) *vṛkṣe vayāṃsi santi* "There are birds in the tree."

42. For example, NSV 3.2.3 (377.20–21): *pradhānakriyāpekṣaṃ tu kārakāṇāṃ kartrādyabhidhānam | tatra yad itarāprayojyam itarakārakaprayoktṛ ca tat kartṛkārakam.* Uddyotakara goes on to take care of a possible objection: an agent thus characterized is also prompted to act by bringing into play other *kārakas*. This is answered by stressing that an agent is prompted to act solely by the desired result of an action, not by any other participant such as an instrument. NSV 3.2.3 (378.1–2): *...nanv ayam api kārakopādānena proyujyate | na prayujyate phalasya prayojakatvāt | phalaṃ kartāraṃ prayojayati na kārakaṃ karaṇādi.* The characterization of an agent as a *kāraka* that causes other participants in an action to act but is itself not caused to do so is widespread; it is cited, for example, by Jayanta (NM II.243: *atha yaḥ kārakāntarāṇi prayuṅkte taiś ca na prayujyate sa karteti...*).

43. NBh. 1.1.1 (1.13): *tatra yasyepsājihāsāprayuktasya pravṛttiḥ sa pramātā* "Among these, the *pramātṛ* is one who acts prompted by a desire to attain (what is desirable, happiness) and avoid (what is undesirable, suffering)."

44. NBhV 1.1.1 (8.11, 12–14): *pramātā svatantraḥ | kiṃ punaḥ svātantryam...yad vā paridṛṣṭasāmarthyāni kārakacakrāṇi prayuṅkte taiś ca na prayujyate.* I have omitted earlier alternatives that Uddyotakara mentions.

(26) speaks of a tree as an agent, since it is independent with respect to its act of standing; in (27), a tree is spoken of as a primary object (*karman*) of viewing because it is what an agent of this act most wishes to reach thereby; the tree spoken of in (28) is given the class name *karaṇa* ("instrument") by virtue of its being, more than any other participant in the act of making known, that which serves to bring this act to accomplishment; the tree of (29) is spoken of as an indirect object that an agent intends through the means of water that is being poured, so that it is classed as a *sampradāna*; in (30) the tree serves as a point of departure relative to a leaf's falling, so that is bears the label *apādāna*; and a tree is spoken of in (31) as a locus relative to being, so that it is classed as *adhikaraṇa*.[45]

A tree is incapable of conscious effort. Consequently, Vātsyāyana's citing (26) and saying that a tree now functions as an agent by virtue of its independence is not immediately compatible with the view that an agent's independence consists in its causing other participants in an action to play their roles while not itself be so caused by any other participant in that action. In this context, Uddyotakara questions what constitutes the independence of the tree referred to in (26) and answers that it is independent with respect to its standing in that it does not require any other *kāraka*. He also notes that this tree does not cause any other *kāraka* to act.[46] Vācaspati connects this with the statement that an agent's independence consists in causing other *kārakas* to act while itself not being caused to act: Uddyotakara's question is motivated, he says, by the fact that here there is no such independence. The import of his answer, notes Vācaspati, is this: one somehow wishes to speak of the independence of an agent by

45. NBh 2.1.16 (63.9–17): *tathā ca loke kārakaśabdā nimittavaśāt samāveśena vartanta iti | vṛkṣas tiṣṭhatīti svasthitau vṛkṣaḥ svātantryāt kartā | vṛkṣaṃ paśyatīti darśanenāptum iṣyamāṇatamatvāt karma | vṛkṣeṇa candramasaṃ jñāpayatīti jñāpakasya sādhakatamatvāt karaṇam | vṛkṣāyodakam ā siñcatīty āsicyamānenodakena vṛkṣam abhi praitīti sampradānam | vṛkṣāt parṇaṃ patatīti dhruvam apāye'pādānam* (A 1.4.24) *ity apādānam | vṛkṣe vayāṃsi santīty ādhāro'dhikaraṇam* (A 1.4.45) *ity adhikaraṇam*. Although only two of the Pāṇinian *sūtras* that serve to assign to *kārakas* the class names *apādāna, sampradāna, karaṇa, adhikaraṇa, karman*, and *kartṛ* (see Cardona 1997: 137–139) are cited, Vātsyāyana obviously refers to *kārakas* as classified by Pāṇinian rules. Moreover, what is said in the *Nyāyabhāṣya* echoes what was said earlier by Kātyāyana and Patañjali, and (30) matches an example cited in the *Mahābhāṣya* (see Cardona 1974: 260).

46. NBhV 2.1.16 (187.2–3): *kiṃ punar vṛkṣasya svasthitau svātantryam | kārakāntarānapekṣitvam | na hi vṛkṣas tiṣṭhan svasthitau kārakāntaraṃ prayuṅkte*. Uddyotakara goes on to consider different meanings one could attribute to *tiṣṭhtati* in (18): standing, not moving; being; being intact, not broken. He also considers the possibility that the tree makes use of part of a whole—its roots—in standing. These and additional details need not be dealt with here.

virtue of its causing others to act, so that it requires other participants for carrying out its action and is thereby dependent on them; all the more, then, does something that does not depend on any other *kāraka* have independence.[47]

The fact remains that the tree of (26) does not conform to what is said to be a true agent. Accordingly, in his *Tātparyaṭīkā* on *Nyāyabhāṣyavārttika* 1.1.1, Vācaspati remarks that what Uddyotakara has in mind when he says that independence on the part of a person who is an agent of an action consists in his causing other *kārakas* to act while not being caused to act by other *kārakas* is this: such a sentient (*cetanasya*) participant has the property of being a causer with respect to all other *kārakas* and is not subject to being caused to act by those *kārakas*; the agency (*kartṛtvam*) of an insentient being (*acetanasya*), on the other hand, is metaphorical (*bhāktam*), not part of such a being's true nature (*na svābhāvikam*).[48]

Arguments Against the Nyāya Position

This position clearly conflicts with the stand of Pāṇinīyas, for whom speaking of an insentient being as an agent involves no metaphor (§ "General Considerations" with note 23). Moreover, the position in question is rejected not only by Pāṇinian grammarians but also by Naiyāyikas, though on different grounds.

Bhavānanda's Objections

Bhavānanda[49] brings up the view that a participant's being an agent (*kartṛtvam*) consists in its causing other participants to act (*kārakāntaraprayojakatvam*) while it is itself not caused to act by others (*kārakāntarāprayojyatve*

---

47. NVT 2.1.16 (320.14–19): *svasthitau vṛkṣaḥ svātantryāt karteti bhāṣyam | tatra svātantryaṃ pṛcchati vārttikakāraḥ: kiṃ punaḥ svātantryam iti | itarakārakāprayojyatvaṃ prayojakatvaṃ ca kārakāṇāṃ madhye kartuḥ svātantryam uktam | iha tu kārakāntarābhāvāt tādṛśaṃ svātantryaṃ nāstīti bhāvaḥ | uttaram: kārakāntarānapekṣitvam | kārakāntarāpekṣasya hi prayojakatayā kathañcit svātantryaṃ vivakṣyate tadanapekṣasya punar nitarāṃ svātantryam ity arthaḥ.*

48. NVT 1.1.1 (27.3–5): *lakṣaṇāntaram āha: tatprayoktṛtvam itarāprayojyatā vā | tasya cetanasya sarvakārakāṇi prati prayoktṛtvaṃ taiś ca kārakair aprayojyatā vā | acetanasya tu bhāktaṃ kartṛtvaṃ na svābhāvikam iti bhāvaḥ.*

49. KC 13 (§14): *yat tu kārakāntarāprayojyatve sati kārakāntaraprayojakatvaṃ kartṛtvam iti | satyantāc ca chedyasaṃyogādirūpavyāpārajanake kuṭhārādau nātivyāptir ity apare | tad apy asat īśvaraprayojyānāṃ saṃsāriṇāṃ tattatkriyāsv akartṛtvāpatteḥ.* This and the next passage (note 51) are cited with two typographical errors corrected.

sati).[50] This is unacceptable, argues Bhavānanda, because it results in denying agency in acts by corporeal beings in this world, who are caused to act by Īśvara, since the latter is the cause of all things coming into being that are produced. Moreover, if not being caused to act by another participant consists in not being the locus of an activity that leads to a result and comes about due to another participant, then it fails to apply to a potter, who is the locus of coming into contact with a stick he uses to turn his wheel.[51]

Pāṇinīyas' Objections

Pāṇinīyas reject the view in question for a different reason: agency would thereby not apply to the pot spoken of in (5), the sword referred to in

(32) *asiś chinatti* "A sword cuts"

or the stick spoken of in

(33) *daṇḍaḥ karoti* "The stick (used by a potter) is acting"

since none of these causes other *kārakas* to act and each of them is wielded by another participant.[52]

As grammarians, Pāṇini and his successors let linguistic usage be their guide in making decisions about such a question. In the words of Patañjali, cited at the head of this paper, what words say are our means of gaining knowledge.

---

50. This last condition precludes the possibility of attributing agency to an axe spoken of in a sentence such as *kuṭhāreṇa kāṣṭhaṃ chinatti* "... is cutting wood with an axe." The axe does bring about the act of coming into contact with the object that is to be cut (*chedyasaṃyoga*), but it is in turn caused to do this by the agent who wields it.

51. KC 13 (§15): *aprayojyatvañ ca yadi phalānukūlatajjanyavyāpārāṇāśrayatvaṃ tadā daṇḍādijanyasaṃyogarūpāśrayatvāt kulālādāv avyāptiḥ*.

52. The *Paramalaghumañjūṣā* notes both the conditions appropriate for a true agent and cites (5), (32) as counterexamples: PLM 326: *yat tu kārakāntarāprayojyatve sati kārakacakraprayojakatvaṃ kartṛtvam iti tan na | sthālī pacati asiś chinattītyādau sthālyādeḥ kārakacakrāprayojakatvāt kārakāntaraprayojyatvāc ca tan na syāt*.... Earlier, in his *Vaiyākaraṇabhūṣaṇasāra*, Kauṇḍabhaṭṭa argued against agency being defined by the property of being the locus of a conscious effort (*kṛtyāśrayatva*) or being a participant that causes other participants to act (*kārakacakraprayoktṛtva*) and invoked examples such as (33): *kārakacakraprayoktṛtvaṃ kṛtyāśrayatvaṃ vā daṇḍaḥ karotīty atrāvyāptam* (VBhS 194). I omit consideration of another passage (VBhS 66–67) where Kauṇḍabhaṭṭa also argues against considering agency to be defined by the two properties noted, since this involves details which are not strictly pertinent to my discussion.

Ātman "*Self*"

Ātman versus *Para* "Other"

Pāṇini's emphasis on usage and formal description of the language of his time and place is evident also in what one can see in the use of *ātman* "self."

On the evidence of *sūtras* in the *Aṣṭādhyāyī*, one sees a contrast between *ātman* "self" and *para* "other." This is evident in the grammatical class names *ātmanepada* and *parasmaipada*,[53] used to refer to sets of post-verbal affixes and corresponding roughly to "medio-passive" and "active" of western usage. For example, *ātmanepada* affixes are said to occur signifying an agent after verbal bases that are marked with a low-pitched vowel or *ṅ* (*anudāttaṅitaḥ*); after a base marked with a *svarita* vowel or *ñ* (*svaritañitaḥ*), these occur if the result of the act in question (*kriyāphale*) is intended for the agent (*kartrabhiprāye*); and *parasmaipada* affixes occur under other conditions.[54] Similarly, **A** 3.1.8: *supa ātmanaḥ kyac* (*karmaṇaḥ icchāyām vā* 7) introduces the suffix *KyaC* after a term with a nominal ending (*supaḥ*) to form a derived verb that signifies wishing something for oneself; for example, *putra-am-ya* →...*putrī-ya* "desire a son for oneself, of one's own,"[55] as in *putrīyati* "wishes a son for himself, of his own," equivalent to

(34) *ātmanaḥ putram icchati* "...wishes a son of his own."

Patañjali makes explicit the implicit contrast between *ātmanaḥ* "of oneself, one's own" and *parasya* "of someone else" when he notes[56] that the *sūtra* in question states *ātmanaḥ* in order to exclude the introduction of *KyaC* when the desire is on the part of someone else, since one does not use *putrīyati* as an equivalent to *putram icchati* found in an example such as

(35) *rājñaḥ putram icchati* "...wishes a son for the king."

---

53. The first constituent *ātmane-* in these compounds retains the dative ending *e*. Pāṇini provides (**A** 6.3.7–8: *vaiyākaraṇākhyāyāṃ caturthyāḥ* [*ātmanaś ca* 6, *alug uttarapade* 1], *parasya ca*) that a fourth-triplet ending is not dropped before a second constituent of a compound if it is linked to *ātman-* or *para-* in a first constituent, when the word in question is a conventional technical term used by grammarians (*vaiyākaraṇākhyāyām*).

54. **A** 1.3.12, 72, 78: *anudāttaṅita ātmanepadam, svaritañitaḥ kartrabhiprāye kriyāphale, śeṣāt kartari parasmaipadam*. See Cardona 1997: 87–91.

55. For the derivation see Cardona 1997: 188–189.

56. Bh. II.16.9–10: *athātmagrahaṇaṃ kimartham* | *ātmecchāyāṃ yathā syāt parecchāyāṃ mā bhūd iti*: *rājñaḥ putram icchatīti*. It is not necessary to discuss here the precise syntactic connection of *ātmanaḥ*.

Internal and Corporeal Self

Another contrast involving the term *ātman* is observed by Patañjali. In two different contexts, he distinguishes between a corporeal self (*śarīrātman* "body self") and an internal self (*antarātman*).

One discussion concerns **A** 3.1.87 (see § "Sentences of the Type "The rice is cooking" with note 33). It is proposed that this *sūtra* is not necessary because what it accounts for is successfully accounted for under the assumption that utterances such as (21)–(22) are passives of the same kind as (18). To make this possible, it is assumed that an instrumental term *ātmanā* ("by itself") is to be understood for (21) *odanaḥ pacyate* and that a nominative *ātmā* ("itself") referring to a *karman* is to be understood for (22) *odanena pacyate,* which thus stand for

(36) *odana ātmanā pacyate*
(37) *odanenātmā pacyate.*

In addition,

(38) *hanty ātmānam ātmā* "The self kills the self"
(39) *ātmanā hanyata ātmā* "The self is killed by the self"

are acceptable utterances.[57] This begs the question: what self does the killing and what self is killed? And to this question Patañjali responds that

57. 3.1.87 vtt. 8–10: *siddhaṃ tu prākṛtakarmatvāt | ātmasaṃyoge karmakartuḥ karmadarśanāt | padalopaś ca.* The first *vārttika* asserts that the required result is established (*siddham*) by virtue of the participant in question being an ordinary *karman* (*prākṛtakarmatvāt*)—as provided for in **A** 1.4.49 (note 6) and related rules—instead of involving any extension of operations in the absence of such a *karman,* so that **A** 3.1.87 is not required. This position is then justified by noting that, when the self is conjoined (*ātmasaṃyoge*), one sees a *karman* (*karmadarśanāt*) referred to in the case of an object-agent (*karmakartuḥ*). Patañjali illustrates (Bh. II.68.15–16) with (a) *hanty ātmānam* "... kills (him)self," (b) *ātmanā hanyate* "... is killed by (him)self." The self playing the role of an object of slaying is referred to by *ātmānam* (acc. sg.) in (a); in (b) this self plays the role of an agent, referred to by *ātmanā* (instr. sg.). An objection can be advanced: in (a), only an object—signified by *ātmānam*—is evident, not a particular agent, and in (b), only an agent—signified by *ātmanā*—is evident, not a particular object. This objection is met by assuming that such usages involve the absence of a syntactic constituent (*padalopaḥ*). To illustrate, Patañjali then cites (38)–(39). Bh. II.68.15–17: *ātmasaṃyoge karmakartuḥ karma dṛśyate | kva | hanty ātmānam hanyata ātmaneti | viṣama upanyāsaḥ | hanty ātmānam iti karma dṛśyate kartā na dṛśyate | ātmanā hanyata iti kartā dṛśyate karma na dṛśyate.* II.68.19: *padalopaś ca draṣṭavyaḥ: hanty ātmānam ātmā ātmanā*

there are two selves, an interior one and a corporeal one. One brings it about that the other experiences pleasure and pain.[58]

Another discussion concerns **A** 1.3.67: *ṇer aṇau yat karma ṇau cet sa kartānādhyāne (ātmanepadam* 12). This rule provides that *ātmanepada* affixes signifying an agent follow a verbal base ending with -*Ṇi* on condition that the very entity that functions as *karman* with respect to the act signified by the base without -*Ṇi* (*aṇau yat karma*) plays the role of agent (*sa kartā*) in the causal act signified by the derivate in -*Ṇi*, except where the action in question is remembering something with longing (*anādhyāne*). For example, consider

(40) *darśayate bhṛtyai rājā* "The king is letting his servants see him"

corresponding to

(41) *paśyanti bhṛtyā rājānam* "The servants are viewing the king."[59]

(40) has the causative base *darś-i*, and the stem *darś-ay-a* is followed by the *ātmanepada* ending *te*. The last two *vārttikas* on **A** 1.3.67 bring up a possible problem and an answer thereto. Corresponding to

(42) *hanty ātmānam* (see note 57)

one should have

(43) *ghātayaty ātmā* "The self has (itself) killed."

On the assumption that there is one single self involved, which functions as *karman* in (42), the rule would allow the *ātmanepada* ending *te* after the causative *ghāt-i*—*ghātayate* comparable to *darśayate* in (40)—instead of the *parasmaipada* ending *ti*. Hence, it is argued, a prohibition (*pratiṣedhaḥ*) should

---

hanyata ātmeti. Sentences such as (38)–(39) are found in literary works. A famous example is *Kumārasambhava* 2.10ab: *ātmānam ātmanā vetsi sṛjasy ātmānam ātmanā* "(Brahman,) you know yourself through yourself, create yourself through yourself."

58. Bh. II.68.19–22: *kaḥ punar ātmānaṃ hanti ko vātmanā hanyate | dvāv ātmānāv antarātmā śarīrātmā ca | antarātmā tat karma karoti yena śarīrātmā sukhaduḥkhe anubhavati | śarīrātmā tat karma karoti yenāntarātmā sukhaduḥkhe anubhavati.*

59. (40)–(41) are examples cited in the *Bhāṣya* on 1.3.67 (I.292.7).

be formulated to disallow *ātmanepada* affixes where the *karman* is the self (*ātmanaḥ karmatve*). To this the response is given that such a negation is not required because the causative in -*Ṇi* has an agent distinct from the object of the non-causal (*anyasya kartṛtvāt*).[60] In his *Bhāṣya*, Patañjali then explains that there are two selves, in the same way he does in his commentary on A 3.1.87.[61]

Although Kātyāyana accepts that *ātman* can designate distinct entities and Patañjali specifies that there are two *ātmans*, one the body, the other an interior self, neither elaborates further.[62] In particular, neither scholar insists that only an interior *ātman* that is sentient can be characterized by agency. On the contrary, in consonance with his general view, Patañjali explicitly speaks of the corporeal self as an agent that performs an act (*tat karma karoti*) whereby the interior self experiences pleasure and suffering and also speaks of the corporeal self as an agent that experiences (*anubhavati*) pleasure and pain.[63]

---

60. 1.3.67 vt. 8: *ātmanaḥ karmatve pratiṣedhaḥ*; Bh. I.292.10–11: *ātmanaḥ karmatve pratiṣedho vaktavyaḥ: hantyātmānam ghātayaty ātmeti*. vt. 9: *na vā ṇyante'nyasya kartṛtvāt*; Bh. I.292.13–14: *na vā vaktavyaḥ | kiṃ kāraṇam | ṇyante'nyasya kartṛtvāt | anyad atrāṇyante karmānyo ṇyantasya kartā*.

61. Bh. I.292.13–16: *katham | dvāv ātmānāv antarātmā śarīrātmā ca | antarātmā tat karma karoti yena śarīrātmā sukhaduḥkhe anubhavati | śarīrātmā tat karma karoti yena śarīrātmā sukhaduḥkhe anubhavati*.

62. In the *Pradīpa* on Bh. 1.3.67, Kaiyaṭa notes that under the Sāṃkhya view the interior self is the *antaḥkaraṇa*, since the *puruṣa* is not an agent, but that under the Nyāya position *puruṣa* is the interior self. Pr. II.285: *antarātmeti: sāṅkhyapakṣe 'ntaḥkaraṇam ātmā tasyaiva kartṛtvasambhavāt puruṣasyākartṛtvāt | naiyāyikānāṃ tu mate puruṣasya kartṛtvāt sa evāntarātmā vivakṣitaḥ*. Kaiyaṭa presumably alludes to the Nyāya position that there is an *ātman* inferable as the seat of desire and aversion, conscious effort, pleasure and suffering, and cognition (NS 1.1.10: *icchādveṣaprayatnasukhaduḥkhajñānāny ātmano liṅgam iti*). In consonance with this position, Kaiyaṭa also remarks that Patañjali's statement that the bodily self experiences pleasure and suffering (*śarīrātmā sukhaduḥkhe anubhavati*) is to be interpreted as saying that the body becomes associated with pleasure and suffering, since this is a being that cannot have cognition: Pr. II.285: *śarīrātmā sukhaduḥkhe iti: śarīrasyācetanatvāt sukkhaduḥkhebhyāṃ śarīraṃ sambadhyata ity arthaḥ*. It is not possible to enter here into a discussion of the position that, although Kātyāyana and Patañjali speak of distinct *ātmans*, there is but one such entity (*ekasyaiva*), which is conceived of in different statuses (*buddhyavasthābhiḥ*), a view presented in the *Vākyapadīya* (3.7.104: *ekasyaiva buddhyavasthābhir bhede ca parikalpite | kartṛtvaṃ karaṇatvaṃ ca karmatvaṃ copajāyate*) and referred to in the *Pradīpa* on A 3.1.87 (III.170).

63. See note 62. It is appropriate also to note a passage with a Sāṃkhya tinge from the *Pāṇinīyaśikṣā*, which postdates Pāṇini but was composed prior to the time of Bhartṛhari (fifth century), who cites from it: PŚ 3–4ab: *ātmā buddhyā sametyārthān mano yuṅkte*

Conclusion

Pāṇini recognizes as a category among direct participants in actions one that is given the class name *kartṛ* ("doer, maker, agent"). The participant in question is one that is independent (*svatantra*). However, Pāṇini himself does not tell us what constitutes independence; he allows *svatantra* to be understood according to common usage. Kātyāyana and Patañjali also do not specify what properties qualify a participant in an action as independent. It is Bhartṛhari who enumerates six such properties. Yet he goes on to say that these are considered only with respect to the way the community of speakers talks about things, and his commentator Helārāja remarks that in grammar one operates with meanings as understood from usage, not with respect to what necessarily might be true in a real world of experience. Consequently, there is no requirement that an agent be animate, sentient, or capable of conscious effort. Much earlier, Kātyāyana and Patañjali also held this view. Contrarily, other thinkers—Naiyāyikas primary among them—maintained that a true agent is a participant in an action that is capable of conscious effort, one that operates independently, causing other participants in an act to play their roles while it itself is not caused to play its role. This position was opposed by later Pāṇinīyas, who argued on the basis of commonly accepted usage. In addition, although the notion of a self (*ātman*) was known to Pāṇini and Pāṇinīyas, this was not directly viewed as a characteristic of agency.[64]

References and Abbreviations

A Pāṇini's *Aṣṭādhyāyī*.

Abhyankar, K. V. 1962–72. *The Vyākaraṇa-Mahābhāṣya of Patañjali, Edited by F. Kielhorn, Revised and Furnished with Additional Readings, References, and Select Critical Notes*. 3rd ed. 3 vols. Poona: Bhandarkar Oriental Research Institute.

Bh. *Mahābhāṣya*; see Abhyankar.

vivakṣayā | manaḥ kāyāgnim ā hanti sa prerayati mārutam | mārutas tūrasi caran mandraṃ janayati svaram. In describing the first stages of speech production this passage says the *ātman*, after apprehending through the *buddhi* (*buddhyā sametya*) things that are to be signified (*arthān* "objects, meanings"), associates the *manas* with the wish to speak (*mano yuṅkte vivakṣayā*); the *manas* then strikes the body-fire (*manaḥ kāyāgnim ā hanti*), which sets the breath into motion (*sa prerayati mārutam*); and the breath, moving in the chest (*urasi caran*), produces a low sound (*mandraṃ janayati svaram*).

64. I am grateful to David Buchta for carefully reading my paper and pointing out typographical errors and an infelicity that called for reformulation.

Brahmaśankara Śāstrī. 1942. *Kārakacakram of M. M. Śrī Bhavānanda Siddhānta Vāgīśa Bhattāchārya with the Mādhavī Commentary by Śrī Mādhava Tarkālankāra and the Pradīpa Notes by Vyākaranāchārya Pt. Śrī Sītāśarana Tripāthī.* Haridās Sanskrit Series 154. Benares: Chowkhamba Sanskrit Series Office.

Cardona, George. 1974. "Pāṇini's kārakas: Agency, Animation and Identity." *Journal of Indian Philosophy* 2:231–306.

———. 1975. "Paraphrase and Sentence Analysis: Some Indian Views." *Journal of Indian Philosophy* 3:259–281.

———. 1997. *Pāṇini, His Work and Its Traditions.* Volume 1: *Background and Introduction.* 2nd ed., rev. and enl. Delhi: Motilal Banarsidass.

Chaturvedi, Tarkeshwar Shastri. 1947. *Vaiyakaran Bhusansar of Kaund Bhatt with Prabha and Darpan Commentaries by Pt. Bal Krishna Pancholi and Pt. Hari Vallabha Shastri.* Adarsh Granthamala's 2nd Pushpam. Varanasi: Pt. Tarkeshwar Chaturvedi Shastri. Reprinted 1969: *Vaiyākaraṇbhūṣaṇsāra of Śrī Kauṇḍabhaṭta Edited with "Prabhā" Commentary by Pt. Śrī Bālakṛṣṇ Pañcholi…and with "Darpaṇa" Commentary by Śrī Hariballabha Śāstrī.* Kāshi Saskrit Series 188. Varanasi: Chowkhamba Sanskrit Series Office.

Ghosh, Manomohan. 1938. *Pāṇinīya Śikṣā or the Śikṣā Vedāṅga Ascribed to Pāṇini (being the most ancient work on Indo-Aryan phonetics), Critically Edited in All Its Five Recensions with an Introduction, Translation and Notes Together with Its Two Commentaries.* Calcutta: University of Calcutta. Reprinted 1986, Delhi: Asian Humanities Press. [Reference to the reconstructed text.]

JMS *Mīmāṃsāsūtra* of Jaimini; see Joshi.

Joshi, Ganesh Shastri. 1981–85. *Mīmāṃsādarśanam.* 7 vols. Ānandāśrama Sanskrit Series 97. Pune: Ānandāśrama.

Kapildeva Śāstrī. 1975. *Nāgeśabhaṭṭa-kṛta Vaiyākaraṇasiddhāntaparamalaghumañjū ṣā (Mūla granth, anuvād evaṃ samīkṣātmak vyākhyā).* Kurukshetra: Kurushetra University.

Kāś. *Kāśikāvṛtti*; see Sharma, Aryendra et al.

KC Bhavānanda's *Kārakacakra*; see Brahmaśankara Śāstrī.

NBh. *Nyāyabhāṣya* of Pakṣilasvāmin Vātsyāyana; see Thakur 1997a.

NBhV *Nyāyabhāṣyavārttika* of Uddyotakara; see Thakur 1997b.

Nene, Gopal Śastri. 1929. *The Śabda Kaustubha by Śrī Bhaṭṭoji Dīkshita.* Vol. 2-Fas. 5 to 10: *From the Second Pāda of the Ist Adhyāya to Second Pāda of 3rd Adhyāya and Sphota Chandrikā by Pandit Srikrisna Mauni.* Benares: Chowkhamba Sanskrit Series Office.

NM *Nyāyamañjarī* of Jayantabhaṭṭa; see Varadacharya 1969–83.

NS *Nyāyasūtra* of Gautama; see Thakur 1997a.

NVT: *Nyāyavārttikatātparyaṭīkā* of Vācaspatimiśra; see Thakur 1996.

Pandey, A. N. 1986. *Vāraruchasaṅgraha of Vararuchi with the Commentary "Dīpaprabhā" of Nārāyaṇa.* Kashi Sanskrit Series 237. Varanasi: Chaukhambha Sanskrit Sansthan.

PLM *Paramalaghumañjūṣā*; see Kapildeva Śāstrī.

Pr. Kaiyaṭa's *Pradīpa* on the *Mahābhāṣya*; see Vedavrata.

PŚ *Pāṇinīyaśikṣā*; see Ghosh.

Rau, Wilhelm. 1977. *Bhartṛharis Vākyapadīya, Die Mūlakārikās nach den Handschriften herausgegeben und mit einem Pāda-Index versehen*. Abhandlungen für die Kunde des Morgenlandes Band XLII, 4. Wiesbaden: Steiner.

ŚBh. Śabara's bhāṣya on Jaimini's *Mīmāṃsāsūtra*; see Joshi.

Sharma, Aryendra, Khanderao Deshpande, and D. G. Padhye. 1969–1970. *Kāśikā, A Commentary on Pāṇini's Grammar by Vāmana & Jayāditya*. 2 vols. Sanskrit Academy Series 17, 20. Hyderabad: Sanskrit Academy, Osmania University. Reprinted in one volume, 2008.

ŚK *Śabdakaustubha* of Bhaṭṭoji Dīkṣita; see Nene.

Subramania Iyer, K. A. 1963. *Vākyapadīya of Bhartṛhari with the Commentary of Helārāja, Kāṇḍa III, Part 1 Critically Edited....* Deccan College Monograph Series 21. Poona: Deccan College.

———. 1973. *Vākyapadīya of Bhartṛhari with the Prakīrṇaprakāśa of Helārāja, Kāṇḍa III, Part 2 Critically Edited....* Poona: Deccan College.

Thakur, Anantalal. 1996. *Nyāyavārttikatātparyaṭīkā of Vācaspatimiśra*. Nyāyacaturgranthikā Vol. 3. New Delhi: Indian Council of Philosophical Research.

———. 1997a. *Gautamīyadarśana with Bhāṣya of Vātsyāyana*. Nyāyacaturgranthikā Vol. 1. New Delhi: Indian Council of Philosophical Research.

———. 1997b. *Nyāyabhāṣyavārttika of Bhāradvāja Uddyotakara*. Nyāyacaturgranthikā Vol. 2. New Delhi: Indian Council of Philosophical Research.

Varadacharya, K. S. 1969–83. *Nyāyamañjarī of Jayantabhaṭṭa with Ṭippaṇi-Nyāyasaurabha by the Editor*. 2 vols. Oriental Research Institute Series 116, 139. Mysore: Oriental Research Institute.

VāS *Vārarucasaṅgraha*; see Pandey.

VBhS *Vaiyākaraṇabhūṣaṇasāra* of Kauṇḍabhaṭṭa; see Chaturvedi, Tarkeshwar Shastri.

VBhSD *Darpaṇa* of Harivallabha on the *Vaiyākaraṇabhūṣaṇasāra*; see Chaturvedi, Tarkeshwar Shastri.

Vedavrata. 1962–63. *Śrībhagavatpatañjaliviracitaṃ Vyākaraṇa-mahābhāṣyam [Śrīkaiyyaṭakṛtapradīpena Nāgojībhaṭṭa-kṛtena Bhāṣyapradīpoddyotena ca Vibhūṣitam]*. 5 vols. Gurukul Jhajjar (Rohtak): Harayāṇā-Sāhitya-Saṃsthānam.

VP *Vākyapadīya*; see Rau.

VPHel. *Prakīrṇaprakāśa* of Helārāja on the third kāṇḍa of the *Vākyapadīya*; see Subramania Iyer.

vt(t). vārttika(s) of Kātyāyana; see Abhyankar.

5

Nyāya's Self as Agent and Knower

Matthew R. Dasti

MUCH OF CLASSICAL Hindu thought has centered on the question of self: what is it, how does it relate to various features of the world, and how may we benefit by realizing its depths? Attempting to gain a conceptual foothold on selfhood, Hindu thinkers commonly suggest that its distinctive feature is consciousness (*caitanya*). Well-worn metaphors compare the self to light as its awareness illumines the world of knowable objects.[1] Consciousness becomes a touchstone to recognize the presence of a self. A rock is insentient, void of consciousness, and purely an object. Selves, however, are loci of awareness and thus subjects. Some schools, most notably classical Sāṃkhya and Advaita Vedānta, take this approach to its furthest conclusion: consciousness is not only unique to the self, but is the fundamental feature of selfhood. Other putative features of the self—feelings, memories, moral responsibility, and importantly, agency (*kartṛtva*)—are taken to be the impositions of insentient matter (*prakṛti*) or symptoms of primordial illusion (*avidyā*).[2]

Against this position, Nyāya[3] defends a more robust notion of selfhood, placing desire, aversion, volition, and moral responsibility alongside

---

This chapter was generously supported by a grant from Bridgewater State University's Center for the Advancement of Research and Scholarship. I would like also to thank Edwin Bryant, David Buchta, and Elisa Freschi for helpful comments and discussion.

1. E.g., *Bṛhadāraṇyaka Upaniṣad* 4.3.6: "The self alone is his light"; *Bhagavad Gītā* 13.17: "The light of lights, it is said to be beyond darkness." Translations are mine.

2. Sāṃkhya will be discussed at length below, but also see Bryant's chapter in this volume. Regarding Advaita Vedānta, see Timalsina's chapter in this volume.

3. In this chapter, I will focus on the earlier school of Nyāya (*prācīna nyāya*), with occasional discussion of developments within its sister school Vaiśeṣika and the new school of Nyāya (*navya nyāya*). Recognizing that even the members of conservative *darśana* traditions do not always speak in one voice and that there are various quarrels between philosophers of the same school, I will focus on themes and positions that are central to the schools in question. I should further note that I will focus on Nyāya's metaphysics of agency and not

cognition as the self's distinctive qualities.[4] These various aspects of selfhood come together neatly when we consider agency. An agent performs intentional actions under her volition, which is triggered by her own cognitive and affective states. Her volitional acts further generate moral consequences which she must bear, and which are, in the Indian context, embodied in the form of karmic merit and demerit. For Nyāya, agency is, therefore, a special expression of the self's different capacities and potentialities, which coherently ties them together. Nyāya's view is an important contribution to Indian theories of self as it is a counterpoint to what we may call excessively cognitive accounts of selfhood in other influential Hindu schools, as noted above.[5] The first half of this chapter will consider Nyāya's conception of agency in relation to selfhood. The second half will discuss Nyāya's arguments with other Hindu schools—specifically Sāṃkhya—in support of the thesis that the self must be an agent as well as a knower.[6]

Volition as a Property of the Self

I would like to resist a method of analysis that takes as its point of departure the nature of liberation. Since, for Hindus, liberation presents us with a pure soul, a naked self in its pristine glory, this method would have us begin by considering the nature of a liberated soul, then reading it back into worldly experience, as we sift between the genuine functions of the self and those of the non-self (*indriyas, manaḥ*, etc.). While this approach may have some appeal for both its simplicity and clarity, I suggest that it may lead to confusion. For Nyāya, the self of liberation is in fact *less* than the self of ordinary life, since a number of dispositional properties of the self that are exercised in ordinary life are left permanently unactualized

---

its interpretation of agency within Sanskrit grammar. For further discussion of the latter, see Cardona 1974 and Cardona's chapter in this volume.

4. NS 1.1.10; 3.2.34–40. Also see *Vaiśeṣikasūtra* (attributed to Kaṇāda) [VS] 3.2.4.

5. In this it may be allied with Mīmāṃsā, as seen in Freschi's chapter in this volume.

6. In one instance, Nyāya even argues *from* the agency of the self *to* the conclusion that it must be the locus of awareness (instead of the *manaḥ* or "inner organ"). See NB 3.2.19: "The controller is the knower, and that which is controlled is merely an instrument in knowing" (*vaśī jñātā vaśyaṃ karaṇam*). Since we have some control over our selective attention, we must be the locus of awareness, not the instrument which we use to govern selective attention (the *manaḥ*). Also see NS 3.2.38.

in the state of *mokṣa*.[7] Therefore, it is best for our study to focus upon the world of common experience.

Our point of departure will be *Nyāyasūtra* (NS) 1.1.10, which provides the famous "characteristics of the self":

> Desire, aversion, volition (*prayatna*), pleasure, pain, and cognition are characteristics of the self.[8]

Classical commentators take this verse to enumerate various properties (*guṇa*) of a psychological kind. (These are not the only qualities of the self according to Nyāya-Vaiśeṣika: commonly, karmic merit [*dharma/adharma*] and mnemonic impressions [*saṃskāra, bhāvanā*] are included; Viśvanātha's *Bhāṣā-pariccheda* [BP] 160–161). They are indicators of the self in that they are properties in want of a property-bearer, akin to the way in which an instance of the property *tall* would require the existence of something which is tall. Naiyāyikas use these to infer the existence of the *ātman*, since, as they are psychological properties, a non-material substance is the only kind of property-bearer that will suffice to instantiate them.[9]

We may note that the properties listed in NS 1.1.10 pertain to cognitive states, affective states, and volition (*prayatna*; sometimes *yatna*). Most important to our study is the last. Derived from the verbal root √*yat* ("strive," "endeavor"), the semantic range of *prayatna* includes "volition," "effort," and "impetus to action."[10] Eager as they are to jump right into anti-Buddhist polemics, early Naiyāyikas do not discuss *prayatna* in depth, other than noting that to function, it relies on contributions from memory and recollection, and thus requires an enduring self that synthesizes these various inputs with present experience. But an important analysis is provided by their intellectual cousin, the Vaiśeṣika philosopher Praśastapāda (ca. 575 CE) and explicitly taken up by later Naiyāyikas.

---

7. Here I do not have the space to discuss Nyāya's theory of liberation. See A. Chakravarti 1983, Ram-Prasad 2001, and Phillips (unpublished) for further discussion.

8. *icchā-dveṣa-prayatna-sukha-duḥkha-jñānāny ātmano liṅgam.*

9. See A. Chakravarti 1982, K. Chakrabarti 1999: 55–91, and Ganeri 2007: 178–184 for further discussion of this and other Nyāya arguments for the self.

10. Praśastapāda (PDS; Dvivedin, ed. 1984: 263) glosses *prayatna* as *saṃrambha*, "impetus" and *utsāha*, "effort." Annam Bhaṭṭa (TS §77) glosses *prayatna* as *kṛti* "volition." The *pra-* prefix to the root adds a sense of "emanating forth" out of the verbal locus.

Praśastapāda (*Padārthadharmasaṃgraha* [PDS], *Guṇagrantha*; Dvivedin, ed. 1984: 263) recognizes two kinds of *prayatna*: (i) that produced by the mere fact of being alive (*jīvana-pūrvaka*) and (ii) that produced by desire and aversion (*icchā-dveṣa-pūrvaka*). The former is what motivates various biological and cognitive processes like circulation, digestion, and undirected selective attention. It is sub-volitional, being caused by an *ātman's* innate capacity to provide organization and direction to matter in accord with an individual's karmic merit. The second kind, taken by some to be *prayatna* proper, is "the cause of endeavor directed toward the acquisition of what is beneficial and the avoidance of what is not," being distinctively associated with the agency that is proper to conscious, intelligent beings.[11] An example of this would be volition behind a person's moving her arm in order to drink a desired glass of water.

It is the volitional kind of *prayatna*—again, a direct attribute of the self and not the *manaḥ* or some other cognitive intermediary—with which we are most concerned. *Prayatna* finds its fullest expression within intentional action: action that is impelled by, sensitive to, and explicable by appeal to an agent's objectives (*prayojana, artha*).[12] A robust articulation is provided by the late Naiyāyika Viśvanātha (ca. 1575) (BP vv. 147–151, with corresponding self-commentary), who situates volition within a process that terminates in intentional action.[13] His analysis of this process may be schematized as follows (each arrow represents a causal relation, with "cause" having a wide scope):

> Cognition (of some act as worthy of being performed)→ intention (*cikīrṣā*) → volition (*prayatna*) → bodily action (*karman; ceṣṭā*).

11. Also see VS 3.2.4 and Śaṅkaramiśra's (ca. 1425) commentary. Commentators on Viśvanātha's *Bhāṣā-pariccheda* note that a number of *navya naiyāyikas* reject the category of *jīvana-yoni-prayatna* and take metabolic processes and the like to simply flow either from one's karmic merit or from the fact of being alive, but not from any kind of *prayatna*. On this view, all *prayatna* is volitional. See the Prabhā and Dinakarī commentaries in Shankara Rama Shastry, ed. 1936: 836. Also see Maitra 1963: 28.

12. In their commentaries on NS 3.2.37, Vātsyāyana and Uddyotakara make a clear distinction between action in general (*kriyā-mātra*), which is performed by both sentient and non-sentient things and purposive or intentional action (*hita-ahita-prāpti-parīhāra-artha*), which is the province of sentient beings alone.

13. Here I can provide only a brief description of Viśvanātha's account. See Maitra 1963: 26–79 for a more detailed study.

Intention (*cikīrṣā*)[14] is a desire (*icchā*) whose object is an action that can be accomplished by one's effort (e.g., the desire to cook dinner). It is formed when one cognizes that an act will produce something desirable and that one can accomplish it oneself.[15] A tacit condition on the arising of intention is the absence of cognition that the act in question would have undesirable outcomes of sufficient strength. When coupled with an awareness of the means by which the act may be performed (*upādānasya adhyakṣa*; we may expand this to *awareness that the means to perform the act is now available or appropriate*), intention then leads to volition. As seen above, volition is a direct impetus to bodily movements, and through them, various sorts of intentional action.[16] Though one may have an intention to act and an awareness of the means by which an act may be performed, volition may not be triggered if, like the transition from cognition to intention, there is cognition that the act would have undesirable features of sufficient strength. Once volition arises, there are no cognitive/psychological obstacles to action, although obstacles like bodily malfunction or external force may prevent the performance of an act. I would suggest that like intention, volition must have an object. But while intention is a *desire* whose content is an act or the characteristic result of such an act, volition is a *willing*.

In summary, *prayatna* ("volition") is a property (*guṇa*) unique to the substance *self* (*ātman*) and accounts for the capacity of selves to initiate change or activity. Further, as seen in Viśvanātha's analysis, it serves as the key node through which an individual's agency is expressed in the performance of intentional action.

Cognitive Agency

While Vātsyāyana's (ca. 400 CE) commentary on *Nyāya-sūtra* 1.1.10 is primarily directed against Buddhist flux-theorists, a central feature of

14. The term "intention" has various applications in contemporary philosophy. Here, I am restricting the sense of the term to that intention that directly governs intentional action, as opposed to less immediate senses, like, e.g., the intention to study tai chi one day (perhaps best captured by the Sanskrit word *saṅkalpa*). The noun *cikīrṣā* is formed from a desiderative root derived from the verbal root *kṛ* ("act"), and is commonly translated as "desire to act."

15. *kṛti-sādhya-viṣayiṇī icchā cikīrṣā*...*cikīrṣāṃ prati kṛti-sādhyatā-jñānam iṣṭa-sādhanatā-jñānaṃ ca kāraṇam.*

16. Commenting on VS 5.1.1, Śaṅkara Miśra (Basu, ed. 1923: 151) cites the following verse: *ātma-janyā bhaved icchā/icchā-janyā bhavet kṛtiḥ/kṛti-janyā bhavec ceṣṭā taj-janyaiva kriyā bhavet*: "desire is born in the self/from desire is born volition/from volition is born bodily movement/from bodily movement is born intentional action."

his argument hints at Nyāya's rejection of the dualism between awareness and agency at the heart of classical Sāṃkhya. Setting the agenda for later commentators, he deploys a version of Nyāya's argument from recollection to establish that all of the psychological properties mentioned in the *sūtra* require a cognitive agent whose diachronic identity is maintained in the interim between a cognition and later recognition of a single object. For example, desire is often triggered by cognition of an object that falls under a type formerly experienced as pleasant. This requires a single cognizing subject to endure the gap between the prior experience of a pleasant object and the current experience of an object of the same type that is taken to be desirable. Since, Vātsyāyana argues, one person never recollects the experiences of another, there must be a single, enduring agent, whose desire is triggered by a synthetic judgment that recalls previous experience in the light of occurent experience. Uddyotakara (ca. 550) summarizes the argument (*Nyāyavārttika* [NV] 1.1.10): "since desire and the rest focus upon the same object as memory, they have one and the same agent. For recollection does not occur when there are diverse agents, diverse objects, or diverse instruments of knowledge."[17] The ensuing dialectic centers on the question of whether Buddhists can account for memory by appeal to causal connections between members of the temporal stream that constitute a person. Putting aside the details of this debate, we may note that Nyāya conceives of certain kinds of cognitive process as governed by agential causation. Uddyotakara (NV 3.2.3) says this straightforwardly: "cognition is an act" (*upalabdhiś ca kriyā*). In a similar context, Jayanta (*Nyāyamañjarī* [NM]; Śukla, ed. 1936: *prameya prakaraṇa*, 61) claims that the self is the agent (*kartṛ*) of various effects (*kārya*) like recollection.[18] What we may call cognitive agency is thus another important feature of Nyāya's self.[19]

---

17. *yasmād ete smṛtyā saha eka-viṣayā bhavanti tasmād ekakartṛkatvam pratipādayanti. na hi nānā-kartṛkāṇāṃ nānāviṣayāṇāṃ nānānimittānāṃ ca pratyayānāṃ pratisandhānam asti.*

18. The Śukla 1936 edition of the *Nyāyamañjarī* tends to have a number of minor typos. When required, I have also consulted Tailaṅga 1895.

19. Also see NS 3.1.16 and 3.2.42 with allied commentaries. The notion that cognitive processes are actions of a sort does not contradict another Nyāya claim, that cognition (*jñāna*) is *not* an action as conceived of by Bhāṭṭa Mīmāṃsakas, one which produces a new property (*knownness*) in objects cognized. Jayanta provides a sustained rebuttal of this claim (see Chowdhury 1990: 13–15). Beyond this, as seen in Jayanta's arguments (and notwithstanding

Analyses of Agency

As the bearer of the property *prayatna*, selves initiate and sustain actions and may therefore be spoken of as agents. What, precisely, is agency? There are a number of instances where early Naiyāyikas consider agency according to the *kāraka* schema, developed by Grammarians,[20] which identifies the specific participants in the accomplishment of an action. Uddyotakara (NV 3.2.3) suggests that the direct participant who is an agent (*kartṛ-kāraka*) "(i) employs other direct participants (*itara-kāraka-prayoktṛ*), (ii) without being employed by another (*apara-aprayojya*)." We may note that the second condition is a freedom requirement. A wholly passive member of a causal nexus cannot be a genuine agent. Discussing this requirement, Uddyotakara makes an important point about the causal role of motivation: a desired result or object indeed impels (*prayojayati*) an individual to act. But, Uddyotakara argues, this kind of causal force does not violate the freedom requirement. There are different kinds of causes. Some are entirely external to the agent's "inner" world of motivation and values and others operate within it. Objectives operate internally, as goals or reasons, and the way in which they motivate (or even compel) an individual to act is compatible with the freedom required for genuine agency. Uddyotakara articulates this distinction by noting that the objects or aims that motivate action are not *kārakas*. Therefore, their influence does not violate his requirement that an agent cannot be employed by the other direct participants in the accomplishment of an action.[21]

Aside from this, Uddyotakara's discussion in this section further calls attention to the fact that agency should not be understood to require an unrealistic absolute independence. Agents are dependent on a whole host of factors, including the availability and suitability of the various other *kārakas* needed for the actions in question. Still, so long as the purported agent is not a mere passive instrument of other causal factors, he is sufficiently autonomous, acting with their assistance (or, to put it slightly differently, acting through them).

Uddyotakara's comments on NS 3.2.3), Naiyāyikas typically conceive of cognition as a property (*guṇa*) and a *result* of knowledge-processes, not an action (*karman*) itself. But in any case, the deep point, accepted by Naiyāyikas, is that insofar as the self engages in practices of knowledge, it participates in a form of agency.

20. See Cardona's chapter in this volume.

21. I think we could reasonably say that here, Uddyotakara gestures toward the reasons/causes distinction that is well known in contemporary action theory.

In his discussion of the *kārakas (Nyāyabhāṣya* [NB] 2.1.16), Vātsyāyana seems to endorse an attenuated notion of agency. He remarks that a tree is spoken of as an agent (*kartṛ-kāraka*) in relation to the act of its own standing, though the tree lacks conscious volition and other features of full-blown agency (later Naiyāyikas suggest that this is a metaphorical extension of the term). It is important, however, to make a distinction between discussion of *kārakas*, which are centrally for the purpose of characterizing language, and straightforward metaphysical analysis.[22] Clearly, as a metaphysical category, Naiyāyikas restrict agency to sentient, volitional beings.[23] Vācaspati Miśra (ca. 900 CE) suggests that

> Being an agent (*kartṛtva*) is to be characterized by the inherence of volition (*prayatna*), intention (*cikīrṣā*), and cognition (*jñāna*).[24] (*Nyāyavārttikatātparyaṭīkā* [NVT] 4.1.21)

Importantly, he further argues that these three features of agency cannot easily be separated. "Because of their inseparable connection, when any one is established, so are the others."[25] This claim further supports what we have noted above, that Nyāya considers the nexus of properties associated with agency to be profoundly intertwined. Annam Bhaṭṭa (ca. 1650 CE) largely follows Vācaspati.

---

22. See Cardona 1974: 238, 246, 284n24 and his contribution to this volume, which stress the Grammarians' principle of focusing on common language to guide conceptual analysis.

23. Even in his discussion of the *kārakas*, Uddyotakara (NV 2.1.16) leans in this direction as he defines the power (*śakti*) of an agent to perform an act: "It is a property of the agent (*kartṛ-dharma*)—both a capacity to act (*sāmarthya*) and an ascertainment of the means by which the act may be performed (*upāya-parijñāna)*—that manifests in relation to action." Such ascertainment would be the province of volitional agents, whose purposeful actions are informed by cognition and governed by intention.

24. *jñāna-cikīrṣā-prayatna-samavāya-lakṣaṇatvāt kartṛtvasya*. Note that in Nyāya's typology, intention (*cikīrṣā*) is simply a subspecies of desire (*icchā*), a direct property of the self.

25. *teṣāṃ ca paraspara-avinābhāvād anyatara-siddhau itarayoḥ siddheḥ*. The context of this passage is that Vācaspati is trying to prove the existence of God by a version of the argument from design. He argues that we may infer the existence of a maker upon observation of an artifact which exhibits the marks of design. What do we learn about such a maker? Minimally that it possesses cognition, along with the intention and volition that govern the act of making, since these three features of agency are inseparably connected (*paraspara-avinābhāva*). As a relevant aside, it is noteworthy that despite the severe ambiguity of the theistic *sūtras* of the *Nyāya-sūtra* (4.1.19–21), they strongly evince a concern to demarcate a place for human freedom in relation to a God who influences worldly processes. See Ingalls 1957.

> An agent (*kartṛ*) is to be characterized by a direct cognition (*jñāna*) of the material cause of an effect, by intention (*cikīrṣā*) and by volition (*kṛti*). (*Tarkasaṃgraha* [TS] §17)

From these accounts, agency is a capacity to initiate action with some degree of independence, in the sense that an action flows from (and, we may add, is responsive to) the objectives, decisions, and efforts of an individual who has the cognitive capacity to superintend the action. And while the *kāraka* analysis is not the final word in terms of metaphysics, it does underscore that one must not merely be a passive instrument of some other causal factor. In its most robust sense, agency requires the capacity for cognition, desire, and volition, and as the fundamental bearer of all of these, an individual *ātman* is held to be an agent. Vardhamāna (Tarkālaṅkār, ed. 1890: 166) therefore comments that agency is "being the locus of volition" (*kṛti-āśraya*).

It should be noted that to exhibit or actualize its capacity for agency, a self requires various sorts of instruments—most importantly, a body/*manaḥ* complex. A body, including sense-faculties, is required to allow the self to entertain information about the world and act upon it. A *manaḥ* is needed to regulate the input of the senses and to apperceive one's own mental states and memory traces (NS 1.1.16 and allied commentaries). This dependence upon instruments does not, however, undermine the self's agency any more than does a racecar driver's reliance upon her vehicle or a carpenter's reliance upon his tools.[26] It is true that an *ātman's* reliance upon its most immediate instruments—a body and *manaḥ*—is profound: while a carpenter cannot build a house without his tools, he can still think, feel, and perform other tasks. But a self needs a body and *manaḥ* to engage in even the most basic cognitive, affective, or conative functions. Nevertheless, these instruments do not share or compromise the self's agency (NV 3.2.3); they merely provide the conditions by which its potential for agency may be actualized. When such potential is actualized it is a property of the self alone.[27]

---

26. See NS 3.1.16–19 and 3.2.34–7 with allied commentaries. Also see NB 3.2.8, "It is the person (*puruṣa*) who cognizes, not the inner organ."

27. It may help to distinguish between a property that, when actualized or possessed, (i) flows from the essence of the substance and one that (ii) is itself constitutive of the substance, part of its essence. The former would not be a necessary feature of the substance, but when it does exist, it is the property of the substance alone and not an artificial or alien imposition. The latter, on the other hand, would be necessary for the substance's existence.

Against Sāṃkhya's Frictionless Self

In debates over the existence of the self, Buddhism is Nyāya's great opponent; but when discussing the nature of the self, Nyāya often takes aim at the Sāṃkhya school.[28] This is largely due to the fact that Sāṃkhya displaces most of the properties of Nyāya's self to the *antaḥkaraṇa* ("inner organ"; an insentient psychological apparatus apparently related to, yet completely external to the self), and specifically to *buddhi* (a primary component or aspect of the *antaḥkaraṇa*; see Bryant's chapter of this volume).[29] The following chart (table 5.1) illustrates some of the differences between the two schools. (Sanskrit terms given here are representative; synonyms proliferate.)

Compared to Sāṃkhya, which accepts a tripartite "inner organ" of *manaḥ, buddhi, and ahaṃkāra* ("false conceit") along with the self, Nyāya merely posits a *manaḥ*. The functions of *buddhi* are largely performed by the self, while *ahaṃkāra* is at most merely a special kind of false cognition, not a self-standing category (NB 4.2.1).

Although it is not as explicitly developed as Nyāya's well-known arguments in support of the self as a unified cognitive agent, Nyāya also argues that a self is required to synthesize various aspects of volitional action and its moral and metaphysical consequences: Intention is informed by the memory and cognition of the very person who intends to act; her

For Nyāya, the self's agency exists in the former way. A self may exist, albeit in an attenuated form, when agency is not present (as many hold to be the case in the state of *mokṣa*, "liberation"). Agency is not, therefore, constitutive of selfhood, but when the self does exhibit or possess agency, it flows from the self's essential nature and is possessed by the self alone. Taking Viśvanātha's definition of self into account (in the section immediately below), we may say that it is necessary for self to possess the capacity for agency.

28. As is well known, the Sāṃkhya tradition had enormous and wide-ranging influence on various ancient and classical traditions of thought in India, and existed in a large number of iterations and branches. The school or family of schools that we will focus upon here are those which rose to prominence in the middle of the first millennium CE and are exemplified in the *Sāṃkhya-kārikās* of Īśvarakṛṣṇa (ca. 400 CE). It is this brand of Sāṃkhya, or something very close to it, with which Naiyāyikas are concerned (e.g., Jayanta's NM; Śukla, ed. 1936: *prameya prakaraṇa*, 59–61; anti-Sāṃkhya polemics are also found throughout the third book of the *Nyāya-sūtra*). I will also include the commentators on the *Yoga-sūtra*—members of the "Yoga" school—as Sāṃkhya philosophers. In support of this inclusion, see Nicholson 2010: 79–83.

29. *Sāṃkhya-kārikā* 19, 20, 23. We could add that in the language of the *Yoga-sūtras*, these functions are properties or modes of the *citta*, not the self.

Table 5.1 Differences between the Nyāya and Sāṃkhya schools

Function or Property	Its locus for Nyāya	For Sāṃkhya
Consciousness (*caitanya*)	Self	Self
Propositionally structured cognition (*adhyavasāya; jñāna*)	Self	*antaḥkaraṇa*
Memory (*smṛti*)	Self	*antaḥkaraṇa*
Desire/Aversion (*rāga/dveṣa*)	Self	*antaḥkaraṇa*
Volition/agency (*prayatna/kartṛtva*)	Self	*antaḥkaraṇa*
Moral responsibility/karmic merit (*dharma/adharma/adṛṣṭa*)	Self	*antaḥkaraṇa*

intention then triggers volition and her ensuing intentional action.[30] Given that an individual self is the agent responsible for such acts, it is also the bearer of both moral responsibility and its concretization in the form of karmic merit (*dharma*; *adṛṣṭa*). As is well known, such responsibility and merit may span many lifetimes; therefore, Nyāya contends that the self bears them from body to body.[31] These various features of action are not easily separated from the rest; they are a nexus of traits that mutually express the fullness of selfhood. Viśvanātha (Shankara Rama Shastry, ed. 1923: 381) therefore succinctly states that "the category of self (*ātma-jāti*) is delimited by the condition of being a substratum of pleasure, pain and the rest."[32]

30. NB 3.2.34: "Thus, cognition, desire, volition, pleasure and pain each share an intimate relationship. Desire and the rest share the same agent as cognition and reside in the same locus."

31. See NB 3.2.38, 3.2.72 and various commentaries on NS 3.1.4. Also see Ram-prasad 2001: 20 for discussion of a similar position held by Kumārila Bhaṭṭa. That the self functions well as a locus of continued moral responsibility is suggested by the need felt by early Buddhists to explain how no-self theories do not undercut moral responsibility (e.g., *Questions of King Milinda* 3.2.6).

32. *ātma-jātis tu sukha-duḥkhādi-samavāyikāraṇatā-avacchedakatayā sidhyati.* Interestingly, in the same section, his very definition of self focuses upon the need to have an agent which superintends the functioning of the body and senses: "The self is an overseer (*adhiṣṭhātā*) of the body and senses, as instruments (*karaṇam*) require agents (*sakartṛkam*)."

Sāṃkhya, as seen above, allows only unqualified consciousness or awareness *simpliciter* to be a property of the self. In the *Nyāyakusumāñjali*, Udayana (ca. 975 CE) summarizes the Sāṃkhya position.

> Neither cause nor effect, the pure self (*puruṣa*) has the nature of unchanging consciousness (*kūṭastha-caitanya-rūpa*). The original cause of the manifest world is primordial nature (*prakṛti*), which is insentient and capable of modification. From it springs the creation of *buddhi* and the rest...That single thing which functions in all of the conditions of life (waking, dreaming, deep dreamless sleep), and is the support of impressions left by cognition, is the inner organ (*antaḥkaraṇa*). Objects become impressed upon it and are thus made available to the pure self. Though it does not do anything, the self is thought of as an agent (*kartṛtva-abhimāna*) owing to non-recognition of its distinction from the *buddhi*. And the insentient *buddhi* is thus taken to be sentient. In *buddhi* alone rest the impressions and results of action. But the *puruṣa* is ever untouched, like a lotus leaf on the water.[33] (*Nyāyakusumāñjali*, First Stabaka; Tarkālaṅkār, ed. 1890: 161–166)[34]

Why would Sāṃkhya endorse such an attenuated notion of selfhood, one that likely seems quite unattractive to an outside observer? To understand this, I would suggest that one keeps in mind a concern to unearth and embrace the essential and hidden self, common in Hindu schools, which may be traced to the speculations of the Upaniṣads. The hidden self is that kernel of our psychic being that survives death and is, owing to its being our true essence, the very content of enlightenment or liberation. A primary motivation for Sāṃkhya, therefore, is the need to create a buffer between the deep self and the world in order to protect the deep self's changelessness and, therefore, the possibility of its liberation from this world of constant change.[35] As Larson (1979: 171) notes, consciousness *simpliciter* "is the fact of man's experience which provides the basis for his

33. Vardhamāna glosses this as "it is not touched by religious merit or its fruits, as the *śruti* claims it is changeless and the like" (Tarkālaṅkār, ed. 1890: 164).

34. I have followed Vardhamāna on a few points of interpretation of this passage.

35. Sāmkhya's view is surely also informed by reports of yogīs that all discursive thought and the like is absent in their *samādhi* experiences, which are taken to be experiences of the pure self (cf. *Yoga-sūtra* 1.2–3). See Phillips 1985 for a powerful critique of this latter claim.

freedom precisely because it is not a part of or determined by the world." If, Sāṃkhya contends, the self were a locus of volition and the rest—properties that come and go—it would be beset by change, and therefore be ephemeral (See Bryant's chapter in this volume). This would make liberation impossible, as there would be no part of the self that can escape the clutches of time. Sāṃkhya therefore conceives of the true self as what we may call "frictionless," never truly touched by the world.[36] *Sāṃkhya-kārikā* 62 accordingly states that "No *puruṣa* is therefore ever bound, released, or the subject of transmigration. It is *prakṛti* alone in its various modes of being, which is bound, released, and undergoes transmigration." Sāṃkhya thinkers thus walk a very fine line, citing the existence of a *puruṣa* or self in order to account for conscious experience, while simultaneously holding that strictly speaking, the self has nothing to do with the vicissitudes of life as experienced.

In defending the self's agency, the central case Nyāya makes is that there must be more friction between the self and world for various sorts of widely held philosophical commitments to make sense. To do this, Nyāya need not argue about agency directly, but rather that at least some of the cluster of properties associated with agency must belong to the self. If this can be established, then naturally the rest may be too, for two reasons. First, this would be enough to rebut the theoretical support for Sāṃkhya's great divorce. If the self is capable of bearing some properties beyond unqualified consciousness, it can in principle possess others. Second, given the interdependence of the various features of agency, establishing that some of them are direct properties of the self would provide a wedge by which the others may be reasonably included.

Below, we consider two sets of arguments: first, that for religious/ethical acts—and ultimately the very pursuit of liberation—to make sense, the self must be the direct generator and bearer of karmic merit, and second, that the Sāṃkhya divorce between cognition (a property of the *antaḥkaraṇa*) and consciousness (a property of the self) is unsustainable. To be conscious requires that one has the capacity to undergo cognition, which ultimately entails being a cognitive agent.

36. My use of the term "frictionless" is partly inspired by John McDowell's (1994: 11) provocative phrase "a frictionless spinning in the void," by which he describes contemporary epistemologies that are not, in his analysis, sufficiently world-engaging.

Udayana's Argument from Religious Merit

As part of its broad defense of theism, Udayana's *Nyāyakusumāñjali* advances the thesis that "there is a transcendental means to achieve the world beyond" (Dravid, ed. and trans. 1996: 6). In this context, Udayana seeks to articulate the way in which religious acts produce karmic merit. Our passage, near the end of the first chapter of the *Kusumāñjali*, is centered on Udayana's appeal to "the rule that enjoyment of karmic results is tied to the self who produces the karma" (*prati-ātma-niyamāt bhukteḥ*). He resists the notion that in ritual acts, insentient materials themselves become affected. Rather, it is the agent who performs the act—the self—who is directly affected by the potency of ritual and the production of karma more generally. Udayana argues that unless the individual selves who experience the fruit of their actions are also the direct bearers of karmic merit, there would be no appropriate metaphysical tie between selves, their actions, and the consequences of their actions (including the physical bodies that they inhabit owing to past karma). This is opposed to the Sāṃkhya view that holds that volition, action, and karmic merit are features of *buddhi*, while the self is an experiencer (*bhoktṛ*) of karmically created bodies and circumstances.

> The individual selves who experience the fruit of actions are eternally all-pervasive[37] and are thus, in the absence of a distinguishing property like karmic merit, equally connected to each and every body. And even if the material elements were invested with some kind of distinguishing property, the tie between individuals' actions and their enjoyment of karmically merited results would still be unfounded, since there would be no appropriate causal mechanism that connects individuals to particular bodies (*pratiniyata-bhoga-asiddheḥ*): even if a body, mind, and senses had some distinguishing properties, there is no rule (*niyama*) that they be tied to a particular self, since there is no mechanism to underwrite such a rule (*niyāmaka-abhāvāt*). Accordingly, there would be the unwanted conclusion that many selves would share a single body. (Tarkālāṅkar, ed. 1890: 158)

37. This position is shared by both Naiyāyikas and classical Sāṃkhya thinkers.

Udayana starts from the widely held view that a self's enjoyment of karmically mediated experience requires it to have a particular body that allows for such experiences. But if, like Sāṃkhya, one holds that karmic merit is only a property of insentient *prakṛti*, and not selves, then one still lacks the resources to account for why a particular self should be tied to this or that bit of karma-invested *prakṛti*. By analogy, we may imagine a factory that produces trophies with engraved names. One of them says "Ian Jones." But even if my name is "Ian Jones," unless there is something distinct about *me* that warrants my receiving that particular trophy, I lack a connection to it such that I deserve it. In his commentary, Vardhamāna explains: "Regarding things like a body, it must be accepted that these are produced by the karma of a specific self. Since there's no special connection between a body and a particular self, you cannot otherwise explain specific experiences (i.e., that a specific body produces experiences for just one specific person)." (Tarkālaṅkār, ed. 1890: 158).[38]

This is a distinctively Indian take on the familiar problem of mind-body dualism (here, *self-body* dualism, since among scholars of Indian thought, "mind" is often a translation of *manaḥ*, an aspect of the inner organ). In short, this problem arises when the self is taken to be of a radically different kind than body, such that there would be no available causal relations by which their interactions may be underwritten. In the Indian context, karmic merit (karma, *adṛṣṭa*, *dharma*, sometimes *daiva*, etc.) often serves to tether individual selves to the unique constellation of body and experiences merited by their acts (in this discussion, I am using the term "body" to refer to the "inner organ" as well as the physical body). Karmic merit has the capacity to tie selves to certain aspects of the world. While Nyāya is, like Sāṃkhya, a dualistic school, it has a much more robust notion of self, which allows for self-body interaction.[39] This includes the idea that selves are directly the loci of karmic merit. Sāṃkhya's frictionless self is, however, incapable of storing karmic data (and, analogously, of being the seat of moral responsibility). What mechanism, then, governs the connection of a self to any particular body—and most problematically, to a particular karma-encoded *buddhi*? Udayana considers a number of possible responses, which place all of the causal power on the "body" side

38. *Bhoktṛ-pratyāsatter aviśeṣāt kiṃcic charīraṃ kasyacid eva bhogaṃ janayati iti pratiniyata-bhoga-anyathā-anupapattyā pratiniyata-bhoktṛ-karma-upārjitatvaṃ śarīrādāv abhyupeyam.* Also see NS 3.2.66.

39. See Chakrabarti 1999 for a thorough treatment of Nyāya's interactionist dualism.

of self-body dualism, and which try explain how bits of matter may be invested with special properties that underwrite their connection to particular selves. They all fail, however, since in each case, the explanatory power of each account depends upon there already being some kind of self/body connection in place.[40] They never account for the fundamental connection itself. The correct rule or principle, Udayana argues, is that the elements that make up a body are invested with certain special properties only when they are *already* connected to a particular self, which influences them through top-down causation. Therefore, to make sense of the relation between selves and their bodies, the self must be understood as a direct locus of the karmic merit that ties it to certain bodies, and the volition which governs karma-producing actions.

At this point in the argument Udayana explicitly identifies Sāṃkhya as his opponent and summarizes the central planks of Sāṃkhya dualism, including its rejection of the self's agency (quoted above, in the beginning of this section). Against this view, he provides two key arguments (Tarkālaṅkār 1890: 166). First, our common experience (*anubhava*) is that we are both conscious *and* agents; that is, we experience ourselves as the locus of both consciousness and agency. "The conscious being is truly the agent, as there is direct experience of consciousness and volition as co-located."[41] Vardhamāna notes that such experience takes the form of apperceptive awareness: "I, the conscious being, am acting." Nyāya accepts and defends the principle that cognition that appears to be true should be taken as such unless called into question by stronger *pramāṇas*.[42] And apperception (*anuvyavasāya*) is a subspecies of perception, the chief *pramāṇa*. Therefore, Udayana suggests, the information conveyed by this experience stands as true unless his Sāṃkhya interlocutor can refute it. He argues that Sāṃkhya can appeal to no principle, whether theoretical

---

40. For example, one account holds that the distinguishing information could be invested in material elements by something like *apekṣābuddhi*, a mental act by which an individual invests external things with number, by cognizing the elements as such. The cognition "there are four jars on the table" thus invests the jars with number. But, as Udayana notes, for such an act to take place, one must already have a body and mind. Therefore, the fundamental issue remains unsolved.

41. *cetano 'pi kartā eva kṛti-caitanyayoḥ sāmānādhikaraṇyena anubhavāt.*

42. See Dasti 2012 for some of the theoretical motivations behind this principle. As an example of a putatively veridical cognition which is defeated, Nyāya holds that the cognition "I am my body" is defeated by inferences that establish that the self is a substance that is other than the body.

or experiential, that has a stronger evidential basis than the cognition in question.[43]

In principle, Udayana could rest his case now, having traced his view to a properly functioning *pramāṇa*. But he makes a more radical second argument, turning the Sāṃkhya concern for liberation on its head: if, as Sāṃkhya contends, volition and karmic merit are properties of *buddhi* and not the self, then we would be either eternally bound in *saṃsāra* or eternally liberated (Tarkālaṅkār, ed. 1890: 169). His argument takes the form of a dilemma: is *buddhi* eternal or not? If eternal, then the self to which it is tied will never gain release, being eternally shrouded by *buddhi* and lost to its own true nature.[44] If *buddhi* is temporary and subject to destruction, then (according to a widely held principle in Indian thought) it must also have a beginning. But since, for Sāṃkhya, it is the *buddhi*—and not the self—that stores karmic merit, there would be no mechanism to underwrite and regulate its initial deployment in relationship to a particular self. Since there would be no appropriate initial conditions for *buddhi's* ensnaring any particular self, no self could be ensnared, and there would be no onset of *saṃsāra*. Thus, on the Sāṃkhya view, we should either be eternally bound or eternally liberated. Since both views are untenable, Udayana rejects the Sāṃkhya bifurcation of conscious selfhood from volition and karmic merit. His *kārikā* for this section of the *Kusumāñjali* (Tarkālaṅkār, ed. 1890: 166) thus reads:

> An agent's own merit fixes his place,
> cognition is his alone.
> Else liberation would be a fancy,
> or seeds of bondage never sown.[45]

---

43. This section of Udayana's argument is, true to his general style, quite condensed and resists concise summary. After claiming that experience supports the Sāṃkhya position no better than the Nyāya position, Udayana proceeds to bring up a number of theoretical difficulties with Sāṃkhya metaphysics, especially the fundamental principle of *satkāryavāda* (see note 48 for further discussion of *satkāryavāda*).

44. *puṃsaḥ sarvadā sopādhitve svarūpeṇa anavasthānāt*. The seeds of this argument may be found in NS 3.2.38–9 and NS 3.2.68. Especially note Uddyotakara's commentary on the latter.

45. The last line is rendered quite loosely. More literally, the entire verse reads "The Nyāya view is that an agent's *dharmas* govern his situation in the world, while he alone is the conscious knower. Otherwise, there would be no possibility of liberation; or conversely, freedom from *saṃsāra* would be constant" (*kartṛ-dharmā niyantāraś cetitā ca sa eva naḥ/anyathā anapavargaḥ syād asaṃsāre 'thavā dhruvaḥ*).

The final task of Udayana is to respond to the primary theoretical motivation for Sāṃkhya's great divorce: the need to preserve the self's changelessness (*kauṭasthya*) and thus, its immortality. If, as Nyāya holds, the self is the direct locus of volition, cognition, and merit, would it not then be beset with change and thus impermanence? Udayana responds to this concern by appealing to the distinction between properties and property bearers. "Given the complete distinction between properties and their bearers (*dharma-dharmiṇor atyanta-bhede*), there is no violation of changelessness (*kauṭasthya-avirodhaḥ*)."[46] The self is a property bearer, while cognitive states, karmic traces, and individual volitions are its properties. An individual self may remain the same despite the changes in its properties.[47] This response suggests that a large part of Sāṃkhya's motivations for denying volition, et cetera, to the self stems from its *satkāryavāda* metaphysics, which does not distinguish between properties and property bearers.[48]

Let us pause here for some reflections on this discussion: Our chief concern is Nyāya's defense of the view that the self is an agent. In the above passage, this defense is nested within a larger argument about the mechanism that undergirds karmic merit. The reason for this is important: the function of karmic merit is to generate certain experiences, or a possible range of experiences, in response to an individual's actions. It therefore has both a *moral* and *metaphysical* function. Morally, it ensures that an individual receives her just deserts. It is because of the functioning of karma that the diverse distribution of life-conditions we see at a single moment is explicable by appeal to individuals' past behaviors (see NB 3.2.67). This is a primary reason that the tie between an individual's volition and her karmic merit is so important. Clearly, if I were to willfully

---

46. Tarkālaṅkār, ed. 1890: 171. See NVT 3.2.2–3 for a similar application of this distinction.

47. Some changes in a property entail a change of or destruction of their property bearers, especially if such bearers are composite wholes. But the self is a single, non-composite substance for Nyāya and is not threatened by destruction. See Ramaiah 1987 for discussion and critique of Nyāya's account of metaphysical change and identity.

48. *Satkāryavāda* is the doctrine that effects preexist within their causes, and thus that causation is simply the manifestation of an effect which is already existing (*satkārya*). Classical examples used to support this theory include the manifestation of a clay pot from a lump of clay. It is suggested that the pot is already there before its formation, and this preexistence of things like the pot is required to allow for causal regularities found in nature: a lump of clay does not produce a cotton shirt, for example. Udayana and Jayanata provide sustained attacks on *satkāryavāda* within or immediately after their criticism of Sāṃkhya's account of the self. I think that they strongly suggest that Sāṃkhya's fear of the self's mutability is largely due to the limitations of *satkāryavāda*.

perform some evil deed in this life and yet someone else were to suffer its karmic consequences in the future, such would be unjust and absurd. The moral consequences of an act should be tied to the very agent, the bearer of volition, who performs the act. On Nyāya's view, this is done straightforwardly: an individual *ātman* is the bearer of volition and of the karmic merit tied to volitional acts, and is further the direct experiencer of the outcomes produced by its karma.[49] For Sāṃkhya, the situation is much more complicated and, as Udayana argues, problematic. An individual *puruṣa* has no volition or karmic merit. These are both located in *buddhi*, which is entirely alien to the true self. Yet, the *puruṣa* is supposed to be the sufferer (*bhoktṛ*) of karmic consequences—and more importantly, the liberation or bondage generated by the decisions of *buddhi*.

Udayana chooses not to focus on the problems involving the seeming injustice of a situation where the self suffers, powerless and devoid of agency, because of the actions of *prakṛti*. He focuses on the metaphysical role of karmic merit, tying individual selves to their current bodies, and by extension to their current circumstances. Udayana notes that an individual self has no inherent connection to the constellation of material elements which make up this or that body. In principle, it is equally related to all material elements. What distinguishes elements such that they become the body of a certain self is karmic merit. We may think of such merit as an informational state, which encodes directives to produce and maintain bodies of a certain kind. Udayana notes that on the Sāṃkhya account, this information is encoded in *prakṛti*, particularly the *buddhi*, and not the self. There is nothing about the self itself that contributes to its situation in the world. But this still leaves us with the question of why any particular self should be joined with any particular information-laden bit of *prakṛti*. Unless the self is able to bear some kind of merit or informational content, there is no causal mechanism to appropriately underwrite the connection between a self and its body (and more generally, its situation in the world). Sāṃkhya's dualism is complete and unremitting: morally and metaphysically, the self has no causal relationship with the world. By granting all agency to *prakṛti*, including that which supports religious and

49. See NS 3.2.38 and 60, with allied commentaries. Also note Potter's (1980: 263) comments for a similar perspective in other *darśanas*.

meditative practice, Udayana argues that it has made the entire quest for liberation either useless or unnecessary.[50]

A possible Sāṃkhya response may be to urge that Udayana poses a false dilemma. Why can't *buddhi* be eternal, but still become "separated" from a particular self in the course of time? But this line of thinking is problematic precisely because Sāṃkhya places all causation and agency on the side of *prakṛti*. As Jayanta (NM; Śukla, ed. 1936: *prameya prakaraṇa*, 62) forcefully argues, should someone become liberated, what guarantee is there that *prakṛti* will not simply snatch him up again, as it did at least once before? The "lack of discrimination" that binds one to *saṃsāra* is indeed a feature of *buddhi*, not the bound self, since on the Sāṃkhya view, selves are as incapable of being mistaken as pots or the color red. And as the self is unable to store any content, karmic, mnemonic, or otherwise, it cannot encode directives to prevent re-entanglement.[51]

Knowledge as an Expression of Agency

In its attempt to safeguard the changelessness of the self, Sāṃkhya further articulates a complicated relationship between the *puruṣa* and *buddhi* within the act of cognizing. In outline, it holds that *puruṣa* is the only locus of consciousness, as *prakṛti* is insentient. But *puruṣa* is incapable of discursive, concept-laden experience, engaging in concept deployment, or being the locus of memory. Any of these would entail that it could suffer modification and change. Therefore, while *puruṣa* emits consciousness, this is all it can do; all propositionally structured cognition takes place within the *buddhi*, which, somehow or other, "reflects" the consciousness of the self.[52]

---

50. Dravid (1995: 3, 9) criticizes Nyāya's view, claiming it is no better than Sāṃkhya's dualism in this regard. Since the body/*manaḥ* complex is required for an individual's conative or cognitive functioning to occur, he asserts that "in no sense, therefore, the self can be regarded as the agent of the activities." But Dravid's criticism is based on a misunderstanding of Nyāya's metaphysics of agency. As discussed above (note 27), for Nyāya, while the body/*manas* complex provides causal conditions for the self's expression of agency, it does not partake in such agency. Dravid fails to recognize that causal conditions may be necessary conditions for agency without themselves being agents and therefore, he does not sufficiently distinguish between Nyāya's integrated dualism and Sāṃkhya's absolute dualism.

51. Related to this issue, Udayana argues that *satkāryavāda* metaphysics cannot provide a coherent account of how *buddhi* may exist yet fail to entrap a self, since on the Sāṃkhya account, traces of conditioning (*vāsanā*) should never really be destroyed. *Satkāryavāda* holds that things are never really created or destroyed, but eternally existing. Also see NB, NV, and NVT on NS 3.2.68.

52. See Bryant 2009: 14–16, Rukmani 1988: 369–72, and Whicher 1998: 135–142. Also see Bryant's essay in this volume.

As we have seen, Nyāya holds that the self performs various acts of cognition and that cognitive agency is a central feature of selfhood. Nyāya therefore rejects the existence of *buddhi* as conceived by Sāṃkhya, holding that the correct referent of word *buddhi* is simply cognition itself, a property (*guṇa*) of the self (NS 1.1.15). For Nyāya, there is no organ akin to *buddhi;* there is only the self and the *manaḥ*, which governs selective attention, apperception, and memory (compare with Mīmāṃsā, as discussed in Freschi's chapter). In the argument below, Uddyotakara, following Vātsyāyana, argues that Sāṃkhya's division between consciousness (*cetanā*), the exclusive property of the self, and cognition (*jñāna, adhyavasāya*), the exclusive property of *buddhi*, collapses under scrutiny (NV 3.2.3).

UDDYOTAKARA: If *buddhi* cognizes things (*adhyavasyati*), then what does the conscious being (*cetana*) do with the cognition (*jñāna*) that exists in the *buddhi*?

SĀṂKHYA: It is conscious (*cetayate*).

U: Then who exactly is conscious (*kaś cetayate*)? If the very being who possesses cognition (*adhyavasāya*) is conscious (*cetayate*), this would contradict your position (that *buddhi* is insentient). If, on the other hand, the self (*ātman*) is conscious (but does not possess cognition), how could it be conscious by dint of cognition (*pratyayena*) that takes place within the *buddhi*? For one cannot act through an action performed by another.

S: The self (*puruṣa*) is conscious (*cetayate*), while the *buddhi* cognizes (*jānīte*).

U: But what is being spoken of (in both cases) is nothing other than cognition (*jñāna*). Saying that something is conscious (*cetayate*) is equivalent to saying that it cognizes (*jānīte*).

S: What if *buddhi* is what causes (*jñāpayati*) the self to cognize?

U: Then your notion is that the *buddhi* causes the self to cognize (*jñāpayati*), while the self is the cognizer (*jānīte*). And clearly, it is the *puruṣa* who knows and the *buddhi* that causes him to know. (This is the very position which Nyāya defends, taking *buddhi* to simply be the self's state of cognition). Given this, you must explain what you take to be the deep distinction between ascertainment (*adhyavasāya*) and awareness (*cetanā*).

The core of Uddyotakara's argument is that dividing consciousness and cognition between two separate substances is unsustainable, as it is impossible to effectively bifurcate the locus of propositionally structured cognition and the locus of consciousness. Better, from Nyāya's perspective, is to hold that one substance is the locus of both consciousness and cognition. Though it takes a different form than Udayana's arguments above, here we again find an attack on the radical dualism of Sāṃkhya. A simple metaphor for this dualism is provided in *Sāṃkhya-kārikā* 21: "The connection of *puruṣa* and *prakṛti* is like that of a lame person and a blind person...." The basic idea is that *puruṣa*, the lame person, has the capacity for awareness but not for activity, while *prakṛti*, the blind person, has the capacity for activity but not awareness; in this world the two band together to accomplish various ends. The upshot of Uddyotakara's critique is that this image is deeply misleading and collapses under scrutiny. Awareness involves a kind of activity, something that must be performed by the very being who is aware. This makes sense, since awareness involves a process (paradigmatically, the operation of *pramāṇas*) that terminates in a result (awareness, cognition, knowledge, etc.). Therefore, given Sāṃkhya metaphysics, the metaphorical lame person should also be blind, deaf, and incapable of thought, as these are all activities governed by *prakṛti* and not the province of Sāṃkhya's self. If we are to speak of the self as a knower in any meaningful way, it must be directly involved the process of knowing. There must be some cognitive friction between the self and world.

To elaborate: the Sāṃkhya position is that *buddhi* is the seat of cognition (*jñāna, adhyavasāya, pratyaya*), while the self is the seat of consciousness (*caitanya*). Uddyotakara's argument tries to expose the fault lines in this account, stressing the incongruity of claiming that for a single cognitive event (e.g., seeing a tree in the distance), one entity provides the consciousness, while another unconscious entity is the substratum of cognition. *To cognize* simply means to be conscious of a particular fact or object, while *being conscious* means having the capacity to undergo experience. Indeed, it is very difficult to conceive of consciousness in a way that dislocates or transfers it from its locus. Sāṃkhya again appeals to metaphor to make sense of this, the metaphor of reflection (*pratibimbana, chāyā*): *buddhi* reflects the consciousness of the self as a mirror reflects light. But Naiyāyikas contend that this too is a false analogy. Jayanta (NM; Śukla, ed. 1936: *prameya prakaraṇa*, 61): "Since the capacity for consciousness (*citiśakti*) is not liable to modification and is *not transferrable to another*, there can be no transference from the *puruṣa* to the *buddhi*" (emphasis added).

Nyāya's arguments may be bolstered by considering the way in which we are said to possess or own our cognitive states. My cognition is "mine" in that I have a special and intimate sort of participation with it.[53] Clearly, I have a (limited) sort of power to control my cognitive life from within in a way that I cannot control another's. I can (again, within some limitations) sort and frame my cognitions in ways that I cannot for another, at least not with the directness of my own. Conversely, I cannot disregard my own cognitions in the way I can another's. How to account for this sort of ownership? Nyāya's account answers this question straightforwardly: cognition is a property of the self and therefore the self is said to possess it. But despite the fact that Sāṃkhya philosophers sometimes speak of the self as "owning" the *buddhi*,[54] such a relation is impossible. There is no real relation between Sāṃkhya's self and the *buddhi*, and therefore no real ownership of propositionally structured cognition. Like the above arguments about karma and moral responsibility, Nyāya's case that the self must be the seat of propositionally structured cognition may serve as a wedge for the inclusion of other information-bearing states in the self's own properties.

Conclusion

We have considered three ways that Nyāya accounts for the self's agency: (i) its categorization of volition and agency as features of the self and not some faculty like the *buddhi* or *manas*; (ii) its argument that for karma/moral responsibility and the pursuit of liberation to make sense, the self must be the direct bearer of various properties, which are synthesized in agency; and (iii) its attempt to undermine the dualism of knowledge and action at the heart of classical Sāṃkhya, by arguing that knowing is itself an expression of agency. I would like to close our discussion by recognizing the way the question of agency reflects a more general issue of personhood. To speak in broad terms, I would suggest that Nyāya's metaphysics of personhood stands in the middle of the two poles occupied by Sāṃkhya and Buddhism. In the effort to protect the self's immortality, Sāṃkhya isolates it entirely from the fluctuations of the world. The real self never engages with the world, and to think that the changing empirical person

53. See Ganeri 2007: 175–177 for discussion of individuals' ownership of their own cognitive states.

54. See Vyāsa's comments on *Yoga-sūtra* 1.4.

is the true self is a falsehood based on misidentification. On the other side, Buddhists commonly reduce what is thought of as a person to nothing more than a stream of fleeting, world-engaging states, with no enduring self behind them. Nyāya's account of personhood involves substances and properties: an enduring substantial self *with* its fluctuating, world-engaging properties like memory, awareness, and volition allow for full personhood. Like Sāṃkhya, Nyāya allows for a self which endures through time, survives bodily death, and participates in ultimate liberation. But like the Buddhists, Nyāya's person is directly engaged in the world. We are here now.

References

Basu, Major B. D. ed., Nandalal Sinha, trans. 1923. *The Vaiśeṣika Sūtras of Kaṇāda.* Sacred Books of the Hindus 7. Allahabad: Vijaya Press.

Bhattacarya, Gopinath, ed., trans., and commentator. 1976. *Tarkasaṃgraha and Tarkasaṃgraha-dīpikā of Annaṃbhaṭṭa.* Calcutta: Progressive Publishers.

Bryant, Edwin F. 2009. The Yoga Sūtras of Patañjali: *A New Edition, Translation, and Commentary.* New York: North Point Press.

Cardona, George. 1974. "Pāṇini's Kārakas: Agency, Animation, and Identity." *Journal of Indian Philosophy* 2: 231–306.

Chakrabarti, Kisor. 1999. *Classical Indian Philosophy of Mind: The Nyāya Dualist Tradition.* Albany: State University of New York Press.

Chakravarti, Arindam. 1982. "The Nyāya Proofs for the Existence of the Soul." *Journal of Indian Philosophy* 10: 211–238.

———. 1983. "Is Liberation (mokṣa) Pleasant?" *Philosophy East and West* 33 (2): 167–182. (Author's name is listed as "A. Chakrabarti" in this publication.)

Chowdhury, Santimoy. 1990. "Is Knowledge an Act (Kriyā)?" *Vishwabhāratī Journal of Philosophy* 27 (1): 10–17.

Dasti, Matthew. 2012. "Disjunctivism and Parasitism in Nyāya Epistemology." *Philosophy East and West* 62 (1): 1–15.

Dravid, N. S. 1995. "Anomalies of the Nyāya-Vaiśeṣika Concept of Self." *Indian Philosophical Quarterly* 12 (1): 1–12.

Dravid, N. S., ed. and trans. 1996. *Nyāyakusumāñjali of Udayanācārya.*Vol. 1. New Delhi: Indian Council of Philosophical Research.

Dvivedin, V. P., ed. 1984. *The Praśastapāda Bhāṣya with Commentary Nyāyakandalī of Śrīdhara.* 2nd ed. Delhi: Sri Satguru Publications.

Ganeri, Jonardon. 2007. *The Concealed Art of the Soul.* New York: Oxford University Press.

Ingalls, Daniel H. H. 1957. "Human Effort Versus God's Effort in the Early Nyāya." In *Felicitation Volume Presented to Professor Sripad Krishna Belvalkar,* ed. S. Radhakrishnan et al., 228–235. Benares: Motilal Baranasidass.

Larson, Gerald. 1979. *Classical Sāṃkhya.* 2nd ed. Delhi: Motilal Banarsidass.

Maitra, S. K. 1963. *The Ethics of the Hindus.* 3rd ed. Calcutta: University of Calcutta.

McDowell, John H. 1994. *Mind and World.* Cambridge, MA: Harvard University Press.

Nicholson, Andrew J. 2010. *Unifying Hinduism: Philosophy and Identity in Indian Intellectual History.* New York: Columbia University Press.

Nyaya-Tarkatirtha, Taranatha and Amarendramohan Tarkatirtha, eds. [1936–1944] 2003. *Nyāyadarśanam: with Vātsyāyana's Bhāṣya, Uddyotakara's Vārttika, Vācaspati Miśra's Tātparyaṭīkā & Viśvanātha's Vṛtti.* Reprint, Calcutta: Munshiram Manoharlal.

Phillips, Stephen H. 1985. "The Conflict of Voluntarism and Dualism in the Yoga-sūtra." *Journal of Indian Philosophy* 13: 399–414.

———. Unpublished. "Liberation: Gaṅgeśa's *mukti-vāda* and Nyāya on the Supreme Personal Good."

Potter, Karl. 1980. "The Karma Theory and Its Interpretation in Some Indian Philosophical Systems." In *Karma and Rebirth in Classical Indian Traditions,* ed. W. O'Flaherty, 241–267. Berkeley: University of California Press.

Ramaiah, C. 1987. "The Problem of Personal Identity—Nyāya Vaiśeṣika Perspective." *Indian Philosophical Annual* 20: 68–84.

Ram-Prasad, Chakravarthi. 2001. *Knowledge and Liberation in Classical Indian Thought.* London: Palgrave Macmillan.

Rukmani, T. S. 1988. "Vijñānabhikṣu's Double Reflection Theory of Knowledge in the Yoga System." *Journal of Indian Philosophy* 16: 367–375.

Shankara Rama Shastry, C. 1923. *Kārikāvalī with Muktāvalī, Prabhā, Mañjūṣā, Dinakarīya, Rāmarudrīya, and Gaṅgārāmajaṭīya.* Madras: Sri Balamanorama Press.

Śukla, Pandit Śrī Sūrya Nārāyaṇa, ed. 1936. *The Nyāyamañjarī of Jayanta Bhaṭṭa.* Kashi Sanskrit Series, no. 106 (Nyāya series, no. 15). Benares City: Jaya Krishna Dās Haridās Gupta.

Tailaṅga, Mahāmahopādhyāya Gaṅgādhara Śāstrī, ed. 1895. *The Nyāyamañjarī of Jayanta Bhaṭṭa.* Vizianagram Sanskrit Series, ed. Aurthur Venis, vol. 8, no. 10. Benares: E. J. Lazarus & Co.

Tarkālaṅkār, Mahāmahopādhyāya Candrakānta, ed. 1890. *Nyayakusumanjali prakaranam by Udayanacarya, First Part, Containing the 1st, 2nd and 3rd Stavakas, with the Commentary of Ruchidatta and the Gloss of Vardhamana.* Calcutta: Baptist Mission Press.

Thakur, Anantalal, ed. 1996. *Nyāyavārttikatātparyaṭīkā of Vācaspati Miśra.* New Delhi: Indian Council of Philosophical Research.

——— 1997. *Nyāyabhāṣyavārttika of Bhāradvāja Uddyotakara.* New Delhi: Indian Council of Philosophical Research.

Whicher, Ian. 1998. *The Integrity of the Yoga Darśana: A Reconsideration of Classical Yoga.* SUNY Series in Religious Studies, ed. Harold Coward. Albany: State University of New York Press.

6

Freedom Because of Duty

THE PROBLEM OF AGENCY IN MĪMĀṂSĀ

Elisa Freschi

What is Mīmāṃsā?

Mīmāṃsā (lit. "desire to think," hence "reflection") is one of the six traditionally recognized Brahmanical philosophical systems (*darśana*). It was born out of an ancient tradition of exegesis of sacred texts and keeps as its primary focus the Veda ("knowledge," Indian sacred texts, not accepted as such by Buddhist and Jaina schools). Thus, just as other philosophical systems generally look at Vaiśeṣika for natural philosophy and at Nyāya for logic, so they look at Mīmāṃsā as a reservoir of exegetic rules, making it possibly the main source for the Indian approach to hermeneutics in general. This influence is particularly evident in the case of Vedānta, where Mīmāṃsā rules of interpretation, adjusted to the Vedānta view of the Veda or other sacred texts, have been systematically applied and constitute the background of most theological discussions.

The bulk of the system is based (as usual in India) on a collection of *sūtra* "aphorisms," Jaimini's *Mīmāṃsāsūtra* (henceforth MS), which would be quite obscure without Śabara's *Bhāṣya* ("commentary," henceforth ŚBh). There is no direct evidence for the date of Śabara, other than that he knows some sort of Mahāyāna Buddhism and is aware of a theory of *sphoṭa* (but one that seems more primitive than Bhartṛhari's one[1]), and does not refer to any known author after Patañjali (ca. 2nd cent. BCE). Some centuries later, around the 7th century, Kumārila Bhaṭṭa and Prabhākara Miśra wrote philosophically engaged commentaries on the ŚBh. These

1. Bhartṛhari's date is itself controversial, but scholars tend to agree on the 5th century CE.

commentaries have been again commented upon by later Mīmāṃsā authors (Pārthasārathi, e.g., wrote a line-to-line commentary on Kumārila's *Ślokavārttika* [henceforth ŚV] and Śālikanātha a similar gloss on Prabhākara's *Bṛhatī*). According to the different tenets of these two main thinkers, Mīmāṃsā is traditionally distinguished in two schools, the Bhāṭṭa Mīmāṃsā, which follows Kumārila, and the Prābhākara Mīmāṃsā, which follows Prabhākara. Mīmāṃsā may also be referred to as Pūrva Mīmāṃsā, to distinguish it from Uttara Mīmāṃsā (or Vedānta). For brevity's sake, I shall restrict the use of "Mīmāṃsā" to Pūrva Mīmāṃsā only. A thinker belonging to the Mīmāṃsā school is called Mīmāṃsaka "follower of the Mīmāṃsā."

The main Mīmāṃsā tenets originated out of issues connected with Vedic exegesis. Mīmāṃsā authors following Śabara uphold the default validity of cognition (and, consequently, the general reliability of our cognitions), accept linguistic communication as an instrument of knowledge,[2] and focus on philosophical issues involving action and exhortation. The default validity of cognition (called *svataḥ prāmāṇya* by Kumārila) is the basis of an apologetics of the Veda. Kumārila explains at length that our sense faculties only regard what is (directly or indirectly) perceptible, that common human beings have no independent access to morality (defined as *kārya* "what has to be done"), and that there is no reason to believe that there have ever been exceptional human beings who could have access to it. Thus, the Veda is the only instrument of knowledge regarding what has to be done instead of what there is. Or, from a different perspective, unless we accept the Vedic word, we have no way to access the realm of what has to be done.

To sum up,

1. A cognition is valid unless and until the opposite is proved.
2. Sense-perception (and the other instruments of knowledge, which ultimately rely on perceptual data) only regards what exists (cf. MS 1.1.4: "Sense perception is not a suitable instrument [to know dharma] because it grasps only present things [*vidyamānopalambhanatvāt*]").
3. The Veda, by contrast, regards what ought to be done, and, consequently, it has a completely different scope (in other words, the Veda

2. Linguistic communication as an instrument of knowledge (*śabdapramāṇa*) includes all instances of language as a source of knowledge, thus first and foremost the Veda. Unlike in the Nyāya school and among the Western authors who accept testimony in their epistemology, the Mīmāṃsā *śabdapramāṇa* does not depend on a speaker to be valid.

conveys prescriptions of what ought to be, instead of descriptions of what there is).[3]

4. In this field, the Veda is the only instrument of knowledge (see below, note 4 for the Mīmāṃsaka definition of instrument of knowledge).
5. There is no reason to think that there have ever been human beings whose sense perception was able to grasp dharma.
6. Thus, the Veda remains uncontradicted and, hence, valid.

By the same token, the same principle entails that the Veda is only an instrument of knowledge in its unique field, namely, what has to be done.[4] As for the field of what there is, sense perception and the other instruments of knowledge based on it (inference, analogy, cogent evidence, and absence) are the only valid sources of information. Consequently, unless and until contrary evidence arises, the world is the way we perceive it.

Last, the Mīmāṃsakas' focus on the Brāhmaṇa part of the Veda, which mainly consists of exhortations, and their awareness of the importance of this topic led them to investigate the mechanisms, within language, which make one undertake an action. More importantly for the present topic, it also made Mīmāṃsakas consider the issue of agency from the viewpoint of how one is made into an agent by a (Vedic) injunction.

---

3. The one between description and prescription is a crucial distinction. Both schools of Mīmāṃsā agree that the Veda is an instrument of knowledge insofar as it conveys something *sādhya* "to be realized" and not something *siddha* "already established." In this terminology, the choice of a gerundive (*sādhya*) is revealing. The point is not that the Veda conveys something not yet established, as would have been expressed by a future participle, but, rather, something that could be done or should be done. In other words, the Veda is not a fortune teller. It does not tell one today what will happen tomorrow (or in any other moment of the future). If this were the case, it would be relatively easy (within one's lifespan or with the collaboration of one's children or grandchildren) to prove it right (or wrong) and its precinct of knowledge would no longer be exclusive. This is the approach of Nyāya authors. The Naiyāyika Jayanta Bhaṭṭa gives, in fact, as evidence of the Veda's validity the fact that after having performed a *grāmakāma* sacrifice, his grandfather actually conquered a village. For Mīmāṃsakas, no verification of the Veda through other instruments of knowledge is possible. In fact, the Veda regards something altogether different, which can never fall within the precinct of our other instruments of knowledge.

4. For an instrument of knowledge to be acceptable, a necessary requirement in Mīmāṃsā is that it must grasp something not known before by the other instruments of knowledge. Thus, the Veda is an instrument of knowledge because it is the only source of information as for the *kārya*, whereas sense perception is our fundamental instrument of knowledge about the world. For a discussion of this requirement and its consequences, see Kataoka 2003.

Is there an Analogue of Free Will in Indian Philosophy?

This volume deals with free will, agency, and selfhood. However, a search for a precise synonym of free will in the South Asian context is most probably going to be vain, insofar as "free will" is, in Western culture, a concept loaded with history, especially Christian history, and is thus unlikely to have a direct equivalent in a different cultural and historical context.[5]

Granted that the definition and the semantics of the syntagm "free will" are historically loaded, one can more easily determine the set of questions or scenarios within which it typically arises in Western philosophy and theology. In this way, one may not find a precise synonym, but perhaps a functional equivalent[6] of this term in India. Four leading questions, or issues, are roughly:

1. The problem of the agent's causation: how does the process of volition lead to an action?
2. Moral responsibility vs. determinism
3. The psychological experience of freedom
4. Individual freedom vs. God's omnipotence

We will see ("Epistemological Basis of Compatibilism in Mīmāṃsā") that the psychological experience of freedom, though not thematized, is often the implicit departure point for Mīmāṃsā authors, who describe the

5. In fact, although arguments against or in favor of determinism are very ancient, the usage of "free will" (translating *liberum arbitrium*) is a relatively recent label (possibly 13th century CE) and might seem partly redundant, insofar as its opposite ("bound will," or *servum arbitrium*) entails paradoxical elements (how can one's will be bound? Would not it cease to be a will if it were bound?) and only makes sense within certain perspectives, such as Martin Luther's soteriology. The disproportion of God's omnipotency and an individual's free will has turned, in contemporary philosophy, into that between the evidences of natural scientists, which seem to weigh in favor of determinism (or at least this is their reception among lay people), and the psychological experience of freedom. Classical Indian philosophy, it goes without saying, predates these developments.

6. A functional equivalent is not a synonym, but a concept or institution which is seen as performing the same function that, e.g., the concept of free will is supposed to perform in the Western culture. The concept of a "functional equivalent" has been developed by Raimon Panikkar in the context of his comparative approach to Christian, Buddhist, and "Hindu" terms. As an instance of functional equivalent one might suggest that the authority of the Veda is, for the Prābhākaras, the functional equivalent of the categorical imperative in Immanuel Kant, since both fulfill the same role, namely, providing a fixed term of reference for what ought to be done.

phenomenology of will without taking into account whether it is ontologically legitimate to speak of freedom.[7]

Thus, in the following, the first two issues will be examined in some more detail. Not much space is needed for the fourth, since Mīmāṃsā authors deny any role to God as a philosophical entity. They may subjectively adore a personal God (this is especially true in the case of later authors; see below, "Desireless Actions and Dedication to God"), but tend to be quite strict in denying to him or her the role of ontological foundation of the world or of their system. In other words, God has no place as a justification for the system and there is, consequently, no need to discuss one's freedom in respect to his omnipotence.

Agent's Causation

Epistemological Basis of Compatibilism in Mīmāṃsā

In addition to the general epistemological points brought forward above ("What is Mīmāṃsā?"), it is worth remembering that Mīmāṃsā authors in general favor accounts that mirror common experience. Let us consider, for instance, the cognition one has upon entering a dark room. At first, one hardly sees anything at all, but in a few seconds, one starts distinguishing pieces of furniture, et cetera. Is this later experience still a case of sense perception (*pratyakṣa*)? Buddhist epistemologists deny it this status, since it is the result of conceptual thinking, insofar as one only distinguishes, for instance, a table, insofar as she expects to see one and, hence, conceptually organizes her vague sensory data in order to fit her expectations. By contrast, Mīmāṃsā authors contend that, since one experiences it as a case of sense perception, one could only refute it this status if one has very strong reasons for doing so (*Ślokavārttika* [ŚV], Pratyakṣa 126–127; see Taber 2005: 24, 37). The Buddhist Pramāṇavādins state that the notion of a table

7. This turn has occurred only recently in Western philosophy, where, following P. F. Strawson 1962, Brian Earp (and others) have welcomed the shift of focus on the question "What it is like to feel free?" rather than on the older one "Are we free?": "It is worth saluting this shift in emphasis from the millennia-old, seemingly intractable debates about free will to current philosophical and psychological work on the empirical questions surrounding *belief* in free will, and how it may be influenced by context, motivation, and other factors" (Earp 2011: 25). Johannes Bronkhorst, though not explicitly making this point, discusses Indian conceptions of free will favoring an "experiential" approach, which takes into account our decisions within the process of undertaking actions, independently of whether they are absolutely free (i.e., if determinism is wrong) or not (Bronkhorst 2012). Bronkhorst's choice is probably determined by the similar attitude of Indian authors.

ought to be due to conceptual thinking, since perception has been a priori defined as only grasping the ultimate particular. But this response seems to prefer preservation of the consistency of the Buddhist epistemological system over that of our experience of the world.[8] Similarly, since one obviously feels that one's will has a role in the process of undertaking an action, Mīmāṃsakas do not dispute this. Unlike their Western colleagues, Mīmāṃsā philosophers do not question the degree of freedom of the decisions one experiences as free. They do not, for example, argue for the fact that our experience of freedom might just be an epiphenomenon accompanying the process of undertaking an action[9] or that our experience of freedom might be in fact fake, since our decisions are completely determined by who we are, something which is a priori determined by facts we cannot interfere with, such as genes and early education (cf., by contrast, G. Strawson 1998). The fact that decisions are *experienced* as free is enough for Mīmāṃsā authors to treat them accordingly. Within this framework (which basically takes our intuitions about freedom at face value), one could also just speak of "will," since from the point of view of the way a single action is caused, nothing changes if the general laws of the universe allow freedom or not—one would nonetheless believe one has freely decided to do X. Thus, and given that Mīmāṃsakas accept the laws of karma and the ritual causality linked to *apūrva*, Mīmāṃsakas adopt what Western authors would label a compatibilist stance.[10]

8. This is, e.g., also Kumārila's answer to the Buddhist Pramāṇavādin who contends that it is illogical to claim that a single perceptual act can grasp both the individual and the universal inhering in it. Kumārila maintains that this must be the case, because so runs our experience, ŚV Pratyakṣa 117–118 and 175, see Taber 2005: 41.

9. Conscious will, writes for instance the psychologist Daniel M. Wegner, "is not a direct perception of relation [between thought and action] but rather a feeling based on the causal inference one makes about the data that do become available to consciousness—the thought and the observed act" (Wegner 2002: 67). And, even more clearly: "The experience of will...is the way our minds portray their operations to us, not their actual operation. Because we have thoughts of what we will do, we can develop causal theories relating those thoughts to our actions on the basis of priority, consistency, and exclusivity. We come to think of these prior thoughts as intentions, and we develop the sense that the intentions have causal force even though they are actually just previews of what we may do" (Wegner 2002: 96). Both passages are quoted in Bronkhorst 2012.

10. The theory of karma introduces a loose determinism as a pre-condition for all Indian schools, in that the karmic momentum of the past severely circumscribes our present possibilities. I would suggest that the only option left for the Indian thinkers is some sort of compatibilism. Most Indian authors assume automatically that we are heavily determined by karma, but also that karma is not an inextricable chain. If it were, no liberation would be possible (or, according to how strict one's interpretation of karma is: no liberation would be possible without a divine intervention). Predestination is, accordingly, only admitted by the

The Vedic-Exegetical basis of the Concept of Agenthood in Mīmāṃsā: Consciousness and Ability

Mīmāṃsā authors dealing with agenthood (*kartṛtva*) primarily focus on the sacrificial agent and the lack of energy spent on issues of free will allows for them to discuss technical problems (such as to whom does agenthood pertain in case there are several ritual performers [MS book 3] or several sacrificers [MS book 6]) without having to question the very concept of agenthood. Of chief importance, in this case, is that the agent is the one who consciously undertakes actions. Thus, to be an agent, one needs to be aware of what one is doing. For instance, in a rather late compendium of Mīmāṃsā rules, the *Mīmāṃsānyāyasaṅgraha* (henceforth, MNS), it is said that—although they seem to figure as agents in a certain Vedic statement—"the bones [of a dead sacrificer] are not the agents, either on their own or through an arrangement; only living persons, who are (indirectly) indicated through them (i.e., their bones), are the sacrificers."[11] Consequently, automatic movements are not enough to be an agent, whereas the same movements, if performed on purpose, are the activity of an agent (for the difference between movement and action, see Freschi 2010). An agent may also not perform any movement at all and yet be called an agent, if she[12] instigates another to undertake a certain action (see ŚV, Ātmavāda 75–87). Accordingly, both the person who commissioned the sacrifice (*yajamāna*) and the officiating priest are said to be agents.[13]

---

theistic school of Dvaita Vedānta, founded by Madhva (see Buchta's chapter in this volume. See also, e.g., Zydenbos 1991 and Pandurangi's review of Zydenbos' article, Pandurangi 2012).

11. MNS and MS 10.2.17, The Sanskrit text runs as follows: *asthnāṃ svataḥ saṃvidhānena vākartṛtvāt tallakṣitā jīvanta eva yaṣṭāraḥ*. A parallel passage of Pārthasārathi Miśra's *Śāstradīpikā* has "It is never possible, either directly or through an arrangement, that a dead person is an agent" (*na kathaṃ cid api mṛtasya sākṣād vā saṃvidhānād vā kartṛtvaṃ sambhavati*, quoted in MNS in Mahādeva Vedāntin 2010: 239).

12. The usage of feminine pronouns is not only due to gender-correctness. MS 6.1.13 asserts that women are entitled to perform sacrifices exactly because "the desire for the results is equally [present] [in men and women] (*phalotsāhāviśeṣāt*)."

13. See MNS 3.7.8, which depicts an objection claiming that the sacrificer should perform the sacrifice himself and a reply explaining that he might be an agent also if he has priests officiate instead of him. In Benson's translation (slighly adapted): "[Obj.:] Because the agent and the enjoyer (of the result) are in syntactic agreement in the statement, 'One desirous of heaven should sacrifice (*yajeta*),' because the suffix of the middle voice (i.e., in the verb *yajeta* 'let him sacrifice') is taught by *smṛti* (i.e., grammar) to be employed when the result of an action accrues to the agent, and because the rite, together with its subsidiaries, produces the result, the actions of sacrifice etc., together with their subsidiaries, should (all) be performed

However, being conscious is not enough, insofar as one must also be able to perform the action, even if one does not actually perform it. This requisite has an evident ritual origin, since lame and blind people, or animals, cannot accurately perform the sacrifice and thus they cannot be ritual agents.[14] It is, however, applied also outside the ritual sphere, for instance when Kumārila argues against the possibility of a God by saying that omnipotence (*sarva-kartṛtva*, literally "omni-agenthood") would only be possible for an embodied agent, since without a body, one is not able to undertake all possible actions.[15]

Bhāṭṭa and Prābhākara Mīmāṃsā versus Nyāya

The philosophical school Mīmāṃsā authors mostly engage with is the Nyāya school.[16] Thus, a comparison of Mīmāṃsā and Nyāya views usually throws additional light on both. Naiyāyika authors usually detect a sequence leading from cognition (e.g., of the pleasant flavor of an apple) to volition (*icchā*) to the action (see Dasti's contribution in this volume). Mīmāṃsā authors of the Bhāṭṭa school usually start with desire (e.g., to eat something fresh and healthy), which leads to the effort (*prayatna* or *pravṛtti*, e.g., the fact that one undertakes the action of eating an apple). Prābhākara Mīmāṃsākas complicate the picture by adding the role of injunctions, so that one desires something (e.g., a long life), one consequently identifies oneself as the addressee of a certain injunction (e.g.,

---

by the sacrificer. [Reply:] No. In as much as the action of hiring (the priests) would otherwise be inapplicable, the meaning of the text (*śāstra* [the Veda]) is only that at a rite which has subsidiaries, the condition of being an agent is common to the direct agent and the instigating agent," (MNS in Mahādeva Vedāntin 2010: 446–7, square brackets are mine). The Sanskrit text runs as follows: *svargakāmo yajeteti kartur bhoktuś ca sāmānādhikaraṇyāt, kartṛgāmiphala ātmanepadasmaraṇāt, sāṅgasya phalajanakatvāc ca sāṅgaṃ yāgādi yajamānena kāryam. na. parikrayānyathānupapattyā sāṅge sākṣātprayojakasādhāraṇakartṛtvasyaiva śāstrārthatvāt* (the transcription has been slightly changed to fit the conventions of the present chapter). See also ŚV, Ātmavāda 74. For the underlying Grammatical conception of agenthood, see Cardona's contribution in this volume.

14. The *sūtra* expressing this point is MS 6.1.2. The suggestion regarding animals is found in commentaries and Mīmāṃsā textbooks, such as the MNS on 6.1.2.

15. But—Kumārila's argument continues—the notion of an embodied God is inherently contradictory (how could he be revered by different people in different places simultaneously, if he were linked to a body?). Hence, there is no God. On Kumārila's arguments against the existence of God, see Krasser 1999.

16. On the parallel and contrastive development of the two schools' views on the key issue of linguistic communication/verbal testimony, see Freschi and Graheli 2005.

"if you want to live a long and healthy life, eat apples regularly"), and the fact that one feels enjoined leads to one's effort. Both schools of Mīmāṃsā tend not to focus on whatever happens after the effort, namely, on the actual performance of the action. In this sense (just like pre-contemporary Christian thinkers) they focus on "free *will*" and disregard the actual performance of the action. Accordingly, Mīmāṃsakas would define free will as just the *capacity* to do what one wishes, independent of whether one actually does it or not. What one needs in order to be an agent is just the capacity to fulfill the action (see above, "The Vedic-Exegetical Basis of the Concept of Agenthood in Mīmāṃsā").

As for the cognitive element, a previous cognition is indeed mentioned in the ŚBh as preceding desire and, therefore (like Nyāya, but contra Buddhist Epistemologists), as an evidence of a self enduring from the moment of cognition to that of desire:

> Through desire we grasp a self.
> [Obj.:] How?
> [Reply:] Because desire regards something coveted which has been known before, not something which has not been known. For instance, we do not desire those sweet tree-fruits found north of the Mount Meru (i.e., in an unattainable place), which no human being has ever experienced. Nor does one knower desire what has been grasped by another person.... Therefore we understand that this [desire] has the same agent as that grasping.[17]

Unlike Nyāya authors, however, Mīmāṃsakas do not always stress the connection of desire with cognition. Furthermore, unlike in Nyāya, Prābhākaras deem desire to be important not as the direct antecedent of the action; it is important only insofar as the subject identifies herself as the addressee of a prescription that engages with her specific desire:

> It has been explained that the one who desires heaven, etc., has to be understood as the enjoined one, since duty is connected to himself [in sentences such as: "The one who desires heaven should

17. *icchayā ātmānam upalabhāmahe. katham. upalabdhapūrve hi abhiprete bhavati icchā, nānupalabdhapūrve. yathā merum uttareṇa yāny asmajjātīyair anupalabdhapūrvāṇi svādūni vṛkṣaphalāni, na tāni praty asmākam icchā bhavati,... tenopalambhanena samānakartṛkā sā ity avagacchāmaḥ* (ŚBh ad 1.1.5, pp. 60–72, Frauwallner 1968: 52).

> sacrifice"]. And it has been explained at the beginning of the eleventh [book of the MS] that the desire for heaven is a specification of the enjoined person.[18]

Thus, for Prābhākaras, desire is only an indirect cause of action (the direct cause being the prescription).

To sum up, an agent is identified as one who undertakes an action, who has the capacity to perform it in full, and who does it consciously. At least in ordinary experience (outside it, see "Desireless Actions and Dedication to God"), she also needs to have a goal in view while undertaking the action, as expressed in a well-known verse by Kumārila: "Without a goal, even the fool does not undertake any action."[19] In short, according to Nyāya:

> cognition → desire → effort → action.
> According to the Bhāṭṭa Mīmāṃsā:
> desire → effort.
> According to the Prābhākara Mīmāṃsā:
> desire → recognition of oneself as the addressee by the prescription → effort.

The Role of Commands

A related problem, crossing over the boundaries described in the section "Is There an Analogue of Free Will in Indian Philosophy?", is that of the role of commands in Mīmāṃsā, which can be seen as concerning both the psychological experience of freedom and at the same time the agent of causation. Commands are often neglected in Western philosophy,[20] just like exhortative language is usually neglected in Western linguistics (see Freschi 2008, Freschi forthcoming a). By contrast, they play a fundamental role in Mīmāṃsā (see Freschi 2007, Freschi 2012a, Freschi 2012b).

---

18. *kāryasya svasambandhitayā bodhyaḥ svargakāmādir niyojya iti vyutpāditam. svargakāmanā ca niyojyaviśeṣaṇam ity ekādaśādye vyutpāditam* (VM {{*Vākyārthamātṛkā*}}II ad 23, *Prakaraṇa Pancikā* [PrP] in Śālikanātha Miśra, 1961 p. 440, Sarma 1990: 44). I could not find any passage at the beginning of ŚBh ad MS 11 which could be the one Śālikanātha has in mind. Thus, he probably refers to Prabhākara's lost commentary thereon. See also *Tantrarahasya* [TR] IV, sections 10.2–10.3.2 in Freschi 2012b.

19. *prayojanam anuddiśya na mando 'pi pravartate* | (ŚV, Sambandhākṣepaparihāra 55ab).

20. A notable exception is Bocheński 1974.

A command, Mīmāṃsā authors maintain, only provides for one to feel enjoined (*niyojya*). It does not make one necessarily *perform* what is enjoined by the command. For an action to be undertaken and then performed, one still needs the whole process described above, in the section "Epistemological Basis of Compatibilism in Mīmāṃsā," to take place. However, people who have been trained (see below, "Is There Room for Freedom...?") to hold in high esteem a certain authority (notably, the Veda), will rejoice at undertaking the actions enjoined (see *Tantrarahasya* [TR] §10.11 in Freschi 2012b and cf. the notion of *ātmatuṣṭi*, on which see note 39) and are thus very likely to undertake them. (People for whom a certain text or person is not authoritative simply do not feel enjoined by it.)

Can one still speak of free will if one undertakes an action due to a prescription? Is there room left for free will, after having heard a Vedic command? Before answering, it is worth remembering that prescriptions only regard specific people, that is, the ones identified by the desire mentioned in the prescriptive sentence. Hence, a specific prescription applies to an individual according to what she desires. Does this prescription apply in a deterministic way, according to whom she is? The case of the Śyena (see below, "Immoral Sacrifices Prescribed by the Veda"), where people who desire to harm their enemies are blamed, hints at the opposite. Such people are blamed because one can train oneself to desire something ethically better than harming one's enemy.[21]

Once one has been enjoined to do something, one is thus free not to perform the action enjoined, but one is not free not to feel enjoined. Furthermore, one is free not to desire a certain goal, in which case the corresponding prescription will not apply. This applies to optional goals, such as sons, rain, cattle, villages. In exceptional cases (see below, "Desireless Actions and Dedication to God"), it seems to apply also to the general goal of happiness.[22]

21. One might suggest that these people are blamed for desiring to harm, although they cannot help it, because of their nature. However, this paradoxical interpretation (one can be blamed although one could not have done otherwise) would not suit the legalistic attitude of Mīmāṃṣā (about which, see for instance Lingat 1973). Similar claims have been made only within a strong theistic context (e.g., in some branches of Lutheranism emphasizing responsibility even over things one cannot control, or in the discussion about the paradox of responsibility by Emmanuel Levinas).

22. It is probably worth remembering that this degree of freedom only regards male Brahmins. Śūdras, women, etc. undergo many more constraints due to their own nature,

The agent: same through changes

Naiyāyikas and Vedāntins tend to speculate on how agenthood can refer to an underlying self (called *ātman*). By contrast, Mīmāṃsakas generally discuss empirical agents and refrain from discussions on the *ātman*, unless they need to polemically address their Buddhist opponents (like in the ŚBh passage quoted in "Bhāṭṭa and Prābhākara Mīmāṃsā versus Nyāya"). Even when this is the case, most notably in Kumārila's works, Mīmāṃsakas are keen to prove the existence of something closer to the Western common-sense notion of "subject" or "person" than to that of an underlying *ātman*. This means that what they envision is a subject that is intrinsically an agent, rather than a changeless *ātman* to which agenthood later accrues as an adventitious quality. Kumārila opposes the two aspects with the terms *puruṣa* "person" and *ātman* "self" in ŚV, Ātmavāda 22–29.[23] Kumārila is even ready to go as far as to risk denying the fixedness (*nitya*) of the self, in order to make room for the possibility of its undergoing change:

> It is not prohibited to say that the self is not fixed (*nitya*) |
>
> if what one means is just that it can undergo change (*vikriyā*), [since this does] not [mean] at the same time that it comes to an end ||
>
> If there were an absolute destruction of the [self], there would be destruction of the actions performed and accrual of actions non-performed [hence, there would be a disruption in the relationship between individuals' actions and their corresponding results] |
>
> but this does not occur when [the self] just attains to a different state, just as it does not occur when, in ordinary experience, a child,

---

so that it is possible that they cannot freely train their desires in whatever direction. I am not overstressing this point here because it seems to be rather a sociopolitical issue, inherently linked with the history of classical India, rather than a specific feature of Mīmāṃsā *philosophy*.

23. For a similar terminological opposition in Prābhākara Mīmāṃsā, see Freschi 2012a.

> youth or [adult] [attains to a different age] (and yet he is still the same person) ||[24]

His commentator Pārthasārathi explains further:

> If [you claim that it is] not fixed simply because it changes, then let it be so (as you prefer)! In fact, there is no cessation of one's own nature simply because one changes, since one is recognized[25] [as the same person]. And the [false] dilemma between "different" and "not different" should be in any case avoided by relying on an approach that does not rule out the one or the other.[26]

Thus, argues Kumārila, if one were to deny the continuity of the self, one would be forced to conclude that the actions performed by a certain self would lead to a result enjoyed by another, and this is paradoxical and runs against common sense. By contrast, the self can change, just like a person changes from being a child to an adult. To this a Buddhist Pramāṇavādin might reply that it is precisely the case that the current experiencer is different from the previous doer. Against this view Kumārila replies that the self is both constant and non-constant:

> According to me, even when the person (*nara*) attains to a new stage of pleasure or pain |
>
> it never relinquishes its nature of being conscious, a substance and something which exists ||
>
> ....
>
> Therefore, since both options (i.e., total fixedness and total destruction) have been rejected, a person must be accepted as consisting of

24. *nānityaśabdavācyatvam ātmano vinivāryate | vikriyāmātravācitve na hy ucchedo 'sya tāvatā || syātām atyantanāśe 'sya kṛtanāśākṛtāgamau | na tv avasthāntaraprāptau loke bālayuvādivat* || ŚV, Ātmavāda 22cd-23cd.

25. *Pratyabhijñāna* may refer both to other people recognizing one as the same person and to one's own apperception of oneself as the same person. On *pratyabhijñā* in Mīmāṃsā and in the Śaiva Pratyabhijñā school, see Ratié 2011: 60–62.

26. *yadi vikāramātram anityaṃ tad astu, na hi vikāramātreṇa svarūpocchedo bhavati pratyabhijñānāt. anyānanyavikalpaś ca sarvatrānekāntavādāśrayaṇena parihartavya iti* (*Nyāyaratnākara* ad loc.).

> something that disappears and something that recurs, like gold in an ear-ring, etc. ||[27]

He further adds (possibly against Sāṃkhya and what came to be known as Advaita Vedānta) that there is no intermediate entity that changes instead of the subject:

> Nor is it the case that the condition of being an agent and that of being an experiencer have as substrate the stages of a person | therefore, the agent himself reaches his fruit, because [the condition of being an agent and that of being an experiencer] belong to the [same] person, who is the possessor of [all] stages | ||[28]

Thus, Kumārila's treatment suggests that he presupposes the notion of a subject as a knower and agent, who is able to change through time. At this point, one might argue, what enables one to recognize her as a single subject? To this general problem, the Nyāya and some Vedāntins answer by delineating an underlying character which does not change, namely the *ātman*. This would remain stable, allowing accidental qualities to change without altering it. By contrast, Kumārila seems to imply that no such distinction makes sense, and that, on the contrary, there is no need to postulate a subtle, changeless *ātman*. The subject itself guarantees continuity, though in flux, and one can recognize the continuity as constituted by the changes, just in the case of the subsequent stages of a river. Just like a river or a child becoming an adult, the subject changes continuously, but she is still the same person because each stage is essentially identical with the preceding one (insofar as each stage is conscious, etc.). By contrast, it is not the case that there is a solid "core" (the underlying *ātman*) to which adventitious qualities are added. The agent is, in other words, constant in a dynamic way, through his changes.[29]

---

27. *sukhaduḥkhādyavasthāś ca gacchann api naro mama / caitanyadravyasattādirūpaṃ naiva vimuñcati //...tasmād ubhayahānena vyāvṛttyanugamātmakaḥ / puruṣo 'bhyupagantavyaḥ kuṇḍalādiṣu svarṇavat //* (ŚV, Ātmavāda, 26 and 28)

28. *na ca kartṛtvabhoktṛtve puṃso 'vasthāsamāśrite / tenāvasthāvatas tattvāt karttaivāpnoti tatphalam //* (ŚV, Ātmavāda 29).

29. One is reminded of the Mīmāṃsā concept of *kuṭastha-* and *pravāha-nityatva*. The first one is immutable fixedness, the second one is fixedness through change. The former is the permanence of something that never changes through time, like a mountain (as, rhetorically speaking, compared to the lifespan of a human being). The latter is the permanence of something that changes continuously, but whose later stages are identical with the former

Furthermore, Kumārila states that the subject is knowable through *aham-pratyaya* "notion of an I," that is, the notion one has of oneself when one refers to oneself in sentences like "I am going," or "I am making an effort." This stance has been opposed exactly by the schools who consider the *ātman* to be an underlying entity, which is not to be confused with the empirical "I."[30] The fact that Kumārila and his commentators stick nonetheless to this position most probably means that they implicitly deny any sharp distinction between the empirical "I" and an underlying *ātman.*

The Prābhākaras dispute this view out of a different standpoint, namely because they deem it impossible for the subject to be at the same time the knower and the known entity. They maintain, instead, that the subject is knowable in each act of cognition since all cognitive acts simultaneously throw light on themselves, on their content, and on their knower *qua* knower, that is, as a subject and not as an object (see TR, chapter 1, partly translated in Freschi forthcoming b). Thus, Prābhākaras are even stricter in underscoring the active nature of the subject, though in both sub-schools, one grasps the subject while it is "doing" something. For this reason, other psychic organs (such as *buddhi* or *antaḥkaraṇa*) are hardly mentioned at all (see Freschi forthcoming b).

Although I am not aware of any explicit statement about this in Mīmāṃsā texts, the general attitude of Mīmāṃsā authors is to deal with a complex subject—as opposed to an abstract *ātman*—who acts (knowledge is included in action), desires, and experiences. Its possible subdivisions are irrelevant because the only entity one actually experiences is such a subject (and because, once again, Mīmāṃsakas are more interested in accounting for our experience than in creating an alternative explanation of it).

Exceptions: Ontological Discussions About the Subject

Discussions about the self in itself (i.e., independent of any action it might be performing) are strikingly rare in Mīmāṃsā. So rare that a reader might suspect that Mīmāṃsā authors were not interested in investigating about

ones, like a river, which is always the same notwithstanding the fact that the drops of water composing it change at every second. Similarly, the *ātman* of Nyāya, Vedānta, etc. is stable, whereas the flow of consciousness of Yogācāra Buddhists continuously reproduces itself.

30. For an instance of the kind of problems raised by the identification of "self" and "I," see Watson 2006, chapter 3 (especially pp. 276–277, on the difficulties of the Śaiva Siddhāntin Bhaṭṭa Rāmakaṇṭha when faced with this argument).

an hypothetical *ātman* underlying all experiences, given that their focus was much more on the active subject of all these experiences. Moreover, Mīmāṃsā arguments about the *ātman* as a substance derive much from their Nyāya antecedents and are hardly original (see Freschi 2012a).[31]

In one of the few extensive ontological descriptions of the self I am aware of, found in Śālikanātha Miśra's *Tattvāloka*, the *ātman* is said to be inseparably linked to its attributes (*guṇa*) ([PrP], Śālikanātha Miśra 1961: 343). These arise only when the *ātman* is in contact with the inner organ (*manas*). This, in turn, is only present in a body. Thus, although an *ātman* is theoretically conceivable also without a body, its attributes, the ones through which one grasps it, are only possible within a body. Mīmāṃsakas are quite clear in distinguishing the subject from its external body,[32] nonetheless, the body understood as an organism is said to be the only possible substrate of activities which are typical of the subject, such as being an agent (see above, "The Vedic-Exegetical Basis of the Concept of Agenthood in Mīmāṃsā") and undergoing experience (see PrP, *Tattvāloka*, p. 331). In TR 2 it is said that plants do not have bodies (*śarīra*) because they are not able to experience, and bodies are exactly defined as the instrument for realizing experience (*bhogasādhana*).[33] Thus, the individual subject and the body are most probably mutually dependent: although a bodiless subject might be theoretically conceivable, in ordinary experience subjects can only be such insofar as they are embodied. Conversely, bodies are defined insofar as they enable one to experience reality. Corpses are not bodies and, after death, subjects will probably need some new form of (subtle?) body.

A further case in which the notion of *ātman* is discussed in the *Tattvāloka* is the context of *dharma* and *adharma* ("merit" and "demerit") of each individual. Śālikanātha is absolutely unwavering in his refutation of the Advaita Vedānta notion of a single *ātman*, also because this would

31. For instance, a later Bhāṭṭa author, Gāgābhaṭṭa (16th c.), mentions the *ātman* in connection with his argument that pleasure (*sukha*), cognition (*jñāna*) and desire (*icchā*) do not reside in the body, nor in the sense organ, nor in the inner organ (*manas*). Therefore, they must reside in the *ātman*, which is thus established (*tasmāt tadāśrayatayā ātmasiddhiḥ*) (*Bhāṭṭacintāmaṇi*, Gāgābhaṭṭa 1933: 53–54). Further psychic entities are not mentioned at all and the whole argumentation repeats a Naiyāyika scheme (see the Naiyāyika commentaries on NS {{Nyāya Sūtra}}1.1.10).

32. See the discussion in ŚBh ad 1.1.5, Frauwallner 1968, p. 34, and then PrP Tattvāloka, p. 320 and pp. 327–329.

33. This passage is discussed and partly translated in Freschi 2012a.

lead to a confusion of karmic merit and demerit, along the lines of that discussed by Kumārila above. (PrP, *Tattvāloka*, p. 345).

Causality and Determinism

Is There Determinism in Mīmāṃsā?

From the literal point of view, one's will can only be defined as "free" if there is the chance for it to be bound. Is this possibility ever mentioned by Indian authors? A similar hint may be detected in some theistic schools, where it is said that God alone is free (as reflected in such terms as, e.g., *īśvara* and *svatantra*), whereas we are all bound (i.e., *paratantra* "eteronomous," or like *paśu* "cattle"). Furthermore, one might suggest that the karma might be thought to obstruct one's will (this view can be found in dramas; cf. the attitude of minor characters in the *Abhijñānaśākuntala*, on which see Nuckolls 1987). However, in philosophical schools one does not encounter a deterministic view of karma being explicitly endorsed.[34] Does this non-determinism intersect with the Mīmāṃsā account of causality? Or does the non-determinism only refer to the moral level, whereas accounts of causality regard the ontological realm? In other words, does the Mīmāṃsā account of natural causality interact with its understanding of the agent's causality? Do they represent distinct descriptions of different approaches to reality, which do not need to intersect? Or even: is there a concern with mere physical reality in Mīmāṃsā?

Causality

Within Mīmāṃsā, different accounts of causation intersect. One is the (almost) pan-Indian account based on *karman*. Another is the ritual paradigm, linked to the *apūrva* that one accumulates during rituals. This *apūrva* is a force, "which was not there before" but is generated by the ritual and lasting until its result, thus explaining how the ritual one performs today can be the cause of one's conquering a village at a future time, and so on. It is not clear whether the two paradigms might clash, for instance, if a person whose karma does not allow him to have sons

34. I am very much inclined to think that also the Buddhist Pramāṇavāda (notwithstanding what seems a mechanistic account of causality) is not deterministic, as shown by the fact that Dharmakīrti refutes the possibility of inferring a result from its causes, so that even a karmic cause cannot be said to invariably lead to a certain result.

may perform a Putrakāmeṣṭi (a sacrifice meant for people who want to have sons) and eventually get a son. The topic is not explicitly dealt with, as far as I know, in Mīmāṃsā.[35] The general idea seems to be that both paradigms express rules about the world and that the *karman*-paradigm rules the "natural" world whereas the *apūrva*-one rules the human world. In case of conflict, the *apūrva* paradigm might be thought to override the other just like human causation overrides the tendencies of undirected nature. But it could also be suggested that if one can be the *adhikārin* "responsible agent" for a certain sacrifice (i.e., if one has enough wealth to perform it, and is not disabled in any limb, etc.), this must mean that one's karma has led him or her to this goal.[36]

Is There Room for Freedom Given the Causal Weight of the Past and the Authority of the Veda? Training Desires

The question as to whether deterministic causation (be it through karma or through *apūrva* or both) could ever hinder one's free will seems to be resolved in Mīmāṃsā through a compatibilistic approach. Compatibilism in a nontechnical sense is in fact one of the distinctive marks of Mīmāṃsā authors, who seem to prefer to adhere to our complex experience rather than to reduce it to some basic and consistent principles (see above, "Epistemological Basis of Compatibilism in Mīmāṃsā"). Mīmāṃsā thinkers describe agent causation as a complex process, in which a role is played by the agent's initial desires and a role by the exhortations they receive and accept because of these desires. That the latter role does not rule out the former is taken for granted and is not the object of a separate treatment.

The key point that does not make the laws of karma end up in a rigid determinism probably lies in the fact that Mīmāṃsā authors seem to presuppose that one can influence one's likes and dislikes. Since one can decide, for instance, not to want more cattle, or at least train oneself to want just a little bit more, one will not be liable to the authority of the

---

35. On causality within and outside Mīmāṃsā, see Halbfass 1980.

36. Furthermore, it might be argued that the theory of karma derives from some form of ritual causation or has been influenced by it (evidences for this thesis are discussed in Göhler 2011: 135), and this historical connection could partly explain why the two paradigms seem to be seen as compatible by Mīmāṃsā authors. By contrast, Johannes Bronkhorst and other authors identify the *karman*-theory as a non-Brahmanical addition of foreign (possibly Buddhist) origin (Bronkhorst 1993: 92–95, chapter 9.2.7).

prescriptions concerning the Citrā sacrifice. Similarly, one might infer that the same applies in ordinary experience. Freedom would then, within Mīmāṃsā, be negotiated within the parameters given by the authority of the Veda over a ritual agent (and, more generally, of an adult over a child, a landlord over his servants, etc.) together with the ritual agent's past karma, and these are not incompatible with her freedom to adhere to the Veda (etc.) or not. Of course, adherence is the preferred option, the one that the agent should long for, since the Vedas tell us it is the right decision. This precinct of freedom is stressed by Prabhākara in sentences such as

> The [Vedic] injunction tells one what to do, it does not tell one that one has to do it.[37]

This puzzling statement relies on the distinction between (in Western terms) imperatives and injunctions. The Veda tells one what has to be done (injunction), but it does not make one do it (as an imperative would do). The burden of choosing to do or not to do what has been prescribed by the Veda remains entirely on the addressee of the prescription.

This again leads to a wider question, namely, are we free only when we act independently of desire? Or can one speak of free will also in the case of acts impelled by desire? In other words, is eating while hungry an instance of free will? Or is only the whimsical movement of one's arm with no exact reason a free act? Indian schools such as Mīmāṃsā have naturally acknowledged the role of desire. Accordingly, the implicit answer seems to be that one can train oneself to desire the right things, since desire is part of one's rational behavior and not outside it. For Mīmāṃsā authors, desire is part of the natural world, which is governed by the laws of karma and restricted by the Vedic injunctions and prohibitions. And karma, most probably, inclines one toward doing something, but does not completely determine one to do it. An evidence of this attitude is found in discussions concerning the *parisaṅkhyāvidhi, pañca pañcanakhā bhaktavyāḥ* "the five five-nailed ones are to be eaten." The *parisaṅkhyāvidhi* is a prescription restricting something else. In this case, Mīmāṃsā authors explain, it restricts one's natural appetite—which would be directed to everything—to these five animals only:

---

37. *kartavyatāviṣayo niyogaḥ. na punaḥ kartavyatām āha* (Bṛhatī, I/38, 8-9. For an insightful discussion of this topic, see Yoshimizu 1997.)

> Here it is not the eating which is prescribed, since this course of action is already determined by one's desire (*rāga*) for it, and an activity produced by a desire (*rāga*), which has been initiated prior [to the injunction], cannot be prescribed (since prescriptions only provide knowledge of something previously unknown).[38]

This means that one naturally desires eating flesh, but that an injunction can make one restrict one's natural appetites. This implies that one has enough freedom to operate on one's desires and restrict them.

A further evidence is the concept of *ātmatuṣṭi* (see note 39), according to which one can train his desires and emotions so that one ends up rejoicing when a Vedic command is fulfilled and regretting when this does not happen.

Thus, if we try to get a coherent picture out of these elements, karma lies at the origin of the natural desires one experiences. Vedic prescriptions and prohibitions rule them and if one is addressed by a Vedic prescription or prohibition, one cannot but feel enjoined by them. Consequently, one will restrict one's natural desire to only the things which are permitted by the Veda. Here lies the precinct of application of one's free will—one's response to the Vedic word. In sum, free will in this view is not tantamount to one's whims, but rather to one's faculty to consent or dissent to a Vedic injunction.

Source of Ethics

Mīmāṃsā authors uphold the externality of moral authority. There is no inner source for morality, they maintain, because all human instruments of knowledge ultimately rest on sense perception, and sense perception cannot fill in the gap between the is and the ought (in Sanskrit terms, between what is *siddha* "already established" and what is *sādhya* "to be brought about"). The only source for morality is, hence, the Veda as instrument of knowledge. The Veda is the only way to know about what one ought to do. Other sources, such as *smṛti* ("traditional texts," e.g., the

38. *atra ca na bhakṣaṇaṃ vidheyam; rāgataḥ prāptatvāt. nāpi rāgaprāpteḥ pūrvapravṛttyā vidheyatvam* (Śambhubhaṭṭa's *Prabhāvalī* on Khaṇḍadeva's *Bhāṭṭadīpikā* 1.2.4, Khaṇḍadeva 1987: 33). The text was written in the mid-17th century. On the requirement for Vedic prescriptions to cause one to know something new, see above, fn. 4. The technical meaning of *prāp-* is out of the focus of this chapter and has, thus, been disregarded.

Mānavadharmaśāstra and the other Dharmaśāstras) and *sadācāra* ("behavior of good people") are valid insofar as they are based on the Veda. People who are versed in the Veda and who have studied the Mīmāṃsā rules to interpret it may end up developing an inner feeling for what ought to be done, as suggested in the Dharmaśāstras[39] and in Kumārila's TV,[40] but this is nothing other than an analogical extension of the hermeneutic rules they learnt and hence not an independent source.

Desireless Actions and Dedication to God

The Veda is an instrument of knowledge about what one ought to do, because it *prescribes* something to be done instead of *describing* a state of affairs. It is thus a collection of commands. The Vedic commands are of two sorts. On the one hand there are commands that regard compulsory sacrifices, which are to be performed regularly throughout one's life (*nitya*) or on certain occasions (*naimittika*), such as the birth of a son. On the other hand, there are optional sacrifices (*kāmya*), dependent on one's wishes. Thus, one needs to perform an Agnihotra every day, whereas a Citrā is only performed if one wants cattle. In the Mīmāṃsā classification, however, all sorts of sacrifices relate to one's desires. The first group applies throughout one's life because such sacrifices identify as the person who has to perform them "the one who desires happiness," and the desire for happiness accompanies one throughout one's life.[41]

The above has been concerned with the "pure" (i.e., Vedic-exegetical) Mīmāṃsā core. However, Kumārila[42] and most later Mīmāṃsakas seem

39. See, e.g., *Mānavadharmaśāstra* 2.6: *vedo 'khilo dharmamūlaṃ smṛtiśīle ca tadvidām / ācāraś caiva sādhūnām ātmanas tuṣṭir eva ca* Olivelle translates as follows: "The root of the Law is the entire Veda; the tradition and practice of those who know the Veda; the conduct of good people; and what is pleasing to oneself" (Olivelle 2004), but the context and the position of *sādhūnāṃ* suggests that also "what is pleasing to oneself" only regards good people who know the Veda.

40. TV ad 1. 3.7, *passim*. On the topic of *ātmatuṣṭi*, the whole Davis 2007 is insightful and intriguing. See also Francavilla 2006: 165–176, which dissents with Davis as for the importance of *ātmatuṣṭi*, but agrees as for its being dependent on the authority of the Veda.

41. On the equivalence of *svarga* and happiness, see ŚBh ad 6.1.2. The goal of happiness identifies the one who has to perform the sacrifice, and the MS and the ŚBh explain that happiness is everyone's goal, see MS 4.3.15.

42. See Mesquita 1994, whose thesis is discussed in Taber 2007.

to admit that it is theoretically possible to extirpate one's desires. At that point, one would no longer be under the influence of Vedic and non-Vedic commands, since commands depend on the identification of a desire of the person who should fulfill them (see Freschi 2007). In this case, one would be left with the possibility to act focusing only on the actions, since one would no longer long for their results. This could be labeled freedom, although it is a very abstract degree of freedom, in which no room for acting whimsically is left. Later Mīmāṃsakas tend to interpret this stage as that in which one dedicates to God all actions, so that one no longer performs them for the sake of their results, but rather for the supreme purpose of pleasing God (see the closing verses of Āpadeva's *Mīmāṃsānyāyaprakāśa* [MNP], in Edgerton 1929). This would be a relative freedom (freedom from the common desires, but dependence on a higher-order desire).[43] It is difficult to establish whether the acceptance of a desire-free action is a move of Kumārila, influenced by Vedānta (as maintained in Mesquita 1994), or whether this possibility has always been held in account by Mīmāṃsā authors. This issue has to do with the relation between Mīmāṃsā and Vedānta and with the problem of their historical connection. It might in fact be suggested (see Parpola 1981 and Parpola 1994) that the fact that these two schools were known as Pūrva- and Uttara-Mīmāṃsā (see above, "What is Mīmāṃsā?") points to a remote time in which their basic texts formed a single *sūtra*, initially commented upon as a whole and only later parted into two. If this were the case, then one could easily imagine that the "Vedānta development" was in fact already part of the background of Mīmāṃsā authors, who however left its discussion to commentators on the *Brahmasūtra* (against the view of a single *Mīmāṃsāsūtra*, later split into *Pūrva-Mīmāṃsāsūtra* and *Uttara-Mīmāṃsāsūtra*, see Bronkhorst 2007).

Immoral Sacrifices Prescribed by the Veda

Given that the Veda is the only source of morality, one might expect the Veda to prescribe only rituals having objectives that are clearly acceptable, such as sons or cattle, and that it would avoid prescribing rituals whose results run against the very Vedic rules. In fact, since the Veda (see above, "Source of Ethics") is the only source of ethical norms, how can

43. The issue of theism in later Mīmāṃsā is quite complicated. Suffice it here to say that after the 13th century and especially in South India, Mīmāṃsā moves very close to Śrī Vaiṣṇavism (for further references, see Freschi 2012b, chapter 1.1.2).

it prescribe one to do something which it prohibits elsewhere? How can one decide that what is prescribed by the Veda should not be performed, unless through another Vedic prescription that tells us not to perform it? And would not this second Vedic prescription invalidate the first? And if so, would not this mean that the Veda as a whole is no longer absolutely valid? Furthermore, the fact that undertaking a ritual actually prescribed results in a punishment leads one to question the origin of morality. If the Veda is the only source of morality, how could it be that something it prescribes is immoral?

The problem is dealt with in regard to the Śyena sacrifice, which is performed in order to destroy one's enemy (and about which, see Kataoka 2012). Now, if one performs this sacrifice, one will obtain the annihilation of one's enemy, while at the same time being guilty of violence, since one would have transgressed another Vedic command, namely "one should not perform violence on any living being" (*na hiṃsyāt sarvā bhūtāni*[44]). Thus, that person will end up in hell. So far, the *apūrva*-causality seems to work in a rather mechanical way. If the slaughter of her enemy is so important that she is ready to endure the consequences, she might perform it (and literally go to hell as a consequence). Basically, the Veda tells her how to obtain the slaughter of her enemy; it is up to her whether to perform it or not. In each case, she will endure the corresponding consequence. Thus, the Veda does not enjoin one to perform the Śyena (see Prabhākara's quotation in "Is There Room for Freedom...?"). It only tells one *how* to perform it, in the event that one had freely chosen to perform an illicit (*qua* violent) act. In fact, only "one who is desirous to harm [one's enemy]" (*hiṃsākāma*) is a suitable candidate for the performance of the sacrifice. She alone would be the addressee of the prescription and have the status (*adhikāra*) required to perform the sacrifice. However, the condition of being desirous to harm one's enemy is itself forbidden by the prohibition to perform any sort of violence. Consequently, and in accordance with the principle expressed in the section "Is There Room for Freedom...?", one might speculate that one's general appetite (i.e., unspecified desire) to harm one's enemies falls within the restrictive power of the prohibition to perform any violence, so that one ought never get to the stage of becoming "one who desires to harm one's enemy." This also means that if one

44. Like in the case of another well-known Mīmāṃsā "quotation" from the Veda, i.e., *darśapūrṇamāsābhyāṃ svargakāmo yajeta*, the passage is not found in this form in any extant Vedic text of my knowledge.

becomes one who desires to harm one's enemy, one has already violated a Vedic prohibition and is therefore to be ethically blamed.

Conclusion

The basic Mīmāṃsā approach to the issue of agency and free will takes the psychological experience of one's freedom of action to be valid, given the default validity of ordinary experience, and, further, since the *karman-* or *apūrva*-based causalities are not found to eliminate all precincts of the application of free will. In fact, human beings are led to act, according to Bhāṭṭa authors, by their desires, and, according to Prābhākara authors, by injunctions that identify their addressees through their desires. Consequently, their precinct of free will seems exactly to lie in their faculty to train their desires. Even from the point of view of the Prābhākaras, who stress the role of Vedic commands, free will is presupposed by the claim that, although the Veda *tells* one what to do, it does not *make* one do it.

Agency does not accrue to an underlying *ātman*, but rather seems to constitute one of the subject's essential characters. Accordingly, the agent subject is said not to be immutable and does instead change through time.

References

Abhyankar, Kashinath Vasudev and Ganesasastri Ambadasa Jośī, eds. 1971–1980. *Śrīmajjaiminipraṇite Mīmāṃsādarśane: Mīmāṃsakakaṇṭhīrava-Kumārilabhaṭṭapraṇita-Tantravārtikasahita-Śābarabhāṣyopetaḥ*. 2nd ed. Ānandāśramasaṃskṛtagranthāvaliḥ 97. Poona: Anandasrama. (1st ed., 1929–1934).

Bocheński, J. M. 1974. *Was ist Autorität?* Freiburg: Herder.

Bronkhorst, Johannes. 1993. *The Two Traditions of Meditation in Ancient India*. 2nd ed. Delhi: Motilal Banarsidass.

———. 2007. "Vedānta as Mīmāṃsā." In *Mīmāṃsā and Vedānta: Interaction and Continuity*, ed. Johannes Bronkhorst, 1–91. Delhi: Motilal Banarsidass.

———. 2012. "Free Will and Indian Philosophy." *Antiquorum Philosophia* 6: 19–29.

Davis, Donald R., Jr. 2007. "On Ātmatuṣṭi as a Source of Dharma." *Journal of the American Oriental Society* 127.3: 279–296.

Earp, Brian D. 2011. "Do I Have More Free Will Than You Do? An Unexpected Asymmetry in Intuitions about Personal Freedom." *New School Psychology Bulletin* 9.1: 21–27.

Edgerton, Franklin. 1929. *Mīmāṃsānyāyaprakāśa of Āpadeva*. Introduction, Sanskrit Text, English Translation and Notes. New Haven, CT: Yale University Press.

Francavilla, Domenico. 2006. *The Roots of Hindu Jurisprudence: Sources of Dharma and Interpretation in Mīmāṃsā and Dharmaśāstra*. Vol. 7. Corpus Iuris Sanscriticum. Torino: Cesmeo.

Frauwallner, Erich, ed. 1968. *Materialien zur ältesten Erkenntnislehre der Karmamīmāṃsā*. Kommission für Sprachen und Kulturen Süd- und Ostasiens; Philosophisch-Historische Klasse; Sitzungsberichte. Wien: Österreichische Akademie der Wissenschaften.

Freschi, Elisa. 2007. "Desidero Ergo Sum: The Subject as the Desirous One in Mīmāṃsā." *Rivista di Studi Orientali* 80: 51–61.

———. 2008. "How Do Exhortative Expressions Work? Bhāvanā and Vidhi in Rāmānujācārya and other Mīmāṃsā Authors." *Rivista di Studi Orientali* 81: 149–185.

———. 2010. "Indian Philosophers." In *A Companion to the Philosophy of Action*, ed. Timothy O'Connor and Constantine Sandis, 419–428. Hoboken, NJ: Wiley-Blackwell.

———. 2012a. "Action, Desire and Subjectivity in Prābhākara Mīmāṃsā." In *Self and No-Self: Hindu and Buddhist Ideas in Dialogue*, ed. Irina Kuznetsova, Jonardon Ganeri, and Chakravarti Ram-Prasad. Dialogues in South Asian Traditions: Religion, Philosophy, Literature, and History. Farnham: Ashgate.

———. 2012b. *Duty, Language and Exegesis in Prābhākara Mīmāṃsā: Including an Edition and Translation of Rāmānujācārya's* Tantrarahasya, Śāstraprameya-pariccheda. Jerusalem Studies on the History of Religion 17. Leiden: Brill.

———. (forthcoming a). "The Study of Indian Linguistics. Prescriptive Function of Language in the *Nyāyamañjarī* and in the Speech Act Theory." In *Open Pages in South Asian Studies. Proceedings of the Workshop held in Moscow.27–28th April 2011*, ed. Alexander A. Stolyarov. Leiden.

———. (forthcoming b). "Does the Subject Have Desires? The Prābhākara Mīmāṃsā Answer." In *Pushpika: Tracing Ancient India Through Text and Traditions. Contributions to Current Research in Indology. Number 2*, ed. Giovanni Ciotti, Paolo Visigalli, and Alastair Gornall. Oxford: Oxbow Books Press.

———, and Alessandro Graheli. 2005. "Bhāṭṭamīmāṃsā and Nyāya on Veda and Tradition." In *Boundaries, Dynamics and Construction of Traditions in South Asia*, ed. Federico Squarcini, 287–323. Kykéion Studies and Texts I. 3. Firenze and New Delhi: Firenze University Press and Munshiram Manoharlal.

Gāgābhaṭṭa. 1933. *Bhāṭṭacintāmaṇi*. Ed. Sūryanārāyaṇa Śarmaśukla. Chowkhamba Sanskrit Series 25 and 27. Benares: Vidya Vilas Press.

Göhler, Lars. 2011. *Reflexion und Ritual in der Pūrvamīmāṃsā. Studie zur frühen Geschichte der Philosophie in Indien*. Beiträge zur Indologie 44. Wiesbaden: Harrassowitz.

Halbfass, Wilhelm. 1980. "Karma, Apūrva and 'Natural' Causes: Observations on the Growth and Limits of the Theory of Saṃsāra." In *Karma and Rebirth in*

Classical Indian Traditions, ed. Wendy Doniger O'Flaherty. Berkeley: University of California Press.

Kataoka, Kei. 2003. "The Mīmāṃsā Definition of Pramāṇa as a Source of New Information." *Journal of Indian Philosophy* 31: 89–103.

———. 2012. "Is Killing Bad? Dispute on Animal Sacrifices between Buddhism and Mīmāṃsā." In *Samskṛta-sādhutā "Goodness of Sanskrit." Studies in Honour of Professor Ashok N. Aklujkar*, ed. Yohichika Honda, Michele Desmarais, and Chikafumi Watanabe, 349–367. New Delhi: D.K. Printworld.

Khaṇḍadeva. 1987. *Bhāṭṭadīpikā, with the Commentary Prabhāvalī of Śambhu Bhaṭṭa*. Ed. Ananta Krishna Sastri. 2nd ed. Sri Garib Dass Oriental Series, no. 50. Delhi: Sri Satguru. (1st ed., Bombay, 1921–22).

Krasser, Helmut. 1999. "Dharmakīrti's and Kumārila's Refutations of the Existence of God: A Consideration of Their Chronological Order." In *Dharmakīrti's Thought and Its Impact on Indian and Tibetan Philosophy*, ed. Shoryu Katsura, 215–223. Wien: Verlag der Österreichischen Akademie der Wissenschaften.

Kumārila and Pārthasārathi. 1978. *Ślokavārttika of Śrī Kumārila Bhaṭṭa with the Commentary Nyāyaratnākara of Śrī Pārthasārathi Miśra*. Ed. Dvārikādāsa Śāstrī. Prāchyabhārati Series 10. Varanasi.

Lingat, Robert. 1973. *The Classical Law of India (Translated with Additions by J. Duncan M. Derrett)*. Berkeley: University of California Press.

Mahādeva Vedāntin. 2010. *Mīmāṃsānyāyasaṅgraha: A Compendium on the Principles of Mīmāṃsā*. Ed., trans. James Benson. Wiesbaden: Harrassowitz.

Mesquita, Roque. 1994. "Die Idee der Erlösung bei Kumārilabhaṭṭa." *Wiener Zeitschrift für die Kunde Süd-Asiens* 38: 451–484.

Nuckolls, Charles W. 1987. "Causal Thinking in Śākuntala: A Schema-Theoretic Approach to a Classical Sanskrit Drama." *Philosophy East and West* 37.3: 286–305.

Olivelle, Patrick. 2004. *Manu's Code of Law: A Critical Edition and Translation of the Mānava Dharmaśāstra*. Oxford: Oxford University Press.

Pandurangi, Veeranarayana. 2012. "A Review of 'Jaina Background of Dvaita Vedānta' by Robert Zydenbos." *Saṃskṛta Vimarśaḥ* 6 (Special issue released during the WSC, New Delhi): 280–318.

Parpola, Asko. 1981. "On the Formation of the Mīmāṃsā and the Problems Concerning Jaimini with Particular Reference to the Teacher Quotations and the Vedic Schools (Part I)." *Wiener Zeitschrift für die Kunde Südasiens* 25: 145–177.

———. 1994. "On the Formation of the Mīmāṃsā and the Problems Concerning Jaimini with Particular Reference to the Teacher Quotations and the Vedic Schools (Part II)." *Wiener Zeitschrift für die Kunde Südasiens* 38: 293–308.

Prabhākara. 1934–1967. *Bṛhatī ad Śābarabhāṣya*. Ed. S. K. Rāmanātha Śāstrī and S. Subrahmanya Sastri. Madras: University of Madras.

Rāmānujācārya. 1956. *Tantrarahasya. A Primer of Prābhākara Mīmāṃsā, Critically Ed. with Introduction and Appendices*. Ed. K. S. Rāmaswami Śāstri Śiromaṇi. Baroda: Oriental Institute.

Ratié, Isabelle. 2011. *Le soi et l'autre: identité, différence et altérité dans la philosophie de la Pratyabhijñā*. Jerusalem Studies in Religion and Culture 13. Leiden: Brill.

Śālikanātha Miśra. 1961. *Prakaraṇa Pañcikā of Śālikanātha Miśra with the Nyāya-Siddhi of Jaipuri Nārāyaṇa Bhaṭṭa*. Ed. A. Subrahmanya Sastri. Darśana Series 4. Benares: Benares Hindu University.

Sarma, Rajendra Nath. 1990. *Verbal Knowledge in Prābhākara Mīmāṃsā*. Sri Garib Das Oriental Series 60. Including the text of Śālikanātha Miśra's *Vākyārthamātṛkā*. Delhi: Sri Satguru.

Strawson, Galen. 1998. "Free Will." *Routledge Encyclopedia of Philosophy*, ed. Edward Craig, 743–753. Vol. 3. London: Routledge.

Strawson, Peter Frederick. 1962. "Freedom and Resentment." *Proceedings of the British Academy* 48: 1–25.

Taber, John. 2005. *A Hindu Critique of Buddhist Epistemology: Kumārila on Perception: The "Determinatin of Perception" Chapter of Kumārila Bhaṭṭa's Ślokavārttika/translation and commentary*. RoutledgeCurzon Hindu Studies Series. London: RoutledgeCurzon.

———. 2007. "Kumārila the Vedāntin?" In *Vedānta and Mīmāṃsā: Interaction and Continuity*, ed. Johannes Bronkhorst. Delhi: Motilal Banarsidass.

Uṃveka Bhaṭṭa. 1971. *Ślokavārttikavyākhyatātparyaṭīkā*. Ed. S. K. Rāmanātha Śāstrī, rev. by K. Kunjunni Raja and R. Thangaswamy. 2nd rev. ed. University Sanskrit Series 13. Madras.

Watson, Alex. 2006. *The Self's Awareness of Itself: Bhaṭṭa Rāmakaṇṭha's Arguments against the Buddhist Doctrine of No-Self*. Wien: De Nobili.

Wegner, Daniel M. 2002. *The Illusion of Conscious Will*. Cambridge, MA: The MIT Press.

Yoshimizu, Kiyotaka. 1997. *Der "Organismus" des urheberlosen Veda: eine Studie der Niyoga-Lehre Prabhākaras mit ausgewählten Übersetzungen der Bṛhatī*.Wien: De Nobili.

Zydenbos, Robert. 1991. "On the Jaina background of Dvaita Vedānta." *Journal of Indian Philosophy* 19: 249–271.

7

Just Another Word for Nothing Left to Lose

FREEDOM, AGENCY AND ETHICS FOR MĀDHYAMIKAS

Jay L. Garfield

Freedom of the Will and Theodicy

The problem of the freedom of the will appears to the modern Western sensibility as an obvious and natural problem, and is often taken to be one of those perennial philosophical questions that arises simply upon reflection. Nonetheless, the problem as we know it in the Western philosophical and religious tradition is in fact a very specific cultural and religious artifact. For this problem to arise at all, one needs to have a *will*, and a sense of the possibility of uncaused *agent causation*, as well as a thesis of causal determinism. Only with these three ideas in place can one ask the question whether that will is subject to a universal determinism or is capable of causing acts without its own activity being caused.

Of course once one poses that question, one can immediately perform the intellectual rope trick that makes philosophy possible, and ask not only whether the will is free in this sense, but also ascend to the question of whether the freedom of the will is or is not compatible with determinism, if so, how, and if not, whether one opts for the libertarian or determinist view. And of course this set of questions has engendered a massive literature in the West, remaining active topics of philosophical research to the present day. (See Pereboom 2009, Watson 2005, Kane 2005, Campbell et al. 2004 for surveys of these debates, and Meyers 2010 for a superb

Thanks to Edwin Bryant, John Connolly, Matthew Dasti, Bronwyn Finnigan, and Karin Meyers for very helpful comments on earlier drafts of this paper.

discussion of this meta-issue.) It is not, however, my purpose to survey that literature or to weigh in on any of these questions in this essay.

It is important to note that none of these problems have ever been raised in the Buddhist philosophical tradition. (But see Gómez 1975, Harvey 2007, and Rhys Davids 1898 for contrary views.) That is not because Buddhist philosophers were just too dumb to think about it, nor because they had somehow solved it. It is because the presuppositions that raise these questions are not satisfied by the Buddhist tradition. Consideration of that fact may lead us to the kind of hermeneutic distance that will allow us first to see the problem as peculiar, and then to set it aside in favor of more productive lines of inquiry. I hope that this is indeed one of those cases where attention to another philosophical tradition can indeed help us to advance our own. The plan, then, is first to show why the problem of the freedom of the will as it is posed in the Christian context, and as it comes to be addressed in much of the Western philosophical tradition, cannot arise in the context of Madhyamaka Buddhist philosophy, and then to show how concerns related to those that motivate that problem arise and are addressed within that tradition.

Let us begin with the idea of *will*. It is ubiquitous in the West, not only in technical philosophical and religious discourse, but in the law and popular culture. "Did you perform this act of your own free will?" we might ask when deciding whether to blame or to excuse an apparent wrongdoer, or we might have to answer when having a document notarized. We explain our inability to stop smoking or to lose weight through appeal to weakness of will (a topic that enjoys its own vast literature. See Hoffman 2008 and Stroud 2008 for surveys.) Even contemporary cognitive science is concerned to locate and understand the will, or at least our conception thereof (Dennett 1984, 1992, 2003, Libet 1985, 1999, Mele 1995, 2001, 2010).

But what is this thing called "will"? We do not come by the idea that we have wills through observation, either of ourselves or of others. Just try introspecting and finding a will. What does it feel like? Nor is it the theoretical posit of any science. Nor has it always been the case in Western intellectual history that persons took themselves to have wills—faculties of action per se. (Despite the infelicitous but perniciously and ubiquitously influential translation of *akrasia* as *weakness of will,* Aristotle never identified a faculty of will.)

The will as we (seem to) know it is in fact the legacy of St. Augustine, and of his struggle to solve the theodicy problem raised by the Fall of Adam and Eve in Eden. If God is indeed the cause of all things and is indeed omniscient, then the primal fall from grace would appear to have been caused by God, in which case God would not appear to be very nice, particularly since he then punished not only Adam and Eve, but also the entire human race for the affair. The only way to preserve God's omnibenevolence, saw Augustine, was to absolve him from the causation of Adam's and Eve's disobedience. And that required them to be the original authors of their own actions. Augustine posited a faculty of producing uncaused (free) action in order to show how *that* could be the case and argued that only action produced by that faculty (free action) is morally praiseworthy or blameworthy; that all other behavior, in virtue of being heteronomously caused, is mere natural event. (See Stump 2001 for an excellent introduction.)[1]

This linkage of morality and indeed even personhood to freedom in this rich sense ramifies through St. Thomas and eventually to Kant. It grounds the political and legal theory of the enlightenment to which we are heirs, and infuses our high and popular culture with a presupposition of the reality of the will and its freedom. It also leads us to take for granted the idea that we are only persons in the full sense to the degree that we are free, and that moral responsibility is possible only in the context of this freedom. (See Frankfurt 1969, 1971.)

Now to be sure, there are many who take the story of Eden and the Fall seriously and who may be sanguine about the foundation of this aspect of our culture and the nest of philosophical problems to which it gives rise on this curious theological myth. But for those who would prefer a secular ground for culture and a secular premise for philosophical inquiry, this genealogy of metaphysics might suggest that it is time for a reassessment of this way of seeing things. In any case, this much is clear: If there are

---

1. While this is not an essay primarily about the views of Augustine, it is useful to introduce a bit of nuance here, as Augustine's views seem to have undergone some evolution, and he has been cited both as the father of libertarianism (Plantinga 1967; Berthold 1981) and as a determinist and compatibilist (Baker 2003). And indeed both attributions are correct. In *On Free Will* Augustine clearly defends a very explicitly libertarian account according to which the will (*voluntas*) is entirely under our control, and that free will (*liberum aritrium*) is a necessary condition of the justice of divine reward and punishment. (See Berthold 1981: 528–529.) Plantinga 1967 defends the necessity of this libertarian doctrine for the solution of the problem of theodicy. But as Baker 2003 points out, in his refutation of the Pelagians in *On Nature and Grace*, Augustine defends a universal Divine determinism alongside a doctrine of freedom, arguing that freedom in the relevant sense and universal determinism are compatible, and that all of our free choices are in fact also determined. (Further complications arise when we ask whether, even if Adam was completely free, post-Fall humans are. But this really takes us too far afield in an essay on Madhyamaka!)

reasons to worry about the freedom of the will, and in particular, reasons to ask what Mādhyamikas should think about freedom and determinism, Christian theodicy is not the main issue.

Why Worry about Freedom and Determinism?

But why do we worry about freedom and determinism in the first place? Surely not because of a massive cultural obsession with theodicy. The motivations for most modern thought about this network of questions are twofold. The first motivation is metaphysical—a concern to understand the nature of agency and of personhood more broadly, and the distinction between what we as agents *do* and what merely *happens*. The second—closely connected—is ethical and legal. We must draw a distinction between those actions for which we are morally or legally responsible and those events for which, even though we may be causally implicated, we are not responsible. This distinction is often taken to be that between free acts of will and caused behavior. Determinism is taken to be a threat on both fronts. All of this is well-worn territory, and none of my reflections are at all original. It is, however, useful to remind ourselves of what is at stake in this discussion before turning directly to the Madhyamaka tradition.

Let us consider the metaphysical problem first. When we take ourselves to be personal agents, we take ourselves to be capable of choosing and directing our own actions, to make choices between alternative possibilities. We take ourselves to act for *reasons,* and reject the notion that our behavior is simply *caused* by external events.[2] This authority over our actions is what makes us who we are, and what qualifies us in the law to be taken seriously as citizens. But choice, one might think, requires that the alternatives between which we choose are each open to us, and that deliberation is an effective consideration of reasons for each and not a

2. We must be careful about the sense of "external" here. To be external in the relevant sense is to be external to the *self,* or the agent, not necessarily to the *body*. So, for instance, being caused to do something by a device implanted in the brain, or even by mental illness, would count for these purposes as being externally, and hence *heteronomously*, determined. This distinction is often put in terms of the distinction between being determined by *reasons* and being determined by *causes.* So, one might think, following Locke and Kant, that an action is free to the degree that we can provide reasons for it, and that it is for those reasons that we undertake it. An action is unfree to the extent that it is merely caused, and that its causes are not reasons that we could give for so acting. We will see this distinction play out in the discussion below, and we will see that—suitably transformed—it re-emerges in the Madhyamaka account of moral responsibility we will develop at the end of this essay.

sham to which we are spectators (Frankfurt 1971) If, and only if, multiple alternatives are genuine possibilities, can one choose action, instead of performing causally determined behavior. So, this line of reasoning continues, genuine agency requires an exemption from determinism; while acts of will may have effects, they cannot have sufficient causes, as sufficient causes in this sense would place the explanation of behavior outside of the agent him/herself.[3]

Similar considerations are advanced in defense of moral responsibility. The locus classicus, of course is Kant's *Foundations of the Metaphysics of Morals.* Kant argues that freedom is a transcendental condition of moral responsibility and that in order to think of ourselves and others as morally responsible agents, we must regard ourselves as free. Of course he also argues that we can never *know* that we are free, but that also amounts to the claim that we can never *know*, though we must *assume*, that we are morally responsible, and hence that we must *assume* that we are free. That freedom is again parsed as the determination of the will not by *causes*, but by *reasons.*

This line of argument has proven to be both intuitively plausible and influential. If someone acts in a morally or legally blameworthy way, and we can find no exculpatory external cause for her action, we take her action to have been free and hold her responsible. If she is successfully able to defend herself by appealing, say to mental illness or a horrible childhood, and if we agree that those are the *causes* of her behavior, we absolve her of blame, arguing that she was causally compelled and not free to act. Determination by causes hence undermines moral agency; if ethical assessment is possible, we require that agent causation be exempted from determinism. The Kantian transcendental argument is easily joined with the premise that ethical and legal assessment must be possible to yield the conclusion that the will is free.

There is, of course, an older strand of analysis of freedom or choice defended by Locke, with ancestry in Aristotle. On this view, for an act to be free (Locke) or chosen (Aristotle) is for the cause of the act to be the intention or desire of the agent, not for the salient cause to be *external* to the agent. This is an analysis of freedom in terms of absence of constraint. The advantage of this approach over Kant's is that instead of exempting

3. So, for instance, Plantinga (1967: 134) writes, "It seems to me altogether paradoxical to say of anyone all of whose action are causally determined that on some occasions he acts freely."

the will from causation it ties responsibility and agency to the appropriate kinds of causes that are operative. The idea is that when our actions are determined by our own intentions and desires they are free acts of will; when they are otherwise caused, they are not; the will is not involved.[4] When I consider my prospects and decide that I would be better off dead and jump from the window, I am acting freely; when you lift me bodily and toss me from the window, my defenestration is unfree; the relevant distinction is nicely captured by attention to the most salient proximal cause of my exit.

The Aristo-Lockean view is not unproblematic, however. At least two kinds of considerations cast doubt on its ability to articulate a robust free/unfree distinction sufficient to underwrite the requisite notions of agency and responsibility. First, there is the issue of coercion. Suppose that you don't toss me from the window, but threaten to torture my children if I don't jump. There is a sense in which I then jump freely; I consider living with the knowledge that my children are being tortured or dying in the knowledge that they are safe; I hence freely sacrifice myself for them. But there is an equal pull in the opposite direction. I did not freely commit suicide; I was driven to it by a threat; you, not I, are the cause of my death. There is no need to figure out which of these intuitions is better; the point is only that they are both robust, and a clean distinction may not be forthcoming.

Second, there is the problem of extended causal chains. I worry about the future of the world, what with a bad housing market, global warming, terrorist threats, the unlikelihood of a resurgence of Australian cricket in my lifetime, and I decide to end it all. It sure looks free from here, and if this is a morally wicked decision (after all, I cause needless grief to my spouse, children, and dog) I appear to be responsible precisely because it is free, and neither caused by force nor even coerced. The cause is just my

---

4. Such positions are *compatibilist*. Baker 2003 sets up the contrast between libertarian and compatibilist positions nicely:

> Let us say that an account of free will is *libertarian* if and only if it entails that a condition of a person S's having free will with respect to an action (or choice) A is that A is not ultimately caused by factors outside of S's control. Let us say that an account of free will is *compatibilist* if and only if it entails that a person S's having free will with respect to an action (or choice) A is compatible with the A's being caused ultimately by factors outside of S's control. . . .
>
> On a compatibilist conception of free will, a will can be caused and still be free in the sense required for moral responsibility.

desire to avoid the sufferings I contemplate. But now a dilemma ensues. Either that desire is caused or uncaused. If it is uncaused, then it is a random occurrence for which I can hardly be responsible; in such a case I am not the author of my own action. But if it is caused, then it must be caused by prior events, many of which (global warming, the poor housing market, the failure of Australian cricket selectors, etc.) lie outside of myself. In this case, too, I fail to meet the conditions of free-agent causation. I am not the author of my own action. One can see what drives one to a metaphysical causeless will acting purely on reasons, however little sense that really makes.

All of these considerations lead us almost inexorably to the denial that anything that can count as a genuine action—anything for which we are responsible—can be subject to causal determination, and hence to the conclusion that the distinction between agency and the mere causation of behavior seems to vanish. Freedom seems both necessary for these essential categories of personhood and inconsistent with universal determinism. But hold on. As Schopenhauer argued in what is arguably still the best treatment of this question, his *Essay on the Freedom of the Will* (an argument Dennett rediscovered much later in 1984, encapsulating ideas developed with great sophistication by Frankfurt 1969 and Davidson 1980 in different ways), the freedom of the will is not only compatible with, but in fact *demands* determinism.

After all, Schopenhauer points out, when we say that an action is free, we mean that is *caused* by our desires and intentions. If it were not, it would not be *our* action, and we would be neither agentively nor morally responsible for it. When we wish for freedom, we don't wish that our bodies and mouths moved randomly; we want to be able to *cause* them to move in the ways we desire. Moreover, we want those desires and intentions to be caused; randomly, spontaneously occurring conative states do not make us *free*; they make us *insane*; not *responsible*, but *excusable* on grounds of that insanity. In short, we want our own desires and intentions—the proximal causes of our actions—to be caused in turn by our own more general standing beliefs, desires, traits, et cetera, which are also plausibly, and desirably caused, and so on... Freedom is hence not the *absence* of determination, but *self*-determination. It is not inconsistent with determinism, but entails it.

But now we seem to be chasing our own tails: freedom requires determinism; determinism entails that our actions are ultimately caused by chains of causation originating outside of us; authority and responsibility require agent-causation through choice among real alternatives (see Plantinga 1967, Pereboom 2009). These three premises seem to entail that freedom in the morally relevant sense is impossible. It is time to recall what we care about here. We care about making sense of our moral lives and of our agency. While it might have appeared that a discourse of freedom and determinism and a metaphysics of will would be the best way to do this, this way of seeing things may be a dead end. And it may be only the relic of a very particular Hebrew myth, a myth of little interest to Buddhists, of course.[5] Perhaps it makes sense to look elsewhere in order to find a Buddhist—and in particular a Madhyamaka Buddhist—account of action.

This set of problems, it may also be worth noting, also presupposes another metaphysical doctrine anathema to Buddhists—that of a self or a soul as the center of agency. For a Christian, such as Augustine, the reality of the soul requires no argument, and for many of his more secular successors, such as Kant, while the idea of a transcendental subject or agent may have required argument, that argument was provided (whether it was successful or not is another matter). While these ideas are literally independent (one could imagine an unfree soul, or an soulless free agent), the doctrine of the reality of the soul is connected to the idea that the will is free in the sense we have been scouting in that it is natural in the post-Christian European tradition to imagine the soul as an autonomous entity, capable of initiating its own actions, and so as that which is ultimately morally responsible. We can then even draw the distinction between responsible human agents and non-responsible animals, for instance, on the basis of soul-possession, and provide the hope for future reward or punishment in heaven or hell on the ground of the soul's responsibility and survival after physical death. Once again, since a distinctive feature of all Buddhist philosophical systems is their *rejection* of the view that there is a metaphysical soul (the doctrine of *anātman*), there is no basis here for formulating the problem of the freedom of the will in the manner in which it develops in Europe.

5. This is not, however, to say either that the Hebrew myth is the only possible source of theodicy or that theodicy is the only possible root of puzzles about agency. I only want to emphasize that in the Christian West this is the root of this cluster of problems, that this root gives them their particular character, and so that we should not be surprised to find other traditions in which they either do not arise at all, or, if they do arise, arise in very different forms.

Pratītyasamutpāda *in Action: Why these Problems Can't Arise for a Mādhyamika*

With a clear view of the issues at stake when we ask whether we have free will and whether this is consistent with determinism, and the theological background of that question as it is posed in the West, let us see why *this* problematic can't arise in a Buddhist context. A fundamental tenet of any Buddhist school is that all phenomena are dependently originated. In Madhyamaka Buddhist thought, following Candrakīrti (1992, 2003), this dependency is glossed in three ways.

(1) All phenomena come to be in dependence on causes and conditions, and cease when those causes and conditions are no longer present.

> All things arise in dependence on causes and conditions, and this is the meaning of dependent origination. [*Prasannapadā* 2b][6]

(2) All wholes are dependent upon their parts, and the parts of wholes are dependent for their existence on the wholes of which they are parts.

> Although both from the standpoint of reality and from that of everyday life,
> The sevenfold reasoning shows that a chariot cannot be established,
> In everyday life, without analysis
> It is designated in dependence on its parts. [*Madhyamakāvatāra* 6: 159]

The reciprocal dependence of parts on their wholes is taken up a few verses later:

> If the chariot were not to exist,
> Without that which possesses parts, there would be no parts either.
> Just as when the chariot is burned, there are no longer any parts,
> When the fire of understanding consumes the chariot, it consumes its parts as well. [*Madhyamakāvatāra* 6: 161]

---

6. All translations are my own, from Tibetan.

(3) The commentary on 6: 169 nicely connects dependence of wholes on their parts with the third sense of dependent origination, namely, that entities are also dependent for their existence as entities on conceptual imputation, a theme taken up in greater detail in subsequent verses and comments in this text. (See Garfield 1994 and Cowherds 2010 for more detail.)

> ...Therefore, although dependent origination is generally maintained to be dependence upon conditions, from our perspective, this is not inconsistent with it also being dependent upon mundane nominal conventions.... In this context, to be recognized in everyday life, the conventional designation is clearly understood without the slightest bit of analysis necessary. [*Madhyamakāvatāra-bhāṣya*, p. 259]

The universality of *pratītyasamutpāda,* or dependent co-origination, ensures that persons and their mental and physical states and actions also arise in this thoroughgoing interdependence. In fact the emptiness of persons of any more substantial being than this, such as the possession of a unitary soul or self, is a central insight to be achieved in one's moral and metaphysical development on the *Bodhisattva* path to full awakening. Candrakīrti puts the points this way in the next few verses:

> In the same way, although in everyday life, the self is maintained to be
> The appropriator of the aggregates, it is designated on the basis of
> The aggregates, the sensory domains and the six sense faculties.
> The appropriated taken as the object and the self as the agent. [6: 162]

> Since it does not exist, it is neither continuous
> Nor discontinuous, neither arisen nor ceased;
> It has no properties such as permanence,
> Existence, nonexistence, identity or difference. [6: 163]

> The self is simply whatever it is towards which
> Beings constantly develop the attitude of ego-grasping.
> The self arises out of the attitude that something is *mine*.
> Since it becomes manifest unreflectively, it arises from confusion. [6: 164]

So long as one takes oneself to be a substantial center of subjectivity or agency, as opposed to a causally connected stream of momentary psychophysical phenomena, one is mired in primal confusion that makes the cultivation of compassion and the liberation from suffering impossible. Only by recognizing that our identities arise only from our own imposition of a unity and coherence on a complex, multifaceted stream of events and processes can we escape that confusion (Siderits 2005, Garfield 2010/2011 press).

This philosophical position entails that all actions, all thoughts, all intentions, and all character traits are causally dependent, and that any unity we ascribe to ourselves over time is merely imputed. This in turn entails that any ethical assessment in which we engage is the assessment of caused events or of merely conventionally designated persons. Agent causation in the sense imagined by the will-libertarian is simply inconceivable in this framework. Moreover, Buddhist psychology, not surprisingly, does not posit a general faculty for action—a will (Siderits 1987, 2008).[7] There is no need to posit anything like this, for there is no theodicy problem for it to solve. Actions, according to Buddhist psychologists, are caused by intentions, but this causation does not require mediation by any special conative faculty. So without a truly existent personal agent, without a category of uncaused events, and without a faculty of will, the "problem of the freedom of the will," let alone the question of whether a free will is compatible or not with determinism, can't be formulated. The problem seems just as weird from the perspective of a Mādhyamika as would the problem of explaining the Buddha's omniscience be to a Catholic.

Despite the weirdness of the metaphysical problem as it is formulated in the Christian tradition and taken up in supposedly more secular Western philosophy, however, Mādhyamikas such as Nāgārjuna, Candrakīrti, Śāntideva and others are committed to the view that as agents we are responsible for our own situations and destinies (after all, this the heart of the doctrine of *karma*). Moreover Buddhist moral texts such as *Ratnāvalī, Catuḥśatakaṭīkā, Bodhicāryāvatāra* and others are replete with admonitions to perform certain actions and to refrain from others, and accounts

7. Or anything that would correspond to an Augustinian notion of *voluntas* at any stage of his philosophical development, or, for that matter, to a Kantian *Wille*.

of mental episodes as the primary causes of actions. Reconciliation of this position in the context of *pratītyasamutpāda* is hence of real concern to any Mādhyamika.

Some Bad Arguments for Supposed Buddhist Doctrines of Freedom of the Will

The fact that it is impossible to formulate the thesis of the freedom of the will in a Buddhist framework or to pose the question of whether free actions are independent of the causal nexus, authored by independent agents, has not stopped recent Buddhist philosophers from doing so or from arguing that Buddhist philosophy entails a doctrine of the freedom of the will. Each of these attempts is motivated by the desire to present Buddhism as a "modern" and hence Western doctrine, one that somehow comes to many of the same conclusions to which Western thinkers have arrived. Here is a brief sampler. See Meyers (2010) for a more extensive survey and a more detailed critique.

Bhikkhu Bodhi (1995), Potter (1963), and Rhys Davids (1898) each argue in somewhat different ways that *pratītyasamutpāda* is consistent with the freedom of the will because dependent origination is not deterministic. The idea is that dependent origination specifies only that conditions *occasion* events, but not that they *cause* them, where this is supposed to mean that they somehow *give rise to* events, but do not *necessitate* them. Given that there is no necessitation, there is room for freedom to choose.

This argument actually looks best in the context of Madhyamaka given Nāgārjuna's critique of causal powers (Garfield 1994, 1995) But it is still a terrible argument. All Buddhist philosophers, Mādhyamikas included, give universal scope to the thesis that "when this arises, so does that; when this fails to arise, so does that," namely., that any event can be completely explained by reference to prior and simultaneous causes and conditions. Nāgārjuna himself in the famous first verse of *Mūlamadhyamakakārikā* rejects arising from nothing at all.

A cousin to this argument is Griffiths's (1986) claim that the formula of dependent origination entails only that causes or conditions are necessary for the arising of events, but not that they are sufficient. So, this argument goes, initiation of an action may require the presence of a number of conditions. But these are not sufficient. An act of free will is also required. This is also a terrible argument. First of all, there is no textual evidence whatsoever of a Buddhist doctrine of necessary but insufficient conditions or of the necessity of an uncaused act to potentiate action. But second, even if this view were accepted as a rational reconstruction of Buddhist action theory, it would be incoherent. For if we are operating even within this novel understanding of the doctrine of dependent origination, the posited act of free will would itself require conditions, and those would be insufficient, resulting in an embarrassing regress.

Jayatilleke (1963) argues that the doctrine of karma necessitates a doctrine of free will. Karma (in the sense of *karmaphala)*, this argument continues, is the reward or punishment for action, and reward or punishment would be inappropriate and unjust if action were simply caused behavior.[8] So, since the doctrine of karmic consequence is central to Buddhist action theory and ethics (it is) and since it is a doctrine of reward and punishment, Buddhist ethics and action theory would be unacceptable if actions are not freely chosen. This argument from justice, however, substantially mistakes both the Buddhist account of karma and the structure of Buddhist ethics more generally. This is a consensus among even those who disagree dramatically among themselves about what the structure of Buddhist ethics is (see Goodman 2009; Garfield 2010/2011; and Keown 2001) that karmic consequence is *not* reward or punishment; it is causal consequence, pure and simple. As such, there is no question of justice or injustice, just as there is no question of the justice or injustice of a billiard ball moving in response to being struck by a cue ball. And so there is no argument in this quarter for a doctrine of free will, either.

Payutto (1990) argues that since all Buddhist schools accept the claim that action is caused by *cetanā*, and since *cetanā* can be translated as *choice*, it is essential to Buddhist action theory that choice is involved in action. Since choice involves the freedom to opt for any of the open alternatives, Buddhists, this line of argument continues, are committed to free will. This argument relies on a tendentious translation and a tendentious account of choice. *Cetanā* is indeed a difficult word to translate (see Meyers 2010 on this), but there is a broad consensus that its central meaning is captured by *intent, intention, intending, volition*, et cetera, none of which implicate the idea of *choice*. Even if one were to translate *cetanā* as choice, though, it would be a further task to argue that a Buddhist, as opposed to

8. Augustine makes an argument of exactly this sort in *On Free Choice of the Will*.

a libertarian, doctrine of choice would require our choices to be causeless, a hard row to hoe, as noted above. While this is not an exhaustive survey of arguments to this conclusion, I hope that it makes the case that it is hard to get a discourse of freedom in the (libertarian) Augustinian sense or in the Kantian sense going in this tradition. If we are after an account of agency and responsibility in Madhyamaka thought, we will have to look elsewhere.

Madhyamaka and Persons: The Two Truths

Central to Madhyamaka philosophy is the doctrine of the two truths.[9] (Newland 1992, 2009, Cowherds 2010) Now many Buddhist philosophical schools distinguish between two truths, and they do so in different ways and even for different purposes. Sautrāntikas and Vaibhāṣikas, for instance, argue that conventional reality (or truth) is erroneous in that it comprises (refers to) composite entities, which are regarded by adherents to these philosophical schools as illusory or fabricated. So, one might argue, forests aren't real; their trees are; trees aren't real; leaves and trunks are; and so on.... On the other hand, Sautrāntikas and Vaibhāṣikas argue, these illusory conventional entities reduce to ultimately real, simple, momentary, causally interacting constituents of reality called *dharmas*. Things that might be conventionally true about wholes (the persistence of the person, for instance) are shown to be literally false, but to reduce to claims that are literally true about *dharmas* (the momentariness but causal connectedness of the constituents of persons).

While, from a Sautrāntika or a Vaibhāṣika point of view, we might wonder whether an account of action involving some measure of freedom and responsibility for persons at the conventional level might reduce to an impersonal account of causal processes at the ultimate level (for an excellent articulation of such a position, see Siderits 1987, 2008), this option is not open for the Mādhyamika, for the Madhyamaka account of the two truths neither exempts the conventional from dependent origination nor leaves us with an ultimate truth comprising fundamental constituents. For Madhyamaka is not reductionist at all (Garfield 2006). For a Mādhyamika,

9. It is important in this context to remember that the Sanskrit *satya* is ambiguous between the English *truth* and *reality*, an ambiguity not salient in Sanskrit philosophy, where this distinction is not really drawn.

nothing exists ultimately, and to say truly that anything exists is to say that it exists conventionally. As Nāgārjuna puts it,

> That which is dependent origination
> Is explained to be emptiness.
> That, being a dependent designation
> Is itself the middle way.
>
> There does not exist anything
> That is not dependently arisen.
> Therefore there does not exist anything
> That is not empty. (*Mūlamadhyamakakārikā* 24: 18, 19)

(See Garfield 1995 and Cowherds 2010 for more on this topic.) If we are interested in an account of agency and responsibility in Madhyamaka, then, it is important to be clear that we can only be addressing the realm of dependent origination, that is, the realm of conventional truth.

Of course, this applies to persons, and it is into the freedom, responsibility, and agency of persons that we inquire. So what can we say about the person? Candrakīrti, in *Madhyamakāvatāra-bhāṣya* (1992; see also Huntington and Wangchen 1989), argues that the person is neither identical to the psycho-physical aggregates, nor different from them, nor a single one of them, nor the collection of them, nor even the owner, controller, or possessor of them. None of these alternatives, he argues, can be made intelligible. Instead, the person is a conceptual imputation, a convenient designation, with no reality apart from that designation. Candrakīrti puts it this way in *Madhyamakāvatāra*:

> The self is not the aggregates; and the aggregates
> Are not the self. If there were any difference
> Between them, such ideas would make sense.
> But since there is no such difference, these are just ideas. [6: 142]
>
> The self cannot be maintained to be the possessor of the body;
> Because the self does not exist, it cannot be the possessor of anything.
> Only where there is difference can there be possession, as when one has a cow.

> Or without difference, as in the possession of the body; but the self is neither different nor non-different from the body. [143]
>
> The self is not the body; the self does not possess the body;
> The self is not in the body; the body is not in the self;
> All four aggregates are to be understood in this fourfold way. [144]
>
> Therefore, the basis of self-grasping is not an entity.
> It is neither different from the aggregates nor the essence of the aggregates.
> It is neither the basis of the aggregates nor their possessor.
> Instead, it is posited in dependence on the aggregates. [150]
>
> The self can thus be said to be no different from a chariot.
> It, in the same sense, is neither different from, nor identical with its parts.
> Nor does it possess its parts; it does not contain them, and they do not contain it.
> Nor is it the mere structure or mereological sum of its parts. [151]

We are, as Dennett (1992) felicitously put it, "centers of narrative gravity." That is not to say that persons or their actions do not exist, but rather to say that our mode of existence is merely conventional, merely imputed. (For more on this see Garfield 2006 and Newland 2009.)

If we are to ascribe agency and responsibility or to engage in moral evaluation in a Madhyamaka framework, then, we will be ascribing agency and responsibility to these nominal entities and evaluating actions without ultimately existent agents. This may seem a tall order, and one might despair of any discourse of ethics and agency in such a framework. But that would be to give up too soon. After all, even Mahāyāna Buddhism—perhaps especially Mahāyāna Madhyamaka Buddhism—has the cultivation of the path to liberation at its core, and that cultivation involves the cultivation of moral qualities, and a commitment to action on behalf of the welfare of all sentient beings so eloquently expounded by Śāntideva in *Bodhicāryāvatāra*. But how is this possible?

Agency and Responsibility in Madhyamaka

For a Mādhyamika, we have noted, our selves are *constructed*. They are constructed through the appropriation of aggregates, through recognizing a body as mine, thoughts as mine, values, dispositions, and intentions as mine. In turn, those physical and cognitive processes are also constructed in relation to that self, and it, then, is appropriated by them. That appropriation and narration of a life is, moreover, not a solo affair. We narrate and construct each other constantly in the hermeneutical ensemble act that is social life. (See Hutto 2008, and Bogdan, 2011, for more recent Western developments of this idea, but of course, as Nehamas 1985 points out, this idea goes at least back to Nietzsche.) None of us is innocent in our own creation; but at the same time none of us is *autonomous* in that creative activity. Our identities are negotiated, fluid, and complex in virtue of being marked by the three universal characteristics of impermanence, interdependence, and the absence of any self. It is this frame of context-governed interpretive appropriation, instead of the frame of autonomous, substantial selfhood, that sets the metaphysical questions regarding agency, and the moral questions regarding responsibility in Madhyamaka.

What is it to act? As we noted above, it is for our behavior to be determined by reasons, by motives we and/or others regard as our own. On a Madhyamaka understanding, it is therefore for the causes of our behavior to be part of the narrative that makes sense of our lives, as opposed to being simply part of the vast uninterpreted milieu in which our lives are led, or bits of the narratives that more properly constitute the lives of others. This distinction is not a *metaphysical* but a *literary* distinction, and so a matter of choice and sensitive to explanatory purposes. That sensitivity, on the other hand, means that the choice is not *arbitrary*. We can follow Nietzsche here. For what do we take responsibility and for what are we assigned responsibility? Those acts we interpret—or which others interpret for us—as our own, as constituting part of the basis of imputation of our own identities.

Let us return to the three cases of defenestration considered earlier. When I propose to jump in order avoid living through global warming and the decline of Australian cricket, the conditions that motivate my act are cognitive and emotional states I take to be my own, and which others who know me would regard as mine. The narrative that constructs the conventional self that is the basis of my individuation includes them, simply in virtue of our psychology and social practices. This, then, is, uncontroversially, an action. When you toss me from the window against my will, the causes of my trajectory lie in what we would instead, and uncontroversially, but again, on conventional, hermeneutical grounds, interpret as parts of *your* biography. This is no action of *mine*. The agency lies with *you*, not on metaphysical grounds, but on conventional grounds, not on the discovery of agent causation in your will, not in mine, but based upon the plausible narrative we tell of the event and of each other's lives as interpretable characters.[10]

The interesting questions arise concerning the intermediate case of coercion, where you threaten my children with torture if I do not jump. We have seen that there are two ways to take this case, and this is as it should be. For there are many ways we might construct a narrative of this case. In one story, I am the passive victim of your blackmail; seen in that way, what we read as the causes of my jumping are your actions not mine. Reading the case this way, agency is assigned to you and not to me. In another narrative, I make the noble sacrifice in the face of circumstances beyond my control. Here we explain the jumping on the grounds of my own character and desires, locating the agency in my person, not yours. And of course there is a richer, more nuanced story in which we say that while I may not be responsible for the circumstances that forced me to make the ultimate sacrifice, when faced with the hard choice I made it, nonetheless, assigning responsibility according to the assignment of causes to bases of personal imputation. How to choose between narratives in particular legal or moral discourses is, as it should be, an interesting and difficult question. But the important point from a Madhyamaka perspective is this: In asking how best to tell this story, and so in asking where to assign agency, we are never forced to look to a will, to its freedom, or to a metaphysics of agent causation.

On this Madhyamaka understanding of personal identity established through imputation—a view with important affinities to those of Hume and Nietzsche in the West—we *do* make choices, often hard choices; we do perform acts that merit moral assessment; we do assign responsibility to agents for their actions, and absolve others; and we do assess acts morally. But none of this requires us to talk about freedom or about a faculty of will. All of these moral practices can be better understood in the framework of

10. It is important to remember that not all narratives are equally good. Some make good sense of our lives or those of others; some are incoherent; some are facile and self-serving; some are profound and revealing. It is possible for people to disagree about whether a particular event is an action or not, or about the attribution of responsibility. It is possible for us to wonder about whether we should feel remorse for a particular situation or not. These questions are in the end, on this account, questions about which narratives make the most sense. While these questions may not always be easy (or even possible to settle), the fact that they arise saves this view from the facile relativism that would issue from the observation that we can always tell *some* story on which this is an action of mine, and *some* story on which it is not, and so that there is simply no fact of the matter, and perhaps no importance to the question.

pratītyasamutpāda. From this perspective, a choice occurs when we experience competing motives, consider alternative reasons, some of which could, if dominant, occasion alternative actions, and one set of reasons dominates, *causing* the action, and *caused to cause the action* by our background psychological dispositions and other cognitive and conative states. Some actions are expressive of and conducive to virtue, happiness, liberation, and the welfare of others and merit praise; others are not. But there need be no more to moral assessment than that.[11] Everything that the post-Augustinian libertarian West buys with the gold coin of the freedom of the will, along with all of the metaphysical problems it raises, are bought by the Mādhyamika much more cheaply with the paper currency of mere imputation.

Freedom on the Path; Freedom from Saṃsāra

Mādhyamikas do talk about freedom however—they pursue liberation from suffering, and so from cyclic existence, freedom from the *kleśas*, or maladaptive psychological processes. And this, to be sure, is a kind of freedom. It is the freedom of our actions—mental, verbal, and physical—from determination by those aspects of our personality we wish to write out of the narrative. At present, many of my actions are driven by fear, anger, despair, greed, and so forth, states that I appropriate or that others assign to me as part of my biography. As a consequence, I interpret a great many of the events in which I participate as occasioned by the acts of others—those who threaten or annoy me or with whom I see myself in competition—and react to them on that basis. This is the basis of vice (See Garfield 2010/2011).

But the path to liberation, seen in the context of a self that is but a conceptual imputation, is a path to the authorship of a narrative in which a better self is the protagonist, a self whose actions are conditioned by compassion, sympathetic joy, generosity, and confidence, by responsiveness as opposed to reaction. The self I imagine at the higher stages of the path is free in ways that the self I construct now is not. More of its acts are actions it claims to author, and the conditions of those actions are morally salutary rather than counterproductive. But the freedom achieved

11. This also indicates why, on a Madhyamaka view, persons can be held responsible for actions even when they involve no explicit choice, as in Frankfurt-style cases. Choice is not necessary to the kind of interpretation and authorship at issue in this account of action.

through the cultivation of this path, understood in the Madhyamaka framework of Candrakīrti and Śāntideva, is not a freedom of the *will*, but *authority*—a freedom of a conceptually imputed person from the bars of a self-constructed prison, a freedom that in no way demands any causal indeterminism. And when that freedom is complete, there is simply nothing left to lose.

References

Baker, L. R. 2003. "Why Christians should not be Libertarians: An Augustinian Challenge." *Faith and Philosophy* 20.4: 460–478.

Berthold, F. 1981. "Free Will and Theodicy in Augustine: An Exposition and Critique." *Religious Studies* 17.4: 525–535.

Bodhi Bhikkhu. 1995. *The Great Discourse on Causation: The Mahānidāna Sutta and Its Commentaries.* Kandy: Buddhist Publication Society.

Bogdan, R. 2011. *Our Own Minds: Sociocultural Grounds for Self-Consciousness.* Cambridge, MA: MIT Press.

Campbell, J., M. O'Rourke, and D. Shier, eds. 2004. *Freedom and Determinism.* Cambridge: Cambridge University Press.

Candrakīrti. 1992. *Madhyamakāvatāra-bhāṣya (dBu ma 'jug pa'i rang 'gral).* Sarnath: Kagyud Relief and Protection Society.

———. 2003. *Prasannapadā. (dBu ma tshig gsal).* Sarnath: Gelukpa Student Welfare Committee.

Cowherds. 2010. *Moonshadows: Conventional Truth in Buddhist Philosophy.* New York: Oxford University Press.

Davidson, D. 1980. "How is Weakness of the Will Possible." In *Essays on Actions and Events,* by D. Davidson, 21–42. Oxford: Oxford University Press.

Dennett, D. 1984. *Elbow Room: Varieties of Free Will Worth Wanting.* Oxford: Oxford University Press.

———. 1992. *Consciousness Explained.* Cambridge, MA: MIT Press.

———. 2003. *Freedom Evolves.* New York: Penguin.

Frankfurt, H. 1969. "Alternate Possibilities and Moral Responsibility." *Journal of Philosophy* 66.23: 829–839.

———. 1971. "Freedom of the Will and the Concept of a Person." *Journal of Philosophy* 68.1: 5–20.

Garfield, J. 1994. "Dependent Origination and the Emptiness of Emptiness: Why Did Nāgārjuna Start With Causation?." *Philosophy East and West* 44: 219–250.

———. 1995. *Fundamental Wisdom of the Middle Way: Nāgārjuna's Mūlamadhyamakakārikā.* New York: Oxford University Press.

———. 2006. "Reductionism and Fictionalism: Comments on Siderits." *APA Newsletter on Asian and Comparative Philosophy* 6.1: 1–8.

———. (2010/2011). "What Is It Like To Be a Bodhisattva? Moral Phenomenology in Śāntideva's *Bodhicāryāvatāra*." *Journal of the International Association of Buddhist Studies*, Vol 33: 1–2. 327–351.

Gómez, L. 1975. "Some Aspects of the Free Will Question in the Nikāyas." *Philosophy East and West* 25: 81–90.

Goodman, C. 2009. *Consequences of Compassion*. New York: Oxford University Press.

Griffiths, P. 1986. *On Being Mindless: Buddhist Meditation and the Mind-Body Problem*. LaSalle: Open Court.

Harvey, P. 2007. "Freedom of the Will in Light of Theravāda Teachings." *Journal of Buddhist Ethics* 14: 271–291.

Hoffman, T. 2008. *Weakness of the Will from Plato to the Present*. Washington DC: Catholic University of America Press.

Huntington, C., and Geshe N. Wangchen. 1989. *The Emptiness of Emptiness: Candrakīrti's Madhyamakāvatāra*. Honolulu: University of Hawai'i Press.

Hutto, D. 2008. *Folk Psychological Narratives*. Cambridge, MA: MIT Press.

Jayatilleke, K. 1963. *Early Buddhist Theory of Knowledge*. London: Allen and Unwin.

Kane, R., ed. 2005. *The Oxford Handbook of Free Will*. New York: Oxford University Press.

Keown, D. 2001. *The Nature of Buddhist Ethics*. New York: Palgrave.

Libet, B. 1985. "Unconscious Cerebral Initiative and the Role of Conscious Will in Voluntary Action." *Behavioral and Brain Sciences* 8.4: 529–539.

———. 1999. "Do We Have a Free Will." *Journal of Consciousness Studies* 6: 47–57.

Mele, A. 1995. *Motivation and Agency*. New York: Oxford University Press.

———. 2001. *Autonomous Agents: From Self-Control to Agency*. New York: Oxford University Press.

———. 2010. *Effective Intentions: The Power of Conscious Will*. New York: Oxford University Press.

Meyers, K. 2010. *Freedom and Self-Control: Freedom in South Asian Buddhism*. PhD diss., University of Chicago.

Nehamas, A. 1985. *Nietzsche: Life as Literature*. Cambridge, MA: Harvard University Press.

Newland, G. 1992. *The Two Truths*. Ithaca, NY: Snow Lion.

———. 2009. *Introduction to Emptiness*. Ithaca, NY: Snow Lion.

Payutto, P. 1990. *Freedom, Individual and Social*. Bangkok: Buddhadhamma Foundation.

Pereboom, D., ed. 2009. *Free Will*. Indianapolis: Hackett Publications.

Plantinga A. 1967. *God and Other Minds*. Ithaca, NY: Cornell University Press.

Potter, K. 1963. *Presuppositions of India's Philosophies*. Englewood Cliffs, NJ: Prentice Hall.

Rhys Davids, C. 1898. "On the Will in Buddhism." *Journal of the Royal Asiatic Society of Great Britain and Ireland*. http://enlight.lib.ntu.edu.tw/FULLTEXT/JR-ENG/dav.htm. Retrieved August 7, 2013.

Siderits, M. 1987. "Beyond Compatibilism: A Buddhist Approach to Freedom and Determinism." *American Philosophical Quarterly* 24: 149–159.

———. 2005. "Freedom, Caring and Buddhist Philosophy." *Contemporary Buddhism* 6: 87–116.

———. 2008. "Paleo-Compatibilism and Buddhist Reductionism." *Sophia* 47: 29–42.

Stroud, S. 2008. "Weakness of Will." *Stanford Online Encyclopedia of Philosophy*, http://plato.stanford.edu/cgi-bin/encyclopedia/archinfo.cgi?entry=weakness-will.

Stump, E. 2001. "Augustine on Free Will." In *The Cambridge Companion to Augustine*, ed. E. Stump, and N. Kretzman. 124–147. Cambridge: Cambridge University Press.

Watson, G., ed. 2003. *Free Will: Oxford Readings in Philosophy*. New York: Oxford University Press.

8

Self, Causation, and Agency in the Advaita of Śaṅkara

Sthaneshwar Timalsina

[Brahman is] similar to the fire that has consumed the fuel. [It is] devoid of parts, free from actions, motionless, stainless, tranquil, and [is] the highest bridge to immortality.

—ŚVETĀŚVATARA UPANIṢAD 6.19

Arjuna! Even when in the body, this supreme and changeless self neither acts nor is attached [to the results of actions], because it has neither a beginning nor any guṇas.[1]

—BHAGAVAD GĪTĀ 13.31

WHETHER SUBJECTS ARE autonomous in determining their own course of action is a thorny question with a range of different and often contradictory answers. This volume makes it clear that there is not one way to address this question, even within the schools of Indian philosophy. This essay examines the issue through the lens of Advaita Vedānta, the exegetical tradition that rests primarily on the Upaniṣadic literature. This essay also

I am immensely thankful to Professors Edwin Bryant and Matthew Dasti for their insightful comments and corrections to the earlier draft of this chapter.

1. *anāditvān nirguṇatvāt paramātmāyam avyayaḥ |śarīrastho 'pi kaunteya na karoti na lipyate || Bhagavadgītā* 13.31. Although I have translated the term *nirguṇa* here as "devoid of *guṇas*," I will be generally translating it as "devoid of properties," following Śaṅkara's understanding.

illustrates that there is not one Advaita, as even Śaṅkara's school (710 CE)[2] develops multiple sub-schools that address the issue of agency in different ways. What readers need to keep in mind is that the historical context in which the issue of agency emerges in Advaita is different from the contemporary discourse on agency and free will. Although some arguments may reflect the contemporary Western debate, the pivotal arguments in Advaita arise from different and multiple cultural and philosophical contexts. To introduce the issue without a discussion of this background results in breaching multiple hermeneutic barriers. I will, therefore, provide such contextualization as a precursor for the specific consideration of agency. I cannot claim that this essay does full justice to the school of Śaṅkara; rather, it is a modest attempt to engage Advaita upon the issue of agency.

An agent endowed with free will may freely choose to shoot an arrow, but his freedom does not extend to determining the exact course of that arrow after it has been launched. Persons, for Śaṅkara, are placed in a chain of cause and effect that constitutes the world wherein the embodied subject undergoes the consequences of his previous actions while being autonomous in creating a new chain of events. Most schools of Indian philosophy accept this law of karma, and while doing so, they do not equate the experience of a karmic flow with a lack of agency. The concept of karma, either as actions and their consequences in general or as the acts prescribed by the Vedas, relies on an agent that is autonomous in determining whether or not to conduct such an act. Śaṅkara agrees that a cause exists behind every effect, but whether the events experienced in this life are the consequence of past actions or are determined by a free agent acting in the present time is a complex issue. If current actions are determined by the past ones, this leads to infinite regress, as those actions will also rely on previous ones. The problem becomes explicit when we realize that there are infinite previous lives and no primordial life that has initiated action. Advaitins therefore do not take this theory too seriously because following Advaita, this whole action-and-consequence paradigm becomes a moot point, since this philosophy challenges the absolute reality of both the transmigrating self and the phenomenal world that relies on actions and their effects.

---

2. I am not making any original claims regarding the dates of the scholars discussed in this paper. I am primarily relying on Potter 2011, Sastri 1984, and Thrasher 1993.

Similar to the Mādhyamika Buddhists (see Garfield in this volume), Śaṅkara adopts the model of describing reality in two tiers, consisting of the conventional (*vyāvahārika*) reality that corresponds to our phenomenal experiences and the absolute (*pāramārthika*) reality of the Brahman. The issue of agency arises in Śaṅkara's philosophy when he discusses phenomenal reality. However, he rejects the paradigm of agent and action when postulating the absolute viewpoint. This being the case, the dialectical context is crucial to understand Śaṅkara's arguments. On the one hand, when he engages the Mīmāṃsakas, he may appear to be rejecting the entire karmic complex that relies on the triad of agent, action, and effect, while, on the other hand, when he confronts the Buddhist philosophers, he will be defending the foundational consciousness whereby or wherein the chain of events manifests. Śaṅkara thus places himself in the middle. From the perspective of absolute reality, when establishing oneness of the phenomenal self and the absolute reality, the Brahman, he maintains that the self is devoid of agency. When engaging in his relative perspective, however, his is not a case of either free will or determinism: it is a compromise between free will and a mild determinism that is based on the karmic residue of an agent's previous actions that were effected with his own free will.

The philosophical background in which this issue evolves contains both ontological and soteriological aspects. At the ontological level, we will find Śaṅkara closer to his predecessor Gauḍapāda (600 CE) who proposed the doctrine of "non-origination" (*ajāti*) that reflects in some respects the position of the Mādhyamikas.[3] With an analogy of a dream, Gauḍapāda maintains that there is no actual origination in the Brahman that is free from any mutation. One needs to nonetheless be aware that Gauḍapāda's position of non-origination (*ajāti*) is not identical to the Mādhyamika position of absolute emptiness (*śūnyatā*). While accepting Gauḍapāda's teachings of non-origination at the absolute level, Śaṅkara is interested in engaging Advaita in the phenomenal level, and in addition to establishing the philosophical foundation, he is keen to address soteriological issues. In Gauḍapāda's philosophy (which is adopted by Śaṅkara as well), there is neither karma nor is there its applicability for liberation. This shift in understanding the role of karma in liberation clearly differentiates Śaṅkara's philosophy from the position of early Advaitins such as

3. For non-origination in Gauḍapāda's philosophy, see King 1995: 119–140.

Brahmadatta (660 CE) and Bhartṛprapañca (550 CE).[4] Śaṅkara maintains that the wisdom imparted by the Upaniṣadic sentences such as "you are that"[5] suffices to grant liberation independent of performing rituals or any other actions for that matter. For him, the self is devoid of action, and action and wisdom are as contradictory as light and darkness. On the contrary, the early Advaitins such as Bhartṛprapañca maintained that while the Upaniṣadic passages direct one toward some form of self-realization, one cannot dissociate from actions and actualize liberation. This position relies on the meta-thesis that the individual self is intrinsically dynamic, and the self qua Brahman emanates the world that is as real as the diversity of the branches of a tree or the waves of an ocean. These Advaitins therefore prescribe a course of contemplative practice that is generally identified as *prasaṅkhyāna*.[6] The heart of the problem is whether the self is dynamic or devoid of action: if the self is essentially dynamic, certain actions reveal its intrinsic nature and the agent is free to determine the course of action in a compromised way; if the self is static and devoid of action, no action can reveal its intrinsic nature. This issue will be further explored in the section on Sureśvara (740 CE).

Any discussion of agency is not possible without addressing action. If agents act, in other words if there exists any action, the question arises whether the agents are autonomous in such actions. On the other hand, if the self is devoid of action (as Śaṅkara maintains in the absolute sense), the issues of agent and the will to act are irrelevant. This absolute position of Śaṅkara reflects the philosophy of Gauḍapāda who maintains that there is no origination as such to ground the theory of cause and effect. The chain of events that we perceive in the world, following this paradigm, is a grand misconception, either defined in terms of a metaphysical illusion (*māyā*) or described in terms of subjective ignorance (*avidyā*). What exists in reality is just Brahman or the self. This self, due to forgetting its real nature, imagines itself both as agent and effects. The phenomenal world, or the reality as we see it, is the creation or imagination of this self.

---

4. For the philosophy of Bhartṛprapañca, see Nakamura 2004: 128–152; Timalsina 2006: 156–169.

5. The hermeneutic distinction can be drawn from the Advaitins interpreting *tat tvam asi* (*Chāndogya* 6.8.7) independently of the initial sentence that can be interpreted as injunction.

6. *Prasaṅkhyāna* refers to the contemplative practice in Advaita where the specific thought, such as "I am Brahman" is repeated silently to actualize a deeper conviction. For discussion on this method, see Alston 1997: 187–191.

This imagination is twofold: at the subjective level, the self imagines itself as an agent engaged in action and as the locus of sensation; on the objective level, it constitutes the external reality that accommodates its own fancies. In this picture, behind every action and effect is desire, and behind desire exists a separation of the self from its original nature, the Brahman. The self distanced from its primordial nature, or confined due to ignorance that results in it having subjectivity, is identified by the term *jīva*. Just like a man covered in mud is still a man, the individual self is nonetheless always the Brahman. The defining characteristics of the Brahman are *sac-cid-ānanda*, "being, awareness, and bliss," and while the blissful nature is covered with the metaphoric mud of ignorance, being and awareness are constantly experienced even when the self undergoes bondage.

We first need to decide how to engage with the Advaita of Śaṅkara. On the phenomenal level, most of the categories acceptable to the Mīmāṃsakas (between the two sub-schools, I am keeping the Bhāṭṭas in mind here) are also acceptable to the Advaitins: they do not deny the subject-object duality and the actions and agencies that occur as a consequence of agency when immersed in common-sense experience. But leaving the categories of ordinary experience to the Naiyāyikas and the Mīmāṃsakas, Advaitins instead explore what lies beneath. If we address the issue of agency and free will while somehow bracketing this distinction between the ultimate and conventional levels of reality, we will be violating the fundamental premise of the philosophical system.

So when engaging the absolute perspective, we need to begin with what constitutes a person in Advaita. From the absolute viewpoint, the self qua Brahman is all that is there, and the issue of agency arises due to ignorance. Although there is no creation in this sense, if the absolute perspective is engaged to describe phenomenal reality, the entire manifestation is the projection of the self, independent of anything other than the self itself. When engaging the conventional perspective, agents are bound due to ignorance, and what these agents undergo is largely determined by their earlier actions. Even this determinism is relative, as these agents are endowed with the latent potential of self-realization and liberation. Due to self-imposed bondage, the phenomenal self undergoes karmic flux. There are two ways to understand karma: initial acts, where the acts of an agent will have certain consequences, and residual karma from previous lives that conditions current situations. *Avidyā* is a precondition for both to exist. Noteworthy, however, is that when addressing the efficacy of karma, Advaitins mean the first. The scope of Advaita is not to explain why we are bound in the first place. Although they accept the law of karma and its consequences, they also maintain that there is no first beginning of the world. They engage the concept of karma only to explain the circumstances in which we find ourselves. Like the character Gregory Samsa in Kafka's *The Metamorphosis*, the real quest of an agent is to be emancipated from bondage. And at this conventional level, the Advaita of Śaṅkara accepts agency and free will.

The fundamental issue, then, is how to understand creation so that we can engage the concept of being an agent in the world to examine the scope of determinism. Yet again, when considering the absolute Advaita viewpoint, no creation has ever occurred, while from the conventional viewpoint, creation has no first beginning. The notion that creation is circular without a first beginning is shared by most Indian philosophical systems. Relying on two different perspectives, Advaitins, on one hand, maintain that creation springs forth from the Brahman, while on the other hand, they also claim that there is no origination. In order to explore the Advaita position regarding causality, I will briefly summarize the pertinent issues addressed by Śaṅkara in his commentary upon the *Brahmasūtra* (BS).

Śaṅkara on Causality

The issue of agency cannot be relevant if there is no causation as such, which, when engaged from the absolute viewpoint, is the case with Advaita. Whether the events are predetermined or whether agents are free is not an issue if there are no events or agents to begin with. Gauḍapāda adopts this absolute perspective that resonates with the Mādhyamikas. There is, however, no compromise among the Advaitins as far as the metaphysical foundation for the manifestation of subject-object duality is concerned. The self or Brahman is the precondition for any speculation, any being. No negation can nullify the Brahman, as even this act of negation relies on the negating subject. Expanding the scope of Advaita from the position of Gauḍapāda, Śaṅkara attempts to provide a coherent picture of the world at the conventional level. There are a number of reasons that lead Śaṅkara to adopt this practical approach in addressing Advaita. If only the absolute viewpoint is maintained, there is no need of teachings since there is neither creation nor bondage. Furthermore, he could not engage in the classical philosophical battle and at the same time explore a rational approach to the non-dual experience of Brahman without speaking of experience at the phenomenal level. Rather than the teachings in the absolute sense, it is this conventional position that provides a better platform for our discussion on topics such as agency.

When Śaṅkara states that the very Brahman is the cause of the world, comparing the world to the show of a magician, we should not conclude that he is describing creation. What we need to keep in mind is that the model of causality where the Brahman or the deep self gives rise to manifoldness without going through an actual transformation, addressed in terms of *vivartta*, is distinct from the actual causation where the effect has been transformed from its original state, addressed in Indian philosophy as *satkāryavāda* (if any original state existed). This is relevant only to the extent that something is phenomenally felt or experienced, although what is supposed to be felt is not ultimately ontologically "there" in Advaita. Even when terms such as "transformation" (*pariṇāma*) or "creation" (*sṛṣṭi*) are used, these philosophers do not accept ontological transformation. The first exegetical battle of Śaṅkara is therefore against the Sāṃkhya philosophers. For the Sāṃkhyas, as clearly explicated in Bryant's essay in this volume, although the self or *puruṣa* is not an agent, it nonetheless is the enjoyer (*bhoktṛ*), and the insentient *prakṛti* causes a real mutation, *satkārya*. Therefore, the first challenge Śaṅkara faces is to reconcile the Upaniṣadic passages that contradict the doctrine of "non-origination" (*ajāti*), as many of them can be read as describing creation.[7]

Keeping this in mind, Śaṅkara's commentary on the Brahmasūtra (BS) (2.2.1–10) counters the Sāṃkhya account of creation, rejecting their theory of actual transformation. While it is not necessary to address all these arguments here, it is noteworthy that his objections respond to the Sāṃkhya positions that accept (1) real causation and (2) insentient *prakṛti* as the cause of the world. Śaṅkara argues, what possible motives could insentient *prakṛti* have behind creation? *Prakṛti* is nothing but the three *guṇas*, none of which have any purpose of its own. Śaṅkara fundamentally disagrees with the premise that something insentient can act, since any "act" is directed toward achieving a goal and is carried out by a conscious agent. While Sāṃkhya does accept a proximity of the conscious self in initiating the chain of creation, Śaṅkara rejects this idea by saying that events are not

7. Śaṅkara's first attempt is to demonstrate that, just like there are texts describing the Sāṃkhya model of causality, there also are texts proposing the monistic model where Brahman itself is the cause (BSbh 2.1.1–2).

caused by the mere proximity of an agent. If proximity could cause action and effect, coming close to a snake could poison an individual, and mere proximity could lead to conception. The Sāṃkhya strategy—keeping the self isolated from being actively engaged in causation while accepting a real transformation—is not acceptable to Śaṅkara, who carries the premise to its logical fallacy when he argues that *prakṛti* causing creation would be similar to grass turning into milk (without a cow or in proximity of a cow). While the rejection of the model of transformation could lead to a monistic paradigm of the early Advaitins wherein the Brahman emanates in the form of the real world just like gold in different forms of ornaments, Śaṅkara maintains that there is no actual transformation at all in the first place.

The problem for the Advaitins, then, is to describe everyday experience where there is causation, there are agents, and events happen in the world that do not seem to be erroneous. Śaṅkara first attempts to describe causation by maintaining that the Brahman is metaphysical source or ground of all causal relations. When this position is adopted, since the self is nothing but Brahman in reality, the self is autonomous in giving rise to the world of common-sense experience. In order to defend this monistic model, Śaṅkara has to justify the contrast between the insentient world and the Brahman that is also identified in terms of pure consciousness. This is because nothing that is radically different originates from something dissimilar: chickens do not lay mangos but eggs. Śaṅkara responds to this problem by saying that insentient effects originate from a sentient cause and vice versa: "It indeed is witnessed in the world that the insentient [effects] such as hair or nails originate out of persons established as sentient and the beetles et cetera [come out] of cow-dung, which is established as insentient."[8] The opponent can argue, however, that the above example cannot describe the relation of the Brahman and the world because the examples of cause and effect share common properties while this is not the case here. Advaitins respond to this objection by saying that both the Brahman and the world share the fundamental constituent of "being" (*sattā*). Here, the opponent can argue further by saying that the Brahman is consciousness and the world is insentient, and if the insentient entities return back to the Brahman, this will pose a contradiction. Śaṅkara responds to this objection by saying that entities that are

8. *dṛśyate hi loke cetanatvena prasiddhebhyaḥ puruṣādibhyo vilakṣaṇānāṃ keśanakhādīnām utpattir acetanatvena ca prasiddhebhyo gomayādibhyo vṛścikādīnām* | BSbh 2.1.6.

considered distinct from their cause, for example a pot, which is different from the soil that comprises it, are recycled back into the primordial substance without maintaining their individual identities. Brahmasūtra (2.1.21) utilizes the metaphor of a cloth to describe the distinction between cause and effect, comparing the Brahman to the wrapped cloth and the world to the spread cloth. This example describes the difference only in form and not in essence.

Since the arguments above lead to a monistic picture of the world that is identical to the Brahman, one can surmise that Śaṅkara does adopt some form of causality. However, a close reading of other passages provides a different picture. In the section entitled "The Beginning" (BS 2.1.14–20), Śaṅkara expands in great detail the theory that Brahman and its effects are identical. Some of the passages in this context are noteworthy for our discussion on agency. For example:

> Plurality is displayed by false cognition.[9]
>
> Just like the transaction in a dream is established as real before awakening, so also are all transactions, prior to the awareness of [the self] as the Brahman.[10]
> The one bitten by a rope snake does not die. Neither are the purposes of drinking or plunging [into water] fulfilled by the mirage of water.[11]

This rejection of creation underlies the Advaita concept of the non-agency of the self. As Śaṅkara has addressed in BS (2.2.1–10), something insentient cannot be the cause, and if the self is considered the cause, it will have to undergo transformation. Advaitins maintain that Brahman and the phenomenal self are identical in essence. This being the case, if there were any creation, the phenomenal self could then be considered the autonomous personal creator of the world (BS 2.1.21). To prevent this conclusion, Śaṅkara responds that the Brahman transcends individuality because it is eternally pure, constantly free, and always in the state of

9. *mithyājñānavijṛmbhitaṃ ca nānātvam* | BSbh 2.1.14.

10. *sarvavyavahārāṇām eva prāgbrahmātmatāvijñānāt satyatopapatteḥ, svapnavyavahārasyeva prākprabodhāt* | BSbh 2.1.14.

11. *na hi rajjusarpeṇa daṣṭo mriyate* | *nāpi mṛgatṛṣṇikāmbhasā pānāvagāhanādiprayojanaṃ kriyata iti* | BSbh 2.1.14.

liberation (*Brahmasūtraśāṅkarabhāṣyam* [BSbh] 2.1.22). One can further argue that the self is the creator with regard to the person who has realized the identity of the self and the Brahman. Śaṅkara counter-argues, "in that state, what is creation [there?]"[12]

The conversation above regarding causality is noteworthy for the argument that if by the term "self" (*ātman*) we mean the Brahman, then it is eternally free (and has no agency); but if this term is referring to the phenomenal self, then it is bound due to the karma generated by its own acts. Either way, there is no entity extrinsic to the self that determines its agency. A common Advaita metaphor is that of a silkworm that is caged inside its own cocoon. One needs to nonetheless keep in mind that the conversation regarding creation applies only on the phenomenal level. Śaṅkara reminds us repeatedly that the instances where creation is discussed are not meant to describe or endorse the notion of a real creation as such, but only to affirm the oneness of the Brahman and the world. For instance:

> When we hear [the Vedas] as [describing] creation, one should also not forget that [this] is not [to propound creation] as an absolute object, because the [worldly] transaction is [just] the name and the form assumed due to ignorance, and [these passages are in fact] directed to establish identity with the Brahman.[13]

One can, then, say that this position is tantamount to accepting that the cognitive faculty (*buddhi*) is the cause of the world. The Advaitins would then be accepting that the mind is the sole cause of creation. If we read texts such as the *Yogavāsiṣṭha*, we encounter a similar position. This position in essence attributes to the mind its own agency. Śaṅkara is not willing to accept this position. In the section on "Agent" (BS 2.3.33–39), he expands upon the concept that a cognitive faculty cannot be the agent and gives the following reasons:

1. The injunctive sentences in the Vedas presuppose an agent that is distinct from the cognitive faculty to act on what has been enjoined.

---

12. *tatra kuta eva sṛṣṭiḥ?* BSbh 2.1.22.

13. *na ceyaṃ paramārthaviṣayā sṛṣṭiśrutir avidyākalpitanāmarūpavyavahāragocaratvāt, brah-mātmabhāvapratipādanaparatvāc cety etad api naiva vismartavyam* | BSbh 2.1.33.

2. Accepting an agent that is other than the cognitive faculty is congruent with the Vedic passages that describe that the agent strolls out when in dream.[14]
3. The phenomenal self is described as the agent that retains information processed through the cognitive faculty.
4. There is a separation between agency and instrumentality, and if the cognitive faculty is considered the agent, this will contradict the above distinction.
5. The *samādhi* experience, which describes the state devoid of cognitive functioning, will not be established, if the phenomenal self is not considered distinct from the cognitive faculty.

The above discussion demonstrates Śaṅkara's willingness to engage his philosophy at the phenomenal level. Śaṅkara alludes to his position regarding agency with a brief statement pertaining to the phenomenal self: "There is no absolute autonomy of the self in carrying out actions, because [actions are] contingent upon space, time, and particular instruments. However, it is not [the case] that an agent will not have agency if it is dependent upon the accessories. A cook is still a cook even when he relies on wood, water, et cetera."[15] This position echoes that of the Grammarians, as Cardona has pointed out in this volume.[16] Here, instruments are distinguished from the agent in terms of his autonomy, although an agent cannot in practice carry out something in absence of the instruments. Returning to our discourse on the cognitive faculty, in which the independence of an agent similarly relies on instruments, the phenomenal self is autonomous, although it relies on its cognitive faculty.

In conclusion, according to Śaṅkara, the conventional agent is autonomous, albeit only at the conventional level of reality. The meta-narrative of Advaita, that all that exists is the Brahman alone and there exists no action

---

14. The analysis of dream to analyze reality comes frequently in the Upaniṣadic literature itself but receives prominence with Gauḍapāda. Noteworthy is the fact that the dream analogy leads the Mādhyamikas to absolute emptiness, the Yogācārins to the doctrine of momentary instances of cognition, and the Advaitins to the undifferentiated consciousness that has never come to any defilement.

15. *api cārthakriyāyāṃ nātyantam ātmanaḥ svātantryam asti, deśakālanimittaviśeṣāpekṣatvāt | na ca sahāyāpekṣasya kartuḥ kartṛtvaṃ nivartate | bhavati hy edhodakādyapekṣasyāpi paktuḥ paktṛtvam* | BSbh 2.3.37.

16. Particularly the *sūtra* of Pāṇini, *svatantraḥ kartā* (*Aṣṭādhyāyī* 1.4.54), is noteworthy for this discussion.

or agency at the absolute level, nonetheless remains untouched, as this statement supersedes all other statements. At the level of the Brahman, Śaṅkara wastes no time in discarding this "autonomous" agent, as the very concept of agency is a product of ignorance (*avidyā*) that needs to be shunned. The paradox generated by this view is apparent: when you are free (i.e., self-realized) you have no will to act, and when you have the will, your autonomy is compromised by *avidyā* and karma. As an agent in the form of the phenomenal self (*jīvātman*), the subject is under its own spell and its powers are limited, while, from the position of the Brahman, there is just the non-dual awareness that does not retain any agency or action. When we see creation and causality, we are bound and our actions are somewhat determined, but when we are liberated, there exists neither act nor agency. Advaitins therefore describe liberation in terms of an awakening, compared to waking up from a perpetual dream. From the Advaita standpoint, the discourse on the autonomy of an agent is a quest to alter one's own dreams, and the Advaitins are interested not in changing the dream but in waking up. In light of the higher awakening, there exists no agent or action and the issue of free will is a moot point.

Sureśvara on "Non-action" (naiṣkarmya)

In the interests of brevity, I will address in this section only the arguments on agency that Sureśvara discusses in his "Establishment of Non-action" *Naiṣkarmyasiddhi* (NS). The focal point of this text is to establish that the comprehension of Vedic passages alone is sufficient for liberation. In his opinion, no meditative practice (or any action for that matter that relies on agency) stands between the understanding of sentences such as *tat tvam asi*, "you are that," and attaining liberation. This position emerges from the broader metaphysical position that the self qua Brahman is devoid of action, free from qualities and parts, and also that Brahman cannot be an effect of any action, as it cannot be originated, altered, reached, or transformed.

Various Advaitins prior to Śaṅkara, however, maintained that Brahman is active and the world is its modification. Brahmadatta, for instance, held that sentences such as *tat tvam asi* are to be interpreted in light of other Upaniṣadic passages such as "one should meditate upon the self."[17] If we

---

17. *ātmety evopāsīta* (Bṛhadāraṇyakopaniṣad (BĀU) I.iv.7). For discussion, see Hiriyanna 1928: 1–9; Hiriyanna 1980: xxiii.

read sentences such as "you are that" as injunctions, this requires an agent with the will to act on them. Accordingly, the philosophers that maintain agency of the self hold that one has to act on the knowledge of the deep self to attain liberation. They argue that just as a mere understanding of the commands such as "one should offer *soma*" does not translate into acquiring virtue, so also is it with these Upaniṣadic passages. Action, in their opinion, is the only means to virtue. Congruent with this position, Bhartṛprapañca maintains that an infusion of knowledge and action (*jñāna-karma-samuccaya*) is mandatory for liberation.

Maṇḍana (690 CE) advocates a modified version of this position. The difference in Maṇḍana's position is that he maintains that meditation gives rise to a different type of knowledge, a deeper knowledge compared to that of a mere linguistic comprehension. He thus accepts wisdom as the absolute means but also holds that this wisdom is a consequence of contemplation and not merely of comprehending the Vedic passages. The main argument of Sureśvara against this position is that all the means of veridical awareness (*pramāṇas*) are independent in giving rise to awareness. For instance, we do not rely on inference to confirm what has been directly apprehended; or, we do not need to touch the object to verify its smell when we receive the sensory information through our olfactory system. Along the same lines, if verbal testimony is accepted as a valid means of cognition, and this is the case with all these Advaita philosophers, then *śruti* should suffice in generating the corresponding awareness independent of any other means.

Mīmāṃsakas give a linguistic turn to this issue of Advaita soteriology, arguing that there is always an injunction in the Vedic texts, even in the context of declarative sentences such as "you are that." This position is not acceptable to the Advaitins, and their response is that, while there are Vedic sentences that enjoin actions, the scope of the Upaniṣads is different; they are primarily meant to provide knowledge of Brahman. The sentences that establish the identity between the phenomenal self and Brahman are ones that just describe the facts, such as the sentence, "this is Mr. Fox."

If there is a gap between knowing the deep self and being liberated from *saṃsāra*, this would suggest that something else is required for liberation besides simply knowing the self. While this is the case for Brahmadatta, Sureśvara rejects this position. Simply put, Sureśvara argues that you do not meditate upon a rope once you realize that what you conceived of as a snake is in fact a rope. The liberation from fear of a snake does not require meditation, as it is instantaneous to the realization that the object is just a rope. Sureśvara has no shortage of examples. He says that one does not make an extra effort to find the necklace that was lost once one realizes that it was right on the neck all along (NS 1.31), nor does the individual make an extra effort to remove the demon, once the person realizes that it is his own shadow (NS 1.32). Actions are similar to a child conceiving of a mascot as a real elephant (NS 1.59), or thinking of a stump as a thief (NS 1.60). For Sureśvara, both the duality in the form of subject and object, and the problems that arise from our misconceptions regarding the subject (thinking that I am the agent of such an act) and objects (desiring to acquire or avoid something) vanish once ignorance (*avidyā*) is removed: "Since liberation is only the removal of ignorance, action cannot be an instrument. Action does not remove ignorance, just as darkness [cannot remove the superimposed object] manifest in the dark" (NS 1.24).

Sureśvara argues that actions create, achieve, reform, or transform something. The liberated state is not something that you can create, alter, or transform. Actions thus cannot grant liberation (NS 1.52). When one is liberated, no ontological change has occurred. The removal of misconception only requires knowledge of the reality and not doing something about it. For Sureśvara, there is not even room for the fusion of action and wisdom as the means for liberation. In his opinion, this union is like that of darkness and light (NS 1.56, 66), completely incompatible.

Appealing to the example that fire cannot burn itself, Sureśvara rejects any agency in self-realization. His general point is that one cannot simultaneously be the agent and object of the same action. This argument stems from a refutation of the Bhāṭṭa Mīmāṃsakas (NS 2.23–24).[18] One can argue that there is a fallacy in Sureśvara's position, since counterexamples are available: one directly apprehends that "I am aware of myself." Sureśvara argues that this mode of awareness is manifest in *buddhi* and therefore is a property of *buddhi* and not of the witnessing self. According to Sureśvara, what has been grasped when one objectifies the self is merely the inner modalities collectively identified as the "internal cognitive faculties" (*antaḥ-karaṇa*[19]). The ego that has been objectified is thus a property,

18. Prābhākaras had already pointed out this particular objection against the Bhāṭṭas. For discussion, see Freschi's chapter in this volume.

19. The term *antaḥ-karaṇa* collectively refers to *manas*, *buddhi*, *citta*, and *ahaṃkāra* that describe all the internal cognitive modalities. Mind, intellect, and egoity are its primary expressions.

and it belongs to the substrate wherein it appears. This ego is manifest in the internal cognitive faculty, and this faculty is not the phenomenal self. Therefore what is manifest to the experience, "I know myself," is not the self since it cannot be objectified, but rather the ego that is witnessed by the self in the background of the internal cognitive modality.[20] Sureśvara also does not accept the idea that the very self divides itself into two parts as the agent and object of cognition. If this position is accepted, Sureśvara points out that this will establish identity between the subject and the object (NS 2.26). Furthermore, if the self were to manifest as subject and object in different modes of time, there would be no subject to cognize it when it manifests as an object. Something cannot be called an "object of cognition" in the absence of an agent that cognizes it.[21]

One can argue that the ego (*ahaṃkāra*) is the property of the self, since even in realizing the Brahman, one states, "I am Brahman." Advaitins maintain that this identity is nothing more than the identity of the ego and the body superimposed on the *ātman* as is the case in the statement "I am slim." Sureśvara compares the sentence "I am Brahman" with the sentence "the stump is [in fact] a person" (NS 2.29). When one realizes that what one saw as a stump in the distance was in fact a person, this realization does not confirm the stump's presence. Along the same lines, what is mistakenly construed as an agent, when truly realized, is nothing but the non-agential Brahman. Sureśvara gives an additional reason to reject that the ego is the property of the self, saying that the ego would be then eternal, just like the self, if it were its property. And since its removal would not be possible, liberation would then be impossible (liberation being construed in all Indic soteriological traditions as freedom from the ego; NS 2.33).[22] Nor can one argue that the phenomenal self transforms into the Brahman just like a sour mango turns into a ripe and sweet mango, because the self is free from transformation (NS 2.34). Furthermore, the agency imposed upon the self is not permanent, as one can see its absence in the deep sleep state, and if the self were composed of impermanent properties, this would lead to the impermanence of the self.

For the Advaitins, then, the properties imposed on the self are similar to the property of fire imposed on a hot iron rod, when one says, "this rod

---

20. NS 2.25, and the *Candrikā* commentary thereon.

21. NS 2.27, and the *Candrikā* commentary thereon.

22. For discussion of the self having properties, see Bryant in this volume.

burns." In this example, although the rod is not fire, the property of burning inherent to fire has been superimposed (*adhyasta*) on the rod. In essence, the phenomenal agent finds himself with different subjective identities, having external properties superimposed on him. The deep self, on the other hand, transcends these changing identities. The soteriological aspect of this removal of agency lies in the elimination of attachment that arises from the ego being linked with objects. This leads in consequence to the rejection of the phenomenal self in Advaita. As Ram-Prasad (2011: 229) points out, "the 'I' itself is part of egoity; everything about it is made up. The 'I' simply does not pick out *ātman*." Whether arguing that the true self cannot act or following the rejection of the "I," the issues of agency and free will do not occupy a relevant space within the domain of Advaita metaphysics from its perspective of ultimate reality.

One of the central Advaita premises is that the deep self, identical to consciousness, is immediately given in every mode of experience. Whether or not concepts exist in ultimate reality, the self that is witnessing the being or nonbeing of concepts is always there. Relying on this premise, Sureśvara argues that the phenomenal world that comprises agents, acts, and objects of cognition—and indeed, cognition itself—rests on the ignorance of the true self. The manifestation of this ignorance is a consequence of the self not being aware of itself. This being the case, the phenomenal world manifests in the very platform of the self qua consciousness.[23] For Sureśvara, the self is transcendent to the triad of the subject, object, and act of cognition, and while it is witnessing the events of cognition, it does not in itself undergo these events (NS 2.108).

According to Sureśvara, both the body and the agent are contingent upon higher cognitive mechanisms to be affirmed as phenomenally existing. Just as experiencing the body entails the existence of sense organs, so also does the experience of oneself as the subject necessitate the deep self (NS 3.56). This experience is the superimposition of the ego upon the deep self—the superimposition which constitutes agency—akin to the superimposed properties between fire and the iron rod (NS 3.59). One can argue that if the ego is placed among external objects, why do we not say "I am experienced" instead of "I experience"? Sureśvara responds to this question by saying that the concept of agency arises being contingent upon external objects that are to be

23. Synthesized from NS 2.96 and Sureśvara's auto-commentary thereon.

grasped by the internal cognitive complex (*antaḥ-karaṇa*).[24] To the question, why does this ego not appear equivalent to the external objects?, Sureśvara responds that there is no subject anticipating the act of objectifying the ego (NS 3.60–61). In other words, the transcendent self does not act or objectify anything, and there is no other higher mechanism to cognize this ego and make it as its object. In fact, it is not even the nature of the self to witness entities, as there are no entities to be witnessed in reality. One may then ask, "how is the internal cognitive modality cognized?" Sureśvara responds to this by proposing two tiers, where the deep self is conditioned by the concept of "I" and this phenomenal self is what grasps the internal cognitive modality.

It is due to ignorance (*avidyā*) that agency is perceived and has been witnessed by the self. In the deep sleep state, although there is latent ignorance, it is not active, and so there is no subject or object to be witnessed. Since there never is an absence of the self, the Upaniṣadic sentences only affirm what is already there. This can be compared to the statement, "you are the tenth."[25] A common example in Advaita, this sentence epitomizes the narrative of ten people crossing the river and counting heads to make sure that all have crossed the river alive. Coincidentally as everyone counts only the others and not themselves, they come up with only nine. Seeing the group of quizzical travelers, the wise man points out that the counting subject had forgotten to include himself in the total. In another example, if a prince is raised by a hunter since early childhood, he will assume himself to be a hunter. The sentence, "you are the prince" does not create a prince out of a hunter, but only helps to remove the misconception of the prince regarding himself and allows him to regain his lost identity. Just like there is no action sought in the case of the prince believing himself to be a hunter, actions are inconsequential with regard to liberation.

Alternate Models of Causation in Advaita

Setting aside the issue of agency and action as a precondition for liberation, the issue of causation and an allied question of the possible scope of the self's creative potential warrant deeper analysis. If we closely read

24. *evaṃ tāvad avidyotthasyāntaḥkaraṇasya bāhyaviṣayanimittarūpāvacchedāyāhaṃvṛttir vyāpriyate* | NS 3.59, auto-commentary of Sureśvara.

25. This example is common in Advaita literature after Śaṅkara. Sureśvara, for instance, uses this example in *Taittirīyavārttika* 2.8.77; 2.1.39; *Bṛhadāraṇyakopaniṣadbhāṣyavārttika* 1.1.208; 1.4.602; and NS 3.64.

various Advaita texts on these issues, we come to realize that there is not one single philosophy that we can call Advaita. Relying on some common categories, Advaitins develop distinct models that respond to different challenges raised by different schools of Indian philosophy. I will offer a brief treatment of the alternate models of causation given by Advaitins so that we can contextualize the issue of agency in a broader sense.

The Advaitins subsequent to Śaṅkara respond in multiple ways to the question "what level of agency do the subjects (*jīvas*) enjoy in giving rise to the phenomenal world?" This diversity stems from their positions regarding ignorance (*avidyā*). Although all the Advaitins maintain that individuality is due to *avidyā,* not all explain its scope the same way. Maṇḍana, who most likely was a senior contemporary to Śaṅkara,[26] maintains that the substrate of ignorance (*avidyā*) is the individual self and not the Brahman. The very Brahman is perceived as conditioned and in the form of the world by the subjects undergoing *avidyā.* It needs to be noted at this point that the term *avidyā* refers both to misperception and non-perception. So, due to *avidyā,* persons not only do not see the way things are (as the singular Brahman) but also perceive them otherwise (as the phenomenal world), thus sustaining a grand illusion of cause and effect. The plurality of the phenomenal selves, following the model of Maṇḍana and Vācaspati, is due to multiple *avidyās,* with each person being confined by her own *avidyā.* Although this model will not settle the issue of whether subjects enjoy free will, it nonetheless gives scope to the notion of subjects who construct their own reality. The reality as we see it is either a causation of an individual self (one understanding of the Advaita model that there exists a single phenomenal self) that projects its own world like in a dream or hallucination, or a collective causation, a transaction in the world. Just as subjects are diverse with distinct interests, so also is the world manifold. The world as we see it is thus our own collective creation, constructed by our responses to particular events, our embodied states, and our active engagement in the world.

Even when this perspective that provides some apparent agency and creative initiative to the self that projects a world of experience is adopted, the agent still undergoes the consequences of his previous karma. Following Advaita, people are miserable, simply put, because they put themselves in misery. According to this perspective, the material cause behind the

26. For the time of Maṇḍana, see Sastri 1984. For the philosophy of Maṇḍana, see Thrasher 1993; Acharya 2006.

world, *avidyā*, is the power inherent to the Brahman. Brahman, as previously identified, is consciousness in itself. Following Maṇḍana, the self or the Brahman is also capable of being ignorant of itself or of knowing itself other than what it really is. This, however, does not require that Maṇḍana accepts real causation as understood in the world of common experience. The noteworthy element in this position is that there is no ultimate causation, and the world of common-sense perception is collectively *construed* as such by the *jīvas*. On the other hand, following Padmapāda (740 CE) and Prakāśātman (975 CE), the founders of the Vivaraṇa sub-school of Advaita, the Brahman is the locus of *avidyā*, and not the individual selves. However, if by agency we mean the subjectivity imposed upon the phenomenal selves, the above model of Advaita proposed by Maṇḍana provides a higher autonomy, since these subjects collectively construe their own reality.

Besides the phenomenal selves that experience agency, Advaitins identify another category, that of Īśvara (or Hiraṇyagarbha), broadly interpreted as the collective ego. This collective subject enjoys the highest level of autonomy, as it is the free will of this agent that gives rise to the phenomenal world. However, this collective self is not the agent whose free will is under consideration. In order for us to address the agency of the phenomenal self, we need to bracket this meta-agent or Īśvara from the discourse.

In order to contextualize agency in Advaita, it is essential for us to comprehend the relation of the phenomenal self to the collective self identified as Īśvara. For the Advaitins, Brahman does not have selfhood or agency of any sort. When this transcendent category assumes selfhood, it experiences itself as Īśvara. Advaitins have a varied response to how this collective self is related to individual agents. According to Sureśvara, the very Brahman when conditioned by *avidyā* assumes the collective subjectivity of Īśvara and when conditioned by *buddhi* becomes the phenomenal self. This position, however, is not acceptable to many other Advaitins. Sarvajñātman (1027 CE), for instance, rejects the idea that Īśvara is pure consciousness delimited by *avidyā*. Pure consciousness, for him, is like the surface, where what is reflected due to *avidyā* is Īśvara. In his opinion, Brahman or pure consciousness is both the substrate and the object of *avidyā*. Following this model, the plurality of the phenomenal self is due to the plurality of the cognitive faculty and not *avidyā*. On the other hand, Prakāśātman maintains that the phenomenal self is consciousness reflected upon ignorance that is conditioned by the internal cognitive modalities. The varied scope of the phenomenal self within Advaita demonstrates the problem in identifying one Advaita position regarding agency as definitive.[27]

One of the reasons for introducing the Advaita concept of Īśvara (or Hiraṇyagarbha) here is that some Advaitins maintain that this Īśvara is actually the single phenomenal self (*jīva*), and what maintains individuality and agency is the individual's mind (*antaḥ-karaṇa* to be precise). This means that what we have considered to be the self is merely a reflection of the self (the mirror image of the self in our mind), where what is meant by the self is the individuated state of Brahman. Noteworthy is the fact that the mind is not a beginningless entity, in contrast to the phenomenal self. Although Advaitins maintain that individuality is a consequence of *avidyā* conditioning the Brahman, they consider the relation between Brahman and *avidyā* as beginningless. This makes the agency underlying the phenomenal self as beginningless. However, this is not the case if agency is linked merely with the mind. This position of Advaita heads to the direction of the more radical form of subjective idealism.

This gloss does not sufficiently detail the nature of the phenomenal self in Advaita, nor is this the place for that. What is explicit, nonetheless, is that not all Advaitins agree upon what constitutes a person. While these differences appear to be minor exegetical divergences, a closer study reveals that they give rise to different epistemologies. The following statements are very distinct: (1) a person is the mirror image of the Brahman, similar to the sun reflected in multiple puddles and (2) a person is the very Brahman conditioned by ignorance, similar to the space conditioned by the walls inside the house. In all contexts, Advaitins maintain that subjectivity is phenomenal and also that, in whatsoever form, *avidyā* does play a role in constituting this subjectivity. It is not necessary that the subject is whatever he believes himself to be. Just because the Daoist philosopher Zhuangzi dreamt of himself as a butterfly does not make him a butterfly, even if that is what he believed himself to be while in the dream.

There are ample examples in texts such as the *Yogavāsiṣṭha* that resonate with the dream of Zhuangzi. But the characters in this text do not just simply "have" a dream; instead, through some spell or their own yogic abilities, they actually enter those states. If we consider the example of Gādhi,[28] the protagonist does not simply find himself in his alternate subjective state,

---

27. For discussion of the different models of Advaita, see Timalsina 2006: 20–42.

28. *Yogavāsiṣṭha*, Upaśama Prakaraṇa, chapters 44–50.

but this parallel existence is subsequently affirmed even when the character returns to his previous identity. In this narrative, Gādhi wishes to experience the illusive power (*māyā*) of Viṣṇu, and he soon finds himself in a strange situation. When he entered the waters to take a bath, he experiences his death and a rebirth in a lower-caste family. When grown up, this alternate Gādhi becomes the king and eventually gets rejected when the people learn about his bloodlines. When he immolates himself upon finding this turn unbearable, he wakes up to his previous identity. While recovering from this dreamlike experience, a guest verifies the narrative of an actual kingdom ruled by a lower-caste individual where the king kills himself. Further puzzled by this affirmation, Gādhi embarks upon an adventure to explore that kingdom. The narrative comes to the climax with the protagonist finding his abandoned home and the forsaken kingdom. In the narrative of Līlā,[29] the protagonist goes to the parallel world to meet her deceased husband only to find him as a king engaged in battle. The narrative takes a turn with the protagonist finding her identical twin in this parallel world. She convinces the king and another Līlā to join her in her homecoming. This utterly fictional nature of reality that maintains equal status to the common-sense experience is what gives rise to the Advaita model of "creation as seeing" (*dṛṣṭisṛṣṭivāda*).[30] Creation, following this model, is identical to awareness, or alternatively, perceptual modes. Although this model of Advaita accommodates both single and multiple agents,[31] if a single phenomenal self is considered, all events are merely the manifestation of the will of this agent. This model can accommodate the highest degree of autonomy as far as phenomenal reality is concerned. The consequence of adopting this model of Advaita is that there will be no categorical difference between dreams and

29. *Yogavāsiṣṭha*, Utpatti Prakaraṇa, chapters 15–68.

30. One way of understanding this model of Advaita is that creation is coincidental to perception (*dṛṣṭisamakālīnā sṛṣṭiḥ*). When this position is adopted, the term *dṛṣṭi* is interpreted as perception and not pure consciousness. Following another interpretation, pure consciousness itself is creation (or the reality beneath whatever is assumed to be creation). Following the second model, the term *dṛṣṭi* is understood as pure consciousness ("seeing in itself"). When the Advaitins utilize the analogy of a dream to demonstrate creation, it appears at the first glance that they are describing the first model of *dṛṣṭisṛṣṭi*. However, they often add a note that whatever is considered to be a dream (both the dreaming subject and the dream entities) is nothing but consciousness in itself, manifest as both subject and object. Even when adopting *dṛṣṭisṛṣṭi*, Advaitins do not compromise their grand narrative of Brahman as the absolute reality, and this is what keeps them distinct from their Yogācāra counterparts. For an extensive treatment of this model of Advaita, see Timalsina 2006.

31. For discussions regarding the single-*jīva* model of Advaita, see Timalsina 2009: 34–49.

these kinds of creations, as both have the same subjective validity. The subjects are nevertheless autonomous in their imagination, and the scope of this fancy includes bondage and liberation, subjects experiencing collective and individual egos (Īśvara and *jīva*), and subjects and objects. When adopting this position, the entire phenomenal manifestation crumbles when ignorance is removed, that is, when the daydream has finished.

Conclusion

It is not possible to limit the scope of agency in the varied landscape of Advaita to one single model. According to the early Advaitins, some of whom also authored Mīmāṃsā literature, the self is active, liberation[32] is a consequence of action (in the sense of both everyday and ritual acts) as much as knowing, and the world is one mode of Brahman, just like a gold necklace consists of gold. On the other hand, according to Gauḍapāda, the self that is identical to the absolute is inactive, and there never has been any origination—all forms of causation or creation are illusory. While Śaṅkara attempts to negotiate between these two viewpoints, the commentarial literature maintains some of these early divergences. Keeping Gauḍapāda's teachings in the background, Śaṅkara reconciles with the realists by introducing the concept of conventional reality (*vyāvahārika*). Within this scope, there is an agent, and although mediated, this agent is nonetheless autonomous in determining his action. If the reality of convention is a fiction, the role is negotiated between the collective (Hiraṇyagarbha) and the individual selves. If individuals are merely dream objects, their autonomy is inconsequential. On the other hand, if the individuals are the authors of their fiction (one way of reading *dṛṣṭisṛṣṭi*), they enjoy a negotiated autonomy (as creation is each individual's imagination and these are shared). On the other hand, following the doctrine of *ekajīva,* the agent is absolutely autonomous, if a single ego is considered to be the agent. In the absolute sense, the single agent or these agents are autonomous only to the extent that their creation is perceived to actually exist; as far as the absolute reality is concerned, Brahman does not undergo any creation. Just like the protagonist in Borges's *The Circular Ruins,* the agent

32. The early Mīmāṃsakas were not focused on the issue of liberation. Their concept of *niḥśreyas* concerns going to *svarga* rather than realizing the self and being liberated from the chain of karma. The Advaitins, with an influence of Mīmāṃsā, incorporate karma while accepting the concept of liberation.

here finds his autonomy in constructive dreaming. There nonetheless is the moment of realization. The subject that considered himself to be the agent now realizes as the self undivided in the modes of subject and object. In this moment uninterrupted by any rupture, there lies just pure consciousness, undifferentiated, self-aware, and blissful.

References

PRIMARY SOURCES

Bṛhadāraṇyakopaniṣad (see Olivelle 1998).

Brahmasūtraśāṅkarabhāṣyam: Bhāmatī-Vedāntakalpataru-Parimalopa-bṛṃhitam (vols. 1–2). Delhi: Parimal Publications, 1918.

Naiṣkarmyasiddhi (see Hiriyanna 1980).

SECONDARY SOURCES

Acharya, Diwakar. 2006. *Vācaspatimiśra's Tattvasamīkṣā: The Earliest Commentary on Maṇḍanamiśra's Brahmasiddhi.* Stuttgart: Franz Steiner Verlag.

Alston, A. J., trans. 1997. *The Method of the Vedanta: A Critical Account of the Advaita Tradition.* By Swami Satchidanandendra. Delhi: Motilal Banarsidas.

Hiriyanna, M., ed. 1928. "Brahmadatta: An Old Vedāntin." *Journal of Oriental Research* 2: 1–9.

———. 1980. *The Naiṣkarmyasiddhi of Sureśvarācārya. With the Candrikā of Jñānottama.* Poona: Bhandarkar Oriental Research Institute.

King, Richard. 1995. *Early Advaita Vedānta and Buddhism: The Mahāyāna Context of the Gauḍapāda-Kārikā.* Albany: State University of New York Press.

Nakamura, Hajime. 2004. *A History of Early Vedānta Philosophy.* Delhi: Motilal Banarsidass.

Olivelle, Patrick. 1998. *The Early Upaniṣads: Annotated Text and Translation.* New York: Oxford University Press.

Potter, Karl. 2011. *Encyclopedia of Indian Philosophies: Bibliography.* See http://faculty.washington.edu/kpotter/

Ram-Prasad, Chakravarthi. 2011. "Situating the Elusive Self of Advaita Vedānta." In *Self, No Self? Perspectives from Analytical Phenomenological, and Indian Traditions,* ed. Mark Siderits, Evan Thompson, and Dan Zahavi, 217–238. New York: Oxford University Press.

Sastri, S. Kuppuswami, ed. 1984. *Brahmasiddhi of Maṇḍanamiśra: With Śaṅkhapāṇi's commentary.* Delhi: Sri Satguru Publications.

Thrasher, Allen Wright. 1993. *The Advaita Vedānta of Brahmasiddhi.* Delhi: Motilal Banarsidass.

Timalsina, Sthaneshwar. 2006. *Seeing and Appearance: A Study of the Advaita Doctrine of Dṛṣṭisṛṣṭi.* Aachen: Shaker Verlag.

———. 2009. *Consciousness in Indian Philosophy: The Advaita Doctrine of "Awareness only."* New York: Routledge.

9

The Linguistics and Cosmology of Agency in Nondual Kashmiri Śaiva Thought

David Peter Lawrence

AGENCY, THE CAPACITY of a human or non-human agent or actor to act, is a notoriously difficult subject for philosophical inquiry.[1] One must ultimately understand the nature and operation of the agent—including its cognition, choice or what some conceive as "free will" about what to do, and causal efficacy—in the context of numerous other factors that may determine the course of action: physical, biological, cultural, psychological, economic, political, metaphysical, religious or "supernatural," and so on.

The present essay will consist mainly of an exposition of key features of the theories of agency of the nondual Kashmiri Śaiva, Pratyabhijñā philosophers, Utpaladeva (ca. 900–950 CE) and Abhinavagupta (ca. 950–1020 CE). I will first overview and reflect synthetically on my earlier research regarding these philosophers' linguistic understandings of agency, along with the other factors of action, in terms of action syntax and grammatical persons. Sanskritic reflections on a variety of philosophical topics, including agency and action, often has recourse to Pāṇinian and other linguistic considerations. This is particularly the case in schools such as the Pratyabhijñā that follow the legacy of the linguistic philosopher Bhartṛhari (ca. 500–700 CE).

I will supplement the consideration of the Śaivas' linguistic approach to agency with some observations about how they further situate agency within their traditional "theosophical" cosmology of emanation and return. My comparative comments in the essay will be mainly for the sake of elucidating the distinctiveness of the Pratyabhijñā philosophy. At the end, I will

1. I wish to thank Matthew Dasti for his helpful suggestions regarding this article.

mention directions I hope in the future to explore, in pursuit of a more constructive dialogical engagement with the Pratyabhijñā philosophy of agency.

The Quest for Power in Nondual Kashmiri Śaivism, Pratyabhijñā Philosophy, and Pratyabhijñā-Based Hermeneutics

The designation "nondual" or "monistic" "Kashmiri Śaivism" refers to a group of overlapping and interweaving tantric traditions that developed in Kashmir from the latter centuries of the first millennium CE through the early centuries of the second.[2] The classification of such traditions as "tantric" is directly relevant to their understanding of agency. Probably the most generic and distinctive feature of tantra for contemporary scholars is the pursuit of *power*, the practical expressions of which range from limited "magical" proficiencies (*siddhis*), through political power, to the sublimated omnipotence of the liberated person performing the divine cosmic acts. Hindu traditions understand this power as in essence Śakti, the Goddess herself (Woodroffe 1981; Sanderson 1995; Chakravarty 1997; White 2000: 7–9; Lawrence 1999: 53–65 on the *śākta upāya*).

Alexis Sanderson (1985, 1988, 1995) has illuminated the ways in which the tantric pursuit of power transgresses orthodox, upper-caste Hindu norms that delimit human agency for the sake of symbolic-ritual purity (*śuddhi*). Many of the tantric rites were originally performed in cremation grounds, which are traditionally viewed in South Asia as extremely impure. Prescriptions for the sexual ritual commonly advocate adultery and caste-mixing, and perhaps sometimes even incest (Sanderson 1995: 83; Kakar 1983: 159, on the psychology of the sense of power accruing from the tantric fantasy of incest). David White (2003) has recently argued that tantra originated in ancient Siddha practices that endeavored to gain benefits from *yoginīs* through the transgressive offering and ingestion of sexual fluids. In some traditions, there is the ingestion of other impure bodily substances and even, allegedly, human flesh (Parry 1982).

In nondual Śaiva traditions, Śakti is incorporated into the essence of the God Śiva as his integral power and consort through whom, in the

---

2. In this chapter no distinction is made, as is sometimes done, between doctrines and experiences that are "monistic" and "nondual." Likewise, I do not follow any practice of distinguishing between the terms "tantra" and "tantrism."

central myth, he emanates and controls the world. Through diverse ritual practices, ranging from sexual rites to contemplations of the symbolism of *mantras* and *maṇḍalas*, and philosophical speculations, the adept endeavors to recapitulate the basic mythic structure in order to realize salvific identity with Śiva as the *śaktiman*, the possessor and enjoyer of Śakti.

Developing initiatives of his teacher, the philosopher Somānanda (ca. 900–950) (see Somānanda and Utpaladeva 1934; Nemec 2011), Utpaladeva (ca. 900–950) created the foundational texts of the Pratyabhijñā system of philosophical theology, comprising the *Īśvarapratyabhijñākārikā* (IPK),[3] the autocommentaries *Vṛtti* (2002 [IPKV]) and the now fragmentary *Vivṛti*, and the *Siddhitrayī* (1921). While rooted particularly in the tradition known as Trika ("Triadism," named for its advertence to triads of cosmological principles and modes of practice), the Pratyabhijñā became the most influential philosophy for several other traditions of nondual Śaivism and Hindu tantra.

A good portion of the credit for this influence must be ascribed to Abhinavagupta, who further elaborated the Pratyabhijñā in erudite and creative commentaries (1986 [IPV], on the IPK; 1987a [IPVV], on Utpaladeva's largely missing *Vivṛti*). Even more consequential historically was Abhinavagupta's utilization of the Pratyabhijñā theories and categories to formulate what may be called a *philosophical hermeneutics of tradition* (*āgama*), which provided a critical intellectual structure to non-philosophical Trika theology and synthesized under the rubric of the rationalized Trika an enormous range of symbolism, doctrine, and practice from alternative Śaiva, Śākta, and other Hindu and Buddhist schools (important works include 1987b [TA], 1982 [TS], 1985 [PTV], 1921 [MVV]). Abhinavagupta is also renowned for his works on Sanskrit poetics, in which he interpreted aesthetic experience as homologous to, and practically approaching, the nondual Śaiva soteriological realization (1981–1984 [ABH]; 1975–1981 [DHAL]).

The Pratyabhijñā system developed by Utpaladeva and Abhinavagupta is both a philosophical apologetics and a gnoseological internalization of tantric praxis. A central moment of the Pratyabhijñā philosophy is the explanation of Śiva's Śakti, through whom he emanates and controls the universe, as an act self-recognition (*pratyabhijñā, ahampratyavamarśa*). Of special importance for the present essay, Utpaladeva and Abhinavagupta

3. In the present essay, I will refer to this text in the edition of Abhinavagupta 1986. See the critical edition, translation, and notes by Raffaele Torella in Utpaladeva 2002.

further identify Śiva's self-recognition or Śakti with a principle called Supreme Speech (*parā vāk*), which they derive from Bhartṛhari, in order to interpret creation as linguistic in nature (Bhartṛhari 1966–1983 [VP]; Shastri 1959; Lawrence 1999, including comparisons with Western philosophical theologies of Logos). In debates with the Buddhist logical-epistemological school of Dharmakīrti, the Śaivas attempt to show that recognition/Speech is the reality underlying and constituting all states of affairs. As a ritual enactment, by thus disclosing the necessity and ubiquity of Śiva's self-recognition, the system leads the student to complete participation in it (Lawrence 1996).

In the area of philosophical psychology, the Pratyabhijñā thinkers describe the empowered Śiva-identity recognized by the practitioner as a higher sense of "I" (*aham*) or, more abstractly, "I-hood" (*ahambhāva*), which also came to be called "perfect I-hood" (*pūrṇāhaṃtā*) (see Dyczkowski 1992; Lawrence 2008a has analysis and engagement with Western conceptions). The adept endeavors to achieve liberation by recovering Śiva's self-recognition, Speech or perfect I-hood underlying all worldly phenomena.

On the basis of the equation of Śakti with Supreme Speech, Utpaladeva, Abhinavagupta, and subsequent nondual Śaiva scholars advanced Bhartṛharian and Pratyabhijñā metaphysics to interpret the mythico-ritual drama of the Self's/Śiva's creation and control of the world, as a linguistic process—in numerous aspects, such as in terms of the linguistic nature of awareness (in modalities of verbation [*śabdana*] or recognitive apprehension [*vimarśa* or *pratyavamarśa*] integral to all awareness [*prakāśa*]), the semantic relation of words and objects, esoteric symbolic-ritual schemes of mantric phonemes (including those of the mantra, *aham*, "I" itself) and corresponding cosmic principles, Śakti modalities generating linguistic relations (*sambandha*), action (*kriyā*), and time (*kāla*), and other technical features of grammar.

Semantics and Syntax of Action and Agency

The foundation of much of Utpaladeva and Abhinavagupta's theorization on agency is their adherence to Bhartṛhari's Vyākaraṇa (Grammatical Analysis and Philosophy) and related Vedic exegetical traditions in interpreting being or existence (*sattā*), the generic referent of language, as *action* (*kriyā*).[4] Language is said to express being as an action to be accomplished

4. See the more extensive treatment of the topic of semantics and syntax of action and

(see VP, 3.8, 1–40, particularly 3.8.1; and 3.8.27, 22; and 3.8.35, 26). This view extrapolates to all discourse the priestly interpretation of the Vedas as expressing injunctions for the ritual *kriyās* of sacrifice. Furthermore, the word *kriyā*, derived from the root *kṛ*, is cognate to the English word create, and actually means both "creation" and "action." It is Śiva's mythic action, or cre-ation, through Śakti (self-recognition, Speech) that accounts ontologically for all things, and that is ritually reenacted by philosophical discourse.[5]

Now, the Śaivas along with other Indian philosophies further interpret the action of myth and ritual with theories of Sanskrit syntax. This is provided for by the system of the Sanskrit *kārakas*. While the six *kārakas* are historically related to the Indo-European cases, their conception is more subtle and bridges in a particular way the areas of semantics and syntax (besides Cardona's comprehensive and deeply illuminating study for the present volume, see Cardona 1967, 1974; along with Patañjali 1975; VP *Sādhanasamuddeśa*, 3.7, *kāṇḍa* 3, part 1: 230–370 and *Kriyāsamuddeśa*, 3.8, *kāṇḍa* 3, part 2: 1–40; Iyer 1969: 283–344; Al-George 1957, 1968; Rocher 1964; Matilal 1960, 1966, 1990: 40–48; Staal 1969; Gerow 1982). *Kārakas* describe various logical relationships of the referents of declined nouns to the main action expressed by a verb: the action's agent (*kartṛ*), chief instrument (*karaṇa*), object it effects or affects (*karman*), location (*adhikaraṇa*), where it comes from spatially, causally, and so on (*apādāna*), and for whom or what one performs it (*sampradāna*). The same *kāraka* may actually be expressed in more than one case declension. The genitive is not even considered a *kāraka*, as it usually articulates relationships between nouns, rather than between nouns and a verb.

The word *kāraka* is a derivative from the same root as the word action (*kṛ*), having the causal significance of "actor, maker, factor." The *kārakas* are understood as functioning to accomplish the action expressed by the verb. The action is said to be "that which is to be established" (*sādhya*), and the *kārakas* are "establishers" (*sādhanas*). A typical example is: "He cooks rice in the pot with fire." The pot contains the rice and water, and the fire heats them. The rice, that is, the direct object expressed in the accusative,

---

agency in Lawrence 1998.

5. Śiva's capacities pertaining to epistemology and action-ontology are often described respectively as his Knowledge (*jñāna*) and Action (*kriyā*) Śaktis.

is explained to be the locus of the result (*phala*) of the action of cooking, namely, a transformation of the nature of the rice.

Sanskritic speculation about many philosophical topics often has recourse to arguments about the interrelations between the various *kārakas* and the overarching *kriyā*. Even traditions such as Nyāya-Vaiśeṣika, Advaita Vedānta, and Buddhism, which do not accept the notion that semantics is primarily the expression of action, are influenced by the view and also engage in these discussions. I have previously compared Sanskrit speculations on this subject to Kenneth Burke's "grammar of motives." This grammar typifies divergent accounts of the generation of action by their emphasis on, or "featuring," particular factors from a fivefold set, which overlaps with the Indo-European cases (Burke 1962; Lawrence 1998, 1999: 133–154). Burke's scheme and other aspects of his theory of symbolic action have been used in the contemporary human sciences to categorize popular as well as academic explanations of action (Mills 1940; Gusfield 1989; Simons and Melia 1989). Sanskritic philosophers likewise over many centuries developed sophisticated applications of *kriyā-kāraka* theory to elucidate agency and other determinants of action in grammatical terms, and their thought holds much promise for intercultural reflection.

Edwin Gerow and I have separately argued that there is a tendency in many traditions of Hindu and Buddhist philosophy to denigrate the role of the agent (*kartṛ kāraka*) in the syntactic nexus (Gerow 1982; Lawrence 1998). Gerow in particular emphasizes that the dominant feature of syntax is the unity of action and its result (which is indicated by the direct object, *karman karaka*), to which nexus the agent is often seen as an accessory. Among Hindu schools, this tendency appears to be strongest in Advaita Vedānta. Śaṅkara therefore equates liberation with a gnosis beyond agency (1987; see Timalsina's chapter in this volume; cf. Dumont 1980 on the individuality of the renunciant). Along parallel lines, the Viśiṣṭādvaita philosopher Rāmānuja (ca. 1017–1137) elaborates upon the *Bhagavad Gītā's* teaching of *karmayoga*, arguing that it is the performance of ritually appropriate action while the practitioner meditates on Kṛṣṇa/Viṣṇu as the ultimate agent of one's acts (See, e.g., *Gītābhāṣya* 3.30; pointed out by Dasti, personal communication). The mainstreams of Buddhist philosophy entirely negate the role of a substantial and efficacious agent in the syntax of dependent origination. The tendency being described here reflects not only the agent's bondage to karma in rebirth for Hindus and Buddhists—as emphasized by Gerow (1982)—but also its subordination to the order of objective ritual behavior (pertaining to sacrifice, caste, life cycle, and so on, in orthodox Brahmanic norms).

Utpaladeva and Abhinavagupta develop what I have described as a "mythico-ritual syntax of omnipotence" by taking up and radicalizing earlier understandings of the positive albeit delimited role of the agent, particularly from the Vyākaraṇa and Nyāya-Vaiśeṣika traditions. In this they anticipate Burke's typification of various sorts of absolute idealism as placing the greatest emphasis on the role of the motive of the *agent* (1962).

To summarize the most important of these for the Śaivas, all of the *kārakas* are understood to function in accomplishing the overall action or process (*vyāpāra*) expressed by the verb. They do this through their own *subordinate processes.* The pan *holds* the rice, the fire *heats* it, and so on. The agent, in turn, synthesizes the various subordinate processes into the larger one, and thus functions as the locus of the overall process (*vyāpārāśraya*).

Furthermore, according to grammar it is the agent who is instigator (*prayojaka*) of all of the subordinate processes constituting the larger one. He or she arranges the equipment, lights and controls the fire, and so on. Sometimes, further subjective factors in this instigation are identified. The Naiyāyikas in particular stress that the agent is conscious, and that he or she has the intention or desire (*icchā*) and makes the effort (*yatna*) that brings about the action. The followers of Pāṇini state that the direct object (*karman*), as receiving the result of the process, is that which is most desired (*īpsitatama*) by the agent.

Another important point is that, while the agent controls the processes of the other *kārakas,* no other *kāraka* has a similar influence on him or her. The other *kārakas* are "heteronomous" (*paratantra*), but the agent is "autonomous" or "free" (*svatantra*) with regard to their operations.

The Śaivas explain the Lord's/Self's unlimited cosmogonic and cosmocratic power as his creation and control of the universe from his mere intention (*icchā*) and agential autonomy (*svātantrya*). Śiva also serves as the locus of all subordinate processes of all things in the universe, by recognizing himself through the recognitions of each of them. Abhinavagupta uses the analogy of ordinary agency to elucidate that of the Lord:

> Here [according to this system], action is really nothing but the Supreme Lord's intention [*icchā*]. [This intention] consists of uninterrupted self-recognition [*svātmaparāmarśa*], which has the nature of unobstructed agential autonomy [*svātantrya*], and is not

> dependent on another.... For [limited individuals such as] Caitra or Maitra, and so on, the inner intention [*icchā,* such as that expressed] "I cook" is the action. Thus, even though there is the relation of [one who is cooking] with numerous movements [*spanda*] such as putting something on the fire, and so on, the [intention] "I cook" is uninterrupted. It is nothing but the intention [*icchā*] "I cook" which appears as such movements.... Thus is that recognitive apprehension [*vimarśa*] of the Lord, which has the nature of intention [*icchā,* which may be expressed] "I Lord," "I appear," "I manifest in cosmogonic vibration [*sphurāmi*]," "I create through agitation [*ghūrṇe*]"[6] and "I recognitively apprehend [*pratyavamṛśāmi*]." The essential nature [of such recognitive apprehension] is nothing but "I." (IPV 2.1.8, 2:24–25)

We will pick up on this recognition of "I" in the discussion of indexicals below. At present it should be observed that there is a reductionism in a direction opposite to the predominant South Asian tendency, described by Gerow, which features the action-result nexus. In a sentence such as "Devadatta cooks rice in the pan with wood," the factors such as the pan, wood, and rice appear (*prakāśante*) as merged in the action. The action in turn rests (*āśritām*) in the agent (*Sambandhasiddhi* in Utpaladeva 1921: 9). According to the Śaivas, even action that seems to be situated primarily in the object is actually located in the agent through his unifying recognitive synthesis (IPVV 2.4.5, 3:189–190).

The Śaivas elaborate this syntax in a number of different spheres of philosophical explanation. Thus they engage in extensive theorization about the cause-effect relation (*kāryakāraṇatā*). According to Vyākaraṇa, whereas all the *kārakas* are said to have a kind of causal role, it is the *karaṇa* "instrument" case that indicates the cause proper (*kāraṇa*), conceived as the most efficient means (*sādhakatama*) in the accomplishment of an action (Matilal 1960). The effect (*kārya*) is expressed in the *karman karaka,* which more generically indicates the direct object as the recipient of the effect, for example, the rice that has been cooked. In the Śaiva theory, the omnipotent agent Śiva/the

6. The Śaivas commonly describe the unitary, eternal Lord's emanation of temporal diversity as a kind of agitation or vibration. This is the understanding articulated in the doctrine of the Śiva's *spanda*. Abhinava emphasizes the connection with this doctrine here in describing the movements of the one cooking as *spandas*.

Self emanates things through his agential intention (*icchā*) and thus constitutes the substratum that unites the *karaṇa* and *karma kārakas*. Therefore, the cause-effect relation (*kāryakāraṇabhāva*) is in actuality the agent-direct object relation (*kartṛkarmatva*) (IPK and IPV 2.4.1–2, 2:152–154).

The Pratyabhijñā philosophers refute a variety of rival theories on the basis of their reduction of all causality to the syntax of agency. Thus Abhinavagupta applauds the Sāṃkhya doctrine of the preexistence of the effect in the cause (*satkāryavāda*) for "long-ranging insight" and "resorting to recognition (*pratyabhijñā*)" (IPV 2.4.18, 2:194–195). However, he and Utpaladeva argue that the underlying material cause of the universe must be a conscious agent (IPK and IPV 2.4.17–19, 2:193–200). Again, the Śaivas refute the Advaita Vedānta version of *satkāryavāda,* according to which the universe is a projection (*vivarta*) on the Self, because of that tradition's denial of the Self's agency (IPK and IPV 2.4.20, 2:201–206).

The Śaivas also propound a syntactic refutation of the Buddhist understanding of causation as "dependent origination," which is commonly expressed in Sanskrit with a locative absolute construction, such as "When there is this, then there is this" (*asmin satīdam asti.*). The Śaivas argue again that it is necessary to accept the autonomous agent who through his recognitive synthesis (*anusaṃdhāna*) serves as the substratum of the action uniting the constituent processes of the various *kārakas*; it is he who unites what is expressed in the locative with what is expressed in the main clause (IPK and IPV 2.4.14–16, 2:187–193).

The Pratyabhijñā thinkers follow the same approach they use in the explanation of causality to explain the various parameters of the epistemic operation of means of knowledge (*pramāṇa*). They thus reduce the operations (*vyāpāra*) of the means or cause of knowledge (*pramāṇa*), along with related epistemic-syntactic categories such as the object of knowledge (*prameya*), and the result (*phala*), knowledge (*pramā*) itself—to the operation of self-recognition by the universal agent of knowing (*pramātṛ*) (see IPV 2.3.1–2, 2:73–76).[7]

The explanation of all things and all knowledge of things as Śiva's/the Self's cre-ation underlines the fact that the Śaivas are articulating a theory

7. The Pratyabhijñā here refutes Buddhist views that there is no underlying process uniting the means (*pramāṇa*) with the result of knowledge itself (*pramā*). See Lawrence 1998 and Bandyopadhyay 1979.

of existence, an ontology of action, which reductionistically features the agent. Thus Abhinava explains in the conclusion to the discussion of causality:

> [The expression] "The pot exists" has this [true] meaning: The Great Lord, who is awareness [*prakāśa*], desires to exist as the pot and assumes that existence through his agential autonomy [*svātantrya*]. (IPV 2.4.21, 2:207)

To even more explicitly relate ontology and syntax, I quote two more statements by Utpaladeva and Abhinavagupta:

> Being [*sattā*] is the condition of one who becomes [*bhavattā*], that is, the agency of the act of becoming [*bhavanakartṛtā*]. (IPKV 1.5.14, 19)

> Being [*sattā*] is the agency of the act of becoming [*bhavanakartṛtā*], that is, agential autonomy [*svātantrya*] regarding all actions. (IPV 1.5.14, 1:258–259)

This theory of universal syntactic agency is ritually axiomatic as well as mythical. Utpaladeva provides an alternative explanation of how the Pratyabhijñā philosophy leads the student to liberation:

> That one succeeds [*siddhyati*], who places his feet on this [the Pratyabhijñā *śāstra*], and, contemplating that the status of the agent [*kartṛ*] of the world belongs to himself, submerges himself incessantly in the state of Śiva. (IPK 4.1.16, 2:309)

In his TA and TS, Abhinavagupta uses this syntactic theory to explain the inner significance of preliminary ceremonies of the tantric ritual—the divinizing projection of mantric syllables onto the body and other parts of the ritual (*nyāsa*) and purifications with the sacrificial vase. Abhinava identifies various components of the ritual, such as the location, ritual implements, object of sacrifice, for example, flowers, and oblations, with the grammatical cases of *adhikaraṇa*, *apādāna*, *karaṇa*, *karman*, and so on. He explains the overarching ritual process as the aspirant's identification with Śiva as agent of all the cases—the ritual paraphernalia manipulated by the adept epitomizing all other cosmic entities (TA 15.147–158, 6:2516–6:2520; TS 13, 135; Lawrence 1998).

Agency and Linguistic Indexicals

Complementing the Pratyabhijñā theory of agency in action syntax are Abhinavagupta's brief but profound reflections on the semantics and syntax of grammatical persons (*puruṣa*).[8] This theorization may be seen in particular as a linguistic interpretation of Pratyabhijñā conception of I-hood or egoity (*ahambhāva*), which we have observed is also mentioned in discussions of *kriyā-kāraka* relations. The grammatical persons are the familiar triad known in English as I/We, You, and He/She/It/They—which are expressed in corresponding verbal conjugations and pronouns.[9] For the sake of clarity in this essay I will refer to these with the English terms—first, second, and third persons—rather than the Sanskrit terms, which are ordered differently.[10]

Abhinavagupta's most extensive and well-known treatment of the grammatical persons is found in his PTV (especially 117–128), in which he interprets the dialogic process of Śiva's discourses with Śakti in the *Parātrīśikā* and other *āgamas*. He also makes remarks in other writings pertaining to the grammatical persons that in effect constitute rudiments of a "reception theory" of philosophical and aesthetic works. Abhinava's views on the grammatical persons are further elaborated in later texts such as the *Virūpākṣapañcāśikā* with Vidyācakravartin's commentary and Maheśvarānanda's *Mahārthamañjarīparimala* (Lawrence 2008a: 94–96; Maheśvarānanda 1972).

Abhinavagupta's approach to the grammatical persons advances developing Sanskritic reflections on their expression of dialogicity first evinced in Yāska (5th–6th century BCE) and furthered especially by Bhartṛhari (Yāska 1984; Bhartṛhari 1966–1983; Cardona 1973; Haag-Bernede 1998, 2001; Iyer 1969: 344–346). The Kashmiri philosopher's treatment of grammatical persons is also remarkable for ways in which it anticipates theorists on indexicals such as Charles Peirce (Peirce 1982; Singer

---

8. See the more extensive treatment of agency and linguistic indexicals in Lawrence 2008b. Cf. Dupuche 2001; Baumer 2011.

9. Strictly speaking, in Sanskritic theory the grammatical "persons" (*puruṣa*) determine only the classes of verbal conjugations, which correspond to particular sets of pronouns.

10. The third person in Western grammar, He/She/It/They, is called the first person (*prathama puruṣa*) in Sanskritic traditions. The Western second person, You, is the Sanskrit middle person (*madhyama puruṣa*). Likewise, the Western first person, I/We, is the Sanskrit final or ultimate person (*uttama puruṣa*). Some languages distinguish fourth or fifth grammatical persons, sometimes on the bases of distance from the situation of discourse or degrees of generality.

1984, 1989) and Emile Benveniste (1971, particularly chaps. 18, 20, 21)—although he has a very different view about the ultimate nature of the speech situation.

Abhinavagupta concurs with ancient and recent linguistic theorists in viewing the first person, I/We, as indexing the enunciator of discourse—that is, the agent of the speech act. The second person, You, refers to the audience, and the noninterlocutory He/She/It refers to the object of discourse. Also following Bhartṛhari (VP 3.10.7, 4:94), and like contemporary thinkers, Abhinava acknowledges that the three persons in ordinary discourse are arbitrary and interchangeable in their reference (PTV, 121–124).

However, Abhinavagupta ranks the reals underlying the three grammatical persons hierarchically, as reflecting the triadic structure of emanation according to the Trika: Śiva, Śakti, Human (*nara*) (PTV, 117–128). He attempts to demonstrate the primacy of the second person over the third, and of the first over the second, with an observation—anticipating Benveniste (1971: 202)—about their degrees of extension. That is, You can include He, She or They, and We can include both You and He, She or They. The wider extension of the first person points to its still much greater ultimate significance in the Pratyabhijñā concept of Śiva's perfect egoity (PTV, 125–127).

In assimilating the three persons to the Trika triad, Abhinavagupta to some extent agrees with Peirce's correlation of the indices to his own triad of sign, object, and interpretant. According to Peirce, the signs of my first-person discourse in some way convey my identity in giving third-person accounts of people and things, which are understood in your second-person interpretations (Singer 1984, 1989). For Abhinavagupta, I as Śiva am the agent of discourse in the revelation of myself to You as Śakti in the *āgamas*. More broadly, I speak and reveal myself in the whole universe through the grand act of parole that is Supreme Speech (see IPV, 1.5.13, 1:252–254).

A further point may be made with regard to the noninterlocutory He/She/It. Before Abhinavagupta, Bhartṛhari had argued that what we call the third person is actually not indicated by grammar to be conscious (VP, 3.10.2, 4:91). Benveniste for similar reasons would later describe it as a *nonperson* (1971: 198, 200, 217, 221–222). In the same vein, but within a distinctive metaphysical agenda, the Kashmiri philosopher explains that the third person represents the unenlightened human as reduced to the condition of inert objects (*jaḍa*) (PTV, 117).

According to Abhinavagupta, Śiva's foundational agency-cum-act of Speech, with, as, and through Śakti, constitutes all limited circumstances of discourse, including all interlocutors and objects. This theorization provides a contemplation of return in which all forms of He/She/It are *personalized* as absorbed into You, Śakti. And I as cosmic discursive agent realize You to be my integral power and consort (PTV, 117–128).

Singer (1984, 1989) attempted to characterize divergent cultural emphases on one or the other grammatical person, in a manner somewhat analogous to Burke's typologization of alternative grammars of motives for action. However, evidently unfamiliar with tantric linguistic philosophies, he allows that in South Asian traditions there are programs only for the absorption of the individual (first or second person) and/or world (third person) into the impersonal Brahman (third person) or a God (second person) (1989: 239–275; 1984: 174–179). According to Singer, Indian traditions lack an understanding of " 'transcendence' as an act of 'imperial' expansion of the individual self" such that the second and third persons would be reduced to the first (1989: 281, paraphrasing Q. Anderson on the American transcendentalists).[11]

The nondual Śaiva traditions actually do pursue a kind of "imperial expansion" of the self. Sovereignty is in fact an important practical expression of the tantric appropriation of Śakti (Gupta and Gombrich 1986; White 2003: 123–159), and conversely, the soteriologically oriented nondual Śaivas frequently compare the experience of the liberated, empowered adept with that of a king (see IPV 1.1.3, 1:67–68). Abhinavagupta provides a linguistic rationale for this imperial expansion of the self in his theorization on grammatical indexicals (see Lawrence 2008a on the philosophical psychology).

While the Śaiva conception of empowered identity has antecedents in the Upaniṣads and earlier tantra, and parallels in some versions of Western absolute idealism and romanticism, few would follow Abhinavagupta so far in this first-person reductionism. Nevertheless, Abhinava's conception does seem to reflect and radicalize a theorized universal tendency of language in the ascription of agency. Robert M. W. Dixon (1994) has formulated an "animacy hierarchy" of classes of nouns and pronouns to which agency is most likely to be ascribed. Animacy or agency increases in

11. Daniel 1987: 233–287 describes the pilgrimage to Sabari Malai as an immersion in Peirce's category of Firstness, but does not, like Peirce, correlate Firstness with the first person index.

the sequence from common nouns for inanimate things, through proper nouns, and finally the third, second and first person pronouns. There is a general privileging of the participants in the speech act situation. And the I is the quintessential agent, as it is overall more likely (though, of course, it is far from always the case, and is dependent on power) that one will think of doing things to others rather than having them done to oneself (also see Ahearn 2001; and Lyons 1996: 305, 311, 336–342 on linguistic egocentricity, locutionary subjectivity, and agency).

Abhinava indicates in both his Pratyabhijñā and aesthetic writings that the same contemplative agenda should inform the hermeneutic *reception* of philosophy as well as poetry and drama. In the first verse of the IPK, Utpaladeva proclaims that he has attained identity with Śiva, and that for the benefit of humanity he is establishing the recognition of such identity (IPK 1.1.1, 1:18). Abhinava explains that when a qualified person (*adhikārin*) hears this, he or she conceives a transference (*saṃkrānti*) of it into a first-person perspective, in the realization that he or she has already attained that recognition of the perfect and timeless Supreme Lord (IPV 1.1.1, 1:44–46; IPVV 1.1, 1:24).

Paralleling such passages are sections of the ABH and DHAL in which Abhinavagupta—advancing Bhaṭṭanāyaka's earlier appropriations of Pūrva Mīmāṃsā—discusses the universalization (*sādhāraṇīkaraṇa*) of emotions in the aesthetic experience of the qualified spectator (*adhikārin*), as well as the homologies between such experiences and the learning of ethical injunctions (*vidhi*). Abhinava explains that, through identifying with the feelings of a narrative character such as Rāma, one comes to experience *rasas* as universalized emotions and resolves to act according to the ethical lessons provided by the narrative. In these passages he describes a transference (*saṃkramaṇa*) from a third-person to a first-person perspective very similar to that he described in the Pratyabhijñā texts (ABH 1:35; 1:277–279).

Cosmological Transformations of Agency

As explained, the Śaivas' theories of action syntax and indexicals provide a trajectory for intellectual and spiritual realization homologous to the more predominant Pratyabhijñā epistemology of recognition. The prima facie limited "I" realize my true first-person agency to be that of Śiva, the omnipotent possessor of Śakti (*śaktimat*). The Śaivas further map out the path from the limited individual agent to the omnipotent divine one in terms of traditional teachings regarding cosmic principles (*tattva*) and related categories, and typologies of subjects (*pramātṛ*) and states of consciousness.

These topics are treated particularly in the Pratyabhijñā texts' Book on Scriptural Traditions (*āgamādhikāra*) and are further elaborated by Abhinavagupta in works such as the TA, TS, and PTV. Abhinavagupta explains that the limited knower cannot establish everything by means of perception and inference. Moreover, scriptural traditions (*āgama*) are the recognitive apprehension of the omniscient Supreme Lord himself. Therefore, such expositions of cosmology are based largely on scriptural traditions as corroborated by the support of reason (IPV 3.1.Intro., 2:213–214; see Lawrence 2000 on relations of *āgama* to other *pramāṇas*).

We cannot discuss here all details of the Śaiva scheme of the emanation of 36 cosmic principles and subsidiary categories (see Jee 1985: 1–10), and I will confine myself to making a few points regarding how this pertains to agency. It should first be understood that the entire emanation of 36 cosmic principles and subsidiary categories is situated within an overarching exercise of agency. As Abhinavagupta explains, "what is called action [*kriyā*] has the character of manifesting [*avabhāsana*] all the categories [*padārtha*]" (IPV 3.1.Intro., 2:212).

The Śaiva version of a "chain of being" is sometimes analyzed into Pure (*śuddha*), Pure-Impure (*śuddhāśuddha*), and Impure (*aśuddha*) Cosmic Courses (*adhvan*). Śiva by means of Māyā effects the transition from the first to the second courses, which is marked by the entrance of impurity. This impurity is summarized as three taints (*mala*, which are not *tattvas* per se). Issues of agency figure prominently in these. Utpaladeva thus describes the first taint, of limited individuality (*āṇava mala*), as a degradation of one or both of Śiva's intertwined epistemological and agential-active capacities. It is a "loss of the agential autonomy [*svātantrya*] of consciousness, and the lack of consciousness [*abodhatā*] of agential autonomy [*svātantrya*]" (IPK 3.2.4, 2:248; see IPV 3.2.4–5, 2:248–249). This taint contains the seeds of the subsequent two.

The taint of Māyā (*māyīya mala*) pertains specifically to the epistemological aspect and is the misconception that there is a differentiation between the knower and the object of knowledge (IPK 3.2.5, 2:248; IPV 3.2.4–5, 2:248–249). The taint of karma (*kārma mala*) is a delimitation of agency, which has the effect of dragging the individual into the nexus of action and results (IPK 3.2.5, 2:248). Abhinavagupta explains:

> When there is the manifestation of the object of knowledge as differentiated from the agent [*kartṛ*] who is without consciousness [*abodha*, since it is conceived in such limited aspects] as the body, and so on, there is the taint of karma [*kārma mala*]. That has the form of Dharma and Adharma, and due to that there are birth and the enjoyment [of the consequences of actions] for a fixed duration. Thus there occurs karma, which is said to have as its results caste [*jāti*], life and the enjoyment [of the consequences of actions]. (IPV 3.2.4–5, 2:249)

Freedom from karma, conversely, is the realization of the one's omnipotent Action Śakti (see MVV 1.313–315, 30–31; TA and TAV, 13.266–268a, 5:2363–2365; IPK and IPV 3.2.4–10, 2:248–256; Vasugupta and Kṣemarāja 1925: 3.16, 71–72).

Another area relevant to the Śaiva understanding of agency is their conceptualization of certain cosmic principles in the Pure-Impure Course that are known as the coverings (*kañcuka*) of the limited subject. These are contractions of the modalities of the omnipotent Śakti of the Supreme Lord. Of concern here is the covering known as limited agency (*kalā*). Abhinavagupta contrasts this with the omnipotent agency of the Action Śakti in describing it as merely "the affirmation of particular sort of agency [*kiṃcitkartṛtva*] that produces an effect [*kārya*]" (IPV 3.1.9, 2:237). It has the finite expression: "I do a particular sort of thing [*kiṃcit*]" (IPV 3.1.9, 2:237). (The Śaktis of Knowledge [*jñāna*], Intention [*icchā*], Bliss [*ānanda*], and Consciousness [*cit*] are also respectively contracted as limited knowledge [*vidyā*], attachment [*rāga*], time [*kāla*], and causal regularity [*niyati*] [see IPV 3.1.9, 2:238–239].)

Utpaladeva and Abhinavagupta, on the bases of these schemes of taints and coverings, propound a typology of subjects (*pramātṛ*) existing on different levels of emanation—such as Vidyeśvaras, Vijñānakevalas, Pralayākalas, Śūnyapramātṛs, and so on—according to their strengths and deficiencies in consciousness-knowledge, agency, or both (IPK and IPV 3.2.1–7, 2:244–265). The Pratyabhijñā thinkers also analyze the metaphysics and phenomenology of five states of consciousness, that is, waking, dream, deep sleep, the "fourth" (*turya*), and the "beyond-the-fourth" (*turyātīta*). They classify these into the two broad śāstraic categories of what is to be abandoned (*heya*) and what is to be pursued (*upādeya*). Waking, dreaming, and deep sleep are to be abandoned because in them there is the predominance of vital breath (*prāṇa*), and other features of the limited personality, and a concomitant diminution of agency (*kartṛtā*). However, the states of the fourth and beyond-the-fourth are marked by the predominance and stability of agency (*kartṛtā*). Therefore, they are to be pursued (IPK and IPV 3.2.18, 2:268–271; IPKV 3.2.18, 71).

Conclusion: Directions for Further Research

Reflection on the Śaiva conceptions of agency as presented above raises a number of questions. From a purely expository point of view, it would be of great interest to endeavor to relate more explicitly the theory of agency in the semantics and syntax of action, with that of the indexicals. Insofar as Abhinavagupta's comments on the indexicals are rather brief and ad hoc, it may be that he did not think through this issue fully. While there may be further clues regarding the relationship of these theories elsewhere in that scholar's vast corpus, in principle it should also be possible to advance an understanding of it beyond what he has himself stated. Insofar as any action is conscious and in some manner linguistically interpreted, it should have a broadly "dialogic" significance both for the agent and for any others whom there may be. Likewise, speech with another about something is an act.

This question leads to the broader concern about how we may dialogically engage the Śaiva understandings of agency with our own worldview. The outcome of such an engagement may or may not be sympathetic to Pratyabhijñā thought. From the point of view of some contemporary Western-dominated philosophy, it might seem that the synthesis of linguistics and cosmology presented here epitomizes "linguistic confusion," the false abstractions about language and the projection of those onto the universe, that Ludwig Wittgenstein found to underlie much of traditional metaphysics (1991).

In my studies so far of the Pratyabhijñā linguistics of agency, I have expanded on typologies such as Burke's grammar of motives and Singer's anthropology of indexicals mainly to distinguish the philosophy from predominant contemporary orientations. Thus the Pratyabhijñā exaltation of the agent in action syntax may be contrasted with objectivist and instrumentalist deconstructions of it in modern and postmodern thought (Lawrence 1998, 1999). Likewise Abhinavagupta's first-person reductionism may be contrasted with contemporary orientations that make the first-second person dialogicity into a transcendental requirement for both personal identity and ethics (Lawrence 2008a, 2008b). While my own orientation is sympathetic to the Pratyabhijñā, I have not defended the system on linguistic grounds but rather in terms of the philosophical theology of God as the ground of intelligibility (Lawrence 1999), and the philosophical psychology and ethics pertaining to egoity (Lawrence 2008a).

Though I am disregarding the advice of my undergraduate philosophy professor not to introduce new topics in a conclusion, I mention that I am presently exploring the use of Peircean semiotics to address the issues being raised. The following discussion is speculative and programmatic. It seems feasible to me that what Bhartṛhari and the Pratyabhijñā theorists mean by a "subtle language" (*sūkṣmaśabdana*), semantic intuition (*pratibhā*), and linguistic "recognitive apprehension" (*pratyavamarśa, vimarśa*), preceding and grounding ordinary conventional language, could be understood as a process of semiosis or a paradoxically nondual "protosemiosis." Indeed Bhartṛharian and Pratyabhijñā philosophy finds a subtle linguistic process to be present even in animal "instincts" and the behavior of newborn babies, and it would make sense to conceive that more abstractly in terms of semiotics. The Śaiva conceptions of agency in action syntax and discursive exchange also dialectically bridge a paradoxically nondual essence with the structure and expression of concrete sentences and could perhaps likewise be reconceived in semiotic and nondual protosemiotic terms.

Peirce himself endeavored to encompass within his mature categories of Firstness, Secondness, and Thirdness not only the triads respectively of first, third and second grammatical persons; and of sign, object and interpretant, but also that of agent, patient, and action (Peirce 1991). As translated into these categories, the Śaivas' reductions of result (*phala*) and other action factors (*kāraka*) to the process (*vyāpāra*), and that to the agent, would clearly parallel their reduction of the third person to the second, and that to the first.

There have also been fascinating developments of a Peircean philosophy of science in the fields of pansemiotics and biosemiotics, where efforts are underway to identify interpretive processes intrinsic to the nature of all life as self-organizing or "autopoietic" systems. Life is believed to comprise various sorts of agents interpreting and acting, in relations with their own constituent parts, each other, and the broader environment. One of the notable features of biosemiotics is its positing of a natural teleology—through both biological and cultural evolution—toward "semiotic freedom," conceived as more logically rich and agentially efficacious interpretations of the environment (Hoffmeyer 2008). Again, these ideas seem amenable to engagement with the Pratyabhijñā theories of instigative, recognitive-synthetic, and communicative agency. This drive toward semiotic freedom could be well situated within the Śaiva philosophical theology of God's emanation and return through Śakti/self-recognition/ Speech/Action/I-hood.

References

Abhinavagupta. 1921. *Śrī Mālinīvijaya Vārttikam*. Edited by Madhusudan Kaul Shastri. Srinagar: Kashmir Pratap Steam Press.

———. 1975–1981. *Dhvanyālokalocana*. In *Dhvanyāloka of Ānandavardhana with the Locana of Abhinavagupta* (Vols. 1–3), ed. Rāmasāgara Tripāṭhi. Delhi: Motilal Banarsidass.

———. 1981–1984. *Abhinavabhāratī*. In *Nāṭyaśāstra of Bharatamuni with the Commentary Abhinavabhāratī by Abhinavaguptāchārya* (Vols. 1–4), ed. R. S. Nagar and K. L. Joshi. Delhi: Parimal Publications.

———. 1982. *Tantrasāra*. Edited by Mukunda Ram Sastri. Delhi: Bani Prakashan.

———. 1985. *Parātrīśikāvivaraṇa*. In *Śrī Śrī Parātriṃśikā*, ed. and Hindi trans. Nilakantha Gurutu. Delhi: Motilal Banarsidass.

———. 1986. *Īśvarapratyabhijñāvimarśinī* (with *Bhāskarī*) (Vols. 1–2). Edited by K. A. Subramania Iyer and K. C. Pandey. Delhi: Motilal Banarsidass.

———. 1987a. *Īśvarapratyabhijñāvivṛtivimarśinī* (Vols. 1–3). Edited by Madhusudan Kaul Shastri. Delhi: Akay Book Corporation.

———. 1987b. *The Tantrāloka of Abhinavagupta with the Commentary of Jayaratha*.8 vols. Edited by Madhusudan Kaul Shastri and Mukunda Rama Shastri. Kashmir Series of Texts and Studies. Republication, edited by R.C. Dwivedi and Navjivan Rastogi. Delhi: Motilal Banarsidass.

Ahearn, Laura M. 2001. "Language and Agency." *Annual Review of Anthropology* 30: 109–137.

Al-George, Sergiu. 1957. "Le sujet gramatical chez Pāṇini." *Studia et Acta Orientalia Bucaresti 1*: 39–47.

———. 1968. "The Extra-Linguistic Origin of Pāṇini's Syntactic Categories and Their Linguistic Accuracy." *Journal of the Oriental Institute,Baroda 18*: 1–7.

Bandyopadhyay, Nandita. 1979. "The Buddhist Theory of Relation between Pramā and Pramāṇa." *Journal of Indian Philosophy 7*: 43–78.

Baumer, Bettina. 2011. "The Three Grammatical Persons and the Trika." Chapter in *Abhinavagupta's Hermeneutics of the Absolute, Anuttaraprakriyā: An Interpretation of his Parātrīśikā Vivaraṇa*, 101–112. New Delhi: D.K. Printworld.

Benveniste, Emile. 1971. *Problems in General Linguistics*. Translated by Mary Elizabeth Meek. Coral Gables, FL: University of Miami Press.

Bhartṛhari. 1966–1983. *Vākyapadīya of Bhartṛhari* (with commentaries). 4 vols. Edited by K. A. Subramania Iyer. *kāṇḍa* 1, Pune: Deccan College. *kāṇḍa* 2, Delhi: Motilal

Banarsidass. *kāṇḍa* 3, part 1, Pune: Deccan College. *kāṇḍa* 3, part 2, Pune: Deccan College.

Burke, Kenneth. 1962. *A Grammar of Motives*. Berkeley: University of California Press.

Cardona, George. 1967. "Pāṇini's Syntactic Categories." *Journal of the Oriental Institute, Baroda 16*: 202–215.

———. 1973. "On the Interpretation of Pāṇini 1.4.105–108." *Adyar Library Bulletin 37*: 1–47.

———. 1974. "Pāṇini's *Kārakas*: Agency, Animation and Identity." *Journal of Indian Philosophy 2*: 231–306.

Chakravarty, Hemendra Nath. 1997. "Tantric Spirituality." In *Hindu Spirituality II: Postclassical and Modern*, ed. K. R. Sundararajan and Bithika Mukerji, 209–231. New York: Crossroad.

Daniel, E. Valentine. 1987. *Fluid Signs*. Berkeley: University of California Press.

Dixon, R. M. W. 1994. *Ergativity*. New York: Cambridge University Press.

Dumont, Louis. 1980. "World Renunciation in Indian Religions." Appendix in *Homo Hierarchicus: The Caste System and Its Implications*. Translated by Mark Sainsbury, Louis Dumont, and Basia Gulati. Chicago: University of Chicago Press.

Dupuche, John R. 2001. "Person to Person: *Vivaraṇa* of Abhinavagupta on *Parātriṃśikā* Verses 3–4." *Indo-Iranian Journal 44*: 1–16.

Dyczkowski, Mark S. G. 1992. "Self Awareness, Own Being, Egoity." In *The Stanzas on Vibration*, 37–48. Albany: State University of New York Press.

Gerow, Edwin. 1982. "What is Karma (Kiṃ Karmeti)? An Exercise in Philosophical Semantics." *Indologica Taurinensia 10*: 87–116.

Gupta, Senjukta, and Gombrich, Richard. 1986. "Kings, Power and the Goddess." *South Asia Research 6*: 123–138.

Gusfield, Joseph R., ed. 1989. *Kenneth Burke on Symbols and Society*. Chicago: University of Chicago Press.

Haag-Bernede, Pascale. 1998. "Notes sur la personne grammaticale dans la tradition pāṇineene." *Bulletin d'Etudes Indiennes 16*: 7–38.

———. 2001. "Conflicting Views in the Interpretation of Bhartṛhari? The Case of *Madhyamapuruṣa* in the *Vākyapadīya*." *Annals of the Bhandarkar Oriental Research Institute 82*: 233–242.

Hoffmeyer, Jesper. 2008. *Biosemiotics: An Examination into the Signs of Life and the Life of Signs*. Scranton, PA: University of Scranton Press.

Iyer, K.A. Subramania. 1969. *Bhartṛhari*. Pune: Deccan College.

Jee, Swami Lakshman. 1985. *Kashmir Śaivism: The Secret Supreme*. Srinagar: Universal Shaiva Trust.

Kakar, Sudhir. 1983. *Shamans, Mystics and Doctors: A Psychological Inquiry into India and Its Healing Traditions*. Boston: Beacon Press.

Lawrence, David Peter. 1996. "Tantric Argument: The Transfiguration of Philosophical Discourse in the Pratyabhijñā System of Utpaladeva and Abhinavagupta." *Philosophy East and West 46*: 165–204.

———. 1998. "The Mythico-Ritual Syntax of Omnipotence." *Philosophy East and West* 48: 592–622.

———. 1999. *Rediscovering God with Transcendental Argument: A Contemporary Interpretation of Monistic Kashmiri Śaiva Philosophy*. Albany: State University of New York Press.

———. 2000. "Zu Abhinavaguptas Offenbarungstheorie." *Polylog* 5: 6–18.

———. 2008a. *The Teachings of the Odd-Eyed One: A Study and Translation of the Virūpākṣapañcāśikā with the Commentary of Vidyācakravartin*. Albany: State University of New York Press.

———. 2008b. "Abhinavagupta's Philosophical Hermeneutics of Grammatical Persons." *Journal of Hindu Studies* 1: 11–25.

Lyons, John. 1996. *Linguistic Semantics: An Introduction*. Cambridge: Cambridge University Press.

Maheśvarānanda. 1972. *Mahārthamañjarī of Maheśvarānanda with the Auto-Commentary Parimala*. Edited by Vrajavallabha Dvivedi. Varanasi: Varanaseya Sanskrit Vishvavidyalaya Press.

Matilal, Bimal Krishna. 1960. "The Doctrine of Karaṇa in Grammar-Logic." *Journal of the Ganganatha Jha Research Institute* 17: 63–69.

———. 1966. "Indian Theorists on the Nature of the Sentence (*Vākya*)." *Foundations of Language* 2: 377–393.

———. 1990. *The Word and the World: India's Contribution to the Study of Language*. Oxford: Oxford University Press.

Mills, C. Wright. 1940. "Situated Actions and Vocabularies of Motive." *American Sociological Review* 5: 904–913.

Nemec, John. 2011. *The Ubiquitous Śiva: Somānanda's Śivadṛṣṭi and His Tantric Interlocutors*. Oxford: Oxford University Press.

Parry, Jonathan. 1982. "Sacrificial Death and the Necrophagus Ascetic." In *Death and the Regeneration of Life*, ed. Maurice Bloch and Jonathan Parry, 75–110. Cambridge: Cambridge University Press, 1982.

Patañjali. 1975. *Patañjali's Vyākaraṇa-Mahābhāṣya: Kārakāhnika (P.1.4.23–1.4.55)*. Edited with introduction, translation and notes by S. D. Joshi and J. A. F. Roodbergen. Pune: University of Poona.

Peirce, Charles Sanders. 1982. "I, IT, and THOU: A Book Giving Instruction in Some of the Elements of Thought." In *Writings of Charles S. Peirce: A Chronological Edition*, ed. Max H. Fisch et al., vol. 1, 45–56. Bloomington: Indiana University Press.

———. 1991. "A Guess at the Riddle." In *Peirce on Signs*, ed. James Hooper, 186–211. Chapel Hill: University of North Carolina Press.

Rāmānuja. 1991. *Gītābhāṣya: With Text in Devanagari and English Rendering*. Translation by Swami Adidevananda. Madras: Sri Ramakrishna Math.

Rocher, Rosane. 1964. "'Agent' et 'objet' chez Pāṇini." *Journal of the American Oriental Society* 84: 44–54.

Sanderson, Alexis. 1985. "Purity and Power among the Brahmans of Kashmir." In *The Category of the Person*, ed. Michael Carrithers, Steven Collins, and Steven Lukes, 190–216. Cambridge: Cambridge University Press.

———. 1988. "Śaivism and the Tantric Traditions." In *The World's Religions*, ed. Stewart Sutherland et al., 660–704. London: Routledge.

———. 1995. "Meaning in Tantric Ritual." In *Essais sur le Rituel, III* (Colloque du Centenaire de la Section des Sciences Religieuses de l'Ecole Pratique des Hautes Etudes), ed. Anne-Marie Blondeau and Kristofer Schipper, 15–95. Louvain: Peeters, 1995.

Śaṅkara. 1987. *Brahmasūtra Śāṅkara Bhāṣya*. Vols. 1–2. Edited by K. L. Joshi. Delhi: Parimal Publications.

Shastri, Gaurinath. 1959. *The Philosophy of Word and Meaning*. Calcutta: Sanskrit College.

Simons, Herbert W., and Trevor Melia, eds. 1989. *The Legacy of Kenneth Burke*. Madison: University of Wisconsin Press.

Singer, Milton. 1984. *Man's Glassy Essence: Explorations in Semiotic Anthropology*. Bloomington: Indian University Press.

———. 1989. "Pronouns, Persons, and the Semiotic Self." In *Semiotics, Self and Society*, ed. Benjamin Lee and Greg Urban, 229–296. Berlin: Mouton de Gruyter.

Somānanda and Utpaladeva. 1934. *The Śivadṛṣṭi of Srisomānandanātha with the Vritti by Utpaladeva*. Edited by Madhusudan Kaul Shastri. Pune: Aryabhushan Press.

Staal, Frits. 1969. "Syntactic and Semantic Relations in Pāṇini." *Foundations of Language* 5: 83–117.

Utpaladeva. 1921. *The Siddhitrayī and the Īśvarapratyabhijñākārikāvṛtti*. Edited by Madhusudan Kaul Shastri. Srinagar: Kashmir Pratap Steam Press.

Utpaladeva. 2002. *The Īśvarapratyabhijñākārikā of Utpaladeva with the Author's Vṛttti*. Corrected Edition. Edited and translated by Raffaele Torella. Delhi: Motilal Banarsidass.

Vasugupta and Kṣemarāja. 1925. *The Spandakārikās of Vasugupta with the Nirṇaya by Ksemarāja*. Edited and translated by Madhusudan Kaul Shastri. Srinagar: Kashmir Pratap Steam Press.

White, David Gordon, ed. 2000. *Tantra in Practice*. Princeton: Princeton University Press.

———. 2003. *Kiss of the Yoginī: "Tantric Sex" in Its South Asian Contexts*. Chicago: University of Chicago Press.

Wittgenstein, Ludwig. 1991. *The Blue and Brown Books*. Oxford: Wiley-Blackwell.

Woodroffe, Sir John. 1981. *The World as Power*. Madras: Ganesh & Company.

Yāska. 1984. *Nirukta*. In *The Nighaṇṭu and Nirukta*, ed. and trans. Lakshman Sarup. Delhi: Motilal Banarsidass.

10

Free Will, Agency, and Selfhood in Rāmānuja

Martin Ganeri

THE TAMIL BRAHMIN, Rāmānuja (traditional dates 1017–1137 CE), is a major figure both in the development of Hindu theism and of the Vedānta tradition of religious philosophy. The South Indian Śrī Vaiṣṇava tradition, centered on the worship of the male deity Viṣṇu in the form of Nārāyaṇa together with his consort, Śrī, reveres Rāmānuja as its principal teacher (*ācārya*). Śrī Vaiṣṇavism developed as a form of devotional theism (*bhakti*) based on the Tamil hymns of the poet saints, the Āḻvārs (6th–9th centuries CE), while also drawing on the Pāñcarātra tradition of theistic doctrine and ritual. Writing in Sanskrit, Rāmānuja's achievement was to develop a realist and theist interpretation of the Vedānta that established Śrī Vaiṣṇavism's legitimacy within pan-Indian Sanskritic Brahmanical Hinduism.

Rāmānuja's interpretation of the Vedānta represents the first systematic theistic alternative to earlier forms of Vedānta, especially the dominant Advaita (nondualist) tradition, in which both the ultimate reality of the world and of the personal theistic nature of the Ultimate Reality, Brahman, are denied. This system was then preserved and further developed as a sophisticated intellectual tradition within Śrī Vaiṣṇavism. However, the impact of his achievement extended far beyond the concerns of his own tradition. Having shown that Vedānta could provide an intellectual and soteriological system for theism, his account became the model for later Vaiṣṇava traditions to follow or modify, as they themselves sought to establish their own legitimacy within Brahmanical Hinduism. Moreover, within later overviews of Hindu thought Rāmānuja's form of Vedānta is recognized as one of three fundamental varieties of Vedānta, along with Advaita and Dvaita (dualism).

A central concern for all Vedāntic schools is to show how their teaching is an authentic exegesis of the Upaniṣads and the *Bhagavad Gītā,* and provides an accurate commentary on the *Brahma Sūtras*. Building on the work of earlier Brahmin teachers within the tradition, especially Yāmuna (ca. 966–1038 CE), Rāmānuja interprets these authoritative texts as teaching that the world of finite nonmaterial selves and of material entities is real and is the body (*śarīra*) of Brahman. Rāmānuja's system came to be known as Viśiṣṭādvaita (nondualism of the differentiated), meaning that the world is differentiated from Brahman, but is nondual in the sense of being dependent on Brahman for its existence. Brahman is identified with the personal God of theism, who possesses an infinite number of auspicious qualities proper to his divinity, while being free from any of the imperfections that characterize the world.

In this account selfhood exists on two levels: first, there is the Supreme Self, Brahman, who is the universal cause of all other things and, second, there are the many finite selves, distinct from the Supreme Self. An integral part of Rāmānuja's account is to affirm that each finite self is a real agent that exercises genuine freedom of will, in opposition to both Advaita Vedānta and Sāṃkhya traditions. However, Rāmānuja also maintains that the Supreme Self is the universal sovereign agent as the immediate cause of all the actions of the finite self. Indeed, Rāmānuja holds that the finite self should ascribe all its actions to divine agency in order to gain liberation (*mokṣa*) from karma and the cycle of rebirth (*saṃsara*).

Rāmānuja's resultant account would thus seem to be paradoxical, when it comes to what he affirms about the agency of the Supreme Self and about its relation to that of the finite self. Can Rāmānuja affirm all these features of agency without his account becoming incoherent? Modern Indologists such as John Carman (1974, 1994) and Julius Lipner (1986) have helpfully suggested that the complexities in Rāmānuja's account of God and of his relation to the world should be thought of as "polarities," contrasting types of theological discourse that are left unresolved for good theological reasons. Carman defines polarity as "the link between two apparently opposite qualities that belong to or describe the same reality" (Carman 1994: 11). Rāmānuja, he argues, does not settle lightly for paradox and is concerned to develop a harmonious account:

> Even so, despite his concern for consistency, Rāmānuja sometimes affirms two positions that at first seem contradictory, especially when he finds clear support in scriptural statements or traditional interpretations for two apparently opposite qualities or attributes in the divine nature... He regularly tries to resolve apparent

> contradictions in scriptural testimony and to interpret the paradoxes he inherited as complementary poles...however, traces of earlier paradoxes remain and some of his statements, wittingly or unwittingly, suggest new paradoxes. (Carman 1994: 13)

Lipner likewise identifies and explores polarities within Rāmānuja's embodiment cosmology. For his part, Lipner defines a polarity account as follows:

> By "polarity" here I mean a more or less stable tension between two (possibly more) poles such that this tension is resolvable into two mutually opposing but synchronous tendencies. One tendency is "centripetal," whereby the poles are attracted to each other; the other is "centrifugal," keeping the poles apart. Each tendency by itself is destructive of the polarity of the whole, but as simultaneously corrective of each other the tendencies work towards preserving the dynamic equilibrium of the system. (Lipner 1986: 134)

In appreciating why there are theological polarities present in Rāmānuja's account of agency we need to appraise his account in terms of what he is trying to do as a Vedāntic theologian, whose primary concern is to provide an authentic exegesis of the authoritative texts and commentary on the *Brahma Sūtras*. For this reason in what follows we shall keep the texts themselves in clear view in order to see how they shape the account that results. Arguments based on perception and inference support and elucidate this exegetical and commentarial theology, insofar as the matters they deal with lie within the limits of human intellection to comprehend. It is because of Rāmānuja's fidelity to the complex fabric that authoritative texts present and because certain aspects of agency set forth in authoritative texts exceed the limitations of human reasoning that the polarities and the paradoxes they contain arise.

Selfhood and Agency in General

In Rāmānuja's commentary on the *Brahma Sūtras*, the *Śrī Bhāṣya (Ś.Bh.)*, the nature of the self in general is introduced in his refutation of Advaita Vedānta in the vastly extended first *adhikaraṇa* (discursive unit; *Ś.Bh.* 1.1.1). The Advaitin *pūrvapakṣin* (opponent) maintains that there is just one universal self, which is pure undifferentiated and immutable consciousness

(Laksmithathachar 1985–1991 [henceforth cited as Melkote]: vol. 1: 25–57). There is, therefore, ultimately no real distinction between the Supreme Self and finite selves. Rather, the one self is ever liberated, the changeless witness, not an agent or experiencer, nor subject to embodiment and rebirth (cf. Śaṅkara, *Brahma Sūtra Bhāṣya* 2.3.29, Shastri 1980: 538). In the Advaitin's view the self cannot be a knowing agent engaged in different acts of knowledge, since agency involves change, which is excluded from the notion of the self as immutable. Instead, agency occurs only in the form of the material ego (*ahaṃkāra*), which is erroneously superimposed on the self (*Ś.Bh.* 1.1.1, Melkote vol. 1: 55). This material ego, as all other material things, is ultimately illusory in character.[1]

Rāmānuja rebuts the Advaita position point for point, drawing on the authoritative texts as well on observation and reason (Melkote vol. 1: 56–270). Not only are the many finite selves really distinct from the Supreme Self, but any self (whether Supreme or finite) is inherently a conscious subject, with consciousness as its essential nature. Moreover, any self is affirmed to be really a knowing agent, whose agency is, for the most part, realized in relation to forms of real material embodiment. However, Rāmānuja makes an important distinction between a self having the essential form (*rūpa*) of consciousness, something which does not change, because the self never ceases to be a conscious subject, and a self having the quality (*guṇa*) of consciousness, which does change, because particular acts of knowledge are contingent. This complexity in the consciousness of the self is said to be similar to the relationship between a lamp and its light:

> The one luminous substance exists as light and as the possessor of light. Although the light is the quality of the light-possessing substance, nonetheless it is just the luminous substance. It is not a quality like whiteness and such, being dissimilar to whiteness and such like because it exists elsewhere than its own substrate and because it has color. And it is just the luminous substance, because it possesses luminosity and is not a different thing. And it possesses luminosity, because it illuminates both its own form and that of others. But it behaves as a quality of that luminous substance, for the reason that it invariably has it as its substrate and is

1. See Timalsina's chapter in this volume.

> dependent (*śeṣa*) on it... In this same way, the self has the form of consciousness but also has the quality of consciousness. (Melkote vol. 1: 89, 90)[2]

Just as a lamp always shines by its very nature, but contingently brings other things into its light, so the self is always conscious by its very nature, but contingently knows other things. These contingent acts of knowledge inhere in the conscious subject.[3] Thereby, Rāmānuja introduces a distinction that allows contingency and mutability in the self's consciousness, one which makes the Advaitin argument for the material ego (*ahaṃkāra*) unnecessary to explain agency in the self (Melkote vol. 1: 94–107).

Selfhood, Embodiment, and Agency in the Case of the Supreme Self

As we have noted, a central doctrine in Rāmānuja is that the world is the body of the Supreme Self. It is within this relationship that the Supreme Self exercises its own agency. Rāmānuja has a particular definition of what embodiment means, which is intended to apply both to the Supreme Self and the world and to the finite selves and their different bodies:

> Any substance which a conscious entity can completely control and support for its own purposes and whose nature is solely to be accessory of that entity is the body of that entity. (*Ś.Bh.* 2.1.9, Melkote vol. 2: 26–27)

And this is precisely the relation that the Supreme Self has to the world as it is otherwise known from authoritative texts and reason:

> Therefore, since everything is such that it is controlled and supported by the Supreme Person always for his own purposes and has the nature that it is solely the accessory of him, all conscious and non-conscious entities are His body. (*Ś.Bh.* 2.1.9, Melkote vol. 3: 27)

---

2. This and following quotations are my own translations from the Melkote text of the *Śrī Bhāṣya*. The original texts have been slightly recast and abbreviated to allow for clarity.

3. For a further exposition of this distinction see Lipner 1986: 50–52.

The world's relationship to the Supreme Self is thus characterized by the three constituent relationships that make up the definition of embodiment: supported-support (*ādheya-ādhāra*); controlled-controller (*niyāmya-niyantṛ*); accessory-principal (*śeṣa-śeṣin*). In the case of the Supreme Self, the second relation is closely related to another central characterization of the Supreme Self as the Inner Controller (*antaryāmin*) of the world. By the third relation Rāmānuja means that the value and purpose of the world, including the finite selves, is directed wholly to the Supreme Self. Such a relation is otherwise expressed by the servant-master relationship. All things exist to serve the Supreme Self and realize their own proper nature and fulfillment in so doing.[4] All three relationships are important for understanding the nature and expression of the agency of the Supreme Self. Rāmānuja sometimes accepts the use of the term *kartṛtva* of the Supreme Self to denote the Self as the maker of the world as a whole, as long as any suggestion that the Supreme Self is itself subject to karma is excluded (e.g., *Ś.Bh.* 1.4.16).

The Supreme Self's agency is expressed firstly in the Self's universal causality in periodically producing, sustaining, and dissolving the world (*Ś.Bh.* 1.1.2). At the beginning of each cycle the cosmic body is transformed by the Supreme Self from being in a subtle causal state (*kāraṇāvasthā*) to being in its manifest effected state (*kāryāvasthā*), the world of ordinary experience (*Ś.Bh.* 2.3.18). Through an act of his knowledge and will the Supreme Self fashions the general shape of the world on the pattern of the Vedas, while the particular shape of the world is determined by the earlier karma of the selves and what kind of world will allow them to experience the fruits of their earlier deeds (*Ś.Bh.* 2.1.34). Although Rāmānuja accepts that some Upaniṣadic texts teach an emanatory cosmology through a series of causes, he insists that the Supreme Self is the immediate agent in every stage, since the Self is the Inner Controller of the world as the Self's body at every point of its production (*Ś.Bh.* 2.3.10–17). Moreover, the Supreme Self continues to act as the Inner Controller of all things and of all events at every moment of the world's manifestation (*Ś.Bh.* 2.3.40). The Supreme Self, then, exercises a universal and immediate agency over the production, continuing existence, and activity of the world. We have noted, however, that for the Advaitin the idea that the self is a real agent contradicts its immutability. As we have seen, in his general account of selfhood Rāmānuja

4. For more detailed accounts of these relations and their implications in Rāmānuja see Carman 1974 and Lipner 1986.

argues for a distinction between the unchanging form of consciousness and the changing quality of consciousness. However, in the case of the Supreme Self, he affirms that the Self is completely immutable (*nirvikāra*), this being taught by the authoritative texts (*Ś.Bh.* 1.4.26). The Supreme Self is unconditioned being (*satya*), not subject to the forms of change in being that material entities and finite selves undergo (*Ś.Bh.* 1.1.1, Melkote vol. 1: 281). In keeping with this, Rāmānuja argues that, when the Self's cosmic body is transformed from its causal to its effected state, all the change that occurs is extrinsic to the Self within, taking place only in the finite selves and matter (*Ś.Bh.* 2.3.18).

Rāmānuja does not attempt to resolve further the seeming paradox of how the Supreme Self can be completely immutable and yet also act as the universal cause and controller of the world. Nor does he deal with how the Supreme Self can immutably know all the contingent realities that make up the world. Such agency and knowledge would in ordinary human experience involve change in the agent. Here we have, then, one example of the polarities present in Rāmānuja's theistic Vedānta. Rāmānuja affirms on the basis of the authoritative texts that the Supreme Self is changeless, unaffected by the types of change present in finite selves and material entities, but also affirms that it is an agent and is all-knowing, without resolving the apparent paradox this generates. As with other polarities of Rāmānuja's account, later Viśiṣṭādvaitic thinkers sought further to clarify and explain his teaching. Thus Vedānta Deśika (1268–1369 CE) argues that the Supreme Self can be said both to know all the contingent events of the world and to remain changeless because, unlike the finite self, the Self knows them all simultaneously and by direct intuition (Chari 1988: 240).

Selfhood, Embodiment, and Agency in the Finite Self

Like the Supreme Self, the finite self is a conscious subject. However, whereas the Supreme Self is omnipresent, universally and immediately present to all entities at all times, the finite self is limited or atomic (*aṇu*) in being and in scope. The finite self resides in the heart, though extending its consciousness throughout its body (*Ś.Bh.* 2.3.20–25). In saṃsāric embodiments the consciousness of the finite self undergoes real change as it expands and contracts according to what kind of human or non-human body it comes to have and then as particular acts of knowledge arise, in the course of its embodied actions and sensations. The finite self becomes an embodied agent of a particular kind and the experiencer of the pleasures and pain that accord with its embodiment and its actions.

In the third *pāda* of the second *adhyāya* of the *Śrī Bhāṣya*, Rāmānuja has a sustained discussion of the selfhood, agency, and freedom of the finite self in the saṃsāric state. The general purpose of this section in the *Śrī Bhāṣya* is in fact to show that no objection can be made to the Vedāntic teaching that the Supreme Person is the universal and direct cause of all things. This involves discussion of the relationship between the Supreme Self and the finite self and the finite self's own agency. In *Śrī Bhāṣya* 2.3.33–39 (Melkote vol. 3: 215–221), "the agent because of the *śāstra* being purposive," Rāmānuja discusses whether the finite self is a real agent. This time the opponent is from the Sāṃkhya tradition. While the Sāṃkhya view of the self and of reality as a whole is in many respects radically different from that of Advaita, the two traditions have in common that they both view the self as a pure witness and not a real agent. In Sāṃkhya agency is ascribed to the material qualities (*guṇas*) and to the material categories that arise from their evolution, especially to the material intellect (*buddhi*), which is mistakenly superimposed on the self.[5]

The Sāṃkhya *pūrvapakṣin* supports his position that the self is not a real agent by appeal to texts taken from the Upaniṣads and *Bhagavad Gītā* (*B.G.*), the very texts which form the authoritative sources for the Vedāntic system. If these texts can be made out to teach that the self is not an agent, then clearly any claim otherwise cannot purport to be Vedāntic. In support of this, the *pūrvapakṣin* cites the *Kaṭha Upaniṣad*, which would appear to teach that it is deluded to think of the self as the agent:

> If as a killer he thinks (himself) to kill, and as killed thinks (himself) to be killed, both of them do not know. He does not kill, he is not killed. (*Kaṭha Upaniṣad* 2.19)

Then, the *pūrvapakṣin* cites passages from the *Gītā* that appear to teach that it is the material qualities that are the agent, as Sāṃkhya maintains, with the self just the experiencer:

> Everywhere actions are done by the qualities of matter, the one whose self is deluded by the ego (*ahaṃkāra*) thinks, "I am the agent." (*B.G.* 3.27)

5. See Bryant's chapter in this volume.

> When one who sees perceives the agent as none other than the qualities. (*B.G.* 14.19)
>
> Matter is said to be the cause in the agency of cause and effects, self (*puruṣa*) is said to be the cause in the experiencing of pains and pleasures. (*B.G.* 13.20)

On these grounds the Sāṃkhya *pūrvapakṣin* concludes that the self is an experiencer only, not an agent.

In response Rāmānuja argues that when the *sūtra* states, "because of the *śāstra* being purposive," it points to *śāstra* texts as identifying the experiencer with the agent. Moreover, he points out that the very meaning of *śāstra* as a term (from the verbal root, *śās*) is to command and is directed at impelling people to the kind of action that gives rise to knowledge. Thus, the *sūtra* supports the Vedāntic position that the self, as the knower and experiencer, is also the agent. The texts cited by the opponent can, moreover, be interpreted in other ways. Rather than the Upaniṣad denying the self to be the agent in the case of killing, it may be taken simply to be denying that the self can be killed, since it is eternal. An embodied killer cannot actually kill the self of another embodied being, only the body. Again, rather than the *Gītā* texts limiting agency to the material qualities, they should be taken to indicate that embodied self acts together with the material qualities.

Thus, Rāmānuja argues, the *sūtra* and authoritative texts teach that the self is a real agent. Along with this he argues that the agency of an embodied self is actually to be ascribed to the embodied being as a whole, not just to any constitutive element within it. Rāmānuja cites other *Gītā* texts that teach that it is the embodied being as a whole that is the agent:

> This being the case, the one who sees the self alone as the agent because of his intellect being imperfect, wrong headed he does not see. (*B.G.*18.16)
>
> Thus the foundation, agent, the organs of different kinds, and the distinct motions of various kind, and divine destiny here is the fifth. (*B.G.* 18.14)

It is helpful here to refer to Rāmānuja's commentary on the *Gītā (Gītā Bhāṣya)*. In his commentary on the last text (*B.G.* 18.14) he sets out in detail how the agency of an embodied self is the result of a complex causal action involving the finite self, the different elements of its material body and the Supreme Self as its Inner Controller:

> "Foundation" is the body. The body whose nature is the aggregate of the five gross elements is the foundation, because it is established by the individual self. Likewise, "agent" is the individual self. That the individual self is the knower and the agent is established by the [Brahma] *sūtras*, "knowing for this very reason" (*B.S.* 2.3.18) and "an agent because of the *śāstra* being purposive" (*B.S.* 2.3.33). "The organs of different kinds" are the five sense organs of speech, touch and so on, together with the mind, whose operation is of different kinds in the arising of action. "And the distinct motions of various kinds," by the word "motions" is denoted the fivefold vital air by stating its distinct activities; the fivefold varied motion of the vital air, divided by the difference of inhaled and exhaled breath and so on, supporting the body's senses, is activity of various kinds. "And divine destiny here is the fifth," the meaning is that in this collection of the causes of action divine destiny is the fifth, being the Supreme Self, the Inner Controller, the principal cause in the carrying out of action, for it is said, "and I am seated in the heart of all, from me remembrance, knowledge and their loss" (*B.G.* 15.15). And it will be said, "the Lord dwells in the region of the heart of all beings, Arjuna, causing all beings mounted on the machine to whirl round by his *māyā*." (*B.G.* 18.61, Adidevananda 1991: 557–558)[6]

We shall consider the particular relation between the agency of the finite self and the Supreme Self in the next section ("Divine Agency and Human Freedom"). At this point we can just note the full analysis of bodily action given here in terms of five different causal elements. The agency of an embodied self is the result of all five operating as a complex whole.

In the second half of this section of the *Śrī Bhāṣya* (2.3.36–39) Rāmānuja argues that the *sūtras* further advance four rational arguments against the coherence of the Sāṃkhya position. In each case Rāmānuja argues that the Sāṃkhya position contradicts observed reality or the principles that Sāṃkhya otherwise wants to maintain.

First, Rāmānuja considers the implications of locating agency only in matter. If matter were the agent as the Sāṃkhya claims, then since matter

6. All translations of the *Gītā Bhāṣya* are my own from the Sanskrit text in Adidevananda's edition, with the original text slightly abridged in translation.

is common to all selves, all selves would be liable to experience the fruits of all actions. What Rāmānuja is getting at here is the fact there is nothing in matter itself that restricts the properties of one bit from another and so it is matter as a whole that would be the agent. Likewise, he argues, there would be no way of restricting to any particular self the inner organs or other parts of a particular embodied agent and hence there would be no distinction in living conditions between one individual and another (*Ś.Bh.* 2.3.36). Such a situation clearly goes against the observation that there are distinct agents who experience the fruits of their own actions. By implication it also undermines the whole basis for the operation of karma and moral responsibility.[7]

The second argument rests on the connection between being the agent and being the experiencer, something that the authoritative texts have already established. So, if the *buddhi* is the agent, as the Sāṃkhya argues, then it must also be the experiencer. But if that is the case, then the Sāṃkhya position is self-defeating since there are no grounds for knowing that there is a self at all, for Sāṃkhya holds that we know that the self exists precisely because it is an experiencer (*Ś.Bh.* 2.3.37).

The third argument then strikes at the heart of the whole soteriology of Sāṃkhya. If the *buddhi* is the agent, then it is also the agent of the activity of concentrated mediation (*samādhi*), which is the means to get final liberation according to Sāṃkhya. But this would defeat the whole Sāṃkhya enterprise, since such meditation is meant to result in the self realizing its own distinction from matter. Clearly the material *buddhi* by its very nature cannot do this (*Ś.Bh.* 2.3.38).

Finally, an argument is put forward on the basis of the observation that human agents do not keep on acting all the time, but choose sometimes to act and sometimes to desist from acting, just as a carpenter chooses freely to make things using his tools or not to do so. However, if the *buddhi* were the true agent, then we would find human beings acting continuously, since as an insentient thing, *buddhi* lacks the capacity to deliberate and adjust its behavior and its actions would simply flow from its nature. But we do not find that humans always act (*Ś.Bh.* 2.3.39).

These arguments reinforce Rāmānuja's position that the self is a real agent. Moreover, they further support Rāmānuja's analysis of the agency of embodied beings as being the operation of the complex whole, of which the finite self is one causal element, along with the material constituents of the body and the Supreme Self.

---

7. See Dasti's chapter in this volume for Nyāya precursors of this line of argumentation.

Divine Agency and Human Freedom

Rāmānuja thus argues that that the finite self is really an agent. However, a question arises over the scope of such agency when set alongside the agency of the Supreme Self. Rāmānuja's commentary on *Gītā* 18.14–15 affirms that the Supreme Self is included as an integral element in the finite self's actions. How can the finite self genuinely be free and hence morally responsible for its actions, if all actions are dependent on the agency of the Supreme Self? In *Śrī Bhāṣya*, "but from the Supreme Self because of its revelation" (*Ś.Bh.* 2.3.40–41, Melkote vol. 3: 221–225), the discussion moves on to consider whether the finite self acts independently of the Supreme Self or not. Rāmānuja aims to affirm both that the finite self is dependent on the Supreme Self and that it is free enough to be morally responsible for its actions.

The *pūrvapakṣin* argues that the finite self must be independent on the grounds that being subject to moral commands and prohibitions only makes sense if the finite self has freedom of choice to act or not. In response, Rāmānuja points again to the *sūtra* itself and to Vedic passages (as the "revelation" mentioned by the *sūtra*) and the *Gītā*, where the universal and immediate agency of the Supreme Self is taught. The passages from the Upaniṣads are among the standard ones Rāmānuja cites elsewhere as teaching that the Supreme Self is the Inner Controller:

> Entered within, He is the ruler of all things that are born, the Self of all. (*Taittirīya Āraṇyaka* 3.11)
>
> The Self, who being in the self is other than the self, whom the self does not know, of whom the self is the body, who controls the self from within, He is the immortal Inner Controller. (*Bṛhadāraṇyaka Upaniṣad* [Mādhyandina Recension] 3.7.26)

The *Gīta* passages referred to here (*B.G.* 18.15, 18.61) are the same ones that Rāmānuja cites in his commentary on *Gītā* 18.14 to support the idea that the Supreme Self is the fifth causal factor in every action of the finite self.

Rāmānuja argues that the agency of the Supreme Self does not determine the actions of the finite self. Instead, the Supreme Self brings things about as a form of "consent" (*anumati*) to what the self otherwise freely chooses to do:

> In the case of all actions, the Inner Controller, the Supreme Self, having regard for the effort, the exertion, made by the self, by

> giving consent (*anumati*) causes it to act. Without the consent of the Supreme Self its activity would not come about. (*Ś.Bh.* 2.3.41, Melkote vol. 3: 222)

In support of this Rāmānuja goes on to make use of the analogy of joint ownership of property by human beings:

> Just as in the case of two people owning property in common, its handing over to a third party does not come about without the permission of the second owner. Moreover, because it is just on account of the first owner (*svenaiva*) that the permission of the second is given, the fruit of that action belongs to the first. (*Ś.Bh.* 2.3.41, Melkote vol. 3: 222)

In this analogy, then, we see actions that require multiple instances of agency. The first owner cannot bring the action about without the permissive agency of the second owner. However, at the same time, the responsibility of the first owner for the action is in no way undermined by the need to get the permission of the second owner. The choice is very much his own, and so he rightly experiences the good or bad consequences of it. In like manner, the Supreme Self's agency involves granting permission for what the finite agent chooses to do. The Supreme Self's consent is necessary for the action to take place, causing it to come into being, but does not negate that it is a freely willed action on the part of the finite self for which the finite self is responsible. The Supreme Self simply respects the choices the finite self makes and makes it possible for them to be realized.

Julius Lipner has pointed out that Rāmānuja's account of permissive agency and the analogy do not fully explain how the agency of the Supreme Self and of the finite self can operate together without conflict. With reference to a parallel passage in a separate treatise by Rāmānuja, the *Vedārthasaṃgraha*, he comments:

> The indwelling Lord has regard to the "act of will" (*prayatna udyoga*) of the agent and consents to its realisation. This is a minimal form of consent, an "ontological" consent, if you wish. The agent is morally responsible for the deed, not the Lord.
>
> A little reflection will show, of course, that this is hardly a resolution of our dilemma concerning the Lord's universal causality and the possibility of the finite free action. For is the agent's "act of will" in

> the first place dependent upon the consent of the Lord or not? If it is, how is the agent really free to initiate action? If it not, the Lord is not the universal cause... Rāmānuja has sought to do no more than provide an illuminating analogy, by way of partial explanation, for the "co-operation" between the Lord and the individual *ātman* in the performance of free action. (Lipner 1986: 71)

In Rāmānuja's commentary itself the discussion does move on to consider the objection that such a permissive account of the Supreme Self's agency fails to explain other Upaniṣadic texts, where the Supreme Self is said actually to cause some finite selves to do good and so achieve liberation, but others to do bad and so be further enmeshed in rebirths. This seems to affirm a stronger form of divine predestination than mere consent:

> For it is he who causes the one whom he wishes to lead up from these worlds to do work that is good. For it is he who causes the one whom he wishes to lead down to do bad deeds. (*Kauṣītaki Upaniṣad* 3.8)

In reply, however, Rāmānuja, argues that this is still to be understood as the divine response to the free choices that the finite selves have made:

> Favoring the one, who has become fixed in unbounded good will toward the Supreme Person, he causes him to find pleasure (*ruci*) in very auspicious actions leading to attainment of himself. And disfavoring the one, who has become fixed in unbounded hostility to him, he causes him to find pleasure in actions opposed to attaining him, which are the means for going downward. (*Ś.Bh.* 2.3.41 Melkote vol. 3: 223)

Thereby any charge of partiality or cruelty cannot be leveled at the Supreme Self, for the finite self has freely chosen which attitude to develop toward the Supreme Self and is morally responsible for it.

However, this still leaves unresolved how the Supreme Self's agency relates to those actions of the finite self, where the self develops its good or bad will toward the Supreme Self. Are they caused and so determined by the Supreme Self or is the finite self independent? It is here that Rāmānuja's commentary on *Gītā* 18.14–15 again becomes important. Just as this explicitly refers to *Śrī Bhāṣya* 2.3.33–39 and helps give a fuller picture of the nature of the embodied self's agency, so it refers to and picks up on the discussion of the present section of the *Śrī Bhāṣya*. In this commentary on the *Gītā* we find a fuller explanation of the nature of the Supreme Self's agency in terms of the constitutive relationships of embodiment: the Supreme Self is the existential support (*ādhāra*) of the finite self and of its material body and in that sense the cause of the entirety of action for the finite self, including its initial effort:

> The finite self, whose support is the Supreme Self and whose powers are supported by Supreme Self, by means of its sense organs, body, and so on, which are given and supported by the Supreme Self, and by means of the powers supported by the Supreme Self, by its own will begins an undertaking which has the form of directing the sense organs and so on, in order to bring its works to completion. The Supreme Self, established as its end, causes this undertaking to come about by giving his own consent. For this reason the finite self is the cause of its coming into being by the self's own intention. Just as in the bringing about of the moving and such like of very heavy stones and trees by means of many men, the many are the cause and are dependent on command and prohibition. (*Gītā Bhāṣya* 18.15, Adidevananda 1991: 558)

The Supreme Self is the existential support of the other four causal elements that together are constitutive of the agency of an embodied being. Moreover, the Supreme Self is the controller (*niyantṛ*) of all actions, causing them to come to completion. In Rāmānuja's account, then, the finite self is free in that it can choose to act in different ways. It is not free in the sense that either its power of agency or any of its actions are completely independent of the Supreme Self. Rather, without the Supreme Self's gift of existence there would be no power to make free choices, nor would any action come about. As such, the Supreme Self is the agent both of the finite self's own power of free agency and of every action it undertakes. Or, we might say, the finite self is free to act and its actions are free, not despite the agency of the Supreme Self, but because of it.

The Supreme Self is also the end (*anta*) of the finite self's actions, as Rāmānuja's commentary on *Gītā* 18.14–15 states. The finite self is free in its choices whether to be well disposed to the Supreme Self or not, whether to conform its actions to the manifest will of the Supreme Self or not. However, these are not equally good choices to make. The proper nature of the finite self is to be the accessory (*śeṣa*) of the Supreme Self as the Principal (*Śeṣin*). The finite self thus acts well when all its actions are carried out as acts of service and love for the Supreme Self. Moreover, the finite self's final good is to enjoy the blissful knowledge or vision of the Supreme Self. When the Supreme Self rewards the finite selves who have good will toward him or obey his commands, he simply furthers their own desire to progress to this final goal (*Ś.Bh.* 2.2.3). Thus, in choosing to act according to the will of the Supreme Self, the finite self freely chooses to realize the fulfillment of its own proper nature and final ends with the help of divine grace.

The freedom of the finite self's agency is not undermined, because the divine and human wills are not necessarily in competition with each other. However, it remains that we have here a second polarity present in Rāmānuja's account. The proper agency and freedom of both the Supreme Self and the finite self are affirmed on the basis of authoritative texts and human experience. Moreover, reason can show ways to reconcile the apparent conflict between the two. However, since analogies taken from the world of human action do not express fully the relationship between the Supreme Self and finite selves, it remains paradoxical for us to think of an action being caused by the Supreme Self and yet being the free action of the finite self.

In later Viśiṣṭādvaitin scholarship attempts were made to offer a fuller account of the teaching found in the *Śrī Bhāṣya* and *Gītā Bhāṣya*, though with different positions taken on what sense to make of the Supreme Self's agency with respect to the finite self's initial act of will and effort. As Patricia Mumme has pointed out, Sudarśana Sūri (12th century CE), in his commentary on the *Śrī Bhāṣya*, the *Śrutaprakāśikā*, (2.3.40) states that the independence (*svātantrya*) of the finite self (*Ś. Bh.* 2.3.40) means "lack of obstruction in the case of (one having) the capacity to act according to his wish." The finite self's freedom to act is still dependent on the Lord's antecedent gift of the power to know, will and act. Vedānta Deśika, on the other hand, while also affirming the freedom of the finite self, suggests more strongly that the Supreme Self should be said to cause the initial choice and effect, in the sense that the Self is the common cause of all actions including the initial act of will and effort, with the finite self the cause of particular actions (Mumme 1985: 107).

The "Renunciation" of Agency and the Release of the Finite Self

In the previous sections we have seen that Rāmānuja argues for the reality and freedom of the finite self's agency. However, a further aspect of Rāmānuja's account of agency might seem to contradict his affirmation of both these aspects. For Rāmānuja also maintains that if the finite self is to be liberated from karma and the cycle of rebirth (*saṃsāra*), it should renounce any claim to its own agency and instead ascribe all its actions to Supreme Person. This is an important part of the teaching of the *Gītā*, in which Arjuna is taught to practice desireless action (*niṣkāma karma*) and thereby free himself from attachment and concern for the fruits of his actions. Arjuna is exhorted to ascribe all his actions and their fruits to Kṛṣṇa (e.g., *B.G.* 3.30, 18.4, 18.66), with the promise that by so doing Kṛṣṇa will grant him liberation (*mokṣa*). For Rāmānuja's tradition the question of how to reconcile affirmation of the finite self's own agency with such renunciation of it for soteriological and devotional purposes became a major issue that divided the northern and southern branches.

For his part, Rāmānuja interprets the teaching found in the *Gītā* in accordance with his affirmation of the self's genuine agency within his embodiment cosmology. Thus, when in *Gītā* 3.30 Arjuna is told:

> Having abandoned all works in me with your mind on the self free from desire, free of selfishness, wage war with the fever gone.

Rāmānuja interprets this as Kṛṣṇa urging Arjuna to recognize fully that his own agency is grounded in being the body of the Supreme Self and hence subject to the three constitutive relations of embodiment:

> Therefore, having abandoned all works in me, the Supreme Self, thinking that it is by me that all works are done, with the consideration that it is the nature of the self to be set in action by me since it is my body, and performing such actions purely as acts of worship, without desire for the fruits of them, therefore free from selfishness in action, wage war and such like with the fever gone.
>
> The meaning is: contemplating that the Lord of all, the Principal of all, himself causes his own works to be done by the finite self as agent, who belongs to him, for the sole purpose of his own worship

> by his own deeds, free from selfishness in actions, liberated from the fever of death, namely "what will become of me because of the ancient heaping up of endless sin brought into being by beginningless time," remembering that it is the Supreme Person, who having been worshipped will cause you to be liberated from bondage, with your mind at ease, do the *yoga* of works. (Adidevananda 1991: 143)

The "abandoning" of the self's agency here is not the giving up of agency as such. Rather it is the cultivation of a mental attitude of detachment that is an effective means of getting free of self-centered desire for the fruits of its actions. The finite self owns fully the truth that it acts only because the Supreme Self is the support (*ādhāra*) of all its actions and that they find their proper fulfillment in service of the Supreme Self as the Principal (*Śeṣin*). The finite self freely aligns its own will with that of the Supreme Person as the controller (*niyantṛ*), whose agency is exercised to enable the selves making up his body to gain release.

The finite self makes all its actions into acts of worship as an expression of its intense love for the Supreme Self and of its delight in being the accessory of the Supreme Self. As Rāmānuja comments on *Gītā* 9.27:

> Whatever you do, whatever you eat, whatever you sacrifice, whatever you give, whatever austerity you perform, Kaunteya, do that as an offering to me.
>
> The meaning is: since gods and such like, who are thought to be the objects of worship in the case of oblations, gifts, and so on, and you yourself, the agent and experiencer, are mine and since their and your nature, existence, and activity are dependent on my will, offer everything, both yourself as the agent, experiencer, and worshipper, and the clan of gods being worshipped and the set of actions which are the act of worship, just to me, the Supreme Principal (*paramaśeṣiṇi*) and Supreme Agent (*paramakartari*). Filled with unbounded love, contemplate that you have your sole delight in being my accessory (*śeṣa*), based on my being the Controller, and that those who are the objects of worship and so on have this same single nature. (Adidevananda 1991: 316)

In these passages, then, renunciation of agency is really an act of mental realignment, whereby the finite self gets free from attachment to its actions and realizes for itself its nature and bliss as the body of the Supreme Self, rather than any giving up on its own agency as such.

This same teaching is found in the first interpretation Rāmānuja gives for the *carama śloka* (*Gītā* 18.66):

> Completely renouncing all *dharmas*, seek me alone as refuge I will release you from all sins. Do not grieve.
>
> Renouncing all *dharmas* having the form of *karma yoga*, *jñāna yoga*, and *bhakti yoga*, which are the means to the highest end, act as you are entitled to with unlimited love, because these actions are acts of worship of me—with the complete renunciation of fruits of actions and agency and such like, continuously think of me as the sole agent, the object of worship, the end to be attained and the means to it. (Adidevananda 1991: 598)

The second interpretation is that those persons who are unable to perform the expiatory acts necessary to become cleansed of their bad deeds before embarking on *bhakti yoga* can simply abandon themselves to the mercy of the Supreme Self who will release them so that they can begin it.

Thus, the finite self continues to perform acts as an embodied agent according to its class and stage of life. Moreover, these acts are free, since the finite self could act otherwise than it does. But, the finite self chooses to ascribe them to the Supreme Self as the one who is their ultimate basis and whose will it is that they are done, offering them as acts of worship to the Supreme Self of whom the finite self is the *śeṣa*. That this is a purification of agency rather than a giving up of it is clear from Rāmānuja's commentary on the *Gītā* verses (18.15–65) between the analysis of the five causes of the self's agency (*B.G.* 18.14) and the *carama śloka* (*B.G.* 18.66). Here the *Gītā* classifies different people and their actions according to the three material qualities of *sattva*, *rajas*, and *tamas*. As Rāmānuja interprets these verses, sāttvic actions are those where the agency is ascribed to the Supreme Self and where the actions are those prescribed by *dharma*, whereas rājasic actions are those where the actions are done for enjoyment of their fruits, and tāmasic actions are those which are also contrary to *dharma*. It is, then, sāttvic agency that is meant by renunciation of agency. By acting in this manner the finite self realizes the proper nature and fulfillment of its own agency as the body of the Supreme Self, whereas the contrary desire for independent action for one's own benefit and even in acts contrary to the Lord's will is a wrong conception and abuse of that agency.

Julius Lipner finds in Rāmānuja's own account a distinction between what he calls between "*saṃsāra*-immanent (SI)" and "*saṃsāra*-transcendent (ST)" action. The actions are the same, but the intention motivating them is different. In SI action the intention is selfish, to get the fruits of the action for oneself, while in ST action the intention is only to worship the Supreme Self by one's actions and eventually experience the final state of blissful liberation (Lipner 1986: 69–72). By just doing one's dharmic duties and ascribing the agency of all actions to the Supreme Self the finite self transcends the karmic entailment of its actions and hence becomes free from further enmeshment in *saṃsāra*. By such renunciation the embodied self comes even in *saṃsāra* to experience for itself that transcendent freedom that is the permanent character of the agency of the Supreme Self.

John Carman has pointed out that there remains here a further polarity in the relation between human effort and divine grace present within the accessory-Principal or servant-Master relationship itself. On the one hand, there is the law of karma, which is the just outworking of the finite self's own efforts and responsibility, a law that in Rāmānuja's theistic account is executed by God himself. Here God responds to the self's meritorious actions by granting his grace, furthering the finite self in good deeds and then granting final release. The self's acts of devotion are acts of service to the divine Master that merit divine grace. On the other hand, the finite self already belongs to God as accessory or servant, and the self's acts of devotion are acts of service seen as a privilege and joy both because they express the finite self's proper nature and because they are done in response to God's antecedent love and grace (Carman 1974: 214–217; 1994: 95).

The branches of the Śrī Vaiṣṇava tradition themselves came later on to differ markedly over the issue of how to understand the renunciation of the finite self's agency as they sought to further clarify how human effort relates to divine grace in bringing about liberation. As Patricia Mumme has shown, Vedānta Deśika, within the northern tradition, insists on the inherent reality of the finite self's agency at all times (following Rāmānuja's account of agency in the *Śrī Bhāṣya*). He understands such renunciation of agency to be only a form of meditation on the Supreme Self as the universal agent and on the self's dependency on him, especially when it comes to attaining release as a goal that is beyond the finite self's own powers (e.g., in Vedānta Deśika's commentary on Rāmānuja's analysis of the five causes of the finite self's agency on *Gītā* 18.14–15). Such meditation serves to counter the delusion that the finite self is the sole agent of its actions, independent of the Supreme Self (Mumme 1985: 105–109, 113–115).

Thus, Vedānta Deśika develops an account of agency that preserves both the universal agency of the Supreme Self and the particular agency of the finite self. The southern tradition, on other hand, developed the position that the finite self does actually give up its agency in the act of surrender (*prapatti*) to the Supreme Self to obtain release, in which the Supreme Self is seen as the sole agent. This position emphasizes the type of language found in the *Gītā* and in the works of the Āḻvārs, along with the interpretation of Rāmānuja's works by Sudarśana Sūri (Mumme 1985: 109–113).

Agency and Selfhood in the Liberated State

We finish our examination of agency in Rāmānuja by considering what kind of agency the finite self has in the released state. Since for both Advaita and Sāṃkhya agency is located in the material component of the embodied self, it is inherently a feature of saṃsāric embodiment. For Rāmānuja, on the other hand, the liberated self continues to be an agent as part of its own inherent nature. However, the liberated self's agency is now permanently free from any karmic or samṣāric entailment and becomes increasingly like the agency of the Supreme Self.

Thus, the liberated self can now act without a body in order to enjoy itself. Unlike the saṃsāric state, such activity involves no effort on the self's part, beyond the exercise of its free will, just as the Supreme Self brings things about merely through his will (*Ś.Bh.* 4.4.8). At the same time, the liberated self can also take on bodies if it chooses and so act as an embodied agent once more in order to experience bodily pleasures (*Ś.Bh.* 4.4.14). In the liberated state the finite self also regains the fullest expansion of its consciousness, which in *saṃsāra* was contracted along with its agency according to what type of embodiment it had as a result of its earlier karmic actions. The liberated self undergoes no contraction of its consciousness even when it takes on bodies. It is for this reason, Rāmānuja argues, that the liberated self can take on a number of bodies, even though the self is atomic (*aṇu*) in size (*Ś. Bh.* 4.4.15).

In these ways, then, the agency of the finite self comes to be like that of the Supreme Self. The liberated agency of the finite self has the quality of that *līlā* (sport) which characterizes the agency of the Supreme Self, being completely free, unmotivated by any need and having no *karmic* entailment (*Ś.Bh.* 4.4.14). Nonetheless, the finite self remains a finite agent. Even in the liberated state it lacks the universal agency that is unique to the Supreme Self as the universal support and controller of the world (*Ś.Bh.* 4.4.17).

Conclusion

Rāmānuja, then, argues for an account of the self in which the self (whether Supreme or finite) is a conscious subject that exercises real and free agency. His account of the agency of finite embodied beings as being that of the complex whole is one that accords with ordinary experience as well as that taught by authoritative texts. Whereas for Advaita and Sāṃkhya agency is inherently a negative feature of karmic embodiment, for Rāmānuja it is a matter of how that agency is exercised that determines whether it leads to forms of embodiment that cause the self further limitation and misery or becomes an expression of joyful creativity sharing in the transcendent agency of the Supreme Self. Central to the concerns of Rāmānuja's theistic account is the desire to relate the agency of the Supreme Self and finite selves in such a manner as to affirm the proper operation of both, but also recognize that the finite self's fulfillment comes from the recognition of its dependency on and service to the Supreme Self and that it relies on divine agency for final liberation to come about. His account thus maintains a form of compatibilism that is to be found in other classical theistic traditions.

The resultant account is undoubtedly complex. Yet, it would seem more fairly to be characterized as containing unresolved polarities than being incoherent. As a Vedāntic theologian, Rāmānuja works to draw out the teaching found in the textual authorities that form the basis of Vedānta, supported by observation and reasoning. To some extent the polarities that arise are due to the fact that he often does not go beyond what is necessary to explain either the *sūtra* or *Gītā* text sufficiently. However, to some extent the polarities are the common ones that abide in such theistic accounts in many traditions and mark the limits of human reason to make sense of realities that transcend them.

References

Adidevananda, Swami. 1991. *Śrī Rāmānuja Gītā Bhāṣya*. Madras: Ramakrishna Math Printing Press.

Carman, John. 1974. *The Theology of Rāmānuja: An Essay in Interreligious Understanding*. New Haven, CT: Yale University Press.

———. 1994. *Majesty and Meekness: A Comparative Study of Contrast and Harmony in the Concept of God*. Grand Rapids, MI: Eerdmans Publishing Co.

Chari, S. M. Shrinivasa. 1988. *Fundamentals of Viśiṣṭādvaita Vedānta: A Study Based on Vedānta Deśika's Tattva-muktā-kalāpa*. Delhi: Motilal Banarsidass.

Laksmithathachar, M. A., chief ed. 1985–1991. *Śrī Bhāṣyam Melkote Critical Edition* Vols. 1–4. Melkote: Academy of Sanskrit Research.

Lipner, Julius. 1986. *The Face of Truth: A Study of Meaning and Metaphysics in the Vedāntic Theology of Rāmānuja*. Albany: State University of New York Press.

Mumme, Patricia. 1985. "Jīvakartṛtva in Viśiṣṭādvaita and the Dispute over Prapatti in Vedānta Deśika and the Teṅkalai Authors." In *Professor Kuppuswami Sastri Birth-Centenary: Selected Research Papers Presented at the Birth Centenary Seminars*, ed. Kuppuswami Sastri and S. S. Janaki, 99–118. Chennai: Kuppuswami Sastri Research Institute.

Shastri, J. L., ed. 1980. *Brahmasūtra-śaṅkarabhāṣyam*. Delhi: Motilal Banarsidass.

11

Dependent Agency and Hierarchical Determinism in the Theology of Madhva

David Buchta

MADHVĀCĀRYA, OR SIMPLY Madhva, (1238–1317) is the founding figure of the school Dvaita Vedānta, a theistic (Vaiṣṇava) school that contrasts with other Vedānta traditions by strongly affirming duality (*dvaita*) or, more properly, the multiplicity of eternal real entities. Madhva speaks of five types of ultimate difference (*bheda*): (1) between the Lord (*īśvara*) and the finite self (*jīva*); (2) between the Lord and insentient matter (*jaḍa*); (3) between the selves and matter; (4) between distinct selves; and (5) between distinct units of matter.[1] Madhva expressed his doctrines through commentaries on the major canonical foundations of the Vedānta schools—the Upaniṣads, the *Bhagavad Gītā,* and the *Brahmasūtras*—as well as independent treatises, and he inspired a long and rich tradition of theological writing. While Madhva comments on the same core of canonical texts as other Vedānta writers, his interpretations of those texts often differ radically from those of other Vedāntins.[2] Nevertheless, his writings and that of his tradition have had an important influence on the development of other schools, and his views on human agency and free will are distinct in important ways.

1. See Madhva's *Viṣṇutattvavinirṇaya* (Govindacharya 1974: 35). All translations here are my own except where noted.

2. The most famous example is Madhva's resegmentation of the phrase, "*sa ātmā tat tvam asi* (That is the self; you are that)," recurring in ChU 6.8–16 (6.3 in Govindacharya 1969: 437–40, Madhva's comment comes on p. 442), to get "*atat tvam asi* (You are not that)" instead of "*tat tvam asi* (You are that)." See Gerow 1987 for a treatment of this passage in the Mādhva tradition.

This chapter will offer a brief exposition of key passages in Madhva's writing where he addresses issues of agency and free will. After contextualizing Madhva's core ideas against the background of the larger world of Indian philosophy ("Madhva in the Context of Indian Intellectual History"), I focus particularly on the tension between the self's agency and its dependence on God ("Dependent Agency: Madhva on *Brahmasūtras* 2.3.33–42" and "Control and Responsibility: Madhva on *Brahmasūtras* 2.1.35–37") and the eternal hierarchical status that forms part of the self's inherent nature and largely determines each self's destiny ("Determinism and the Hierarchy of Selves"). The claims of two scholars who have championed Madhva's theology as a solution to the problem of theodicy are then considered ("Madhva and Theodicy"). Finally, I acknowledge certain signs of the influence Madhva's ideas have had on later Vedāntins outside of his own tradition ("Considering Madhva's Legacy").

Madhva in the Context of Indian Intellectual History

One of the core disputes about agency in Indian philosophy is whether it is located in our outside of the self. As Bryant's chapter in this volume notes, there was a tendency with roots in the Sāṃkhya-Yoga traditions to deny ultimate agency in the self, a tendency that was motivated by a concern that the self should be unchanging. In Buddhist traditions, as well as in Advaita Vedānta, any personal agency that is acknowledged on the level of conventional reality (*saṃvṛti/vyavahāra*) is denied on the level of ultimate reality (*paramārtha*).[3] In fact, the true self's having any particularizing attributes at all was problematic for many Indian thinkers. The Nyāya school countered this tendency to deny the self's agency (and to deny the self's having particular attributes more broadly), but conceded that the self does not actualize its potential agency in the state of liberation. Madhva follows the Nyāya school in affirming the self's agency (and other attributes)[4] but also claims that the

3. See Garfield's, Meyer's, and Timalsina's contributions to this volume.

4. While the Nyāya school accounts for the self's attributes through the notion of inherence (*samavāya*), Madhva develops a concept of *viśeṣa* (distinction, defined as that which causes the effects of difference in the absence of real difference) to explain the relationship between an entity and its attributes. For an exposition of this theory, see B. N. K. Sharma (2002: 73–91) who deems it to be Madhva's "most outstanding contribution to the stock of philosophical ideas in Indian thought" (44–45).

self actualizes this agency even in liberation, allowing its devotion to God to manifest eternally.[5]

But what does "agency" mean? As many of the chapters in this volume attest, the first word in the available history of discourse on agency in India comes from Pāṇini's (ca. 500 BCE) grammatical treatise, the *Aṣṭādhyāyī*. Pāṇini's *sūtra* (1.4.54: *svatantraḥ kartā*) introducing the term *kartṛ* as a semantic category name for the participant in an action who is independent (*svatantra*) provided a common reference point for much of the subsequent discussion about agency in Indian philosophy. It must be noted that Pāṇini speaks of a *kartṛ* as a linguistic category rather than an ontological one and that later grammarians, beginning from Patañjali, offered nuance to the notion of a *kartṛ* as independent.[6] Still, the idea that a true agent must be, in some sense, independent became a default assumption. Later thinkers either accepted this notion of agency or, if they qualified it in any way, were compelled to justify that qualification.[7]

In Madhva's theology, independence is found only in God, Viṣṇu. Thus, Viṣṇu can properly be said to be the agent of the cyclical process of creation, sustenance, and destruction of the world. Individual selves, however, are eternally subordinate to and dependent on Viṣṇu. Nevertheless, they are held to be responsible for good and bad deeds and are punished and rewarded accordingly. Madhva address this by characterizing finite selves in a way that appears self-contradictory in light of Pāṇini's formulation: they are dependent agents.

Many thinkers in Indian intellectual history recognized limited or qualified modes of independence. Among the Grammarians, we see as early as Patañjali the explicit recognition of the circumscribed agency that

---

5. See in particular, Madhva's commentary to *Brahmasūtra* 4.1.12 (Govindacharya 1969: 197).

6. See Cardona's contribution to this volume, especially the section "Patañjali on Participants in Actions."

7. See, for example, Timalsina's contribution to this volume, where he cites Śaṅkara's acknowledgement (in his *Brahmasūtrabhāṣya* 2.3.37) that the self does not have "*atyantam*... *svātantryam* (absolute independence)," but argues that it may still be understood as an agent, at least on the conventional level of reality. See the section "Divine Agency and Human Freedom" in Ganeri's chapter and the section "Free Will and the Supremacy of God" in Dasa and Edelmann's chapter for discussion on the tension between the free will of the individual and the omnipotence of God. See the section "Analyses of Agency" in Dasti's chapter for Nyāya's claim that the causal role of motivation does not undermine an agent's independence.

each *kāraka* (participant in an activity) has with respect to particular components of a complex activity.[8] Naiyāyikas recognize the dependence of a self as agent on the availability of the necessary instruments and other factors to carry out an action (including a body), arguing that an agent is independent if it directs the other factors without being directed by them,[9] and Śaṅkara makes a similar argument.[10]

Madhva takes a different approach. Rather than acknowledge a qualified independence for the finite self,[11] he explicitly and thoroughly denies that anyone other than the Lord is independent and emphasizes the dependence of the individual on the Lord.[12] I would suggest that there is more to this insistent denial of the self's independence than just semantics. Deepak Sarma comments that "[t]he *svātantrya*, indepedence, of Viṣṇu cannot be underestimated as the lynchpin that holds together Mādhva ontology" (2003: 64). Madhva is unwilling to admit any qualification to the Lord's ultimate control of every aspect of reality. Like Śaṅkara and Rāmānuja, Madhva cites the *Kauṣītaki Upaniṣad's*

8. See Cardona's chapter, the sections "The Roles of Direct Participants (*Kāraka*)" and "Primary Agents." Patañjali's argument that a subordinate entity like a pot is dependent (*paratantra*) in the presence of the primary agent, but independent (*svatantra*) in its absence provides a coherent way of understanding how independence could be contextually circumscribed. However, it does not fit well with Madhva's theology, as the Lord is never truly absent.

9. See Dasti's chapter, section on "Analyses of Agency," and Cardona's chapter, section on "The Nyāya Position".

10. See Timalsina's chapter, section on "Śaṅkara on Causality"

11. Rare exception to this tendency of Madhva's can be found. For example, in his BhGT 3.27–35 (Govindacharya 1969: 45), Madhva states, "Independent agency (*svatantra-kartṛtvam*) belongs to Viṣṇu alone; it is not found in others. The finite self has independence subordinate to the Lord, but only in relation to those lower than oneself. Agency in the form of transformation exists in matter. This is like how, in a [hierarchical] sequence, [it may be said that] a human produces milk, a cow produces milk, and an udder produces milk." Madhva attributes this passage to the *Brahmatarka*. Mesquita 2000 is largely devoted to establishing the thesis that Madhva is the author of all the *Brahmatarka* passages he cites, although Mesquita discusses the view of S. Siauve that this work was composed by someone else during or shortly before Madhva's own time.

12. The characterization of the self as an agent dependent on the will of the Lord is found in the writings of Vaiṣṇava Vedāntins such as Rāmānuja (see the section "Divine Agency and Human Freedom" in Ganeri's chapter) and Nimbārka. However, as I will show, Madhva describes the self's agency as even more dependent on the Lord than other Vaiṣṇavas, or at least describes that dependence more emphatically, claiming that even the self's volition is under the Lord's control.

(3.8)[13] statement that the Lord engages the selves in good and bad deeds. But as per the *Brahmasūtras*, and in keeping with his predecessors, Madhva states that this engagement is based on the volition (*prayatna*) of the self. Where Madhva departs from his predecessors is in insisting that this volition, together with the beginningless cycle of action (*anādi-karman*) and the inherent nature of each individual (*svabhāva*) with which volition is causally tied up, are under the control of the Lord. Like other Vedāntins, Madhva takes recourse to the beginninglessness of karma to exempt the Lord from responsibility for the individual's good or bad deeds and to answer the objection that the Lord is partial or cruel. But he ultimately puts a higher premium on defending the absolute control and autonomy of the Lord.

Madhva's notion of the inherent nature (*svabhāva*) of the individual also puts him at odds with much of Indian philosophical history. For Madhva, this *svabhāva* determines whether a given individual will be able to attain liberation, will forever wander in the cycle of reincarnation, or will be condemned to perpetual suffering in hell. It is not subject to change. This type of predestination brings Madhva's theory close to the fatalism of the Ājīvika school, which became the object of universal and consistent scorn among Indian philosophers all the way back to the Buddha and Mahāvīra.[14] Within Madhva's determinism, volition (*prayatna*) does play a role in the attainment of liberation for those who are so destined, but beyond the fact that volition is under the Lord's control, Madhva further asserts that liberation cannot be attained without the grace of the Lord (*prasāda*).[15] Madhva's ideas on agency and free will thus went against the grain of a number of major trajectories of Indian philosophy up to his time. But as I will demonstrate below, aspects of his theory would find a voice in later Vedānta traditions.

---

13. All citations from Upaniṣads follow the numbering in Olivelle (1998), except where noted.

14. See Basham 2002. For the Buddha's rejection of Ājīvika fatalism, see the conclusion to Meyer's chapter, "Conclusion: Free Persons, Empty Selves." Basham (2002: 282) suggests Ājīvika influence on Madhva's theory, but see note 34 below for other possibilities. Potter (1963: 50) presents a picture of Indian philosophy wherein the refutation of both universal and guarded fatalism is one of its overriding concerns. Potter briefly addresses Madhva's philosophy (249–250), which presents "special problems" (103).

15. Thus, Potter classifies Madhva, "in the last analysis," as a "leap philosopher" as opposed to a "progress philosopher" (1963: 100).

Dependent Agency: Madhva on Brahmasūtras *2.3.33–42*[16]

Like other Vedānta commentators, Madhva most directly addresses this issue of the self's agency in his commentary on a section of the *Brahmasūtras* (2.3.33–42, Govindacharya 1969: 103–104), which begins, "*kartā śāstrārthavattvāt* ([The self is] an agent because the scriptures have a purpose)." However, he addresses a different doubt than his predecessors. Śaṅkara (n.d.: 289–297) and Rāmānuja (1995: 348–352) both ask whether agency should be attributed to the self, or to some aspect of matter—*buddhi* (intellect) or the three *guṇas* (qualities). Madhva instead raises the question of whether agency exists only in God or in the finite selves as well. In Madhva's interpretation, God has already been established in this section as the agent of the creation (2.3.1–12, Govindacharya 1969: 89–95) and destruction (2.3.13–16, Govindacharya 1969: 95–96) of the world. But, one finds statements such as (*Bṛhadāraṇyaka Upaniṣad* [BĀU] 4.4.5), "One attains [the result] of the action one performs," suggesting the agency of the individual self.

Thus, Madhva reads the first four *sūtras* of this section as straightforwardly affirming the agency of the self:

> 2.3.33: The self is **an agent, because otherwise the scripture would have no purpose.**[17]
>
> 2.3.34: The self is an agent even in the state of liberation **because of statements about enjoyment** such as (*Chāndogya Upaniṣad* [ChU] 8.12.3), "[A liberated being] roams there, laughing, playing, and enjoying, together with women, vehicles, and relatives."[18]

---

16. All references to the *Brahmasūtras* follow the numbering found in Govindacharya (1969) with Madhva's commentary. Because of textual variants in the *sūtras*, the numbering can vary slightly from commentator to commentator. I give page number references for other commentators to facilitate cross-referencing when *sūtra* numbering varies.

17. My translations here incorporate both the *sūtras* themselves and key elements of Madhva's brief commentaries on them. Words in bold represent the *sūtras* themselves. *Sūtra* 2.3.33 literally translates as, "An agent, because the scripture has a purpose." The modified wording here is based on Madhva's commentary.

18. This passage is numbered 8.4.3 in Govindacharya (1969: 466). I translate here following elements of Madhva's gloss on this passage, "... *ramate muktaḥ strībhir yānaiś ca bandhubhiḥ*."

2.3.35: The self is an agent **because** it is known **to take up** instruments to accomplish its purposes.[19]

2.3.36.The self is an agent **because of instructions to act**, such as (BĀU 1.4.15), "The world should meditate upon the Lord alone."[20] **Otherwise,** [if the Lord was the only agent] **the statement would have been reversed**, "The Lord alone [should meditate upon] the world."

While Śaṅkara, Rāmānuja, and Nimbārka all interpret *sūtra* 2.3.34 as describing the self's movement within its body,[21] Madhva interprets the *sūtra* as affirming the agency of the self not only in the state of bondage, but even in liberation (*mokṣe'pi*). For Naiyāyikas, the self is an agent, but its agency remains forever unactualized in liberation because the self no longer has a body and other instruments by means of which to act. It is significant, therefore, that Madhva's affirmation of the self's manifest agency in the state of liberation is immediately juxtaposed with the self's employing instruments. Madhva does not elaborate here, but returns to this issue in his commentary to *Brahmasūtras* 4.4.10–16 (Govindacharya 1969: 224–226), which declare that the liberated self may either take on a "luminous" (*tejo-rūpa/jyotir-maya*) body or may act and experience pleasure without a body, as in a dream.[22]

Madhva then raises a possible objection to the agency of the individual in order to introduce the next set of *sūtras*:[23] "Then how [is it said] that the Lord is the sole agent?" In the following six *sūtras*, Madhva spells out the dependent agency of the individual selves, whereby the selves can

19. Madhva's commentary here is extremely terse, but there is an apparent allusion to the description of an agent as directing the other *kārakas*, but not being directed by them. See notes 9 and 10.

20. I translate *ātman* here as "Lord" in keeping with Madhva's clear intention here, and his prevalent tendency to interpret *ātman* as such.

21. All cite BĀU 2.1.18 to this effect. See Śaṅkara (n.d.: 290), Rāmānuja (1995: 350) and Dvivedin (1910: 40).

22. Madhva's commentary is not far from Rāmānuja's (1995: 513–516) here, but they contrast sharply with Śaṅkara (n.d.: 508–510), who interprets the self's taking on a body as referring to a self with a lower-level understanding of a qualified Brahman—that is, an understanding of Brahman on the level of conventional reality (*vyavahāra*).

23. My grouping of the *sūtras* here does not correspond to the traditional grouping of *sūtras* into topics (*adhikaraṇa*), but is meant to highlight themes relevant to the topic of this chapter.

assume moral responsibility without contradicting Viṣṇu's status as the sole *independent* agent:

> 2.3.37: **Just as** the individual self has **no control (*a-niyama*) in the case of knowledge**, such that it cannot say, "I will know this," so it similarly has no control in the case of action. The *śruti* (BĀU) states, "He controls the self from within."[24]
>
> 2.3.38: The individual self's not being independent is understood **because** it has **meager capability (*śakti-viparyaya*)**.
>
> 2.3.39: **And because of its failure to accomplish its actions.**[25]
>
> 2.3.40: **As a carpenter both** is controlled (*niyata*) by an employer and has agency, so the individual self both is controlled by a causal agent and has agency.
>
> 2.3.41: The individual self's power of agency comes **from the Supreme, according to the *śruti* statement,** "Agency, instrumentality, essential nature, consciousness, and endurance—these exist by his grace, and by his neglect they do not exist."[26]

---

24. The citation reads, *ya ātmānam antaro yamayati*. This phrase is absent in the Kāṇva recension (and thus in Olivelle 1998), but is found in the Mādhyandina recension 3.7.30, i.e., *Śatapatha Brāhmaṇa* 14.6.7.30 (Weber 1964: 1074). The passage is also cited by Rāmānuja. See Ganeri's chapter, section on "Divine Agency and Human Freedom."

25. This interpretation of Madhva's extremely brief commentary is necessarily conjectural. Madhva gloss the sūtra, *samādhy-abhāvāc ca*, simply with *samādhānābhāvāc cāsvātantryaṃ pratīyate*. The basic meaning of meditative absorption does not fit well with the context of Madhva's argument, as it does for Śaṅkara and Rāmānuja.

26. Madhva attributes the passage he cites to the *Paiṅgiśruti*. This text, however, has been identified by Mesquita (2000: 119) as one of the fictitious works cited by Madhva that are really his own compositions. Mesquita (2000 and 2008) has examined the vast number of ostensible quotations given by Madhva that are untraceable, concluding that these must be Madhva's own compositions. While the evidence is overwhelming that Madhva did in fact author many of the passages he presents as quotations, there is room for doubt regarding any individual citation, as argument ex silencio is inconclusive. This is especially so in light of the poor state of the critical editing of many Sanskrit texts, especially Purāṇa and Pāñcarātra texts, which have only recently begun to receive careful critical attention. An important qualification is made by Okita's 2011a review of Mesquita 2008. Even if certain untraceable citations do represent the ideas of others cited by Madhva, by citing them as authoritative, Madhva takes ownership of the ideas presented therein. Thus, for simplicity's sake, I will treat untraceable citations as Madhva's own words in the body of the chapter, noting their claimed source in footnotes. In the current case, the claim that the passage quoted represents a *śruti* text is of particular importance, as the *sūtra* itself makes refence to an unspecified *śruti* text (*tac-chruteḥ*).

> 2.3.42: The Lord takes into **consideration the past actions and the volition** of the individual self, as understood **from the non-uselessness of the injunctions and prohibitions** of scripture **and similar reasons** such as the non-partiality of the Lord.

Commenting on this last *sūtra*, Madhva states:[27]

> The Lord causes one to act after taking into consideration one's previous action, volition, and inherent nature.[28] All of it is done by the Lord himself. Because [the cycle of action and reaction] has no beginning, the Lord, who possesses all capability, has no fault.

A few things deserve notice here: Madhva's reading of *sūtra* 37 as acknowledging the individual's lack of complete control reflects the basic theme of Śaṅkara's commentary on this sūtra, although Śaṅkara does, nevertheless, affirm the self's independence. In *sūtras* 38–39, Madhva explicitly denies the self's independence. Madhva offers a distinct interpretation of the word *viparyaya*[29] as indicating that the capability of the individual self is "meager," though not, it should be noted, completely lacking. Madhva interprets the analogy of the carpenter in a novel way to suggest that there is no necessary contradiction between agency and being subordinate or dependent. Finally, Madhva offers his version of the reconciliation of the problem of human agency and divine omnipotence in his commentary on *sūtras* 41–42: while the individual self has agency, this does not contradict divine omnipotence, as that agency itself is a gift from God. The realization of that agency requires facilitation by the Lord, but this is done according to the volition of the individual self. Madhva's commentary to the last *sūtra* alludes back to a related discussion of this problem earlier in the *Brahmasūtras*.

---

27. This is presented as a quotation from a *Bhaviṣyatparvan*, but such a work is not known outside of Madhva's tradition. See Mesquita (2008: 61–62).

28. In light of Madhva's repeated mention of the triad of inherent nature/destiny (*svabhāva*/*yogyatā*), [prior] action (*karman*), and volition (*prayatna*), cited throughout this chapter, I suggest that *saṃskāra* here be understood as roughly synonymous with *svabhāva* in Madhva's usage.

29. Śaṅkara (n.d.: 291) and Rāmānuja (1995: 350; see Ganeri's contribution, the section on "Selfhood, Embodiment, and Agency in the Finite Self") take the word *viparyaya* straightforwardly as a reversal of some sort and discuss why attribution of agency to the *buddhi*/*antaḥkaraṇa* could not be coherent.

Control and Responsibility: Madhva on Brahmasūtras *2.1.35–37*

The tension between the Lord's control over karmic results and the moral responsibility of the individual are similarly addressed in *Brahmasūtras* 2.1.35–37 (Govindacharya 1969: 70–71). As *sūtra* 2.3.42 asserted that the Lord takes the volition of the self into account when causing it to act, *sūtra* 2.1.35 states that the Lord takes the action of the self into account when bestowing karmic results:

> 2.1.35: **There is neither partiality nor cruelty** in the Lord, **because** his role as the bestower of results is carried out **with consideration** of the actions of the individual, **for** the *śruti* passage (*Praśna Upaniṣad* 3.7), "He leads one to a good world because of good [deeds or] to a bad world because of bad [deeds]," **shows this.**

The next *sūtra,* as Madhva interprets it, considers an objection based on the fact that the Lord controls the action of the individual as well.

> 2.1.36: **One may say that it is not the action** of the self that the Lord considers when he bestows results **for there is no difference**: the Lord is also the cause of the self's action according to the *śruti* statement (*Kauṣītaki Upaniṣad* 3.8), "When he wishes to lead someone up from these worlds, he causes that person to perform good acts; and when he wants to lead someone down, he causes them to perform bad acts." **This is not so, for** the cycle of action and reaction **is beginningless**, such that the cause of any action is a previous action. It is said,[30] "Viṣṇu causes one to perform good acts, bad acts, etc. because of one's previous actions. Because action has no beginning, there is no contradiction whatsoever."

The *Brahmasūtras* here punt the problem of the inequality between individuals under the Lord's control back into beginningless time. The Lord does not start individuals off on unequal footing, for their entanglement in actions and reactions has no starting point.

---

30. Madhva attributes this passage to the *Bhaviṣyat Purāṇa*, but the passage is not traceable to that text. See Mesquita (2008: 74).

Madhva interprets the next *sūtra* (2.1.37: **It is reasonable and it is seen)** as reaffirming the Lord's independence. He begins his commentary:

> It is not the case that, by considering the [previous] actions [of an individual when bestowing results], the Lord lacks independence, for the very existence of that action and other factors are under his control, according to the statement, "Substance, action, time, one's inherent nature (*svabhāva*) and the individual itself exist by his grace. By his neglect, they do not exist."[31]

But, if everything is under the Lord's control, then he *should* be held responsible for the inequities of the individual who variously suffer or enjoy. The very charge of partiality and cruelty, which the beginninglessness of action was supposed to address, enters back in. Madhva acknowledges this and makes the surprisingly frank move of accepting the possibility that the Lord may be partial. His commentary continues:

> Nor again is there any fault [on the part of the Lord] by the partiality and the like which results [from the Lord's controlling the individual actions and results], for such partiality is seen in the statement of the *Caturvedaśikhā*,[32] "He causes [individuals] to perform good and bad acts, but the Lord does not have any fault because of this, for the Lord is transcendent with regard to the presence of virtues and faults, being without beginning and being the origin of [all] living beings."

Madhva's priority here is clearly to protect the independence of the Lord and his control over everything, even at the cost of acknowledging the Lord's partiality and the lack of freedom on the part of the individual. The problem is that this seems to shift the burden of moral responsibility from the individual to God, the very problem other Vedāntins try to address in their commentaries on this section. Madhva's response is simply to assert that the Lord is above morality: morality is subject to the Lord, not vice versa. Commenting on the next *sūtra* (2.1.38), the last *sūtra* of the

31. Madhva offers no source for this verse, which cannot be traced.

32. Identified as one of Madhva's fictitious works by Mesquita (2000: 30–31, 103; 2008: 531), who quotes Appayya Dīkṣita's mention of this in a list of unknown (*aprasiddha*) works cited by Madhva.

chapter (*pāda*), Madhva reiterates that the Lord is beyond critique: he possesses all virtues known and unknown, yet has no vices whatsoever. While Madhva does not reconcile the Lord's being transcendent to the presence of both virtue and vice with the apparently contradictory claim of his possessing all virtues, the point is clear: being subordinate to God, we are in no position to find fault with him.

Thus, in Madhva's scheme, only finite selves can be subjected to moral judgment. But even this judgment cannot have any free choice of the self as its object, as the actions of the self are always controlled by the Lord. Rather, as I show in the next section, moral standing is based on the unchanging, inherent nature (*svabhāva*) of each self. Some selves are inherent good, while others are inherently bad.

Determinism and the Hierarchy of Selves

As I suggested above, the Vedāntic doctrine of beginningless action does not by itself solve the problem of the disparity between selves, but merely removes the possibility that the Lord, at some initial point in time, placed individuals variously into advantaged or disadvantaged situations. The question of why one self heads down a positive karmic trajectory while another self heads down a negative trajectory remains. Howsoever other Vedāntins attempt to address this question,[33] they agree that the state of liberation represents the proper condition of the true self, whether it is a singular self, or many selves.[34] Thus, the fact the one person currently performs goods acts and experiences happy results while another is not so fortunate is not caused by and does not betray fundamentally different natures of the true self. Nor, importantly, are those selves engaged in bad action eternally barred from achieving liberation, even if that goal may be out of reach during this lifetime. By contrast, in addressing the inequities between selves, Madhva does not shy away from acknowledging that some selves are inherently and eternally better or worse than others; he outlines

33. Potter 1963 provides a helpful discussion of the various position taken on this question by different schools.

34. Likewise, see the final *Yogasūtra* (4.34, Bryant 2009: 457), where liberation (*kaivalyam*) is defined as the power of consciousness (*citi-śaktiḥ*) situated in its own essential identity (*svarūpa-pratiṣṭhā*). As will be discussed below, Vallabha represent an exception in this regard.

a comprehensive hierarchy (*tāratamya*) of all beings, such that only some selves can ever be liberated.

Of immediate relevance within the full hierarchy is Madhva's threefold classification of the *svabhāva* (inherent nature) or *yogyatā* (fitness/destiny[35]) of living beings as *mukti-yogya* (destined for liberation), *sṛti-yogya* (destined for the cycle of birth and death), and *andha-tamo-yogya* (destined for blind darkness, i.e., hell or lower births).[36] In other words, some selves are destined to be liberated, sooner or later; others will continue to be reborn in this word perpetually; and others will live perpetually in hell. Madhva refers to these natures as highest, middle, and lowest, respectively.[37] He explicitly states that each individual's inherent nature or destiny is beginningless (*anādi-siddhā*) and eternal (*nityā*),[38] and that it cannot become other than it is.[39] As Robert Zydenbos (1991: 252) notes, "*tāratamya* [hierarchy] is considered a basic given fact. Each soul, by nature, belongs to one of the given categories, and this cannot be changed." Thus, attaining liberation is not even within the scope of possibility for many individuals. In *Mahābhāratatātparyanirṇaya* (MBhTN), Madhva aptly calls this ontological status *haṭha* (force/inevitable necessity). The individual does not choose its nature; rather, that nature is the very identity of the self.

35. While the term "fitness" is an etymologically sound translation for *yogyatā*, Madhva's use of the term here may be more richly translated with the word "destiny," given all the usual cautions against importing culturally specific nuances in the translation of technical terms.

36. This classification is found Madhva's BhGT 3.27–35 (Govindacharya 1969: 45), as well as in his MBhTN 30.50–51 (Govindacharya 1971: 434), *Tattvasaṅkhyāna* (Govindacharya 1974: 60), and *Tattvaviveka* 6–7 (Govindacharya 1974: 63) with slightly different terminology. The classification is discussed in Basham (2002: 282), D. Sarma (2003: 54–59), B. N. K. Sharma (2002: 281–305, 359–369), and Zydenbos (1991: 251–253). Basham suggests influence from the Ājīvika tradition (an early ascetic tradition ubiquitously criticized for its fatalist views) and Zydenbos suggests Jaina influence. D. Sarma points to almost identical terminology used by "earlier Pāñcarātrika thinkers" citing Schrader (1916: 86). However, the text Schrader refers to is the *Paramatattvanirṇayaprakāśasaṃhitā*, a text which he describes as "a fairly recent work," "hardly earlier than the 12th century" (1916: 86, 54). Given the identical doctrines and the similarity of the title to some of Madhva's works this was either a text that was greatly influential on Madhva or was a later composition by Madhva or one of his followers. It is noteworthy that the discussion referenced above from the BhGT consists of a citation attributed to a *Prakāśasaṃhitā*, identified by Mesquita (2008: 535) as one of Madhva's untraceable quotes.

37. BhGT 3.27–35 (Govindacharya 1969: 45). This is part of the citation attributed to *Prakāśasaṃhitā*; see note 36.

38. MBhTN 22.81 (Govindacharya 1971: 297).

39. BhGT 3.27–35 (Govindacharya 1969: 45). This is part of the citation attributed to *Prakāśasaṃhitā*; see note 36.

Thus, moral responsibility, virtue and vice, are not questions of choice but of inherent identity. People simply *are* good or bad.

While a given individual's destiny severely curtails the possibilities open to her or him, it is not the only factor determining the cycle of action and reaction. In *Mahābhāratatātparyanirṇaya* (22.81–84b, Govindacharya 1971: 297–298), Madhva states that one's destiny is only the first of three causes (*kāraṇa*) of action; the second is one's beginningless chain of prior action (*anādi-karman*), and the third is the volition of the individual (*jīva-prayatna*). And yet, Madhva again emphasizes that all three of these are always under Viṣṇu's control (*trayaṃ viṣṇor vaśa-gaṃ sarvadaiva*). The beginningless chain of action (*karman*) manifests, Madhva says, from the inevitable necessity (*haṭha*), that is, destiny, and volition arises from the chain of actions. This volition then brings both destiny and the chain of action to bear in manifest action (*yatno haṭha-karma-prayoktā*). Madhva writes,

> Without volition, neither *haṭha* (i.e., destiny) nor action yield their fruit. Vāsudeva [Viṣṇu] is the controller of all power of independence. Even so, he bestows [results upon individuals] after taking those [three factors] into account. His independence manifests in the form of his determination, "I should give a result only after taking those into account."

Thus, while an individual's destiny may be set, he or she will not realize that destiny until they manifest appropriate volition (*prayatna*).

But the interplay of these various factors is only truly meaningful for those destined for liberation. Those of the middle and lowest natures are already living out their destiny in the cycle of birth and death or, in the case of the lowest, in hell or low births. But the highest selves who are living now within the cycle of birth and death have the possibility of getting out of that cycle and attaining liberation. Liberation cannot be attained without the right volition, but other factors are needed as well. Madhva writes in his *Bhagavadgītātātparya* (BhGT) (3.27–35, Govindacharya 1969: 45):

> It is taught that the attainment [of liberation] comes from the fulfillment of the [necessary] means [i.e., the practice of worship]. In the absence of such fulfillment, everyone undergoes the beginningless cycle of birth and death (*saṃsṛti*). And in accordance with Hari's will, it is not the case that, after an eternity of time, everyone fulfills

the means. Thus the beginningless cycle of birth and death continues eternally.[40]

Furthermore, even a person who is *muktiyogya*, whose has the right prior karma, and who manifests the right *prayatna*, needs the grace (*prasāda*) of Viṣṇu to attain liberation. This grace, as Madhva describes it, appears to be a factor over and above the Lord's general control over all aspects of the self's actions and reactions. Madhva formulates the proper attitude of one aspiring for liberation:

> I am not an agent; Hari [Viṣṇu] is the agent. Worship of him is the totality of [proper] action. Even so, the worship which I perform comes about by his grace and in no other way. Devotion to him, the result of such worship, [will develop] in me, again, by his grace.[41]

Thus, to achieve liberation, a given self must: (1) have the right destiny (under the control of the Lord); (2) have the right prior activities (under the control of the Lord); (3) manifest the right volition (under the control of the Lord); (4) engage in and fulfill the practice of worship (by the grace of the Lord); and thus (5) attain devotion (by the grace of the Lord). As one can see, while Madhva asserts that the self is an agent, it has very little if any control over its actions.

Madhva and Theodicy

Both B. N. K. Sharma (1981) and D. Sarma (2003) champion Madhva's hierarchy (*tāratamya*) theory as the best solution to the problem of how to reconcile the experience of evil and suffering in the world with an omnipotent and benevolent God. B. N. K. Sharma writes,

> The theory of Svarūpabheda [difference of inherent natures] and Svarūpayogyatā [destiny based on one's inherent nature] elaborated by Madhva is thus the most *far-reaching* and at the same time highly *suggestive solution* of the problem of plurality of selves and their

40. This is part of the citation attributed to *Prakāśasaṃhitā*; see note 36.

41. BhGT 3.27–35 (Govindacharya 1969: 44–45). Madhva attributes this passage to the *Brahmatarka*. See note 11.

> freedom and freewill and of the presence of evil and suffering in a moral universe under the government of a moral and merciful God. (1981: 367, italics in original)

D. Sarma appeals to what he calls Madhva's "mitigated monotheism" claiming that since the individual souls are eternal and not created by God, "Viṣṇu cannot be held accountable for the behavior of the wicked sentient beings in the universe" (2003: 70–71).

Madhva's position is basically that some of us are just inherently bad, and we suffer as a result. It is *we* who are evil and therefore *we* who are responsible for our suffering, even though we cannot change our evil nature. God does not create us as evil and so cannot be held responsible. Even so, the following question may be asked of Madhva: as God controls all of reality, can he not eradicate such evil and the consequent suffering? A common premise in formulating the problem of evil is that if God is all-powerful, he could remove evil and suffering, and if he is benevolent, he would want to do so. B. N. K. Sharma portrays the Mādhva response thus:

> Theoretically, He may have the power to do whatever He pleases; but the fact remains that He does not choose to upset the moral law or change the nature of beings... The moral character of God is not also challenged on this view. For, one can accuse God of partiality and cruelty only when He changes the nature of some in preference to others. (1981: 366–367)

The first problem with these claims is that Madhva does not sufficiently establish that the Lord is not accountable for the evil deeds and suffering of finite selves. Although in Madhva's theology the Lord does not *create* selves as good or bad, Madhva has repeatedly emphasized that every aspect of the hierarchy (*tāratamya*) framework is under the control of Viṣṇu and plays out according to his desire.[42] Thus, even if God does not create some selves as evil, he continually sustains their inherent evil nature. One may well argue, therefore, that he *can* be held accountable for their evil acts and the attendant suffering. As B. N. K. Sharma has admitted, such an all-controlling God could change the system, but chooses not

42. In BhGT 3.27–35 (Govindacharya 1969: 45), for example, Madhva comments: "*naiva pūrtiś ca sarveṣāṃ nitya-kālaṃ harīcchayā.* (By the will of Hari [Viṣṇu], not everyone has the fulfillment (*pūrti*) [of the means to attain liberation] even after an eternity of time.)"

to. In modern legal parlance, such a failure to prevent harm that is within one's power to prevent can make one guilty of culpable negligence.

Like all Vedāntins, Madhva defends the Lord against the charge of partiality and cruelty by claiming that the Lord's control over the self's actions and results takes that self's volition and its beginningless chain of prior actions into account. Even so, the Lord's control over the self's agency is so absolute in Madhva's theology that the buck must stop with him. Madhva outlines a chain of causes accounting for karmic results with the Lord controlling every step: The Lord rewards and punishes the self, but this is based on the self's action; the Lord engages the self in that action, but this is based on the self's volition; that volition is under the Lord's control, but is based on the inherent nature of each self. But that inherent nature, even if not created by the Lord at an initial point in time, is always under his control and according to his will. The emphasis Madhva places on the need for the highest selves to receive the Lord's grace in order to achieve liberation suggests that similar grace could be made available to the lower selves as well. God need not "change the nature of some in preference to others," but could elevate all souls to the highest nature. But he does not.

This brings us to the second problem with Madhva's theory as a solution to theodicy: his hierarchy essentially denies subjectivity to the lower selves. B. N. K. Sharma (1981: 368–369) suggests that the presence of evil people plays an instrumental role in impelling the volition of the highest souls to reject evil and attain liberation. But the middle and lowest souls have no possibility of even aspiring for, let alone achieving, the ultimate goal of life. Thus, whatever little control the highest souls have over their actions and the attaining of their destiny, the middle and lowest souls have even less. While the unabashed claim that some people are just inherently evil may seem to be an honest assessment of the world as we experience it, it offers no hope for the lower selves. To find hope, one must assume oneself to be one of the highest selves. As Karl Potter puts it, "One must affirm without wavering that one *is* the first kind of soul" (1963: 250). Such an assumption, especially if justified on the basis of religious and sectarian commitments, has the potential to encourage the development of an "us and them" mentality. Although Madhva's theory may be able to account for the suffering that the highest souls occasionally undergo, a comprehensive theodicy must answer for the experience of all selves.

Finally, the claim that God as conceived by Madhva is a moral God is open to question. Madhva himself admits that God may be partial, but denies that this would be a fault as God transcends ordinary morality. This transcendent nature is supposed to make the Lord the appropriate object of worship. But without elaborating a principled justification on terms appropriate to transcendence, the assertion that a God who flouts ordinary morality is ultimately good is not fully theologically satisfying.

Considering Madhva's Legacy

Whatever critique may be offered of the theological sufficiency of Madhva's theodicy, Madhva deserves consideration as a profound, innovative, and influential thinker in Indian intellectual history. Madhva inspired a religious tradition with a robust history of philosophical and theological discourse. Madhva's followers have attempted to address critiques of Madhva's ideas—an attempt that is worthy of serious consideration, though outside the scope of the present chapter. And a number of Madhva's ideas, although against the grain of much of Indian philosophy, found voice and elaboration outside of Madhva's own tradition, especially in the Vaiṣṇava Vedānta traditions established by Vallabha and Caitanya around the beginning of the 16th century.

The most obvious place to find Madhva's influence is in the writing of the 18th-century Gauḍīya Vaiṣṇava Vedāntin, Baladeva Vidyābhūṣaṇa, as he is the main person responsible for promoting the idea of a historical connection of the Gauḍīya Vaiṣṇava tradition to Madhva's tradition.[43] While the promotion of that idea may have been more politically than theologically motivated, Baladeva was trained in the Mādhva tradition in his youth before becoming affiliated with the Gauḍīya Vaiṣṇava tradition, and thus Madhva's influence can be seen in a number of Baladeva's works, including his commentary on the *Brahmasūtras*.[44] Yet, as Kiyokazu Okita has demonstrated, Baladeva quotes and borrows concepts from Madhva, but only "so long as his Mādhva training is useful for strengthening his Gauḍīya predecessor's viewpoint" (2011b: 218).

---

43. Baladeva promulgates a guru succession that connects Caitanya to Madhva in the opening of his *Prameyaratnāvalī*. A similar list can be found in the 16th-century *Gauragaṇoddeśadīpikā* of Kavi Karṇapūra, but its authenticity has been questioned. For a discussion of the legitimacy of the connection and Baladeva's role in it, see Elkman (1986: 25–50, 182–188).

44. This influence has often been exaggerated. B. N. K. Sharma (1981: 596), for instance, claims that "Baladeva is virtually in agreement with Madhva on all the fundamental points of his system." For a more balanced view of Baladeva's indebtedness to Madhva see Okita (2008, 2009, 2011b) and Buchta (2003, 2005, 2007).

Madhva's influence is not, however, limited to Baladeva; it can be seen even in the earliest theologians of the Gauḍīya Vaiṣṇava tradition, including Rūpa Gosvāmin and Jīva Gosvāmin. At least two important ideas that they discuss within the broader context of the self's agency are anticipated in Madhva's theory: the self's manifestation of agency even after liberation through the means of a spiritual body and the acknowledgement of partiality (*vaiṣamya*) on the part of the Lord in relation to his devotees. As discussed by Dasa and Edelmann in this volume, Gauḍīya Vaiṣṇavas speak of a *siddha-deha* (perfected body) by means of which the liberated self in the spiritual world of Vaikuṇṭha acts. While this parallels Madhva's notion of agency and action in liberation and the self's taking on a "luminous" body, the notion of a "perfected body" shows more direct influence from tantra traditions.[45] With Baladeva, however, Madhva's direct influence can be seen. Baladeva follows Madhva's idiosyncratic reading of *Brahmasūtra* 2.3.34 (Kṛṣṇadāsa 1953: 159) as affirming the agency of the self in liberation, citing the same passage from the *Chāndogya Upaniṣad*, as well as his reading of *sūtra* 4.1.12 (Kṛṣṇadāsa 1953: 292–93) as stating that meditation on the Lord (*upāsana*) continues even during liberation.

The Gauḍīya Vaiṣṇava acknowledgement of the Lord's partiality toward his devotees may show more of a direct influence from Madhva, although Gauḍīya Vaiṣṇavas offer a more developed justification for this partiality. In his *Bhaktirasāmṛtasindhu* (2.1.27, 148–153, Śyāmadāsa 1990: 251, 296–97), Rūpa Gosvāmin describes Kṛṣṇa as a "friend to devotees (*bhakta-suhṛt*)" and "under the control of their love (*prema-vaśyaḥ*)." Viśvanātha Cakravartin, in his *Mādhuryakādambinī*, considers whether the Lord's mercy, by which a person develops devotion, makes him guilty of the fault of partiality. While Viśvanātha ultimately relegates responsibility to those devotees through which the Lord's own mercy flows, he first emphatically defends the existence of a certain kind of partiality in the Lord: "But partiality (*vaiṣamya*) in the form of protecting his devotees by suppressing the wicked does not bring about a fault; rather it brings about an ornament [to his character], for the virtue of affection for his devotees [is] the emperor of all [his virtues] and the destroyer of all [ostensible faults]" (Śyāmadāsa 1995: 15).

Again, the clearest evidence of influence from Madhva can be seen with Baladeva (Kṛṣṇadāsa 1953: 111–13). His commentary on *Brahmasūtras* 2.1.35–36 very closely follows that of Madhva, citing the same texts

45. See White (1996) for a discussion of tantric notions of the *siddha-deha*.

(including untraceable passages likely composed by Madhva himself). Baladeva includes within his commentary on *sūtra* 36 the issue addressed by Madhva in the following *sūtra*: whether the Lord's taking the selves' action into consideration when bestowing results contradicts his supposed independence. Baladeva cites Madhva's verse stating that the self, its inherent nature, action, et cetera would not exist without the Lord's grace. Like Madhva, Baladeva speaks of the "beginningless inherent nature of the self (*anādi-jīva-svabhāva*)" as the ultimate grounds of consideration when the Lord engages the self in action, but does not elaborate the same changeless hierarchical triad as Madhva. In reconciling the Lord's independence with his consideration of the self's nature, Baladeva echoes Madhva's statement from *Mahābhāratatātparyanirṇaya* that although the Lord *could* go against the nature of the self, he chooses not to.

In commenting on *sūtra* 37, Baladeva significantly departs from Madhva. Like Madhva, he acknowledges here that the Lord is in some sense partial, but his description of and justification for this partiality is quite different:

> It is reasonable that the Lord, who is affectionate to his devotees (*bhakta-vatsala*) has partiality in the form of taking the side of his devotees for his protecting them and so on is done with consideration (*apekṣa*) of their devotion, which is a function of his own self-same power. Nor is this a contradiction of statements proclaiming the Lord's faultlessness, for such partiality is praised as a virtue. The *śruti*[46] even states that this [partiality] is and ornament on the Lord's virtues, without which all of his virtues, not being pleasing to people, would have no effect. And [such partiality] is seen in *śruti* [and *smṛti*] texts.

Here Baladeva goes on to cite a number of passages, including *Bhagavad Gītā* 9.29: "I am equal to all beings; no one is hated by me or dear to me. But for those who worship me with devotion, they are in me and I am in them." Finally, while Madhva interprets *sūtra* 38 as stating that the Lord has all virtues and no vices, Baladeva takes this *sūtra* to argue that the Lord's partiality toward his devotee can coexist as a virtue with

46. It is not clear here whether Baladeva is quoting or paraphrasing. I have not been able to trace the source of his comment.

his impartiality because all virtues, including mutually contradictory ones, exist in the Lord, whose nature is unable to be understood by reasoning (*acintya*).

While the Gauḍīya Vaiṣṇava tradition strongly affirms the eligibility of all selves for *bhakti*,[47] the predestination that characterizes Madhva's theory of the hierarchy of selves finds echoes in the theology of Vallabha. Vallabha presents a hierarchy of three paths followed respectively by three distinct types of selves: the path of nurturing or grace (*puṣṭi*), the path of rules (*maryādā*), and the path of [going with] the flow (*pravāha*). Frederick Smith (2011: 174) outlines this system in a study of Vallabha's *Puṣṭipravāhamaryādābheda*, seeing it as a form of predestination:

> For a *jīva* [self] of extreme purity, *bhakti* becomes the instrument for realizing the grace (*puṣṭi*) of Puruṣottama, the Supreme Lord. For the studious, religiously inclined, and law-abiding *jīva* without this intense *bhakti*, the maximum achievement can only be a state of limitation (*maryādā*). This experience, which Vallabhācārya describes as ordinary or common (*sādhāraṇabhāva*), becomes the instrument for achieving liberation (*mukti*) as described in lesser forms of Vedānta, notably (and pointedly) that of the earlier *advaitin* Śaṅkarācārya. Other *jīvas* simply participate in the unexamined flow of the world (*pravāha*), in which divisiveness (*dveṣa*) becomes the road to darkness (*andhatamas*).

In Vallabha's system, the Lord may take on an even more decisive role in determining the status of each self. Vallabha states (*Puṣṭipravāhamaryādābheda* 13–14b),

> With respect to their essential natures (*svarūpa*), their incarnation as living beings (*avatāra*), their physical bodies (*liṅga*), and their individual attributes (*guṇa*), there is no natural hierarchy (among these three kinds of *jīva*). Nevertheless, (the Lord) creates these distinctions in essential nature, body, and their respective actions in accordance with his own purpose.[48]

---

47. See, for example, Rūpa Gosvāmin's *Bhaktirasāmṛtasindhu* 1.2.60–62 (Śyāmadāsa 1990: 85).

48. The translation here is Smith's (2011: 204), who relies in his translation on the commentary of Vallabha's follower, Puruṣottama.

Smith considers, but ultimately downplays, the possibility that Vallabha was influenced by Madhva's theory. Nevertheless, the similarities between the two systems are striking (including the description of the lowest selves as destined for *andha-tamas*, i.e., hell). We thus see that the ideas expressed by Madhva, even if out of the mainstream in Indian philosophy, were able to find a voice in the 16th century and beyond, and Madhva may be credited with having helped these ideas to become more acceptable.

Conclusion

On the issue of the self's agency, Madhva was something of an outlier among Vedāntins and Indian thinkers more generally, as he was on many topics. He consistently affirmed the true self's agency, even in liberation, but strongly denied that it had any independence, making for a peculiar notion of an individual free will and moral responsibility. For Madhva, it is *who one is*, not what one *chooses* to do or who one *chooses* to be, that determines one's volition, one's actions, and ultimately one's destination. The Lord does not create the inherent nature of each self, although that nature, like all aspects of reality, is under his control. Yet, the Lord is not morally responsible for the right and wrong actions of the selves, as he is above ordinary morality. For those who are able to attain liberation, agency becomes more meaningful, for such a self will not attain liberation until it manifests the right volition and fulfills the practice of devotion. But even so, liberation comes as a result of the Lord's grace, not merely by the endeavors of the self. Yet as much as these ideas go against common trends of Indian philosophy, Madhva inspired a tradition that remains active to this day, and his ideas found expression in other later traditions as well. Thus, he stands as an important figure in the history of Indian reflections on selfhood and agency.

References

Basham, A. L. 2002. *History and Doctrines of the Ājīvikas: A Vanished Indian Religion*. Lala S. L. Jain Research Series. Reprint of 1st ed. Delhi: Motilal Banarsidass.

Bryant, Edwin F. 2009. *The Yoga Sūtras of Patañjali*. New York: North Point Press.

Buchta, David. 2003. "Gems from the *Gītā-Bhūṣaṇa*." *Journal of Vaishnava Studies* 12.1: 127–147.

———. 2005. "Baladeva Vidyābhūṣaṇa and the Vedāntic Refutation of Yoga." *Journal of Vaishnava Studies* 14.1: 181–208.

———. 2007. "Complexity in Hindu Biography: Baladeva Vidyābhūṣaṇa's Multi-regional Influences." *Journal of Vaishnava Studies* 15.2: 81–93.

Dvivedin, Pandit Vindhyeshvarīprasāda, ed. 1910. *Brahma-mīmāmsā-bhāshya: A Com mentary on Brahma Sutras Called Vedānta Pārijāta Saurabha by Nimbārkāchārya.* Chowkhambā Sanskrit Series, no. 152. Benares: Chowkhambā Sanskṛit Book Depot.

Elkman, Stuart. 1986. *Jīva Gosvāmin's Tattvasandarbha: A Study on the Philosophical and Sectarian Development of the Gauḍiya [sic] Vaiṣṇava Movement.* Delhi: Motilal Banarsidass.

Gerow, Edwin. 1987. "The Dvaitin as Deconstructionist: Viṣṇudāsācārya on 'Tat Tvam Asi': Part 1." *Journal of the American Oriental Society* 107.4: 561–579.

Govindacharya, Bannanje, ed. 1969. *Sarvamula Granthāh* [sic]. Volume 1: *Prasthānatrayi.* Udupi: Akhila Bharata Madhva Maha Mandala Publications.

———. 1971. *Sarva-mūla-granthāḥ.* Volume 2: *[Itihāsa-Prasthānam] Mahā-bhārata-tātparya-nirṇaya & Mahābhārata-tātparya.* Udupi: Akhila Bharata Madhva Maha Mandala Publications.

———. 1974. *Sarva-mūla-granthāḥ.* Volume 5: *[Saṅkīrṇa Granthas] Prakaraṇas, Ācāra Granthas & Stotras.* Udupi: Akhila Bharata Madhva Maha Mandala Publications.

Kṛṣṇadāsa (Kusumasarovaravāle), ed. and trans. (Hindi). 1953. *Śrībrahmasūtragovi ndabhāṣyam: Hindībhāṣānuvādasahitam Śrībaladevavidyābhūṣaṇamahodayaviraci tam.* Mathurā: Puṣparāja Press.

Mesquita, Roque. 2000. *Madhva's Unknown Literary Sources: Some Observations.* New Delhi: Aditya Prakashan.

———. 2008. *Madhva's Quotes from the Purāṇas and the Mahābhārata: An Analytic Compilation of Untraceable Source-Quotations in Madhva's Works Along with Footnotes.* Delhi: Aditya Prakashan.

Okita, Kiyokazu. 2008. "Mādhva or Gauḍīya? The Philosophy of Baladeva Vidyābhūṣaṇa's *Prameya-Ratnāvalī.*" *Journal of Vaishnava Studies* 16.2: 33–48.

———. 2009. "A Bengali Vaishnava Contribution to Vedānta: Baladeva Vidyābhūṣaṇa on the Word '*Atha*' in the *Brahmasūtra* 1.1.1." *Journal of Vaishnava Studies* 18.1: 87–100.

———. 2011a. "Review of Mesquita, Roque, *Madhva's Quotes from the Purāṇas and the Mahābhārata.*" *Indo-Iranian Journal* 54: 185–192.

———. 2011b. "Quotation in Early Modern Vedānta: An Example from Gauḍīya Vaiṣṇavism." *Religions of South Asia* 6.2: 207–224.

Olivelle, Patrick, ed. and trans. 1998. *The Early Upaniṣads: Annotated Text and Translation.* New York: Oxford University Press.

Potter, Karl H. 1963. *Presuppositions of India's Philosophies.* Englewood Cliffs, NJ: Prentice-Hall.

Rāmānuja. 1995. *Śrībhāṣyam of Bhagavad Rāmānuja.* Edited by Scholars of the Academy. Academy of Sanskrit Research Series, no. 22. Melkote: Academy of Sanskrit Research.

Śaṅkara. n.d. *Works of Śaṅkarācārya in Original Sanskrit*. Volume 3: *Brahmasūtra with Śaṅkarabhāṣya*. [No editor listed]. Delhi: Motilal Banarsidass.

Sarma, Deepak. 2003. *An Introduction to Mādhva Vedānta*. Ashgate World Philosophies Series. Hampshire, UK: Ashgate.

Schrader, F. Otto. 1916. *Introduction to the Pāñcarātra and the Ahirbudhnya Saṃhitā*. Adyar, Madras: Adyar Library.

Sharma, B. N. K. 1981. *History of the Dvaita School of Vedānta and Its Literature*. 2nd rev. ed. Delhi: Motilal Banarsidass.

———. 2002. *Philosophy of Śrī Madhvācārya*. Reprint of rev. ed. Delhi: Motilal Banarsidass.

Smith, Frederick M. 2011. "Predestination and Hierarchy: Vallabhācārya's Discourse on the Distinctions Between Blessed, Rule-Bound, Worldly, and Wayward Souls (the *Puṣṭipravāhamaryādābheda*)." *Journal of Indian Philosophy* 39: 173–227.

Śyāmadāsa, ed. 1990. *Śrīmad-Rūpagosvāmī Prabhupāda Praṇīta Śrībhaktirasāmṛtasindhu*. 2nd ed. Vṛndāvana: Vrajagaurava Prakāśana.

———. 1995. *Śrīla Viśvanāthacakravartipāda Praṇītā Mādhurya-Kādambinī*. 3rd ed. Vṛndāvana: Vrajagaurava Prakāśana.

Weber, Albrecht, ed. 1964. *The Çatapatha-Brāhmaṇa in the Mādhyandina-Çākhā*. 2nd ed. Chowkhamba Sanskrit Series, no. 96. Varanasi: Chowkhamba Sanskrit Series Office.

White, David Gordon. 1996. *The Alchemic Body: Siddha Traditions in Medieval India*. Chicago: University of Chicago Press.

Zydenbos, Robert J. 1991. "On the Jaina Background of Dvaitavedānta." *Journal of Indian Philosophy* 19: 249–271.

12

Agency in the Gauḍīya Vaiṣṇava Tradition

Satyanarayana Dasa and Jonathan B. Edelmann

Thus, this [self] who has been completely blessed, having arisen out of this [physical] body approaches the supreme illumination, and he is fully established in his own form. He is a liberated person. In that place, he roams about, [while] laughing, playing, and enjoying with women, vehicles, or relatives, without remembering this physical body.[1]

—CHĀNDOGYA UPANIṢAD 8.12.3

Therein the residents, in vehicles with their wives,
sing about the activities—which can destroy impurities—of the Lord.
The blossoming sweet Mādhavī flower in the water
divides their attention by its fragrance,
yet they scorn the breeze [carrying it].

—BHĀGAVATA PURĀṆA 3.15.17

THIS CHAPTER EXAMINES agency in a Hindu devotional (*bhakti*) tradition known as Gauḍīya Vaiṣṇavism or Caitanya Vaiṣṇavism, which takes its religious inspiration from Caitanya Mahāprabhu (1486–1534 CE). Caitanya was born in the town of Navadvīpa in West Bengal, then called Gauḍa, from which the Gauḍīya Vaiṣṇava tradition gets its name.

---

1. Unless noted, all translations are our own.

As a leading school in the *bhakti* movements of medieval North India, the Gauḍīyas advocated religious practices centered on loving devotion for God, considering the *Bhāgavata Purāṇa* (henceforth *Bhāgavata*) the most important scripture. Gauḍīyas understand the *Bhāgavata* as teaching that one should cultivate love for God through the performance of actions such as hearing and reciting names of Viṣṇu, Kṛṣṇa, Govinda, Rāma, et cetera. These actions are called the means (*abhidheya*) of achieving the ultimate goal of life (*prayojana*), which is such love.[2] For Gauḍīya Vaiṣṇavas, devotion is thus both the means and the end; the soul's devotion for God continues even in the liberated state, which is alluded to in the verses quoted above. Devotional traditions such as this must affirm the self's agency in some manner, since there must be a real connection between scriptural injunctions that one should hear and recite Viṣṇu's names, and the result the soul attains in doing so. Furthermore, a rejection of agency in the self would negate the tradition's belief that there can be relationship between the devotee (*bhakta*) and the Lord through the performance of particular actions even after the separation of the self from the mind-body complex. Thus, while Gauḍīya Vaiṣṇava views on agency are justified by appeal to scripture (and the Gauḍīyas are broadly Vedāntic in orientation, holding the *Bhāgavata* to be an informal commentary on the *Vedānta-Sūtra*), they are also the logical outcome of core theological commitments to the power, efficacy, and reality of devotion as the means of salvation and the truest expression of the soul after liberation.

Gauḍīya Vaiṣṇavas hold that there is a real connection between the devotee and the Lord established by the practice of devotion, a connection that is only possible if there is agency in the self (*ātman*). Furthermore, *Vedānta-Sūtra* (2.3.31–40, the section on agency) argues Vedic injunctions could only be efficacious if the soul is the agent of action. In his commentary called the *Govinda-bhāṣya* (2.3.34), the prominent 18th-century Gauḍīya Vaiṣṇava theologian Baladeva Vidyābhūṣaṇa says: "The self alone is the agent, not the qualities of matter. Why? This is said in scripture: 'If one desires heaven, he should worship' [and] 'one should meditate only on the self in this world' [*Bṛhadāraṇyaka Upaniṣad* 1.4.15]. If the agent is the conscious self, then scripture is meaningful. If the agent is the qualities

2. *Tattvasandarbha*, sections 46–47.

of nature, then that [scripture] would be meaningless."[3] Likewise, if there were no agency in the self, then scriptural injunctions to perform devotion (e.g., *Bhāgavata* 2.1.5) would also be meaningless.

One of the apparent problems with affirming agency in the self on the basis of scripture is that certain passages seem to deny it. The metaphysics of the *Bhāgavata Purāṇa* closely resembles that of classical Sāṃkhya-Yoga as well as Advaita Vedānta (nondualism),[4] yet both of these schools reject agency in the self. There are also passages in the *Bhagavad Gītā*, another important text for Gauḍīya Vaiṣṇavas, that seem to reject agency as a real feature of the self.[5] The argument of this chapter, following Jīva Gosvāmin, is that although the *Bhāgavata Purāṇa* (and other essential texts) appears to negate agency in the self, it in fact argues that agency is a real, inherent, and eternal feature of the self (*ātman*). We argue, therefore, that the *Bhāgavata's* conception of self is inconsistent with Advaita Vedānta's conception of the self. We attempt to show how Jīva and other noteworthy Gauḍīya Vaiṣṇava theologians such as Viśvanātha Cakravartin and Baladeva Vidyābhūṣaṇa interpret the *Bhāgavata Purāṇa* as saying the self has agency, and that this agency is not merely a superfluous by-product of the contact of the self and mind-body complex (i.e., the view of Sāṃkhya-Yoga and Advaita Vedānta). Rather, the innate capacities of the self like agency, the ability to apprehend objects, and the ability to experience pleasure are expressed while in the embodied state through the self's relationship with the mind-body complex. They agree with Nyāya that without a body of some sort, the self is unable to express its latent powers of agency, cognition, volition, apprehension, et cetera.[6] Furthermore, they agree with Sāṃkhya-Yoga that the self is ontologically distinct from matter (*prakṛti*). The school is distinct from Sāṃkhya and Nyāya, however, in that Gauḍīyas argue that after liberation there must be a real and permanent

---

3. *jīva eva karttā na guṇāḥ | kutaḥ śāstreti | svarga-kāmo yajetātmānam eva lokam upāsītety-ādi-śāstrasya cetane karttari sati sārthakyāt guṇa-karttṛtvena tad-ānarthakyaṃ syāt |* (Kṛṣṇadāsa 1963: 259).

4. For an interpretation of the *Bhāgavata Purāṇa* as a nondualistic text, see Rukmani 1970. Bhaṭṭācārya's 1960 and 1962 works are probably the most detailed study of the *Bhāgavata* in the English language, and they tend toward Advaita, although a full study of his interpretation is still wanting. Wilhelm Halbfass said the *Bhāgavata* has an "Advaitic character" (1995: 28), and he writes: "The monistic-illusionistic tendencies of the Vaiṣṇavas (Bhāgavatas) can be explained as being due to their originally close relations with Mahāyāna Buddhism" (ibid.).

5. See Bryant's article in this volume.

6. See §1.3 of Dasti's chapter in this volume.

"perfected" body (*siddha-rūpa*)[7] existing in the spiritual world through which the self eternally expresses its latent powers of agency.

We examine the *Bhāgavata* through the work of Jīva Gosvāmin (ca. 1517–1608 CE),[8] one of the most important scholars in the Caitanya Vaiṣṇava school. Jīva Gosvāmin's method is theological in the sense that it uses logic and reason to interpret what is considered the revealed and perfect words of scripture, and for the most part his efforts revolve around explaining what scripture means.[9] Like other Vedānta thinkers, he accepts the authority of the Vedas, Upaniṣads, *Vedānta Sūtra*, and *Bhagavad Gītā*, and he generates his metaphysics of Brahman through philosophically informed exegetical analysis. Furthermore, and again, like other Vedāntins, he does not give reason authority independent of scripture.[10] The Gauḍīya Vaiṣṇava arguments against Advaita Vedānta and other opposing schools are, therefore, contentions about how scripture is to be interpreted, arguments that use purely philosophical argument in a subordinate capacity. Jīva Gosvāmin, following Caitanya,[11] also argues that in our present age[12] the *Bhāgavata Purāṇa* is the means by which all other authoritative scriptures should be understood. Caitanya was part of a historical tendency that

7. This term is first mentioned in Rūpa Gosvāmin's *Bhakti-rasāmṛta-sindhu* (1.2.295), on which see Haberman 2003: 83. The *Bṛhad-bhāgavatāmṛta* (2.3.9) talks about the attainment of a spiritual body (*pañca-bhautikatātītaṃ sva-deham*). We will also look at *Bhāgavata* 1.6.22 in this regard.

8. For a discussion on the Jīva Gosvāmin's dates, see Brzezinski 1990: 14–57.

9. For instance, Jīva Gosvāmin (Haridāsa 1981: 22) quotes the following (untraced) verse from the *Kūrma Purāṇa* in his *Sarva-saṃvādinī*, an auto-commentary on his *Tattvasandarbha*:

pūrvāparāvirodhena ko nv artho 'bhimato bhavet |
ity-ādyam ūhanaṃ tarkaḥ śuṣka-tarkañ ca varjayet ||

[Proper] reasoning is deliberation on what is the desirable or congruous meaning such that it does not contradict the previous and latter [teachings in a particular text]. Dry logic [i.e., reasoning conducted independently of scripture] should be given up.

10. For a discussion of Śaṅkara's arguments for the validity of scriptural interpretation as the sole means of knowing Brahman, see Rambachan 1991.

11. See *Caitanya Caritāmṛta* (2.25.97, 100, 142) for Kṛṣṇadāsa's characterization of Caitanya's view that the *Bhāgavata Purāṇa* is a commentary on the *Vedānta Sūtra*. It must be noted, however, that Kṛṣṇadāsa was the student of the Vṛndāvana Gosvāmins (Jīva in particular), and thus what he says about Caitanya is mediated by the Gosvāmins.

12. In *Tattva Sandarbha* (section 12) he argues the problem with the Vedas is that right now it is difficult to understand them properly, one reason being that the sages give mutually contradictory interpretations of Vedic meaning. He quotes *Mahābhārata* 1.1.267, which says that one should supplement one's understanding of the Vedas with the Epics and Purāṇas and later in the TS he argues the *Bhāgavata* is the best of the Purāṇas.

had begun much earlier, one that saw the *Bhāgavata* as the quintessential scripture.[13] It was not until the 16th century that *bhakti* theologians Jīva Gosvāmin, Vallabha Ācārya (1479–1531) and Śrīnātha Cakravartin argued in their extensive writings that the *Bhāgavata Purāṇa* holds a status *equal to or even superior to* the Vedas, Upaniṣads, and *Vedānta-Sūtra*. They used it as the source of their theologies and as the lens through which all other Hindu scriptural texts were understood.

Our analysis focuses on Jīva Gosvāmin's seminal work *Six Essays* (*Ṣaṭ Sandarbha*),[14] a massive effort to organize the teachings of the *Bhāgavata*. One of Jīva's concerns throughout this work is to prevent the *Bhāgavata* from being interpreted in a nondualistic manner. The earliest extant full commentary called the *Bhāvārthadīpikā* by Śrīdhara Svāmin (ca. 1350 CE) at times gives a dualistic interpretation of the text that is more in tune with Jīva's theology, but in other places he interprets it according to the school in which he was an initiated member, that of Śaṅkara's (ca. 700 CE) Advaita Vedānta (see Timalsina's chapter in this volume).[15] Jīva Gosvāmin, however, interprets the *Bhāgavata* as saying that there is an individual self (*ātman*) that is real, eternal, and distinct from the absolute reality (*brahman*). It is the same and different from God (*bheda-abheda*), yet this relationship is ultimately beyond reason and known only through scripture (*acintya*). The individual self has the inherent potential to act, know, and experience pleasure, and this potential only becomes actualized through a body, whether that be a material or a spiritual body. Furthermore, unlike the nondualists, for Jīva Gosvāmin the absolute has powers or energies

13. The 13th-century Dvaitin named Madhvācārya wrote a *Bhāgavata Purāṇa* commentary called *Bhāgavata-tātparya-nirṇaya*; the 14th-century Advaitin named Śrīdhara wrote a full commentary called the *Bhāvārtha-dīpikā* although there is a commentary before him by Citsukha that is mostly lost; the 15th-century Advaitin named Madhusūdana Sarasvatī, who lived after Caitanya, wrote a commentary on the *Bhāgavata's* first verse called *Śrīmad-bhāgavata-prathama-śloka-vyākhyā*. See Dasgupta 1961: vol. 4, 1–2 for a list of *Bhāgavata Purāṇa* commentaries.

14. This is a set of six books containing the *Tattva-*, *Bhagavat-*, *Paramātma-*, *Kṛṣṇa-*, *Bhakti-* and *Prīti- Sandarbhas*.

15. For example, Śrīdhara Svāmin writes in his commentary on *Bhāgavata* 3.26.3: "the word 'without qualities' [in the verse] removes the idea that [the self] has the quality of apprehension, etc. (*jñānādi-guṇatvaṃ vārayati nirguṇaḥ*)" (Kṛṣṇaśaṅkara 1965: 959). As we shall see, the issue of apprehension is directly connected with agency. The rejection of apprehension as a real property of the self is precisely the Advaitic position Jīva Gosvāmin will argue against.

(*śakti*) that are also real and eternally part of the absolute's nature.[16] The self (*ātman*) is considered part of a personal God's eternally real nature, thus it shares in some aspects of his divine nature. We begin by examining Jīva Gosvāmin's analysis of the self as found in his *Paramātma Sandarbha*, an essay that is primarily devoted to discussing how the transcendent, supreme Lord (*bhagavān*) is manifest as an indwelling and all-pervasive being in this world (*paramātman*). Since Jīva Gosvāmin argues that the self (*ātman*) is part of the indwelling being, his analysis of the self is included in the *Paramātma Sandarbha*.

Characteristics of the Self in the Paramātma Sandarbha

We begin with a brief outline of Advaita and Sāṃkhya views of agency, since these are the two schools Jīva Gosvāmin opposes. In his commentary on the *Taittirīya Upaniṣad* 2.1, Śaṅkara argues that the three terms describing Brahman—real, awareness, and infinite—are not three distinct qualities, but express the inherent nature of a single, unified pure consciousness. Although he speaks of Brahman here, his views also apply to the self since he holds that Brahman and self are not different. He writes:

> *Jñāna* means awareness. The word *jñāna* is constructed by applying *bhāva*[17] [which signifies a completed state or a nominal verb],[18] but [it does not mean] an agent of awareness because it is an adjective of *brahman*, along with "real" and "unlimited." For if brahman is an agent of cognition, reality and unlimitedness would not be possible. An agent of cognition would undergo transformation, so how could it be real and unlimited, since that which is not divided is unlimited. If *jñāna* is taken [in the sense of] being an agent of apprehension, [Brahman would be] separate

16. According to Jīva Gosvāmin, God has three divisions of powers: *antaraṅgā* (internal), *taṭasthā* (intermediate), and *bahiraṅgā* (external) (see *Bhagavat-sandarbha*, section 16).

17. The addition of *bhāva* to √jñā accounts for the *–ana* suffix in *jñāna*.

18. Abhyankar et al.. 1977: 292 define the third meaning of *bhāva*: "completed action which is shown, not by a verb, but by a verbal derivative noun."

> from apprehension and the object apprehended, thus he would not be unlimited.[19]

Here Śaṅkara wants to say that if Brahman were an agent of awareness and thus had an object of awareness, it would then be divided and separate from another thing, and thus limited; this would contradict the scriptural statements that reality is unlimited and consequently nondual. He likewise denies agency in Brahman and the self for the same reasons. As we discuss later, one of the fundamental ways that Vaiṣṇava and Advaita understandings of Brahman and self differ revolve around how the word *jñāna* is understood. In the *Tattvānusandhāna* of the early 18th-century nondualist Mahādeva Sarasvatī it is stated:

> Consciousness reflected in ignorance is the [provisionally] individual self [and] consciousness delimited by ignorance is the personal God. But others say that consciousness delimited by ignorance which is the cause [of the world] is the personal God [and] consciousness delimited by mind is the individual self.[20]

This passage explains how the illusion of individuality arises, both for the self and for the personal God. Once ignorance is removed from the self, only pure consciousness devoid of any attributes remains, hence it is devoid of any agency also. Thus, in Advaita Vedānta the self (like Brahman) has the inherent nature or essence (*svarūpa*) of pure consciousness or awareness only (*cinmātra*), but apprehension and cognition are not qualities of the self. They propose that the self becomes a knower only when in contact with the mind, which is a property of matter and thus not-self. Being a knower is presupposed in being an agent, since one only acts after deliberation. Sāṃkhya-Yoga also rejects agency in the self, but accepts the self as witness and observer, since this school holds that matter alone

---

19. *jñānaṃ jñaptir avabodho bhāva-sādhano jñāna-śabdo na tu jñāna-kartṛ brahma-viśeṣaṇatvāt satyānantābhyāṃ saha / na hi satyatānantatā ca jñāna-kartṛtve saty upapadyete / jñāna-kartṛtvena hi vikriyamāṇaṃ kathaṃ satyaṃ bhaved anantaṃ ca, yad dhi na kutaścit pravibhajyate tad anantam / jñāna-kartṛtve ca jñeya-jñānābhyāṃ pravibhaktam ity anantatā na syāt* (Aiyar 1910: vol. 3, 63).

20. *avidyā-pratibimbitaṃ caitayaṃ jīvaḥ, avidyopahitaṃ caitanyam īśvaraḥ... anye tu kāraṇībhūta-ajñānopahitaṃ caitanyam īśvaraḥ antaḥkaraṇopahitaṃ caitanyaṃ jīvaḥ* (*Tattvānusandhāna* 1.16, 1.19).

could not account for the fact of experience or *qualia* (*Sāṃkhya Kārikā*, 19). The *Sāṃkhya Kārikā* of Īśvara Kṛṣṇa says the self is a qualitative experiencer or enjoyer (*bhoktṛ*):

> The self exists, (a) because aggregations or combinations exist for another; (b) because (this other) must be apart or opposite from the three *guṇas*; (c) because (this other) (must be) a superintending power or control; (d) because of the existence or need of an enjoyer; (e) because [matter] has functions for the sake of liberation.[21]

Sāṃkhya Kārikā 20 says that the self appears to have the characteristic of agency because of its connection with matter, but in fact agency is located in matter, *not* in the self.

The Caitanya Vaiṣṇava schools accept that the self is aware and that it possesses *qualia* (i.e., it accounts for the qualitative experience of objects), but they add a number of other features to the self, ones that they argue must exist if we are to account for the self's entrapment in the cycle of birth and death, and for the full range of scriptural passages pertaining to the self. To enumerate the characteristics of the self Jīva Gosvāmin refers to the verses of Jāmātṛ Muni (ca. 1370–1443 CE), who is also known as Varavara Muni, a follower of Rāmānuja (ca. 1017–1137 CE):[22]

> *ātmā na devo na naro na tiryak sthāvaro na ca |*
> *na deho nendriyaṃ naiva manaḥ prāṇo na nāpi dhīḥ ||*
> *na jaḍo na vikārī ca jñāna-mātrātmako na ca |*
> *svasmai svayaṃ-prakāśaḥ syād eka-rūpaḥ svarūpa-bhāk ||*
> *cetano vyāpti-śīlaś ca cid-ānandātmakas tathā |*
> *aham-arthaḥ prati-kṣetraṃ bhinno'ṇur nitya-nirmalaḥ ||*

---

21. *saṅghātaparārthatvāt triguṇādi-viparyayād adhiṣṭhānāt |*
puruṣo 'sti bhoktṛ-bhāvāt kaivalyārthapravṛtteś ca || Sāṃkhya Kārikā 17 ||

Translation based upon Larson (2001).

22. Jāmātṛ Muni's views seem to be based on verses from the *Padma Purāṇa*, the likes of which Jīva quotes just prior to his quotation of Jāmātṛ, the only difference being that the PP does not include agency (*kartṛtva*) in its list of the self's characteristics. Jīva provides no explanation as to why he would make a somewhat marginal figure in the history of South Indian Vaiṣṇava thought so central to his doctrine of the self, but we suppose he was drawn to the clarity of Jāmātṛ's expression, as well as his clear affirmation of agency, something Jīva needs given his devotional outlook, as discussed in the Introduction of this chapter.

tathā jñātṛtva-kartṛtva-bhoktṛtva-nija-dharmakaḥ |
paramātmaika-śeṣatva-svabhāvaḥ sarvadā svataḥ ||[23]

> The self is neither a god, nor a human, nor an animal, nor an immovable being, nor the body, nor the senses, nor the mind, nor the life air, nor even the intelligence. It is not inert, it is not mutable, and it is not awareness only. It is aware of itself and it is self-luminous, it has unchanging form, it [always] resides in its true nature, it is conscious, it pervades the body, it is of the nature of consciousness and bliss, it is the referent of [the word] "I," there is a different self in each body, it is indivisible, and it is eternally pure. Furthermore, it has the intrinsic characteristics of being an apprehender, agent and qualitative experiencer, and by its own nature and at all times it is an inherent part of indwelling Lord.

As shown below, Jīva uses the *Bhāgavata* to elaborate upon this, and we supplement the discussion with other sources and argumentation.

The Self is Conscious

The self is not inert (*jaḍa*). As an observer or seer, it is understood to infuse its consciousness into the mind-body complex by its presence in them as a witness. According to the *Bhāgavata*, the subtle body (consisting of the mind, intelligence, ego, and aggregate awareness) and physical body cannot function without being illuminated by self, but the self is self-luminous by its very nature. Thus, whereas the body and mind require the self to function, the self does not require the body and mind for its existence. The self is its own power of illumination, and it has the potential to apprehend, act, and experience, but these latter qualities are manifest only when in contact with a mind-body complex, whether spiritual or material. To dispose of the view that the self is inert, Jīva Gosvāmin quotes *Bhāgavata* 11.13.27:

> Wakefulness, dream sleep, and deep sleep are states of the intellect; they arise out of the qualities of nature. The self is ascertained as distinct from them because of being [their] witness.[24]

23. *Paramātma Sandarbha*, section 19 (Haridāsa 1984: 80). We have been unable to locate the original source of this passage from Jāmātṛ's writings.

24. *jāgrat svapnaḥ suṣuptaṃ ca, guṇato buddhi-vṛttayaḥ |*
tāsāṃ vilakṣaṇo jīvaḥ, sākṣitvena viniścitaḥ || 11.13.27 ||

The argument is that since the self is witness to the three states of intellect (all of which are part of material nature) it must be conscious; Jīva Gosvāmin will, of course, say that the self is more than a mere witness.

The Self is Immutable

If the self is a witness, it must be different from that which is witnessed, and if it witnesses, it must be unchanging. Here we have an axiom in Jīva Gosvāmin's commentary on the *Bhāgavata*: the self does not undergo modifications, for any sort of modification would mean it is temporary and not eternal; it is only the body and mind that are subjected to transformation.[25] While this is an axiom derived from canonical texts, the rationale for this view is that if the self were subject to changes, it could not be a witness to the changes in the body and mind, since to witness a change the observer must remain changeless while observing the changes. If the self were changing and transforming along with the body and mind, it could not recognize the distinction between itself and that which changes.[26]

Jāmātṛ uses the phrase *na vikārī*, that is, the self is not subject to transformation. The *Bhāgavata* (11.7.48) says:

> The various states beginning with birth and ending with death are caused by time, whose function cannot be ascertained, and they belong to the body alone and not to the self, just like the phases of the moon [do not affect the moon itself].[27]

Thus, any modification caused by time only affects the body (and mind) and not the self, just as the moon is unaffected by what appears to be its different phases. The presupposition here is that any modification that could take place has time as its general cause (*sāmānya kāraṇa*). Just as the self can only express its quality-potentials such as agency and apprehension through a mind-body complex, the mind-body complex can only act in time.

---

25. As noted by Bryant in this volume, this is an axiom of Sāṃkhya, and to some degree, Indian philosophy in general.

26. This is also accepted by Patañjali (*Yoga Sūtra* 4.18), "Because the self, the master of mind, is free of any modifications, it always knows the changing states of the mind."

27. *visargādyāḥ śmaśānāntā, bhāvā dehasya nātmanaḥ* |
kalānām iva candrasya, kālenāvyakta-vartmanā || 11.7.48 ||

One might question, then, how actions such as reciting the Lord's names could take place in the spiritual world since the *Bhāgavata* (2.9.10) states that this world is without the power or course of time (*na kāla-vikramaḥ*). In other words, how can one say that Vaikuṇṭha is beyond the scope of time; that all action can only take place in time; and that the self performs actions in Vaikuṇṭha in relation to the Lord? Gauḍīyas interpret the *Bhāgavata* verse quoted above and others like it as only saying there is the lack of time's destructive influence or power, but the spiritual world is still considered sequenced, albeit in a fluid and unfixed manner. While the destructive aspect of time is absent, the expression of the self's agency still requires the existence of sequence (even if nonlinear) as a general cause, just as it requires a spiritual body, mind, et cetera.

Later we shall discuss how the *Bhāgavata* sees agency as an inherent feature of the self, yet one might object that agency entails a transformation in the agent. As noted in Bryant's chapter in this volume, it was for this reason that Aniruddha, an important commentator on the *Sāṃkhya Sūtra*, rejects agency in the self. The *Bhāgavata* holds that the self acts as an agent like a magnet acts as the agent of change upon iron filings; this allows it to be an agent but not undergo modification, as it may modify the shavings "at a distance" through its *śakti*. The self, likewise, performs action at a distance, influencing the changed without itself undergoing modification.[28] In his *Govinda Bhāṣya* on *Vedānta-Sūtra* 2.3.33 Baladeva writes:

> Because it is said [in the scripture] that the self is the agent who controls the life airs, [therefore] the conscious self should be understood to have agency like a magnet attracts [or moves] iron. The life airs and so forth are the means for controlling every other object, but for controlling the life airs there is no other [means] than that [self].[29]

---

28. *Bhāgavata* 5.18.38; this verse is describing the manner in which the Lord gives insentient matter the capacity for action, but it can be applied to the self as well.

29. *jīva-karttṛkasya prāṇopādānasyābhidhānāt lohākarṣaka-maṇer iva cetanasyaiva jīvasya karttrṛtvaṃ bodhyam / anya-grahaṇādau prāṇādi karaṇaṃ, prāṇa-grahaṇādau tu nānyadastīti tasyaiva tat* || (Kṛṣṇadāsa 1963: 159). As noted by Bryant in this volume, Vijñānabhikṣu proposed a similar solution in his own commentary on *Sāṃkhya Sūtra* 2.29, arguing for a type of "passive agency" (Bryant's words) on the part of the self.

While this might explain how the nonphysical self can modify the mind-body complex without its undergoing modification itself, one could further object that the Caitanya Vaiṣṇava tradition recognizes a distinction between the physical body and a spiritual body (*siddha deha*). The *Bhāgavata* (e.g., 3.15.17) talks of a post-liberation world called Vaikuṇṭha to which the self can be transferred upon the perfection of its devotion for Viṣṇu or Kṛṣṇa, and it can live there eternally in an embodied form.[30] Since the self is likened to a finite spiritual spark,[31] the question may be raised as to whether it transforms when it adopts a spiritual body at liberation in the world of Vaikuṇṭha. In reply, it may be argued that the self remains unchanging even in this case because just as in this world the unchanging self identifies with material mind-body complex that undergoes the process of reincarnation, so while in the spiritual realm the self identities with a spiritual body that is eternal or undying. According to the *Bhāgavata* (1.6.29), Nārada said of his own liberation:

> After the exhaustion of my *karma* I discarded [my body] composed of the five material elements and I was united with a pure body that is related to the Lord.[32]

The significant points here are that the self is united with a spiritual body, thus there is a distinction between the self and its newly acquired body. The commentators note that this verse refers back to *Bhāgavata* 1.6.23, wherein the Lord promises Nārada: "after leaving this inferior world, you will attain the position of my personal attendant." To dispel any doubt about the nature of this body, Śrīdhara Svāmin says: "what is implied here is that the bodies of the personal attendants of the Lord are pure, eternal, and not the creation of *karma*."[33] Later we show that the Caitanya Vaiṣṇava tradition recognizes two forms of the ego (*ahaṃkāra*), a material or prakṛtic ego, and a real or spiritual ego (*aham-artha*). Thus, the view

30. See, e.g., *Bhāgavata* 3.15.13. and 10.28.14. For discussion of the differences between the physical and perfected body in Gauḍīya Vaiṣṇavism see Haberman 1988: chap. 5.

31. For example, *Caitanya Caritāmṛta* 2.19.140.

32. *prayujyamāne mayi tāṃ śuddhāṃ bhāgavatīṃ tanum /*
ārabdhakarmanirvāṇo nyapatat pāñcabhautikaḥ || 1.6.28 ||

33. *anena pārṣada-tanūnām akarmārabdhatvaṃ śuddhatvaṃ nityatvam ity-ādi sūcitaṃ bhavati* (Kṛṣṇaśaṅkara 1965: 398). Cf. *Bhāgavata* 7.1.35.

proposed here is that the real, spiritual ego causes the self to identify with the spiritual body, and it acts as an unchanging agent through that body as an eternal attendant of the Lord.

The Self has the Inherent Power of Consciousness

A central question raised by many Indian philosophical schools is whether or not the self is the direct bearer of qualities like awareness or volition.[34] Jāmātṛ Muni says that the self is not mere awareness (*jñāna-mātrātmako na*), but it also has the power to apprehend objects as a real and eternal quality (*jñātṛtva*). In Advaita, by contrast, the self is aware, but the power to apprehend objects is considered extrinsic to its essential nature. The *Bhāgavata* (5.11.12), however, says:

> The pure self sees these manifestations of the mind that continually appear [in waking consciousness and dream sleep] and disappear [in deep sleep], which are actions performed by the impure agent, i.e., the *jīva* [the embodied *ātman*], which is the creation of māyā.[35]

This means that the self has apprehension as an attribute since it knows the body, the presupposition being that only an entity with the power of apprehension could see (*vicaṣṭe*).

This seeing is different from the "awareness only" of Advaita because it is the *pure* self who sees and understands the manifestations of the mind; it is not an action of the mind (*antaḥ-karaṇa*). As shown in this verse, the *Bhāgavata* states that the pure self is a subject who can have an object, whereas for Advaita the pure self is beyond the subject-object distinction. Thus, when Jāmātṛ Muni said, "the self is conscious of itself (*svasmai*) and self-luminous (*svayaṃ prakāśaḥ*)," Jīva Gosvāmin understands this as showing that the self has apprehension as a real attribute and that the subject can become its own object. The word *prakāśa*, or "light," can either refer to something's capacity to illuminate an object or to the inherent luminous nature of an object

34. As noted by Dasti in this volume, Udayana separates properties from the property bearer, which allows him to say the self (i.e., the property bearer) is unchanging, yet its properties (e.g., cognitive states, volition) can change.

35. *kṣetrajña etā manaso vibhūtīr jīvasya māyā-racitasya nityāḥ* /
āvirhitāḥ kvāpi tirohitāś ca śuddho vicaṣṭe hy aviśuddha-kartuḥ || 5.11.12 ||

(like the sun, whose illumination is not derived from another source). A sundial, for example, must be illuminated by an external light source since it lacks an inherent luminosity. The sun, however, has the inherent quality of illumination. The self, on Jāmātṛ's view, has its own power of illumination, and it is conscious of itself—in addition to external objects—by its own self-illuminating power. It is for this reason that Jīva Gosvāmin refers to the self as *cid-rūpa*, or conscious by its own nature, to describe consciousness throughout his *Sandarbhas*. Yet Mādhava in his *Sarva-darśana-saṃgraha* also uses the word *cid-rūpa* to describe the inherent nature of the self as only pure awareness (*jñāna*), but Jīva Gosvāmin uses it to mean that self is aware of itself and of objects.

Since it is often used loosely, an analysis of the word *jñāna* of our own development will help to clarify these issues. *Jñāna* is derived from the verbal root *jñā* meaning "to know" by applying the -ana suffix.[36] One can derive three senses: (1) abstract verbal noun (*bhāva*), (2) an instrument (*karaṇa*), and (3) locus or substratum (*adhikaraṇa*). Therefore we derive the following three senses from the word *jñāna*:

(1) *Jñāna* here refers to understanding, awareness, experience, knowing, consciousness. As per Śaṅkara's usage, *jñāna* in this sense means a state of knowing that is without any content, or "awareness only." It does not reveal anything except the subject itself.
(2) *Jñāna* here refers to that by which one knows an object. *Jñāna* in this sense has content, which is disclosed to a knowing subject.
(3) *Jñāna* indicates here the one in whom there is cognition. *Jñāna* in this sense is a subject that possesses content, or the one in whom reside cognitions.

We showed above that (1) is Śaṅkara's view—the true nature of the self is contentless awareness, revealing only the subject without any object. The *Bhāgavata's* view of God (e.g., 1.2.11) and self is that of (3), since both God and self possess apprehension as natural or innate feature of their being; this entails the existence of (2) in them as well. On this view, (2) is

36. See Pāṇini's *Aṣṭādhyāyī* 3.3.115, *lyuṭ ca*, "The affix *lyuṭ* is added to the root when the name of an action is expressed in the neuter gender." And 3.3.117, *karaṇa-adhikaraṇayoś ca*, "the affix *lyuṭ* comes after a root when the relation of the word to be formed to the verb is that of an instrument or location." Translations based on Vasu (1894: 525–526).

considered a mental state (a *jñāna-vṛtti*), whereas (3) refers to what many Vaiṣṇava thinkers mean by *jñāna-svarūpa*, a subject's inherent capacity for knowledge, that is, its capacity or quality-potential to apprehend. Thus, on the Vaiṣṇava view (3) refers to the essential nature of the self, whereas (2) is its quality (*guṇa*), which manifest when the self is joined with a mind-body complex. We are using the word *guṇa* (quality) loosely here. The relation between the self and its *vṛtti-jñāna* is similar to that of magnet and the movement it creates in the iron shavings. It is none of the conventional relations in Nyāya of contact or inherence because the knowledge, like the movement in fillings, is external to the self.

In summary, when Advaitins use the word *jñāna-svarūpa*, however, they mean it as (1), whereas Vaiṣṇavas mean it as (3). Thus, one might say the fundamental difference between Vaiṣṇava and Advaita theology is in the application of *lyuṭ* as *adhikaraṇa* versus *bhāva*. For Vaiṣṇavas knowledge thus belongs to a subject and it is "contentful," that is, it has reference to an object; but knowledge in this latter sense of (2) is a fluctuation of matter, that is, an inert function of matter in the embodied state, and a function of spiritual substance in the spiritual world.

The Self is the Referent of the Word "I"

Jīva Gosvāmin claims there are two types of ego or identity: an incorrect conception of self that is caused by a function of matter called the *ahaṃkāra*, and a correct conception of self (*aham-bhāva*). He says the self is the meaning or referent of the word "I" (*aham-artha*) because the object of "I" is the feeling or sense of being an "I," and he thinks the sense of self is real, but when that sense of self is focused upon the physical body and mind, it is called the *ahaṃkāra*. In its most pure state, the self knows the "I" as the *ātman* or the real self, whereas in the impure state the self wrongly considers the referent of "I" to be a particular mind-body complex. Whereas the *ahaṃkāra* is extrinsic to the self, the *aham-artha* is intrinsic. As discussed below, much of the argumentation presented by Jīva Gosvāmin in this regard relies on a second axiom: *there must be an ego for there to be any apprehension whatsoever.*

Jīva writes in his *Sarva Saṃvādinī* (an auto-commentary) on *Paramātma Sandarbha* (section 22):

> Because of reflecting "I slept well" immediately after deep sleep it is understood that even in that [deep sleep] there is an inherent ability

> for apprehension, an inherent feeling of happiness and an inherent sense of "I."[37]

Jīva is saying that in deep sleep, when the material or prakṛtic ego is nearly nonfunctional or idle, there must be a capacity inherent within the self that allows it to have the experience of happiness, since all extrinsic and material appendages of the self are nearly nonfunctional. In order to justify the existence of these two types of ego and to show the necessity of the spiritual ego he quotes *Bhāgavata* 11.3.39:

> The vital air follows the self—whether it is born of egg, womb, seed, or other unknown origin—here and there [in the different bodies]. When in deep sleep, when the collection of the senses and the sense of identity is idle, the self remains without the mind. After the deep sleep we remember [the experience of sleep].[38]

This verse says that the material or prakṛtic ego is idle or nearly nonfunctional in deep sleep. Yet, since we remember the experience of sleep upon waking, Jīva Gosvāmin infers that the spiritual ego was active. Thus, the spiritual ego or innate sense of self is being described in this verse.

While not made explicit, in order to render this interpretation of the verse Jīva Gosvāmin relies on the second axiom, that is, *without an ego there is no experience.*[39] In other words, experience, or being a knower, is only possible with an ego. Therefore, Jīva Gosvāmin argues that since the material ego is idle in deep sleep, and since there is still experience in deep sleep because one remembers the nature of that sleep upon waking, there must be second ego that facilitates that experience. This is the real ego, inherent in the self. This is corroborated in *Bṛhadāraṇyaka Upaniṣad* 4.3.11: "When the body is subdued by sleep, the sleepless one sees the sleeping one [i.e., mind-body complex]."[40] Jīva Gosvāmin comments on this as follow: "It was previously established that although the self is

37. *evaṃ sukham aham asvāpsam [na kiñcid avediṣam] iti suṣupty-anantaraṃ parāmarśāt tatrāpy aham-arthatā sukhitā jñātṛtā ca gamyate* (Haridāsa 1984: 21).

38. *aṇḍeṣu peśiṣu taruṣv aviniściteṣu, prāṇo hi jīvam upadhāvati tatra tatra*
sanne yad indriya-gaṇe 'hami ca prasupte, kūṭa-stha āśayam ṛte tad-anusmṛtir naḥ || 11.3.39 ||

39. Like the first, this axiom is accepted by many India schools, e.g., Advaita, Sāṃkhya, Yoga, and Nyāya.

40. *svapnena śārīram abhiprahatyāsuptaḥ suptānabhicākaśīti* | *Bṛhadāraṇyaka Upaniṣad* 4.3.11

awareness only it also has the potential to apprehend; this is not possible without the sense of 'I'."[41]

One might wish to say that there is no experience whatsoever in deep sleep, rather upon waking from deep sleep one *infers* "I slept well" because one's body and mind feel rested, just as one might infer someone had cooked rice in the kitchen because one smells the residual fragrance even if one had not experienced the cooking. This is not Jīva Gosvāmin's interpretation, because to make an inference one must have prior knowledge of the relationship between the cause by which one makes the inference (*hetu*) and the object inferred (*sādhya*). In the above example wherein one infers cooking from the fragrance, one is able to make that inference because one knows of the relationship (*vyāpti*) between cooking rice and its smell. If there is no experience in deep sleep, how is the relationship between cause and the effect established? There is no knowledge of the relationship between deep sleep (the cause) and feeling well (the effect, *sādhya*), so there could not be an inference. We do have a memory of being deep asleep; and if there is a memory, there must have been an ego that produced the experience that allows for the formation of a memory.

From the point of view of Yoga, the experience of deep sleep is the experience of the nonexistence of a mental fluctuation. The *Yoga Sūtra* (1.6) accepts five mental fluctuations or states (*vṛtti*), and the *Bhāgavata* (3.26.30) accepts the same five with slight terminological differences: correct cognition, false cognition, imagination, memory, and deep sleep. All experiences are said to fall under one of these categories. The first four are mental fluctuations that exist (*bhāva-vṛtti*), and the last is the absence of a mental fluctuation (*abhāva-vṛtti*). The latter is known by the experience of its absence, like at night one experiences the nonexistence of the sun—in deep sleep the self experiences the nonexistence of mental fluctuations. Thus, Jīva Gosvāmin means that in waking life the material and spiritual egos are mixed, and in deep sleep the spiritual ego allows for the experience of the absence of any mental fluctuation.

We wish to argue below that there must be a power of identification or an ego *inherent* within the self, otherwise the fact of the self's absorption in matter would not be possible. The problem for Sāṃkhya-Yoga and Advaita Vedānta is that while they agree the self is absorbed in matter, they

41. *jñāna-mātratve'pi jñātṛtvaṃ cātmanaḥ pūrvaṃ sādhitam / tac cāham-bhāvaṃ vinā na sidhyatīti* (Haridāsa 1984: 15–16).

do not provide the self with the inherent power by which it could become absorbed in matter. In a discussion on Sāṃkhya-Yoga, the *Bhāgavata* (3.26.6) says:

> Thus, on account of absorption in the other [i.e., matter] the self attributes agency to himself regarding actions that are [in fact] performed by the *guṇas* of matter.[42]

In distinction from Advaita, the *Bhāgavata* says it is *the self* (the *ātman* or *puruṣa*[43]) that bestows agency to matter because it is the self that is absorbed in matter.[44] Thus the *aham-artha* is alluded to, since without the *aham-artha* the self would not be the agent of absorption in matter, just as an actor without an ego would not be able to adopt the personality of the character he or she acts out.

The verses prior to this describe that the Lord creates the various material forms by the qualities of nature[45] and as soon as the self looks upon (*vilokya*) them, he at once becomes bewildered. The "looking" here is not to be taken literally; it suggests that the self has an inherent power of seeing, comprehension, and action (and thus an ego) since it looked upon matter prior to its connection with a mind-body complex and then identified with it. As a consequence, the self considers the agency of matter to be the agency of the self although it is not; but without an ego inherent in the self, the false cognition "I am matter, my body is acting" could not occur in the mind with which the self identifies. However, this is not to deny that agency is in the self since the *Bhāgavata* (11.25.26) also says that agency remains in the self, even when divorced from all qualities of nature:

> An agent who is free from attachment is qualified by the material quality of goodness, it is said that [an agent] qualified by the material quality of passion is blinded by desire, [and an agent] qualified by the

---

42. *evaṃ parābhidhyānena kartṛtvaṃ prakṛteḥ pumān /*
karmasu kriyamāṇeṣu guṇair ātmani manyate || 3.26.6 ||

43. The grammatical subject of the verb, *manyate*, is not named in 3.26.6, but is carried over from 3.26.3, where it is defined as the beginningless *ātman*, which transcends matter.

44. Although this verse seems to say that agency (*kartṛtva*) is in matter, we shall discuss later why this is not the case.

45. Śrīdhara Svāmin notes this is his play, *līlā*.

material quality of ignorance is lost to introspection. [An agent] who has taken refuge in me is without any quality of nature.[46]

This is another reason why the *Bhāgavata's* conception of self is inconsistent with classical Sāṃkhya-Yoga and Advaita, since it is the self (even when freed from the *guṇas*) who takes refuge in the Lord and not the properties of matter such as the *ahaṃkāra*. Furthermore, this establishes the possibility of agency in the post-liberation state.

If the self is able to become absorbed in matter, it must possess its own innate sense of "I," such that it could be the agent of identification. Unlike the classical Sāṃkhya of Īśvara Kṛṣṇa or the Yoga of Patañjali which say that the sense of "I" is only a function of matter, on the *Bhāgavata's* view there must be an inherent capacity of the self that allows it to cast its feeling of "I" onto the physical body and mind (*manas*). The Caitanya Vaiṣṇava tradition holds that it is impossible to identify with an object if one does not have an ego or "I-maker," so there must be certainly a distinct ego in the self. In this regard, Jīva writes in *Paramātma Sandarbha*, section 29:

> On account of meditating upon matter [see *Bhāgavata* 3.26.6], or, in other words, because of intentness upon matter, one thinks "I am nothing but matter." By thinking thus, one considers the agency of the actions performed by the qualities of nature to be in the self. Since it is not possible for one without a sense of "I" to identify with another, and since the ego is produced from absorption in matter and is a covering [over the self], there must be another distinct sense of "I" in the self. Clearly, then, that [ego] is not the cause of *saṃsāra* since it is located in the pure, essential nature [of the self].[47]

In summary, the *ātman* has its own ego called the *aham-artha*, and it allows it to witness the *ahaṃkāra*. This is justified by the experience of deep sleep, which is the experience of the inactivity of the material ego

46. *sāttvikaḥ kārako 'saṅgī, rāgāndho rājasaḥ smṛtaḥ*
tāmasaḥ smṛti-vibhraṣṭo, nirguṇo mad-apāśrayaḥ || 11.25.26 ||
Śrīdhara Svāmin glosses *kārakaḥ* as *kartā*, or agent.

47. *parābhidhyānena prakṛtyāveśena prakṛtir evāham iti mananena prakṛti-guṇaiḥ kriyamāṇeṣu karmasu kartṛtvam ātmani manyate | atra nirahambhāvasya parābhidhyānāsambhavāt parāveśajātāhaṅkārasya cāvarakatvād asty eva tasminn anyo'hambhāva-viśeṣaḥ | sa ca śuddha-svarūpa-mātra-niṣṭhatvān na saṃsāra-hetur iti spaṣṭam* | (Haridāsa 1984: 99)

Table 12.1. The self's relationship with the mind-body complex

Inherent properties of self (*antaraṅga-śakti-s*)		Extrinsic properties of self (*bahiraṅga-śakti-s*)
FOUNDATIONAL & UNCHANGING	QUALITY-POTENTIALS	QUALITY-MANIFESTATIONS
self-luminous	apprehension	Apprehender
unchanging form	agency	Agent
situated in its own nature	qualitative experience	qualitative experiencer
conscious		external awareness
consciousness		
bliss		
meaning of "I"		identification with body
atomic		

(*abhāva-vṛtti*). Since there must be a witness of this unawareness in deep sleep, since the act of witnessing entails an ego, and since the *ahaṃkāra* is idle, there must be a spiritual ego inherent in the self. The tradition holds that without a real sense of "I" in the self it would be impossible for it to identify with the material mind-body complex, so it rejects the Sāṃkhya-Yoga and Advaita conception of self because they cannot account for the self's absorption in matter. While much of this discussion is on the conditions needed for apprehension (*jñātṛtva*), these are necessary preconditions of agency (*kartṛtva*) since to act entails knowing what to act upon.

At this point we can outline the general scheme of the self and its relationship with the mind-body complex (table 12.1).

By the inherent properties of the self we mean those properties that are the defining features of the self. There are two aspects. The first, foundational, are always present and do not require anything other than their own self-luminous nature to be manifest. The second, quality-potentials, are aspects of the self that require a mind-body complex (whether material or spiritual) to be activated. They are the qualities (*guṇas* or *dharmas*) of the self that are either manifest or unmanifest depending on whether the self identifies with a material or spiritual body. Thus, on this view, to be an apprehender (*jñātṛ*), an agent (*kartṛ*), and an enjoyer or sufferer (*bhoktṛ*) it is necessary to be an *ātman* with apprehension (*jñātṛtva*), agency (*kartṛtva*) and qualitative experience (*bhokṛtva*) as quality-potentials, and an *ātman* with a self-luminous, et cetera foundational (*adhiṣṭhāna*) nature since the quality potentials must be self-revealed to the subject.[48] The "inherent properties" of the self, then, are necessary but not sufficient conditions for one to be an apprehender, agent, et cetera.[49]

The Selves are Multiple and Indivisible

If the sense of "I" or the ego is in fact part of the self's true nature, then it follows, as Jāmātṛ says next, that in each body there is a different self. Jāmātṛ Muni also says that the self is atomic (*aṇu*), that is, it is indivisible. Although atomic, it diffuses its consciousness throughout the entire body. If the self is atomic in size, there must be a separate self in each body. The Upaniṣads also support this: "This soul is atomic and to be known by the intellect; the fivefold life airs are supported by it" (*Muṇḍaka Upaniṣad* 3.1.9). "The size of the self should be known as one ten thousandth part of the tip of a hair" (*Śvetāśvatara Upaniṣad* 5.9). On account of these and other passages Vaiṣṇavas do not accept Advaita Vedānta's concept of one soul that is reflected in different bodies.[50] When the Upaniṣads do speak of the self (*ātman*) as unlimited (*ananta*)[51] or omnipresent (*sarvagata*),[52] Vaiṣṇavas take them as referring to the self's qualities of eternality and its ability to be housed in all forms of life.

---

48. Jīva Gosvāmin's views bear a very close similarity to Nimbārka's, who wrote, among other works, the *Vedānta-pārijāta-saurabha* and the *Daśaślokī*, but his works are interpreted through Śrīnivāsa's *Vedānta-kaustubha* and Puruṣottama's *Vedānta-ratna-mañjūṣā*. Regarding Nimbārka's views of the self, Chaudhuri (1953: 337) writes: "over and above being consciousness in essence passively, the soul is also a conscious knower actively, i.e. it possess the attribute of consciousness [as well as *kartṛtva* and *bhoktṛtva*] which appears or disappears, increases or decreases, with regard to particular things according to circumstances."

49. In Nyāya there is a distinction between the potential capacity (*svarūpa-yogyatā*) and function capacity (*phalopadhāyi-yogyatā*) of objects. A tree branch has the potential to be a cricket stick, but its functional aspect would remain unmanifest until the wood is treated (Bhimacarya Jhalakikar and Vāsudevaśāstrī Abhyaṅkara 1978: 1057). Likewise the self as the potential for agency, etc., but these functions remain unmanifest until the self is connected to a mind-body complex.

50. See Jīva Gosvāmin's *Tattvasandarbha*, sections 37–40 for arguments against these and other Advaita views.

51. *Śvetāśvatara Upaniṣad* 5.9.

52. *Bhagavad Gītā* 2.24.

The Self is the Apprehender, Agent, and Experiencer

Jāmātṛ Muni uses the word *jñātṛtva* to express that the self has the capacity to know. *Jñātṛ* means "a knower" and the suffix *–tva* gives it an abstract sense, often translated as "–ness," to express an a state of being. The body is considered lifeless and without awareness; it appears to become conscious because of the self's presence within it. Likewise, Jīva Gosvāmin argues that the mind-body complex is made of inert matter, but it acquires the power of agency or the ability to act (*kartṛtva*) when it is in relationship with the self. The *Bhāgavata* (6.16.24) characterizes this view as such:

> The body, senses, life airs, mind and intelligence—when all these are contacted by a ray of his [the *ātman*'s] presence, they perform work and not otherwise, just as an unheated piece of iron is not able to [burn or express light]. That [self] acquires the name "seer" in the different states of mind.[53]

The agency that appears to exist within the body is not an innate attribute of the body, mind, et cetera, but it is a characteristic of the self when diffused into the body, et cetera. The analogy here is that heat and light are not innate properties of iron, but when iron has become heated it takes on the properties of fire; likewise, the body, mind, and so forth. take on properties of the self when in contact with the self.

This is the way the Caitanya Vaiṣṇava tradition interprets well-known verses in the *Bhagavad Gītā* (18.13–15):

> Arjuna, hear my explanation of the five causes for the accomplishment of all action according to conclusions of Sāṃkhya: the location, the agent, the various means, the various endeavors, and fate. Whenever an action is undertaken with body, speech, or mind, whether right or wrong, these five causes are present.

The 18th-century commentator Viśvanātha Cakravartin says that the "location" is the body, the "agent" is the connector between the self and inert

53. *dehendriya-prāṇa-mano-dhiyo 'mī, yad-aṃśa-viddhāḥ pracaranti karmasu*
naivānyadā lauham ivāprataptaṃ, sthāneṣu tad draṣṭr-apadeśam eti ||6.16.24||

Śrīdhara glosses *sthāneṣu* as *jāgrad-ādiṣu*, i.e. in the different states of mind starting with waking life.

matter called the ego (*ahaṃkāra*), the "means" are the sense organs, the "endeavors" are the movements of the life airs, and "fate" is the immanent being, the inner impeller of all. By saying the "agent" is the material ego, or the link between inner matter and consciousness,[54] Viśvanātha implies that agency (in this world) has two contributing causes: the innate capacity of the self for agency, and the mind-body complex through which it is enacted. Baladeva Vidyābhūṣaṇa, another 18th-century Caitanya Vaiṣṇava commentator, simply says that "agent" refers to the "self" (*jīva*), and he quotes *Praśna Upaniṣad* and *Vedānta-Sūtra* to justify his position.[55] The *Bhāgavata* (3.26.8) also states:

> The wise know that matter is the cause of the body, the senses, and agency. The self, which is superior to matter, is the cause of the experience of distress and happiness.[56]

While this does seem to locate agency in matter, if this verse is seen in the context of the other verses (discussed above), it can be interpreted as saying that the self is the original source of agency, and it infuses its agency into matter, which in turn becomes the cause of agency for the body and senses.

Other verses seem to explicitly reject agency in the self. *Bhagavad Gītā* 3.27 for example says:

> In all circumstances actions are performed by the qualities of nature, but the self, deluded by the material ego, thinks, "I am the agent."

While prima facie this verse seems to support the absolute rejection of agency one finds in Advaita and classical Sāṃkhya, we argue it does not undermine the view of agency we have argued here. Baladeva Vidyābhūṣaṇa reads *Gītā* 3.27 as speaking to the self in the ignorant state (the *avidvān*, in *Gītā* 3.25) who wrongly thinks he is the independent initiator of activities

---

54. *kartā cij-jaḍa-granthir ahaṅkāraḥ* (Kṛṣṇadāsa 1966: 443–444).

55. *eṣa hi draṣṭā sraṣṭā*, "he is the seer and he is the actor" *Praśna Upaniṣad* (4.9); *kartā śāstrārthavattvāt*, "he is the agent [and not matter, prakṛti] because this gives the scriptures a purpose" *Vedānta-Sūtra* (2.3.31).

56. *kārya-kāraṇa-kartṛtve, kāraṇaṃ prakṛtiṃ viduḥ*
bhoktṛtve sukha-duḥkhānāṃ, puruṣaṃ prakṛteḥ param || 3.26.8 ||

that are in fact conducted by the self in conjunction with the functions of matter, which are themselves moved by the Lord. But let us first consider who or what is the subject of the verb (*manyate*, "he thinks") since it is not fully defined in the verse. It cannot be matter (*prakṛti*) alone, since matter does not think without the presence of the self, and it cannot be the self (*ātman*) considered as entirely unconnected with matter since the verse is directed to embodied selves, and in particular those without knowledge. Furthermore, if the subject of *manyate* were the mind (*manas*) (which can only function or think when animated by the self), then the verse would be muddled because the mind is one of the aspects of matter (cf. *Gītā* 7.4), and thus there would be nothing wrong if it thought itself the agent, for it would in fact be the agent. If the mind were the subject of *manyate*, then it *should* think itself as agent, otherwise it would be deluded, but minds without subjects cannot be deluded anyway. Thus, the subject of *manyate* is the embodied self (the *jīva*, i.e., the *ātman* connected to a mind-body complex), which implies the self has the ability to apprehend (*jñātṛtva*) since "he thinks" (*manyate*). The thinker (i.e., the subject of the verse) is deluded because he thinks he acts *independently* of matter's constraining influences and God's oversight, but this does not deny his agency.[57] That is why *Gītā* 18.16 says he who thinks the self is a completely *independent* agent is wrong. As an aside, we may reiterate that the possibility of being deluded entails the ability to identify with matter, and such identification requires a type of agency. In other words, the ability to think necessitates the self having used its innate agency to identify with a mind-body complex suitable for thinking.

That such verses are meant to teach that the self does not act independently of God is also discussed in the *Vedānta-Sūtra*. While discussing *Taittirīya Upaniṣad* 2.5 in *Govinda-bhāṣya* 2.3.34, Baladeva argues that it is the self (*jīva* = *vijñāna*) who performs the Vedic rituals Darśa and Paurṇamāsa. Furthermore, when it is sometimes said in the scripture that

---

57. Baladeva Vidyābhūṣaṇa is most clear in this regard. He writes: "The self is the agent, whose agency is effected only by the three, i.e., the body, [the senses, and the deities of the senses], and by the immanent Lord whose is the instigator of everything, but not simply by the *jīva* alone. And yet the *jīva*, because of the bewilderment of the material ego thinks 'this is effected by me'."

> *kartur ātmano yat kartṛtvaṃ tat kila dehādibhis tribhiḥ paramātmanā ca sarva-pravartakena ca sidhyati na tv ekena jīvenaiva / tac ca mayaiva sidhyatīti jīvo yan manyate tad ahaṅkāra-vimauḍhyād eva* (Kṛṣṇadāsa 1966: 102–3).

the [self] does not have agency, this is because [the self] does not have independent agency.[58] In his translation and exposition of the *Govinda-bhāṣya*, Śrīśachandra Vasu comments on this that the self's "activities are depending on the will of the Lord" (Vasu 1912: 372). Below we clarify what is meant when one says an agent is not an independent agent.

The Self is Part of the Immanent Lord

Jīva Gosvāmin distinguishes the immanent Lord (*paramātmā*) from the supreme personal Lord (*bhagavān*). According to him, Bhagavān is transcendent God who abides in the spiritual world called Vaikuṇṭha, whereas Paramātmā is a form of Bhagavān that resides in and has dominion over the physical world. This aspect of the singular, nondual supreme being is also called *puruṣa* or *mahā-puruṣa*, and it supervises the emanation, conservation, and dissolution of material universe. This *paramātmā* resides as the immanent being in each physical body that inhabits the created world. To justify this position, Jīva Gosvāmin (*Paramātma Sandarbha*, section 34) interprets the *Bhagavad Gītā* (15.7) as saying the self is eternally part of the immanent Lord, even in the liberated state: "The eternal living being is a part of myself."[59]

Free Will and the Supremacy of God

In this section we look at some traditional Sanskrit grammatical issues relating to agency and free will as discussed in Jīva Gosvāmin's own Sanskrit grammar called the *Hari-nāmāmṛta-vyākaraṇa*. He writes:

> The agent is of three types. It is said[60] that the "agent simpliciter" is independent. The "causative agent" is one who causes another to perform action. The "agent under the control of the causative agent" is one who is made to perform an action. (Haridāsa 1985: 93)[61]

---

58. *evaṃ sati kvacid akartṛtva-vacanam asvātantryāt* | (Kṛṣṇa dāsa 1963: 160).

59. *mamaivāṃśo jīva-loke, jīva-bhūtaḥ sanātanaḥ* | *Bhagavad Gītā* 15.7.

60. Cf. Pāṇini's *Aṣṭādhyāyī* 1.4.54.

61. *kartā svatantra ity ukto hetu-kartā prayojakaḥ*
prayojakādhīna-kartā prayojya iti sa tridhā || *Harināmāmṛta-vyākaraṇa* 4.13.

On one level the self is the second type because it initiates action in the mind-body complex. He is free in doing so, but the action(s) must be approved by the Lord since the Lord is also a causative agent in the sense that he gives sanction to action (e.g., *Bhagavad Gītā* 13.22 says the Lord is the overseer and authorizer). Thus, the self is not an agent simpliciter in an ontological sense. He is the "agent under the control of the causative agent." The Lord is a causative agent because he gives the approval for action, although he is at the same time the agent simpliciter since he is unbounded by time, karma, and other constraining factors. A constraint on the self's free will and agency, however, is its past karma and the latent impressions (*saṃskāra*) with which it is born. These latent impressions create tendencies towards particular actions that are often very difficult to control, thus one's freedom is hampered. While much more could be said about this, we note that it is rooted in the Vedāntic conception that there is one, independent Absolute Reality and everything emanates and is dependent upon it (*Bhagavad Gītā* 7.6, 9.10; *Kaṭha Upaniṣad* 5.12).

Conclusion

The Caitanya Vaiṣṇava doctrine thus holds that the self has the real and inherent powers of knowledge and agency, in other words, it can know and it can act. This is summarized well by Jīva Gosvāmin:

> Moreover, while it is the case that pure [self] has the power of agency,[62] [1] nevertheless when he is conflated with Brahman the power of agency is internalized because of the non-connection with [the items, e.g., the mind-body complex] that link him with karma, and because of the covering caused by the bliss of Brahman. That much we can agree upon. Furthermore, [2] he[63] who is possessed of the internal power (*cit-śakti*) in the form of devotion for the Lord, or [3] he[64] who obtains a [spiritual] body as a companion [of the Lord] that is qualified by a particular aspect of the internal power, they possess agency for the service of that Lord, but it is not

62. He has already argued that there is agency in the pure self, and here he is listing three possible ways that this agency can exist.

63. This is the liberated devotee who still lives in the material world, called a *jīvanmukta*.

64. This is the liberated devotee, who is living in the eternal realm of Vaikuṇṭha.

predominated by matter. In the first case, he has superseded the [predominance of matter] by the internal power; in the second case he is absolutely free from matter.[65]

Thus, the Gauḍīya Vaiṣṇava view is that there are four possible states of agency:

(1) Agency in the embodied state, when the self is acting under the influence of *māyā*—agency is expressed through a material mind-body complex, which is itself under the oversight of the Lord.
(2) Agency in the embodied state when the self is acting in the service of God—agency is expressed through the mind-body complex, but is a form of Lord's own internal power (*cit-śakti*).
(3) Agency in the state when self identifies with Brahman—agency in the self remains as an unutilized quality potential.
(4) Agency in the liberated world of Vaikuṇṭha—agency (as well as apprehension and qualitative experience) in the self is expressed in and through a perfected body (*siddha-deha*).

The Gauḍīya Vaiṣṇava tradition makes a distinction between a material and a spiritual ego; the former causes the self to identify with a temporary mind-body complex, but even this identification depends on the latter, which causes the self to identify with the material ego in the embodied state, and it causes the self to identify with the eternal, perfected body in the liberated state of Vaikuṇṭha. With regard to the former, certain passages in canonical Vaiṣṇava texts (e.g., *Bhāgavata* 3.26.8; *Gītā* 3.27) seem to suggest that the powers of knowing and agency are in matter alone, but we have argued that Gauḍīya Vaiṣṇava theologians interpret these passages as showing that the quality-potentials of the self are only developed in and through the self's connection with a material mind-body or perfected body, but not as denying agency in the embodied self (*jīva*) or the liberated self (*ātman*). We have argued that Gauḍīya Vaiṣṇava theologians believe the powers of agency, apprehension, et cetera are only possible if

65. *śuddhasyaiva kartṛtva-śaktau ca yasyāpi brahmaṇi layas tasya brahmānandenāvaraṇāt karma-saṃyogāsaṃyogāc ca kartṛtva-śakter antar-bhāva evety abhyupagantavyaṃ, yasya ca bhagavad-bhakti-rūpa-cic-chaktyāviṣṭatā cic-chaki-vṛtti-viśeṣa-pārṣada-deha-prāptir vā, tasya tat-sevā-kartṛtve tu na prakṛti-prādhānyam | pūrvatra tām upamardya cic-chakteḥ prādhānyāt | aparatra kaivalyāc ca |* (*Paramātma Sandarbha, Sarvasaṃvādinī*, section 37, [Haridāsa 1984: 110]).

the disembodied self or the liberated self (i.e., the self completely separated from its nonessential, external material casings) has them as part of its inherent nature.

References

PRIMARY SOURCES

Aiyar, T. K. Balasubrahmanya. 1910. *The Works of Sri Sankaracharya. The Upanishad Bhashya.* Volume 3: *Taittirya and Chhandogya I–III.* Srirangam: Sri Vani Vilas Press.

Haberman, David. 2003. *The Bhaktirasāmṛtasindhu of Rūpa Gosvāmin.* Sanskrit Text and Translation. New Delhi: Indira Gandhi National Centre for the Arts and Motilal Banarsidass.

Haridāsa, Śāstrī. 1981. *Tattvasandarbha and Sarvasaṃvādinī by Jīva Gosvāmin.* Vrindavan.

———. 1984. *Paramātmasandarbha and Sarvasaṃvādinī by Jīva Gosvāmin.* Vrindavan.

———. 1985. *Harināmāmṛta-vyākaraṇa by Jīva Gosvāmin.* Vrindavan.

———. 1988. *Caitanya Caritāmṛta by Kṛṣṇadāsa Kavirāja.* Vrindavan.

Satya Nārāyaṇa Dāsa and Bruce Martin, trans. 2005. *Śrī Bhakti Sandarbha of Jīva Gosvāmin.* Vol. 1. Vrindavan: Jiva Institute.

———. 2006a. *Śrī Bhakti Sandarbha of Jīva Gosvāmin.* Vol. 2. Vrindavan: Jiva Institute.

———. 2006b. *Śrī Bhakti Sandarbha of Jīva Gosvāmin.* Vol 3. Vrindavan: Jiva Institute.

Satya Nārāyaṇa Dāsa, Kuṇḍalī Dāsa, Gopīparāṇadhana Dāsa, Draviḍa Dāsa, and Kūrma-rūpa Dāsa, trans. 1995. *Śrī Tattva-sandarbha: The First Book of the Śrī Bhāgavata-Sandarbha also Known as Śrī-sandarbha.* Vrindavan: Jiva Institute for Vaisnava Studies.

Kṛṣṇadāsa, Bābā, ed. 1963. *Śrī Brahma Sūtra Govinda Bhāṣyam by Baladeva Vidyābhūṣaṇa.* Mathurā: Kusumasarovaravāle.

———. 1966. *Bhagavad Gītā with Sārārthavarṣiṇī ṭīkā of Viśvanātha Cakravartin and Gītābhūṣaṇa of Baladevavidyābhūṣaṇa.* Rādhākuṇḍa: Kusumasarovara.

Kṛṣṇaśaṅkara, Śāstrī. 1965. *Śrīmad Bhāgavata Mahāpurāṇam.* Contains Śrīdhara Svāmin's *Bhāvārthadīpikā*, Śrīmad Jīva Gosvāmin's *Kramasaṃdarbha*, Śrīmad Viśvanātha Cakravartin's *Sārārthadarśinī.* Ahmedabad: Śrībhāgavatavidyāpīṭh.

Larson, Gerald. 2001. *Classical Sāṃkhya: An Interpretation of Its History and Meaning [Including Translation of Īśvara-Kṛṣṇa's Sāṃkhya-Kārikā.]* New Delhi: Motilal Banarsidass.

Olivelle, Patrick. 1998. *The Early Upanisads: Annotated Text and Translation.* New York: Oxford University Press.

Vasu, Śrīśachandra. 1894. *Aṣṭādhyāyī of Pāṇini: Translated into English, Book III.* Allahabad: Satyajnan Chaterji at the Pāṇini Office.

———. 1912. *The Vedānta-sūtras of Bādarāyaṇa: With the Commentary of Baladeva [called Govinda Bhāṣya].* Allahabad: Pāṇini Office.

SECONDARY SOURCES

Abhyankar, Kashinath Vasudev, and J. M. Śukla. 1977. *A Dictionary of Sanskrit Grammar.* Baroda: Oriental Institute.

Bhaṭṭācārya, Siddheśvara. 1960. *The Philosophy of the Śrīmad-Bhāgavata,*Volume 1:. *Metaphysics.* Calcutta: Vishva-Bharati Santiniketan.

———. 1962. *The Philosophy of the Śrīmad-Bhāgavata.* Volume 2: *Religion.* Calcutta: Vishva-Bharati Santiniketan.

Bhimacarya Jhalakikar, and Vāsudevaśāstrī Abhyaṅkara. 1978. *Nyayakosa: or, Dictionary of Technical Terms of Indian Philosophy.* Poona: Bhandarkar Oriental Research Institute.

Brzezinski, Jan. 1990. *The Gopālacampū of Jīva Gosvāmin.* Doctoral dissertation no. 1735. London: School of Oriental and African Studies.

Chaudhuri, Roma. 1953. "The Nimbārka School of Vedānta." *The Cultural Heritage of India.* Volume 3: *The Philosophies.* Edited by Haridas Bhattacharyya. Calcutta: Ramakrishna Mission Institute of Culture.

Dasgupta, Surendranath. 1961. *A History of Indian Philosophy: Indian Pluralism.* Vol. 4. Cambridge: Cambridge University Press.

Haberman, David. 1988. *Acting as a Way of Salvation: A Study of Rāgānuga Sādhana.* New York: Oxford University Press.

Halbfass, Wilhelm. 1995. *Philology and Confrontation: Paul Hacker on Traditional and Modern Vedanta.* Albany: State University of New York Press.

Rambachan, Anantanand. 1991. *Accomplishing the Accomplished: The Vedas as a Source of Valid Knowledge in Śaṅkara.* Monographs of the Society for Asian and Comparative Philosophy. Honolulu: University of Hawaii Press.

Rukmani, T. S. 1970. *A Critical Study of the Bhāgavata Purāṇa.* Varanasi: Chowkhamba Sanskrit Series.

Index

Śakti, 211
and omnipotency, 225
as speech, 213
tantric appropriation of, 222
Śiva,
and creation, 216
as higher sense of "I", 213
as possessor of Śakti, 212, 223
in Abhinavagupta, 221
Śrī Vaiṣṇavism, 232, 251
siddha-deha (perfected body), 273, 290, 305
svabhāva (essential nature), 259, 265, 266, 267

tantra, 211, 219
tat-tvam-asi,
in Advaita, 197
in Madhva, 255n 2
theodicy, 269, 272
Two Truths, the doctrine of,
Advaita usage, 188
and free will, 191
as resolution for problem of agency, 207
Buddhist usage,
as correct framework for considering free will, 43, 53
conventional truth within, 43, 53–54, 64,
for Madhyamaka Buddhism, dependent on conceptual imputation, 177–179
ultimate truth within, 43, 53, 63- 64

Udayana, 123, 125–131
Uddyotakara, 101–103, 117–118, 132–133
Utpaladeva, 212, 223, 224
Upaniṣads,
and Gauḍīya Vaiṣṇavism, 280, 282, 284, 294, 299, 301–302, 304
and Kashmiri Śaivism, 222
and Madhva, 258, 260
and Rāmānuja, 232, 239, 240, 245
and Sāṃkhya, 16, 19, 32, 35–36
and Saṅkara, 198,

Vācaspati Miśra, 18, 24, 25, 102–3, 119
Vaikuṇṭha, 37, 273, 289, 290, 305
Vallabha, 272, 275–276, 283
Vātsyāyana, 101–103, 116–17, 119
Veda,
as the source of knowledge regarding moral obligation, 138–139, 156–157
immoral sacrifices prescribed within, 158–159
Vedānta Deśika, 238, 251
Vedānta-sūtra, See Brahma-sūtra
Vijñāna Bhikṣu, 18, 21, 25, 27, 29, 33
Viṣṇu,
in Advaita, 206,
in Madhva 257, 262, 264, 269, 270
in Gauḍīya Vaiṣṇavism, 280
Viśvanātha Cakravartin, 281, 300
volition, 114–5

will, 69, 74,
the notion of as having a distinct genealogy in the Western tradition, 165–167

Yuktidīpikā, 20, 23